Charles S. Peirce
Logic of the Future, Volume 2/1

Peirceana

Edited by
Francesco Bellucci and Ahti-Veikko Pietarinen

Volume 2

Charles S. Peirce
Logic of the Future

Writings on Existential Graphs
Part 1: The Logical Tracts

Edited by
Ahti-Veikko Pietarinen

DE GRUYTER

ISBN 978-3-11-108908-9
e-ISBN (PDF) 978-3-11-065142-3
e-ISBN (EPUB) 978-3-11-064965-9
ISSN 2698-7155

Library of Congress Control Number: 2021932713

Bibliographic information published by the Deutsche Nationalbibliothek
The Deutsche Nationalbibliothek lists this publication in the Deutsche Nationalbibliografie;
detailed bibliographic data are available on the Internet at http://dnb.dnb.de.

© 2022 Walter de Gruyter GmbH, Berlin/Boston
This volume is text- and page-identical with the hardback published in 2021.
Typesetting: Jukka Nikulainen
Printing and binding: CPI books GmbH, Leck

www.degruyter.com

Acknowledgments

The work on the *Logic of the Future* has taken over fifteen years to complete. A considerable number of people and sources of support have accumulated over the years that are to be acknowledged and deeply thanked for their respective contributions.

An edition on Peirce's graphical logic was conceived during the class I gave at the University of Helsinki on *Peirce's Logic and Philosophy* in autumn 2004. At that time, it became obvious to me that Peirce's logic can never be adequately studied, let alone deeply researched, understood and put into a perspective within the history of ideas, without comprehensive editions.

It was the students of that class of 2004 that ignited the work on the present volumes. Its 20-odd students, including Jukka Nikulainen, Henrik Rydenfelt, Lauri Snellman, Lauri Järvilehto, Michael von Boguslawski, Harry Alanen, Peter Schulman and many others whose names I have forgotten, provided initial assistance in manuscript inspection and transcription.

There is one person without whom this edition would not have been possible to be produced at all. My long-term research assistant, Jukka Nikulainen, who has served as a technical editor of these volumes and has provided the first-ever LaTeX package (EGpeirce) by which one can now typeset any graph, special mark or symbol that ever emanated from Peirce's hand, with ease and uniformity. Jukka also encoded a large majority of the hundreds of complex graphs that appear in the volumes, improving the package along the way and adding new features to it. We believe that by now everything that Peirce ever designed and wanted to design as a special graph, type, character, mark or sign—a plethora of his typographical eccentricities notwithstanding—have been incorporated into the functionality of the Peirce LaTeX package. And much more is available in it than is in fact needed for the purposes of compiling the present editions. Peirce's ethics of notation dictates that pieces of notation are just as important as the prose overall, and that whenever new notation is introduced, reasons for it are not to be taken lightly. Design and typesetting practices have to follow suit, and indeed Jukka has considerably assisted the production of the CRCs of these volumes for the press, honing the notations and checking many of the transcriptions as I slowly progressed with them. He has also searched and compiled information on many of Peirce's references as well as prepared both the index of names and the index of words. Nikulainen, above all, deserves to be acknowledged as having done an amount of work vastly exceeding anything that is to be expected of a technical editor—probably years rather than months since 2004—in order to bring the edition into its present shape.

Claudia Cristalli also went out of her way in helping to bring the edition into its near-completion. Without her many suggestions and concrete advice on organisation and presentation of the material, the progress on the edition might have slouched altogether. In particular, she gave valuable proposals on organising the editorial, introductory and survey parts.

Francesco Bellucci deserves an equally immeasurable gratitude for pressing on with finalising the volumes. Not only did he check many of the items and transcriptions but also closely researched their content, coming up with important perspectives concerning their interpretation. The volumes and their editorial introductions have benefitted enormously from our scholarly collaboration over the last several years.

Marc Champagne and Liu Xinwen have followed the progress of this project over the years. Both have provided a number of comments and corrections on the introductory parts, and deserve a special thanks for such laborious deeds.

These editions would probably have not seen the light of day had it not been for the enthusiasm and intellectual support of Nathan Houser, with whom I regularly conversed on the prospects of such a work ever since my stay at the Peirce Edition Project in the autumn of 2005 as a post-doctoral Fulbright grantee. It is thanks to Nathan's vocal accentuation on the importance of bringing about a thematic edition on graphs, and above all the unprecedented scholarship that he represents in the Peirce community, that have kept me going with the work. André De Tienne, Director of the Peirce Edition Project, has been equally supportive of the enterprise from the get-go. Conversations with him have supplied vital links and clues by which one could go about navigating the amazing mazes that the literary output of this American mind puts before us.

Over the years, John Sowa, Matthew Moore and Helmut Pape have all provided experienced advice, John on the topical relevance of Peirce's graphical logic, and Matt and Helmut on the challenges of editing Peirce's papers for a thematic collection. Susan Haack has followed the project with interest, and I do not doubt that any new material that might be found in these texts would only support the conclusions she has already arrived at.

My first graduate class on Peirce was given by Risto Hilpinen, who taught logic and philosophy of science at the University of Turku in early 1990s and who was the first to notice that Peirce had arrived at semantic and logical ideas surprisingly similar to those reached much later by others, in particular the game-theoretical semantics independently discovered by Jaakko Hintikka in the 1960s. I am honoured to have an opportunity of including an Introductory Note from Prof. Hilpinen.

Discussions with the late Jaakko Hintikka in 2000–2015 on Peirce's logic have enabled me to put many of the related contributions into a sharper perspective.

"Peirce—miles ahead of Frege in logic and in the philosophy of mathematics", he once told me. The similarities between Hintikka's and Peirce's philosophies are indeed quite striking (Pietarinen 2018), but can be explained by the similarities in the methods of logic and the significance placed on having good logical notations, the relational apparatus of thought, the value placed on proofs, and the semantic (or model-theoretic, semeiotic, notational) outlook on one's philosophical investigations. Both Peirce and Hintikka had put scientific and human inquiry ahead of bare epistemology: both advocated an *action-first* epistemology. That there is reality and truth in such philosophy is reflected in the comment I once received from Jaakko on my presentation that explored connections between the two thinkers. I had suggested that the sheer number of them makes one almost believe in reincarnation, to which he replied: "Yes, but who incarnated whom?"

Discussions with my father, who together with Risto Hilpinen were Hintikka's first doctoral students in philosophy, helped to clarify several conceptions that relate Peirce to philosophical classics, including Spinoza, Kant, Plato and Aristotle. The edition is dedicated to the memory of my parents.

Along the way, Arnold Oostra and Fernando Zalamea provided valuable advice on both the general conception of the edition as well as on the details of Peirce's graphical notation. Zalamea encouraged me to pursue a resolutely comprehensive rather than a critical and limited collation of texts; his answer to my enquiry on what should be included in an edition about Peirce's graphs was, "Everything!" As usual he was right; Peirce's gardening is too precious to be cut off at any branch or ligature, as it may be just another verso of his folios that has the mutation needed for the germinal idea to evolve into a substantially new insight.

I have space left only to enlist a number of colleagues and Peirce scholars who have contributed to the edition either by way of advancing the research on Peirce's graphical logic or explicitly concerning the edition: Christina Barés Gomez, Reetu Bhattarchajee, Angelina Bobrova, Daniele Chiffi, Matthieu Fontaine, Juuso-Ville Gustafsson, Jelena Issajeva, Ma Minghui, Amirouche Moktefi, Marika Proover and Frederik Stjernfelt. They are all to be thanked for having provided important suggestions during our workshops and Peirce Seminars held at the Tallinn University of Technology.

In addition, Jean-Marie Chevalier and Benoit Gaultier have helped with correcting the transcriptions of the letters Peirce wrote in French (LoF 3). Both have provided helpful comments on the edition at various stages of its development.

Over these 15-odd years, several personal research grants have been instrumental in supporting and sustaining the work on the present edition. They are, in reverse chronological order: Higher School of Economics, HSE University Basic Research Program (*Russian Academic Excellence Project '5-100'*, 2018–2020); Nazarbayev University (*Social Policy Grant*, 2018–2019); Estonian Research Council (*Abduction in the Age of Fundamental Uncertainty*, 2013–2018); Academy of Finland (*Logic and Games*, 2003–2005; *Diagrammatic Mind (DiaMind): Logical and Cognitive Aspects of Iconicity*, 2013–2017); Chinese Academy of Social Sciences (*Peirce's Pragmaticism*, 2006; 2016); Joan Nordell Houghton Library Fellowship of Harvard University (*Peirce's Manuscripts on Logic*, 2011–2012); University of Helsinki Excellence in Research Grant (*Pragmaticism and Its Contemporary Applications*, 2006–2009); Kone Foundation (*Peirce's Scientific and Philosophical Correspondence*, 2008); The Jenny and Antti Wihuri Foundation (*Pragmatic Theories of Meaning*, 2007); ASLA–Fulbright Foundation (*Peirce's Manuscripts on Logic*, 2005), and Finnish Cultural Foundation (*Peirce's Scientific and Philosophical Correspondence*, 2005). These sources of support are gratefully acknowledged. In particular, the staff at Harvard's Houghton Library and curator Leslie Morris are to be thanked for their invaluable assistance during my frequent visits to the library over the years to inspect the Peirce collection.

The publisher's team has seen through the final preparation of the edition. It is only appropriate that Peirce's late works on logic appear with the same publisher as Peirce's late works on mathematics (*New Elements of Mathematics*, NEM I–IV) did nearly half a century ago.

The title "Logic of the Future" comes from Peirce's 1909 Christmas Day letter to William James. That letter also explains Peirce's bequest to have his work appear in places that will, first and foremost, advance inquiry and not the sham and fake reasoning that he saw plaguing scholarly minds of his time. Only then, in addition to the advancement of inquiry, one may recognise the value of ideas as those that their author has instigated along the way:

> Now when I die, I want proper justice done to my memory as to these things. Not at all that they are any credit to me, but simply that, by being made to appear considerable, they may invite attention and study, when I think they will do considerable good. For logic and exact reasoning are a good deal more important than you are able to see that they are. So I hope that some account of my work may appear in some publication that people will look into, and not solely in the Biographical memoirs of the National Academy of Sciences. (CSP to WJ, December 25, 1909)

Soon after, Peirce mentions the "pressing questions of our time" (R 678, 1910). He wanted to resolve them by an application of logic and reasoning. Those questions have not gone away. They can be dispelled only by a collective improvement in the art of reasoning. Everyone involved in advancing the present project has done "considerable good" towards that end.

Ahti-Veikko Pietarinen

Abbreviations of Peirce's Works and Archives

Archives:

R   *The Charles S. Peirce Papers, 1787–1951.* Manuscripts in the Houghton Library of Harvard University, as identified by Richard Robin, *Annotated Catalogue of the Papers of Charles S. Peirce*, Amherst: University of Massachusetts Press, 1967, and in "The Peirce Papers: A Supplementary Catalogue", *Transactions of the Charles S. Peirce Society* 7, 1971, pp. 37–57. Peirce's manuscripts and letters are available, in part, in *The Charles S. Peirce Papers, Microfilm Edition*, Thirty Reels with Two Supplementary Reels Later Added. Cambridge: Harvard University Library Photographic Service, 1966.[1]

HUA   *Harvard University Archives.* Pusey Library, Harvard University.

WJP   *The William James Papers.* Houghton Library, Harvard University.

CLF   *Christine Ladd Franklin and Fabian Franklin Papers.* Butler Library, Rare Books and Manuscripts Collection, Columbia University.

VW   *Lady Victoria Alexandrina Maria Louisa Welby fonds*, York University Archives and Special Collections.

Edited Collections:

SiL   *Studies in Logic, by Members of the Johns Hopkins University.* Edited by Charles S. Peirce, Boston: Little, Brown, and Company, 1883. Reissued as a facsimile reprint in *Foundations of Semiotics*, Volume 1, with introductory essays by Achim Eschbach and Max H. Fisch. Amsterdam: John Benjamins, 1983.

DPP   *Dictionary of Philosophy and Psychology.* Three volumes. Edited by James Mark Baldwin, 1901–1902. New York & London: The Macmillan Company.

CLL   *Chance, Love and Logic: Philosophical Essays.* Edited by Morris Cohen, with a supplementary essay on the pragmatism of Peirce by John Dewey. London: Kegan Paul, 1923.

CP   *The Collected Papers of Charles S. Peirce*, 8 volumes. Edited by Charles Hartshorne, Paul Weiss and Arthur W. Burks. Cambridge: Harvard University Press, 1931–1958. Referred to by volume and paragraph number.

---

[1] The microfilm edition is electronically available at https://rs.cms.hu-berlin.de/peircearchive/ Most manuscript and typescript sheets, notebooks and other material from the Harvard Peirce Papers are included in this microfilm edition, but only a minor part of letters and correspondence was included.

PWP *The Philosophy of Peirce: Selected Writings*. Edited by Justus Buchler. New York: Harcourt, Brace and Company, 1940. Reissued as *Philosophical Writings of Peirce*, Dover, 1955.

CN *Charles Sanders Peirce: Contributions to The Nation*. Four volumes. Edited by Kenneth Laine Ketner and James Edward Cook. Lubbock, TX: Texas Technological University Press, 1975–1987.

NEM *The New Elements of Mathematics by Charles S. Peirce*. Four volumes. Edited by Carolyn Eisele. The Hague: Mouton De Gruyter, 1976.

SS *Semiotic and Significs: The Correspondence between C. S. Peirce and Victoria Lady Welby*. Edited by Charles S. Hardwick with the assistance of James Cook. Bloomington and Indianapolis, IN: Indiana University Press, 1977.

P *A Comprehensive Bibliography and Index of the Published Works of Charles Sanders Peirce*, with a Bibliography of Secondary Studies. Ketner, Kenneth Laine et al., (eds.). Greenwich: Johnson Associates, 1977. Second edition, *A Comprehensive Bibliography of the Published Works of Charles Sanders Peirce*, Bowling Green, OH: Philosophy Documentation Center, 1986.

W *Writings of Charles S. Peirce: A Chronological Edition*. Seven volumes. Edited by Max H. Fisch, C. J. W. Kloesel, et al. and the Peirce Edition Project. Bloomington and Indianapolis, IN: Indiana University Press, 1982–2009.

WMS Manuscripts as cataloged by the Peirce Edition Project, in W.

PLZ *Charles S. Peirce: Phänomen und Logik der Zeichen*. Helmut Pape (ed.). Frankfurt am Main: Suhrkamp, 1983.

HP *Historical Perspectives on Peirce's Logic of Science: A History of Science*. Two volumes. Edited by Carolyn Eisele. Berlin, New York and Amsterdam: Mouton De Gruyter, 1985.

RLT *Reasoning and the Logic of Things: The Cambridge Conference Lectures of 1898*. Edited by Kenneth Laine Ketner. Cambridge, Mass.: Harvard University Press, 1992.

EP 1 *The Essential Peirce: Selected Philosophical Writings*. Volume 1 (1867–1893). Edited by Nathan Houser and Christian J. W. Kloesel. Bloomington and Indianapolis, IN: Indiana University Press, 1992.

PPM *Pragmatism as a Principle and Method of Right Thinking: The 1903 Harvard "Lectures on Pragmatism"*. Edited by Patricia Ann Turrisi. Albany, NY: State University of New York Press, 1997.

EP 2 *The Essential Peirce: Selected Philosophical Writings*. Volume 2 (1893–1913). Edited by the Peirce Edition Project. Bloomington and Indianapolis, IN: Indiana University Press, 1998.

LoI   *Charles S. Peirce: The Logic of Interdisciplinarity. The Monist Series.* Edited by Elize Bisanz. Berlin: Akademie Verlag, 2009.
PoM   *Philosophy of Mathematics: Selected Writings.* Edited by Matthew E. Moore. Bloomington and Indianapolis, IN: Indiana University Press, 2010.
ILoS *Illustrations of the Logic of Science, by Charles Sanders Peirce.* Edited by Cornelis de Waal. Chicago: Open Court, 2014.
PSR   *Charles S. Peirce: Prolegomena to a Science of Reasoning. Phaneroscopy, Semeiotic, Logic.* Edited by Elize Bisanz. Frankfurt am Main: Peter Lang, 2016.
LoF   *Charles S. Peirce: Logic of the Future. Writings on Existential Graphs.* Edited by Ahti-Veikko Pietarinen. Volume 1: *History and Applications*, 2019. Volume 2/1: *The Logical Tracts*, 2021. Volume 2/2: *The 1903 Lowell Lectures*, 2021. Volume 3: *Pragmaticism and Correspondence*, 2021. Berlin and Boston: Mouton De Gruyter.

Introductory Note

Charles S. Peirce was one of the most creative and innovative philosophers of the late 19th and early 20th century. He is known as the founder of American pragmatism, a general philosophical view which he in his later years preferred to call "pragmaticism" to distinguish it from the doctrines propounded by his followers and imitators who, according to Peirce, had "kidnapped" the word 'pragmatism'. He had wide interests, and his pragmaticism permeated his work in many areas of philosophy: logic, semiotics and the philosophy of language, philosophy of science, and metaphysics.

In the 1880s Peirce developed independently of Gottlob Frege a system of quantification theory in which quantifiers were treated as variable binding operators; thus he can be regarded, alongside Frege, as a founder of contemporary formal logic. The standard notation used in contemporary logic is a variant of Peirce's notation rather than that adopted by Frege. As a part of his pragmaticist theory of meaning, Peirce developed a game-theoretical interpretation of logical constants, according to which their meaning is explained by means of a semantical zero-sum game between two parties, an utterer and an interpreter. Peirce also studied modal and many-valued logics, and developed the basic ideas of the possible-worlds semantics for modal logic. In his general theory of reasoning Peirce distinguished three main forms of reasoning, namely abduction, deduction, and induction, and revised the traditional account of non-deductive reasoning. In his work in general semiotics (the theory of signs) and the philosophy of language, he analyzed the sign relation as a triadic relation involving a sign, an interpretant (meaning), and an object, and introduced the distinction between types and tokens into linguistics and the philosophy of language. He made a distinction between iconic, indexical, and symbolic signs, and outlined an account of proper names as "directly referential" indexical signs. Peirce developed a complex classification of signs involving several interpretants and objects, and his rich semiotic system provides a useful framework for the comparison of semiotic theories from the Stoics to the present. He anticipated many significant developments in the later 20th century analytic philosophy and logic.

In the 1890s Peirce reformulated quantification theory by expressing it in a language of diagrams which he called *existential graphs*. The switch from the algebraic notation to the language of graphs seems to have been motivated by his belief that the latter was more suitable for the purposes of logical analysis. According to Peirce, a system of logic can be used as a calculus which helps to draw inferences as economically as possible, or it can be developed for the purpose of representing and analyzing deductive processes. Peirce also thought that a graphical notation was more suitable for logical analysis than an algebraic notation because of its higher degree of *iconicity*. An iconic sign can be said to show what it means in the sense that it resembles its objects in some respect, that is, some features of the sign itself determine its interpretation. Peirce himself regarded the theory of existential graphs as one of his most important contributions to logic and philosophy.

Peirce presented his theory of existential graphs in many papers which also discussed various philosophical topics in semiotics and the philosophy of language. Much of this material remained unpublished during his lifetime, and some scholars became acquainted with it by studying his manuscripts. On the other hand, Peirce was able to get some of these works published, for example, his work *A Syllabus of Certain Topics of Logic* was published by Alfred Mudge & Son, Boston, 1903, and the long paper "Prolegomena to an Apology for Pragmaticism" appeared in the philosophical journal *The Monist* in 1906. However, Peirce's contemporaries ignored these works, perhaps because they were not able to see them as significant contributions to logic and philosophy. It might be said that Peirce was ahead of his times; his work on existential graphs began to receive serious attention only in the 1960s.

The *Logic of the Future* series is the first comprehensive collection of Peirce's writings on existential graphs, especially his previously unpublished writings and unpublished variants of published works. Peirce had the habit of rewriting the same work several times, and the versions often differ from each other in interesting ways. Prof. Ahti-Veikko Pietarinen has performed a valuable service to all students of Peirce's logic and philosophy by making this material easily accessible in book form.

Risto Hilpinen
University of Miami, Coral Gables

Foreword

The *Logic of the Future* edition aims at being both an inclusive and a resourceful set of thematic texts, serving the roles of a diplomatic edition, a handbook, and a set of monographs. Extensive thematic introductions and surveys of selections are included. From editorial points of views, I have attempted to maximise the amount of alternate versions, incomplete drafts and page fragments that one can gather from Peirce's enormous *Nachlass* of over 100 000 surviving pages, while minimising the reader's effort when following his spawning lines of thought and bursts of brilliant insights. The reader will, just as the editor does, despair over the writings that have frequent break-offs, discontinuities and aberrations—explorations left soberly unfinished and rhizoidic—aware as we are that so many of the now-lost pages and forgotten thoughts were once available to fill in the blanks. I hope to share with the reader the view that the numerous alternate versions, even when superficially repetitive, idiosyncratic or seemingly superseded by parallel or later attempts, are all too precious to be left out; too "gravid with young truth" to remain forever undisclosed from the eyes of posterity. If they won't appear in the present edition, chances are that much of that material would never find its way to print.

To wit, let us take to the heart the following passage as an example of such a variant:

> We have only to turn our attention for one moment to a relative term to see that the account given in the logic-books of the composition of concepts is entirely inadequate. The present writer showed the true mode of composition in the seventh volume of *The Monist* by means of graphs. But immediately after that publication he discovered another much better system of graphs, making the whole matter perfectly clear. But he has in vain endeavoured to persuade some journal, academy, or institution to print a sufficient account of it. The time will come when the world will be amazed at this; but then Newton's *Principia* would not have been printed yet if Edmund Halley had not been a very different sort of man from those upon whom publication depends in the United States at this day. (R 280, Alt. pp. 19–20, *The Basis of Pragmatism*, late 1904; LoF 3)[2]

The main purpose of the *Logic of the Future* is to facilitate advancement of inquiry on what has remained one of the most neglected topics in the study of Peirce's

---

[2] The reference R is to the Charles Sanders Peirce papers deposited at Houghton Library, Harvard University, as listed and catalogued by Richard S. Robin. See "Abbreviations for Peirce's Works and Archives" at the end of the General Introduction for the standard references to the archives, collections and editions of Peirce's work. When the material appears in the present edition of the *Logic of the Future* (LoF for short), a reference to Volumes 1–3 is added.

thought, the logic of graphs and their role in the eventual completion of his mature logic and philosophy. This oversight shows up in previous editions of his works, which occasionally but quite routinely have left the graphical account out of the picture. Technical limitations are understandable, but the inevitable consequence has been that his favourite method of analysis became unduly suppressed from the perspectives one hopes to gain over the maturation of his later thought, leading to a de-emphasis of the manifold contributions Peirce calculated logical graphs to make towards erecting a fully articulated, architectonic scientific philosophy.

The volumes on Peirce's logic of graphs should be viewed only as the beginnings of a renewed exposition of the kind of inquiry that a comprehensive access to the largely unpublished late works of this poly-pragmatic American philosopher would facilitate. They do little more than identify the relevant minimal corpus that is not to be neglected in the scholarship on Peirce's method of logical analysis, its history, and its applications to the workings of intellectual cognition. Further editions are needed on Peirce's late writings on the algebra of logic, logic of abduction (retroduction), inductive logic and the logic of science, non-Aristotelian (and non-classical) logics, reasoning, definitions, history of logic, semiotics, methodeutic, modality, continuity, vagueness, imagination and perception; the list goes on with anything that was represented in non-graphical notations (such as Peirce's 1909 work on triadic logics), in order to complete the identification of that minimal logical corpus. Any of these areas, when fully available, will open up new insights on, as well as call for some major revisions to, our current understanding of the logical, philosophical and scientific achievements of this agile mind, and what their proper place in the history of logic will end up being. And although electronic repositories of one's literary remains are certainly useful, and although those, too, will appear before long, they are no substitute for organised, systematic and thematic records of one's profound thoughts.

There are also wider issues that have to do with the kinds of historiographies one gets to write on the development of modern logic, including the virtual histories of what the logic of the later centuries would have looked like had the findings that Peirce produced and presented in various occasions been better and more timely disseminated. Misfortunes happened during Peirce's life all too often—yet on balance, we are also fortunate and privileged as much of his literary estate has been preserved for us to continue its future appreciation and critical scrutiny, however fragmentary or prefatory those surviving segments may appear to be. I hope that the present edition will play its part towards achieving these wider goals.

Preface to Volumes 2/1 and 2/2

The second volume in the series of Charles Sanders Peirce's writings on Existential Graphs (EGs) is arranged in two books, and it bears the theme of the 1903 Lowell Lectures, a series of eight popular public talks arranged by the Lowell Institute Peirce delivered in November and December in Boston, Massachusetts. The selection of texts follows the same criteria as for the first volume: the relevant texts chosen for inclusion are those that concern the topic of Existential Graphs (EGs). The first five lectures were largely concerned with logical graphs, and a great majority of his lecture drafts are indeed on that topic. Roughly two thirds of his overall lecture notes, pre-drafts, supplements and worksheets have made it to the selection of the second book of the volume. An ample amount of preparatory material that Peirce produced during the year has also been included as the first book of the volume, *The Logical Tracts*, a large treatise on logical graphs which Peirce crafted to accompany the planning of his lectures. The introductions are new, including a section on the Gamma part of the theory of EGs in Volume 2/1, a graphical system of modal logic that Peirce had no time introduce during the allotted eight hours. Editorial survey notes are provided on every selection in the introductory essays.

My special thanks are to André De Tienne, Director of the Peirce Edition Project at the Institute of American Thought, IUPUI, Indianapolis, for permission to consult extensive material at the project's possession about Peirce's 1903 Lowell Lectures during my visits there in 2005, 2012 and 2014. Special thanks also go to Helmut Pape, who has studied and worked on these lectures more than anyone else in the past. As before, this volume could not have been completed without the unfailing assistance of Jukka Nikulainen on technical editing matters, and the loving support of my family on matters of vital importance.

Ahti-Veikko Pietarinen, April 2020

Contents

Ahti-Veikko Pietarinen
General Introduction to *Logic of the Future* —— 1

Ahti-Veikko Pietarinen
Introduction to the Theory of Existential Graphs, Volumes 2/1 and 2/2 —— 15

Ahti-Veikko Pietarinen
Introduction to Volume 2/1: *The Logical Tracts* —— 69

References —— 101

Charles S. Peirce's Writings on Existential Graphs

Part IV: The Logical Tracts (1903)

29 Logical Tracts. No. 1 (R 491) —— 119

30 Logical Tracts. No. 2 (R 492) —— 129

31 On Logical Graphs [Euler Diagrams] (R 479) —— 228

Bibliography of Peirce's References —— 238

Catalogue of Peirce's Writings —— 251

Name Index —— 255

Keyword Index —— 257

Ahti-Veikko Pietarinen
General Introduction to *Logic of the Future*

Peirce's Logic

Charles Sanders (Santiago) Peirce (1839–1914) was an accomplished scientist, philosopher, and mathematician, who considered himself primarily a logician. His contributions to the development of modern logic at the turn of the 20th century have been colossal, original, and perpetually influential, albeit his overall influence upon the development of modern logic remained ill-understood for a long time (Fisch 1982, Dipert 1995, Hintikka 1996, Putnam 1982).

Formal, or deductive, logic was just one of the branches in which Peirce exercised his logical and analytical talent. His work developed upon George Boole's algebra of logic and Augustus De Morgan's logic of relations. Peirce worked on the algebra of relatives (1870–1885), the theory of quantification (1880–1885), graphical and diagrammatic logic (1896–1913), trivalent logic (1909), as well as higher-order and modal logics (1898–1911).[1] He also contributed significantly to the theory and methodology of induction, and discovered a third kind of reasoning, different from both deduction and induction, which he called abduction or retroduction, and which he identified with the logic of scientific discovery.

Philosophically, logic became for Peirce a broad and open-ended discipline with internal divisions and external architectonic relations to other parts of scientific inquiry. Logic depends upon, or draws its principles from, mathematics, phaneroscopy (phenomenology), esthetics and ethics (phenomenology), while metaphysics and psychology depend upon logic. One of the most important characters of Peirce's late logical thought was that logic becomes coextensive with semeiotic (his preferred spelling), namely the theory of signs. Peirce divided logic, conceived as semeiotic, into (i) *speculative grammar*, the preliminary analysis, definition, and classification of signs; (ii) *critical logic*, the study of the validity

---

[1] Year ranges are indicative only. The continuous nature of Peirce's explorations and his pluralistic approach to logic routinely challenge pinpointing any definite moment in time when one idea had led to another. For example, higher-order logic was algebraically investigated in his 1885 "On the Algebra of Logic: A Contribution to the Philosophy of Notation" paper but presented in its graphical outfit in 1898. The entire concept of graphical notation for logic is an equally continuous notion and was present in various guises since 1880 (see "Introduction to Volume 1" of Volume 1 of the *Logic of the Future*).

and justification of each kind of reasoning; and (iii) *methodeutic*, or *speculative rhetoric*, the theory of methods and an application of the methods of logical analysis to other fields of science, especially mathematics. Peirce's logical investigations cover all these three areas.

In the early 1880s—roughly at the same time as Gottlob Frege (1848–1925) but entirely independently of him—Peirce discovered a notation of quantifiers and variables for the expression of quantificational logic. Unlike Frege, however, Peirce did not stick to any one formalism. He spent the rest of his logical life experimenting with alternative notations to serve the theory of logic and to advance scientific inquiry. The outcome of his notational researches was a system of logical graphs discovered in 1896, which he termed the system of Existential Graphs (EGs).

Sketchy presentations of EGs appeared in print in 1902 in the *Dictionary of Philosophy and Psychology* (DPP) edited by James Mark Baldwin (entry "Symbolic Logic" in Vol. 2, pp. 640–651; LoF 3), in *A Syllabus of Certain Topics of Logic*, a 23-page printed pamphlet that Peirce wrote to accompany his Lowell Lectures of 1903 and circulated in 100 copies, and in the 1906 *Monist* article "Prolegomena to an Apology for Pragmaticism". Apart from these, his prolific writings on EGs remained unpublished in his lifetime.[2]

Peirce continued working on the theory of logical graphs for the rest of his life. On Christmas Day of 1909 he wrote to William James (1942–1910) that this graphical method "ought to be the Logic of the Future". The next sections explain the rationale behind this phrase.

Structure of the Edition

Logic of the Future: Writings on Existential Graphs is a multi-volume edition providing a comprehensive package of Peirce's late writings on the topic of Existential Graphs (EGs). The first volume, subtitled **History and Applications**, consists of three parts, *Reasoning and Diagrams* (Part I), *Development of Existential Graphs* (Part II), and *Theory and Application of Existential Graphs* (Part III). The aim of Part I is to provide a non-technical introduction, in Peirce's own words, to his

---

[2] There are only a few references and hints to them in his other published papers from the early 20th century, such as the "Some Amazing Mazes" series (Peirce 1908a,b; Peirce 1909a). The second *Monist* paper "Issues of Pragmaticism" (Peirce 1905b) makes one reference; the first, "What Pragmatism Is", does not (Peirce 1905a). Nor does the published version of the "Neglected Argument for the Reality of God" (Peirce 1908c) refer to EGs.

method and philosophy of diagrammatic reasoning, especially as conducted and understood in terms of his theory of logical graphs. Part II tells the story of the discovery of EGs and their relation to what Peirce generally calls the "graphical method of logic"; the discovery that largely happens during his immensely productive year of 1896, followed by two years of significant improvements to that original discovery. Part III, which in many ways comprises the most substantial, detailed and technical set of writings of the entire *Logic of the Future* series, portrays the breath and the depth of the theory of EGs, as well as the impact Peirce took the graphical method to have on the advancement of our understanding of the fundamental nature of reasoning, mathematics, science, mind, and philosophy. This third part covers the period from 1899 until some of his last writings on the topic in 1911.

The second volume, **The 1903 Lowell Lectures**, consists of two parts in two books, *The Logical Tracts* (Part IV) and *The 1903 Lowell Lectures* (Part VI), a selection of the first five lectures from the Lowell Institute Lectures series *Some Topics of Logic Bearing on Questions Now Vexed*. *The Logical Tracts* is Peirce's nearly book-length compendium on EGs written while preparing for his upcoming eight lectures in November and December 1903 organised by the Lowell Institute in Boston. The first five of the Lowell Lectures, in turn, contain the most massive body of texts on EGs that Peirce ever undertook to write. Those lectures, their numerous drafts and the accompanying material in *A Syllabus of Certain Topics of Logic* constitute the centerpieces of Peirce's work on EGs. Chronologically, they mark the half-way point in that dozen or so years during which he produced nearly all of the relevant writings. Content-wise, these lectures portray EGs in their matured form, with the system of conventions fully in place and the sound and complete set of rules of transformation ready to be exposed to the audience.

The most philosophical set of writings is found in the third volume, **Pragmaticism and Correspondence**. In its chapters arranged under Part VI on pragmaticism, Peirce is using EGs to elucidate, and even to prove, his philosophical theory of meaning. Thoughts, signs and minds are extensively discussed, and Peirce sends the graphical method to the service of addressing those difficult and penetrating philosophical questions. Selections from 1904 to 1908 make up this sixth part of the trilogy. The third volume also includes, in Part VII, Peirce's extensive exchange of letters with a number of colleagues, collaborators and friends. Among them is a long letter to William James written on December 25, 1909, in which the allusion to the "Logic of the Future" is made. That final part also presents the dictionary entries and their drafts on EGs that were authored or co-authored by Peirce and which—just as most of the other material in the volumes—have remained largely unpublished to date.

Each selection begins with a headnote, and introductory essays to each of the volumes and their individual parts provide further insight into the textual, substantial and editorial encounters that the production of the present collection has involved over the years. In particular, the introductory essays outline the wider context of Peirce's intellectual life and explain the growth and impact of his ideas within that wider context. They also highlight the major novelties and contributions that Peirce is observed to be making in the texts collected in these chapters.

When discussing Peirce's excursions into the theory of EGs and the numerous ventures he had in trying to get his papers published and acknowledged by his peers, I am following the order of the textual selections in their respective chapters. For most if not for all of the texts included in the volumes, philosophical and technical comments are provided on the content. Those comments aim at being a source of information as much as of inspiration, and have no pretension of exhaustiveness.

Editorial Essay

Text Selection Rationale

The selection of copy-texts and their editorial processing follows a number of general and specific guidelines. As to the general ones, first, the edition aims at being *comprehensive* in its coverage of the material Peirce ever wrote on EGs. The number of such manuscript and letter sheets, notebook pages, worksheets, galley proofs, typescripts and published leaves (inclusive of all variant and incomplete draft pages), is nearly 5 000. Virtually all of them have been used as the material for copy-texts of the volumes of the series. This means that important alternative drafts, variants and fragments have also been included as far as possible. Far from making the text redundant, substantive alternatives often contain information not found anywhere else. Peirce worked incessantly, and routinely did not aim at publishing his findings.[3] Even when he did, his submissions, galleys and offprints can be seen to be superseded by the textual and cognitive context within which they were produced. Variants, alternatives, emendations, parallel and emerging

---

[3] A pertinent example is the destiny of Peirce's 1885 paper "On the Algebra of Logic: A Contribution to the Philosophy of Notation", which was so ahead of its time that is was understood neither by his peers nor the generations that followed (see Ma & Pietarinen 2018a for a recent study). Two decades later Peirce would still feel that it was the aftermath of that paper that led him to give up publishing efforts on the topic of logic altogether; what he would subsequently produce were "written for my eyes solely, like all my logical papers of the last twenty years" (R 253, 1905; LoF 1).

projects, and even substantial rejections, lacunæ and lost pages supply that important context. Although much editorial effort has been expended on identifying, studying, selecting, organising, transcribing and producing the material in its final format, the present series is a *critical edition* only in the sense of having attempted to identify, select and study the thematically relevant material, with much less contemplation whether that material may have accorded with Peirce's intentions and thoughts about the production of final or ultimate versions of any given piece than what is to be expected of critical editions.

Second, the volumes are *chronological* with respect to their internal thematic organisation. Again, Peirce typically worked simultaneously on many projects, writing assignments, letters, proofs and calculations, producing text and delivering results virtually daily on multiple fronts. (Curiously but understandably, nearly all of the pages included in the first volume were written in the warmth of the months between April and August, 1895–1907; his residence was often too cold during winter to support sustained literary engagements.) *Logic of the Future* aims at preserving thematic unities as far as practicable. This is reflected in the organisation of the material in seven distinct parts. The ordering of writings within those parts is chronological, with a few unavoidable concessions. Peirce's letters are organised in sets of exchanges according to the people involved, and the selections in the first part, *Reasoning and Diagrams*, are presented in a roughly reverse chronological order from 1910 to 1895. The reason for the latter is solely didactic: Peirce's wider perspectives and explanations on the value of the method of EGs find their best formulation in his most mature work deriving from not much earlier than 1910. It is hoped that this retrospective glance helps soften the reader's landing on the more demanding pieces that begin to get off the ground during 1896. Retrospection also aids in placing the superabundant ideas of their inventor into wider philosophical and systematic perspectives.

The methods that have guided the selection of present texts also need an explanation. The leading principle for inclusion is that Peirce writes on, or makes substantial references to, his EGs. The present volumes thus do not cover all of his logic: his pioneering work on the algebra of logic, for example, though in many important ways aiding and abetting the development of EGs and being intimately related to their underlying logical ideas, does not belong to the scope of the present collection. His important other logical, philosophical and semiotic writings that were obviously motivated by the discovery and advancement of the graphical method but do not directly engage with it, have likewise largely been left out.

Often the transitions between algebraic and graphical points of view are without much difference. Sometimes Peirce employs terminology in the logic of the algebra of the copula that may be more familiar from his theory of logical graphs (such as "scriptibility", "sheet of assertion"). For example, in the context of the *Minute Logic* (R 430, ms p. 70, 1902), the writing down of a proposition "on some duly validated *sheet of assertions*" makes the proposition so uttered an assertion that "becomes a binding act". This "we will pretend" to be so "[f]or the sake of fixing our ideas" (*ibid.*). The supposition that one takes there to be the "sheet" upon which an utterance or writing down of a proposition makes it an act of assertion is common in Peirce's algebra of logic just as it is in his graphical method. Likewise is the application of the term "to scribe" or "scriptibility": any algebraic or graphical constituent that has a signification by virtue of the fact that it has been asserted as having that signification, is said to be *scriptible* whenever "it is applicable to V, the *veritas*, in some understood sense" (*ibid.*).

As another example, among Peirce's important writings on logic that are omitted from the present collection is R 501 (c.1901, plus adjacent pages in R 9 and R 11), as these worksheets do not directly employ the notation of logical graphs (and as they are to appear elsewhere).[4] In this treatise, Peirce is seen to present both a general theory of deduction and of the consequence relation, the two cornerstones in the development of modern logic. Its importance thus cannot be overestimated. Peirce is led to these theories by three important generalisations: those of (i) propositions to all signs, (ii) truth to *scriptibility*, i.e. "capable of being written conformably to the purpose" (R 501, late 1901), and (iii) derivation to *transformability*, i.e. "capable of being transformed without changing anything scriptible into anything non-scriptible" (R 430, early 1902). One can also find in R 516 (LoF 1), "On the Basic Rules of Logical Transformation", similar definitions of 'scriptible' and 'transformable' in the context of the graphical method of the logic of existential graphs.

A different set of important texts that regrettably does not have space for inclusion in the present edition consists of Peirce's extensive writings, commentaries and criticism on Alfred Bray Kempe's 1886 publication on mathematical graphical forms (R 708–R 715). Although clearly preceding and influencing Peirce's subsequent studies on logical graphs, these and several other writings of his that antedate the year 1896 have to appear elsewhere.[5] It is ultimately only in connection to everything that Peirce wrote, throughout his life, on mathematics and algebra,

---

[4] Ma & Pietarinen (2019) provide a complete transcription of Peirce's "Dragon Logic" of R 501, with an introduction that relate it to later discoveries in modern logic. In brief, Peirce introduces a new Dragon-Head and Dragon-Tail notation: The Dragon Head, Ω, is the implicational sign, and is used in a dual form which Peirce terms the Dragon-Tail, $\hat{C}$, which is an inverse of the head. (Peirce added the circumflex to $\hat{C}$ because C is a singular sign.)

[5] See Grattan-Guinness (2002, 2007) on the account of Peirce's writings on Kempe's theory and their subsequent influence.

both multiple and logical, that we can assess the place of the graphical method and its genesis in the overall development of these interconnected logical, philosophical, notational and mathematical contributions.

The second criterion for inclusion is that the texts *have not been previously published*. Like the first, this principle has its exceptions, but it is a useful one given how long-lasting the lack of access has been to some of the most important writings dating from Peirce's later years. Duplication of EG-related papers that have long been easily available has been avoided, most prominently that of his 1906 "Prolegomena to an Apology for Pragmaticism" paper. There are, however, copious draft versions and leaves pertaining to "Prolegomena" (the galleys have not been recovered) that have not been published before and those are included in LoF 3. Whenever Peirce's writings that have appeared in print before are published in LoF 1–3, the versions that appear are presumed to be more complete versions of their previous publications. The present edition provides not only the alternative and discrete versions and drafts. It also aims to improve upon previous editions by filling in some gaps and omissions. Details are provided in the volume-specific introductions, individual headnotes and annotations.

Editorial Apparatus

The present edition has aimed at narrating the fairly complex technical and graphical notation in a uniform format. The unique 'language' of graphs and other signs and designs peculiar to Peirce's logic and semiotics obviously presents a number of editorial and interpretative challenges. These challenges have been faced by creating a special LaTeX package that produces any graph of whatever kind in a uniform format which is as close to the authorial hand, intentions and explanations as possible. The package includes commands and designs for all logical signs and symbols that have been encountered in Peirce's *Nachlass*. The design of those signs takes into account both (i) how we find them drawn in the relevant autographic sources, and (ii) what Peirce's detailed—and often unfulfilled— instructions to the typesetters were.[6] Fitting several thousand graphs in the vol-

---

[6] For example, in Peirce's algebra of logic the signs similar to sums and products are not the signs of sums Σ and products Π, but those for which "*upright* type should be used without those little finishing-lines the names of which I forget [Sans Serif]. That is *not* $\Sigma\Pi$ but $\mathsf{\Sigma\Pi}$ like inscriptions. You will find many examples in the *Mathematische Annalen*. As a general rule of printing formulae, I like all capitals Roman, all l.c. letters Italics. I only use the small alphabet as subscript letters" (CSP to the Open Court, R S-64, draft, 1896; cf. September 2, 1896 CSP to TJMcC [T. J. McCormack, Assistant Editor at the Open Court]; LoF 3).

umes, both inline and as display items, would have been impossible in any other way than by programming a Peirce-specific LaTeX code, commands and environments that can uniformly produce them all. The next section has more details on editing and typesetting these graphs.

Instead of aiming at a clear-text version, *Logic of the Future* edition follows a quasi-diplomatic protocol. Important changes and alterations have been incorporated into the text, displaying inline Peirce's crossed-out texts, deletions and rejections. The default reading is that any portion of text that is stricken-through or crossed out represents an altered portion of text which Peirce replaced with what immediately follows it in the text. Again, this protocol is fallible as editorial discretion must be exercised on what the most meaningful and significant deletions and alterations are taken to be. The gain is an added insight into the evolution of Peirce's thinking and prose at one glance. Double struck-outs are used when an above-text alteration was itself deleted.

Insignificant changes have been emended silently to improve readability. Accordingly, textual apparatus has been kept to a minimum. The downside is that many of the additions of words, lexical units, phrases and sentences that are found in the manuscripts and papers are non-visibly blended into the flow of the text. Marginalia and corrections from Peirce's galleys, books and offprints have been included whenever available, and collateral and external sources have been resorted to in order to verify details and timings of various episodes as well as to confirm the identity of literary sources.

In short, this is an inclusive, thematic, thematically chronological and quasi-diplomatic edition, which aims at maximising novelty and contribution to the advancement of logic and Peirce's logical philosophy. There is a certain urgency in getting the material to appear in print and to reach audiences beyond the communities of scholars who can work directly with Peirce's manuscripts. The impact of his writings on the development of modern logic and on the improvement of human reason becomes understood only through a widespread access to these complex sources.

The abundance of discrete variant texts that derives from Peirce's later period of life—and especially from his profuse works on logical graphs—has necessitated an inclusive editorial approach that makes room for variant texts and versions that diverge from each other in multiple ways yet pertain to the same authorial project or the line of thought. Often Peirce worked without any expressed authorial purpose of aiming at bringing his thoughts, results and diagrams before the public eye. The present edition aims at maximising the amount of alternative but divergent texts while minimising the amount of effort that the reader needs in order to locate the points in which the variant texts show the beginnings of a divergence. Often this has to be carried out at the expense of sacrificing certain critical editing principles that aim at distilling final authorial intentions from textual masses. But what is gained is the lowering of the risk that significant ideas, terms, definitions or results, which notoriously appear in variants, be left out.

Presenting constantly diverging and evolving sets of texts is hardly possible in a strictly linear format. In the present edition, variant pages and alternative segments have been included in the footnotes or, when they are several pages long, appended to the respective chapters. In both cases it is the vicinity of discrete variants that counts in the final output. The reader can observe where the forking has occurred by following the footnoting and boldfaced references **[Alt. *n*]** prefixed to alternative continuations, where *n* is an index of discrete texts that share the same branching point. Since in many cases there are several substantive alternatives and since at least in some of these cases it is not feasible to venture into guessing whether they represent superseded authorial intentions or whether one or several of them could constitute the final or the maximally authoritative version of the text (or present evidence of the absence of such textual hierarchies), the reader is in such cases presented with options, in hope of furthering the scholarship along the way. It may be that in some cases the alternatives provided in footnotes or appendices in fact represent Peirce's more mature thought, perhaps even those that pertain to some fair copy-text project of his without specific indications. Likewise, substantial deletions and rejections have been retained, either inline or in the footnotes, preceded by editorial tags (**[Del.:]**, **[Rej.:]**). When in rare cases editorial attempts have been frustrated in deciphering a lexical item or a part of an item that occurs in the original source, [*illeg.*] is used in its stead.

When there is an apparent discontinuity in the text either because of physical reasons such as missing, disordered and torn-out pages, or corrupted sheets due to soiling, fire or ink spills, or because of mental reasons such as interruptions of thought, lapses of focus or concentration, but the two texts otherwise can be judged to be parts of the same writing episode, a non-boldfaced flag '[discont.]' is placed in between the conjecturally discontinuous parts. Short editorial omissions and missing text (words or at most a few sentences) as well as incomplete beginnings of alternative texts are indicated by [...]; longer omissions (typically several paragraphs or pages rather than sentences) by [– – –]. Ellipses are used either in order to avoid or curtail excess and irrelevant material or to indicate missing material and lacunæ of any kind, with explanations added. Frequent abrupt endings of the text are indicated by [end].

All editorial annotations are interspersed within the text or given in footnotes and enclosed in upright brackets. Selection titles supplied by the editor are likewise bracketed. Peirce's inconsistent use of brackets has been emended to parentheses to avoid confusion. Identifiers for textual sources are likewise editorial annotations and are included in the text at the beginning of the respective selections, such as **[R 1601]** or [From R S-30] etc. Page references to manuscript sources are to Peirce's own pagination, and when available, are abbreviated by 'ms p.' or 'ms pp.'. ISP pagination numbers are not used.

The editorial approach is thus conservative both as concerns the selection of texts as well as their collation, annotation and textual apparatus. Authorial revisions are visible in the final output with respect to the most significant alterations. Most of the annotations, clarifications and interpretational issues concerning copy-texts and their compositional stages are incorporated in the introductory surveys or in the chapter-wise headnotes. Textual apparatus itself, including detailed information about copy-texts, alternations, variants and editorial emendations, is largely implicit and retained in the source files but not reproduced in the compiled output. Meta-data such as original pagination, running headers and other information about manuscript pages and their organisation are likewise not included in the final output though preserved in the source file layer. Standard and silent normalisations and alterations apply to minor elements of punctuation, such as adding or toggling between single and double quotation marks, typesetting headings and heading punctuation, italization of book titles, and the like. Peirce's original capitalisation of words is preserved. His Latin, Greek, Hieroglyphic, Hebrew, Arabic and other non-English words, phrases, sentences and quotations are given in full but not translated. The sometimes inappropriate vocabulary has been reproduced as is (e.g., "redskin", "negro", "negress", "Flathead Indians", "lover only of a virgin", "lover of every Pope"). In several cases these appear in Peirce's examples (e.g., "Every Hottentot kills a Hottentot") and as such are made up sentences that are entertained, not asserted.

Editing Graphs

In the present edition, graphs are just as important as the text overall. Special note must therefore be made on the methods, techniques and decisions involved in the editorial process of bringing graphs and similar visually pronounced elements into the appearance they have in these volumes. This is not only because of the sheer number of diagrammatic elements involved, but because the totality of instances of graphs also constitutes an actual corpus of a language. As far as the typesetting of the diagrammatic syntax of such graphical languages is concerned, Peirce would typically scribe graphs inline, and only when they grew relatively large in two dimensions, or when there was need to refer to them with running numbers or figure captions, would he display them as individual items or floated or wrapped figures separated from the body of the text. In all cases it is important to keep in mind that graphs are more than mere pictures. They are formulæ of logic and expressions of a language, just as mathematical, logical and natural languages are composed out of designated constituents and lexical units to express relevant and intended meanings. To scribe a graph on the sheet is to assert it. Graphs that appear on the sheet of paper or on the screen of a computer are to be treated as an integral part of the scholarly prose. This needs to be properly acknowledged and accommodated in one's editorial and textual practices, too.

The way the diagrammatic syntax of the language of EGs has been technically handled in the present edition is in terms of developing a special LaTeX package (EGpeirce.sty) that produces uniform, inline-sized graphs that prevent increase in baseline spacing as much as possible. This implies that their "spots" (the predicate terms) that may appear either in natural language, letters (typically upright capital) or some other special marks or mathematical symbols that Peirce used for that purpose, are regularly typeset in small font. For example, A is a graph scribed on a sheet of assertion, and drawing an oval ("the cut") around it produces (A). With two ovals the result looks like ((A)), with three (((A))), and so on. When some added spacing becomes unavoidable, the preference is to typeset graphs within the text in that case, too. In this manner, the meaningful units of Peirce's diagrammatic syntax—its graph-instances—can be adequately treated as lexical units and utterances in their own right and without discriminating them against the prose of natural language. In those places in which Peirce did write the graphs as display items and when incorporation of them into the text would have cluttered the result and made the text jarring to read, the copy-text layout has been followed as far as practicable. Often Peirce used figure captions to index displayed graphs; those are always preserved and graphs produced in the location nearest to their original appearance in copy-text, always with the caption and reference number given by the authorial hand. To accord with publisher's house style, graphs and figures that appear wrapped in the manuscripts are unwrapped, however.

As mentioned, examples of logical graphs amount to several thousand in Peirce's vast corpus on EGs, often drawn with tinctures of red, blue, brown and green. While all of them have been inspected and studied in their original form at relevant repositories, there are also pages after pages of doodles, seriously incomplete and repetitive examples, sketches too faint or smudged to read; and countless obscure or meaningless ornaments that obviously need not or cannot be included even in the most comprehensive edition, at least perhaps for no other reason than aesthetics. This said, thousands of graphs have been produced, in uniform and, whenever possible, compressed and space-saving formats, that reduced excess blank space while sacrificing nothing of the readability of graphical texture. (It was a major challenge in Peirce's time to print the graphs, especially the curved lines, at all.) When there are several nests of cuts with only blanks between them, the resulting and sometimes disturbing Moiré effect has been reduced by applying non-symmetric spacing between the cuts. Caption numbers and their in-text references have been made uniform, standardised and corrected when the occasional slip of the pen has happened. These are all silent emendations and standardisations that pertain to the appearance of graphical forms and change nothing in their meaning.

In all cases, graphs are as close to Peirce's original hand as practicable, and they take into account all meaningful features and information visible in original graphs and their respective explanations. The thickness of the lines as well as the shapes of their loose ends are significant features and need to be accurately reproduced. Likewise, Peirce's occasional use of coloured ink in drawing the graphs is preserved in the electronic edition. Typically, he would draw the thick lines of identity in red and the thin cuts in blue ink, especially in 1903 and later when he had better access to ink palettes. Brown and green ink was also availed of in addition to red and blue by the authorial hand to denote specific logical and notational features, especially in reference to second-order graphs (LoF 2). Peirce also resorted to colours for improved didactic effect when educating his students, audiences and correspondents on the fundamentals of EGs. All colours are preserved in the electronic version of the edition, and its grey-scale rendition is expected to reproduce the contrast between light and dark colours as far as possible.

Several images from Peirce's manuscripts are included, either together with their uniform LaTeX rendition or occasionally as stand alone illustrations. These are marked with **[P.H.]** (standing for "Peirce's Hand"). A couple of facsimiles of entire holograph pages from Peirce's collections have also been included to perfect the material.

While nearly every meaningful piece that Peirce ever wrote or scribed on the topic of EGs is presumed to have been included in the volumes of *Logic of the Future*, this effort is by no means intended to nullify the value of Peirce's original pages, the beauty of which the reader is invited to experience first-hand in the relevant physical and electronic archival locations.

Justification of the Title

It remains to give an explanation of the title chosen to represent the entire edition. On Christmas Day 1909 Peirce wrote to William James that what he had discovered "ought to be the Logic of the Future". What was it that he had discovered? Peirce writes that,

> My triumph in that [algebraic] line, my Existential Graphs, by which all deduction is reduced to insertions and erasures, and in which there are no connecting signs except the writing of terms on the same area enclosed in an oval and heavy lines to express the identity of the individual objects whose signs are connected by such lines. This ought to be *the Logic of the Future*. (R L 224, LoF 3, added emphasis, capitalisation in the original)

This passage epitomises the most important aspects of that new logic. First, historically, EGs represent a natural continuation, application and expansion of algebraic methods that Peirce had worked on for nearly half a century. We now know that everything that can be graphicalised can also be made to work according to algebraic principles. Second, the method Peirce refers to in this passage shows what deduction consists of: a series of insertions and erasures according to certain specified rules of illative transformations. Third, juxtaposition and enclosure completely characterise propositional logic (termed the "Alpha part" of EGs since 1903). These two signs suffice for a system that agrees with a two-element Boolean algebra. An addition of heavy lines moreover extends an Alpha system to (fragments of) first-order predicate logic with identity (termed the "Beta part" of EGs since 1903). Whatever the graphical systems are—and not necessarily only *existential* graphs—they can now incorporate and exploit these three characteristics in full. It is the realisation of the full generality of the graphical method that Peirce predicts is awaiting us in the future.

It may have been only through the advent of modern-day computers, proof theory, mathematics of continuity, cognitive sciences, and a plethora of diagrammatic and heterogeneous notations invented to aid discovery and development of scientific theories, that have put Peirce's prediction into an interesting albeit perhaps somewhat uneasy perspective. How did a single mind not only manage to predict but also contribute to fields that in reality were far ahead in the future? As is the case with a rare number of brains at any epoch of time, Peirce's mind was an anomaly. Largely devoid of academic context and intellectual stimulation of students, in his later years piles of papers accumulated in the attic of his house "Arisbe" in Milford, Pennsylvania, for apparently nothing else than for the sake of advancing the reasoning of posterity. This incremental and exploratory, often painstakingly slow but persistent effort made him realise that an evolution of altogether new logical theories was taking place. This realisation motivated and guided the investigations of this American brain—not the outside influences or recognition expected of them.

"The time will come when the world will be amazed at this" (R 280).

Ahti-Veikko Pietarinen
Introduction to the Theory of Existential Graphs, Volumes 2/1 and 2/2

Introduction

Martin Gardner, in his pioneering book on diagrammatic reasoning, *Logic Machines and Diagrams* (1958), summarised Charles Sanders Peirce's work on the graphical method of logic in the following words:

> We must remember, however, that Peirce undertook his Gargantuan project at a time when symbolic logic was in its infancy. In many aspects of his method he was a pioneer groping in unfamiliar realms. His logic graphs are still the most ambitious yet attempted, and they are filled with suggestive hints of what can be done along such lines. Peirce himself expected successors to take up where he left off and bring his system to perfection. It would be rash to say that no one in the future will be able to build upon it something closer to what Peirce was striving for. In the meantime, it stands as a characteristic monument to one man's extraordinary industry, brilliance, and eccentricity. (Gardner 1958, p. 59)

Peirce self-estimation from mid-1907 was somewhat more modest in kind:

> The author of this book might as well leave his name unmentioned since he has accomplished nothing else but to ~~write this~~ work out the theory sketched in this book and to be more fully set forth and defended in another that he hopes to complete since the day when a diffident boy at this time he picked up from his brother's table a copy of Whatley's *Logic* and asked what logic was and having received an answer stretched himself upon the carpet to devour that book. Now after debating all the points many and many a time within himself a timid old man; he asks himself for the last time whether all this is true. Who can tell? The world will certainly not accept it in a hurry; nor ought it. But the truth will shine clearly out and that in the main the truth is, that which is upheld in these pages is then the belief held with all the strength of head and heart by the author. (R 1608, May 1907)[1]

---

[1] This appears on an unidentified single leaf. It can be dated by the paper type, handwriting status, medical records, and the content that is proximal to Charles's May 1907 letter to his wife Juliette, in which he reveals that "only two things prevent my committing suicide to which I am greatly tempted. One is that I may be useful to you. The other is that I want to write those two little books both of which will do good to many people and bring us money. I am fully resolved to turn over a complete new leaf, give up all my habits of self-indulgence and try to make the rest of my poor life useful" (CSP to JP, May 7, 1907; R L 340).

These words relate to Peirce's planned opening passages for a book (or two) on logic, which he still in his deathbed was convinced is something gravely needed in order to 'make philosophy scientific again'. In his later years, Peirce wanted to save philosophy from the clutches of humanistic studies that scorn scientific practice and pretend to be able to make advances without having to learn and apply the arduous details of methods of logical reasoning.

In that summer, around the time of planning those important books on logic, Peirce receives William James's 1907 book, *Pragmatism*, that contained his popular Lowell Institute Lectures from the previous year, the same series that Peirce had concluded over three years earlier but without success in publishing the lectures. While James's book has often been hailed as no less than the most important contribution to American philosophy, Peirce's 1903 Lowell Lectures were quickly falling into oblivion.[2]

With an allusion to Ferdinand Canning Scott Schiller (1864–1937) among such scholars that had come to deform Peirce's original meaning of pragmatism (Pietarinen 2011b), Peirce had in the meantime drafted a dictionary entry on "Humanism" to drive the point home, with some characteristic satire:

> **Humanism.** Like everybody else I admire humanists and their professed aims. But my admiration of them is by no means unbounded. When they talk of science, as they often do, as abstruse, afflicting, arduous, arid, arenulous, asperous, abstract, abject, apeptic, appallary, abnormal, atrabiliary, abominable, asafetidal, anaclastic, abhorrent, arsenical, abysmal, arithrid, aphagous, and anathema, that simply shows that they ~~like~~ enjoy eating the kindly fruits of the earth better than they do tilling the soil and spreading the manure.
>
> Why should they not abuse the drudges? It is their way of expressing their superior souls.

---

[2] A poignant self-recognition of the implications of his practice of conducting slow science are the autobiographical remarks from the same year, which Peirce recorded on the questionnaire form solicited for the publication of *Men of Science in the United States*, a biographical directory edited by his former student James McKeen Cattell published in 1906:

> **Department of Study:** Logic. [...]
> **Honors Conferred:** Never any, nor any encouragement or aid of any kind or description in my life work, excepting a splendid series of magnificent promises.
> **Books with publishers:** *Photometric Researches* (Leibzig: Wilhelm Engelmann, 1878); Edited *Studies in Logic by Members of the Johns Hopkins University* (Little, Brown & Co, 1883) and B[enjamin] Peirce's *Linear Associative Algebra*, 1882.
> **Chief Subject of Research:** Logic.
> **Where Chiefly Published:** Not published except in slight fragments. See Schröeder's *Logik*.
> **Researches in Progress:** In logic will continue as long as I retain my faculties and can afford pen and ink. (R 1611, 1903)

But ~~personall~~ for my part, not being able to do everything, I limit my endeavors to make philosophy scientific like the sciences that I was bred in, [end]
Many of the recent papers upon Pragmatism, Instrumentalism, Humanism, etc. have been attempts to [end] (R S-82, c.1905)

"[H]ave been attempts to apply those doctrines to notions falling outside the domain of their original conception", Peirce might have continued this abandoned passage. Logic, in contrast, and the analytic method of logical graphs in particular, would show what the real definitions consist of, and how such real definitions would follow from applications of the principle or maxim of pragmati(ci)sm. Without the agility and an unceasing desire to rightly follow up on that chief method of the venerable trivium of the liberal arts, logic or dialectics, humanists' aims would remain forever unfulfilled.[3]

Peirce's idea of logic shows, at the same time, to be equally remote from those emerging conceptions of the early 20th century that took logic to be an exercise in how to promulgate formal systems of inference and proof; systems that may be uninterpreted in their languages, non-anthropological in their epistemologies, and in constant danger of ascribing to an empiricist dogma that implies a strict separation of logical and extra-logical affairs (Pietarinen 2011a). Peirce would see dark clouds gathering over both humanists' noble aims and the logicists' narrowly-conceived impressions. The remedy, as he saw it, was to offer a positive solution to both. This was to be carried out by a massive improvement in the theory of logic,

---

[3] There is a direct and important connection from these remarks to Peirce's 1903 Lowell Lectures: in a letter to F. C. S. Schiller on May 12, 1905, Peirce recollects his course of lectures in Boston in which he "explained at length how reasoning was analogous—and in fact, a particular case of,—moral self-control, how Logic ought to be founded on Ethics and Ethics on a transfigured Esthetics which would be the science of values, although now wrongly treated as a part of Ethics. After the lectures were over on December 17th, I first laid eyes on the outside of *Humanism* [Schiller 1903], and when, long after, I was able to look at the inside, I was sorry I had not seen it when I wrote those lectures" (CSP to FCSS, May 12, 1905, R L 390). Since Peirce was in a hurry to return to his home in Arisbe, Milford, already on the 18th, it might have been that James had just barely managed to show Peirce the cover of the copy of Schiller's new book that James had recently received. Having suffered from influenza (tonsillitis) since December 10, James was indisposed much of that last week of Peirce's course, and apparently did not attend the last two or three lectures (December 10, 14 and 17), having been "cooped up for three weeks" (WJ to CSP, December 31, 1903, R L 224). It is more likely, then, that Peirce had made a brief visit to see James during the day of the final lecture: "I can see you to morrow if you should be able to call" (WJ to CSP, December 16, 1903; James 2002, p. 345, postmarked "Boston Dec 17, 4am", R L 224). Schiller's book contains a footnote in which Schiller tells to have been corrected—probably by James—that the term 'pragmatism' in fact originates from Peirce, adding, quite misleadingly, that according to the doctrine of pragmatism, Peirce does not have a good claim to the ownership of that designation, since the term did not catch on from the writings and communications of its inventor.

unforeseen since Aristotle, that would offer systems of representation applicable, in the best possible fashion, to the analysis of the meanings of our intellectual conceptions, mental states and rational thoughts as well as to our units of language. This was the ultimate aim of the theory of Existential Graphs (EGs), which reached its most extensive expression in 1903, the *annus mirabilis* of Peirce's scientific life.

Basic Notions

Existential Graphs (EGs) are a graphical method of logic which Peirce gravitated to in 1896 and for which he in the 1903 Lowell Lectures coined the now-customary terminology that divided the method into the Alpha, Beta, and Gamma parts. The logic of the Alpha part is a propositional (sentential) logic and agrees with the two-element Boolean algebra. Peirce often began his presentation of EGs with the second, Beta part of the method that corresponds to a fragment of first-order predicate logic with identity. This introduction follows suit and first provides an informal presentation of the Beta part, followed by a slightly more detailed introduction to the Alpha part. The main ideas of the Gamma part had to do with modal logics, and are explained in the introductory essay to the present volume of the *Logic of the Future* series.

Peirce defined the central terms "graph", "graph-replica", "existential graph" and "to scribe" in his 1903 Lowell Lectures as follows:

> Every expression of a proposition in conformity with the conventions of this system is called an *existential graph*, or for brevity, a *graph* (although there are other kinds of graphs). Since it is sometimes awkward to say that a graph is *written* and it is sometimes awkward to say it is *drawn*, I will always say it is *scribed*. A graph scribed on the sheet of assent [the sheet of assertion] is said to be *accepted*. We must distinguish carefully between the *graph* and its different *replicas* [instances]. It is the *graph* which is accepted; and the graph is scribed when a *replica* of it is scribed". (R 450, LoF 2/2)

The distinction between the graphs as *types* and graphs as *replicas* (later renamed *instances*) is one of the central distinctions (see also R S-28), and its articulation in this first version of the second Lowell Lecture (R 450, R S-27, R S-28) from September 1903 triggered Peirce to undertake a complete overhaul of this doctrine of speculative grammar during the last quarter of 1903. What is scribed on the sheet of assertion (or on the "sheet or assent") is the replica (instance) of a graph. What the graphs are in general, correspond to their types. What is asserted (or "assented" to) are the graphs as types. The same graph could be scribed on different parts of the sheet as different replicas or instances without thus producing different graphs.

The invention of EGs was in part motivated by Peirce's need to respond to the expressive insufficiency and lack of analytic power of the two systems described, first in the "Note B: The Logic of Relatives" of the *Studies in Logic, by Members of the Johns Hopkins University* (SiL, pp. 187–203), which Peirce later termed the algebra of dyadic (dual) relatives, and soon after in the 1885 paper "On the Algebra of Logic: A Contribution to the Philosophy of Notation", which he termed his general (or universal) algebra of logic. The analytic power derives from subsuming algebraic operations under one mode of composition. This composition of concepts is effected in the quantificational, Beta part of the theory of EGs by the device of *ligatures*. A ligature is a complex line, composed of what Peirce terms the *lines of identities*, which connects various parts and areas of the graphs (see e.g. Dipert 2006; Pietarinen 2005a, 2006a, 2011a, 2015b; Roberts 1973; Shin 2002; Zeman 1964). Here are three examples:

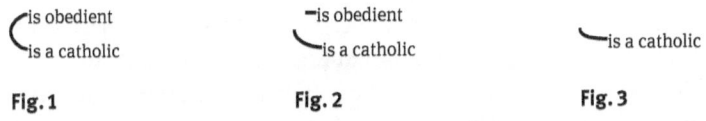

Fig. 1   **Fig. 2**   **Fig. 3**

The meaning of these lines is that two or more descriptions apply to the same thing. For example, in Fig. 2 there is a line attached to the predicate term "is obedient". It means that "something exists which is obedient". There is also another line which connects to the predicate term "is a catholic", and that composition means that "something exists which is a catholic", which is equivalent to the graph-instance given in Fig. 3. Since in Fig. 1 these two lines are in fact connected by one continuous line, the graph-instance in Fig. 1 means that "there exists a catholic who is obedient", that is, "there exists an obedient catholic". Ligatures, representing continuous connections composed of two or more lines of identity, stand for quantification, identity and predication, all in one go.

EGs are drawn on the *sheet of assertion*. It represents what the modeller knows or what mutually has been agreed upon to be the case by those who undertake the investigation of logic. The sheet thus represents the universe of discourse. Any graph that is drawn on the sheet puts forth an assertion, true or false, that there is something in the universe to which it applies. This is the reason why Peirce terms these graphs *existential*. Drawing a circle around the graph, or alternatively, shading the area on which the graph-instance rests, means that nothing exists of the sort of description intended. In Fig. 4, the assertion "something is a catholic" is denied by drawing an oval around it and thus severing that assertion from the sheet of assertion:

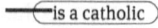

Fig. 4

The graph-instance depicted in Fig. 4 thus means that "something exists that is not catholic".

Peirce aimed at a diagrammatic syntax that would use a minimal number of logical signs, at the same time be maximally expressive while facilitating as analytic a system of reasoning as possible. His ovals, for instance, serve several notational functions: "The first office which the ovals fulfill is that of negation. [...] The second office of the ovals is that of associating the conjunctions of terms. [...] This is the office of parentheses in algebra" (R 430, ms pp. 54–56, 1902; LoF 1). The ovals are thus not only the diagrammatic counterpart to negation but also serve to represent the compositional structure of a graph-formula. Peirce held (see e.g. R 430; R 670, 1911; LoF 1) that a notation that does not separate the sign of truth-function from the representation of its scope is more analytic than a notation, such as that of an ordinary 'symbolic' language, where such a separation is required by the one-dimensional notation. The role of ovals as denials is in fact a derived function from the more primitive considerations of inclusion and implication (Bellucci & Pietarinen 2016; R 300, 1908; LoF 3).

As far as the expressivity of logical languages is concerned, Peirce had already recognised that the notion of *dependent* quantification was essential to the advancement of the theory of logic and that it needed to be captured in any system expressive enough to fully serve the purpose of logical analysis. The nested system of ovals do this in a natural way, much in contrast to algebras that resort to an explicit use of parentheses and other punctuation marks. For example, the graph in Fig. 5 means that "Every Catholic adores some woman". The graph in Fig. 6 means that "Some woman is adored by every Catholic". Peirce notes that the latter asserts more than the former since it states that all Catholics adore the same woman, whereas the former allows different Catholics to adore different women:

Fig. 5   Fig. 6

The graph in Fig. 7 means, moreover, that "anything whatever is unloved by something that benefits it", that is, "everything is benefitted by something or other that does not love it":

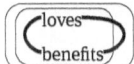

Fig. 7

Graphs can get quite complex, but perhaps still less complex than their natural-language correlates. Peirce occasionally gave examples of some very complicated sentences with intricate quantificational structures, and proposed to model and analyse them with the aid of the graphical method. An example is Fig. 8, which is to be interpreted "in a universe of sentient beings" (R 504, 1898; LoF 1):

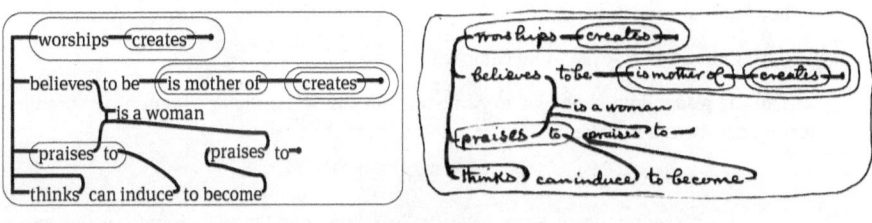

Fig. 8   [P.H.]

The graphical form, Peirce assumes, brings about the meaning of the sentence in a clearer way than what the sentences given in natural language could possibly reveal. For example, the previous graph expresses the following sentence:

> Every being unless he worships some being who does not create all beings either does not believe any being (unless it be not a woman) to be any mother of a creator of all beings or else he praises that woman to every being unless to a person whom he does not think he can induce to become anything unless it be a non-praiser of that woman to every being.

Peirce's example is complicated; the quantificational structure and the dependencies exhibited in the constituents of this sentence are certainly not easily discerned from the linguistic material.

It is on the level of semantics that the power of dependent quantification comes to the fore. Peirce carried his semantics out in terms of defining what today is recognised as two-player zero-sum semantic games that take place between the Graphist/Utterer and the Grapheus/Interpreter.[4] This is explained in a variant of "New Elements (Kaina stoicheia)" (R 517, 1901)[5] as follows. The copulative is *general* and *definite*, as to assert A and B "is to assert a proposition which the interpreter is at liberty to take as meaning A or as meaning B". The disjunctive, on the other hand, is *vague* and thus *individual* in nature, as to assert A or B "is to assert a proposition which gives the utterer the option between defending it by proving A and defending it by proving B" (R 517, ms p. 50). And not only this, Peirce continues that there are strategic advantages according to the order of the choices of selection:

> The asserter of a proposition may be said to [be] *ex officio* a defender of it, or, in the old logical phrase, a respondent for it. The interpreter is, on the other hand, naturally a critic of it and quasi-opponent. Now if a proposition is in one respect vague, so that in that respect the respondent has the choice of an instance, while in another respect it is general, so that in that respect the opponent has the choice of an instance, whichever party makes his choice last has the advantage of being able to adapt his instance to the choice already made by the other. For that reason,
>
> Some woman is loved by all catholics,
>
> where the respondent is obliged to name the woman before the opponent has chosen his catholic, is harder to defend, and less apt to be true, than
>
> Every catholic loves some woman,
>
> where the opponent must instance his catholic, whereupon the respondent can choose his woman accordingly.
>
> It is a curious fact that when there are a number of ~~obvious~~ signified choosings of instances, it is not the later one which has the logical character of an operator upon the one already made, but the reverse. Thus, in the last example [end] (R 517, ms pp. 50–51)[6]

Peircean semantic games were not limited to interpreting natural-language sentences or graph-instances of the theory of EGs.[7] He often applied the same idea

---

[4] Sometimes, and especially in relation to Peirce's *model-building games*, these roles are split so that the Grapheus and the Interpreter are playing separate roles. On this, see Pietarinen (2013). Hilpinen (1982) is the first to notice Peirce's logic as having been importantly erected upon the principles of semantic games. On games in logic, see e.g. Pietarinen (2003b); Majer, Pietarinen & Tulenheimo (2011).

[5] Internal and external evidence suggests that Peirce wrote "Kaina stoicheia" in late 1901 and not in 1904 as has been suggested in the Robin Catalogue and in the publication of that essay in EP 2.

[6] Similar textual evidence for the game-theoretic interpretation occurs in numerous places, see e.g. R 238, R S-64 and the references in Pietarinen (2003a).

[7] How close Peircean semantic games are to contemporary ones has been explored in Pietarinen (2001, 2003a, 2007, 2013).

also to the interpretation of complex quantificational patterns and connectives in his general algebra of logic. In some cases both were considered in unison, as revealed in the following fragment located in R S-64 and probably written sometime in 1893–1894:

> It will be found that the algebraic method is the more convenient; but some persons have such a difficulty with algebra that I add the graphical method.
>
> Given a proposition about two things a and b, if you are to select the thing to be represented by a with a view to making the proposition false, and I am to select b with a view to making the proposition true, it may be an advantage to me, and can be no disadvantage to know what your selection is to be, before I ~~determine~~ fix upon mine. Hence, if the proposition be such that it is true even if I make my selection first, much more will it be true if you make the first selection. Accordingly, if a proposition be written either in the algebraic or the graphical system, and that proposition be true, much more will it be true when any letter in a square or affixed to a Π is moved to the left. For a similar reason, of two letters both in circles or in squares, or both attached to Σs or to Πs, it is indifferent which comes first. Thus, to say that every man loves every woman is the same as to say that every woman is loved by every man; and to say that some man loves some woman is the same as to say that some woman is loved by some man; but to say that some man loves every woman is to say much more than that every woman is loved by some man.
>
> [Alt.] There are other interesting systems of representing propositions; but it is not necessary to consider them here. The above algebraic system is the most convenient; but I add the graphical for the sake of the many readers who do not take kindly to algebra.
>
> Given a proposition about two subjects, A and B, if *you* are to select the subject A with a view to making the proposition false, if you can,—in which case, plainly, A is universal, for the proposition asserts itself to be true, and hence that you cannot succeed in this,—while *I* am to select B with a view to making the proposition true,—so that B is particular,—then it may be of advantage to me, and can at any rate be no disadvantage, to know what your selection for A is to be, before I fix upon mine for B. That is, if the proposition be true though the particular subject be selected first, much more will it be true if the universal subject be selected first.

The "circles" and "squares" Peirce talks about pertain to the notation of protographs that preceded the discovery of the logical method of EGs (see Introduction to Part II, LoF 1). Importantly, he also emphasises the 'strategic' advantage to those who know what the earlier selections have been, which indeed is a standard property of semantic games (of perfect information) for classical logics.

In another, proof-theoretic sense, it nevertheless speaks to the superiority of EGs over algebraic systems that in it deduction, as follows from Peirce's Johns Hopkins graduate student Oscar Howard Mitchell's (1851–1889) work (Mitchell 1883), is reduced to a minimum number of permissive operations. Peirce termed these operations *illative rules of transformation,* and in effect they consist only of two: *insertions* (that is, permissions to draw a graph-instance on the sheet of assertion) and *erasures* (that is, permissions to erase a graph-instance from the sheet). More precisely, the *oddly-enclosed* areas of graphs (areas within a non-even number of enclosures) permit inserting any graph in that area, while *evenly-enclosed* areas permit erasing any graph from that area. Furthermore, a copy of a graph-instance is permitted to be pasted on that same area or any area deeper within the same nest of enclosures. This is the rule of *iteration*. A copy thus iterated is permitted to be erased by the converse rule termed *deiteration*. An interpretational corollary is that a *double enclosure* with no intervening graphs (other than the blank graph) in the middle area can be inserted and erased at will.

A more detailed exposition of these illative rules of transformation would need to show their application to quantificational expressions, namely applying insertions and erasures to ligatures. Some flavor of such transformations can be gotten from examples. Regarding the graphs in Figs. 1, 2 and 3, an application of a permissible erasure on the line of identity in Fig. 1 results in the graph-instance in Fig. 2, and that another application of a permissible erasure on the upper part of the graph-instance in Fig. 2 results in the graph-instance as depicted in Fig. 3. Thus what is represented in Fig. 2 is a logical consequence of the graph-instance in Fig. 1, and what is represented in Fig. 3 is a logical consequence of the graph-instance given in Fig. 2.

Roberts (1973) has shown that the transformation rules Peirce had reached by 1903 form a semantically complete system of deduction. Roberts did not mention, however, that Peirce had demonstrated their soundness in 1898 and again in 1903 and that he had argued for their completeness in a couple of places, including in unpublished parts of *A Syllabus of Certain Topics of Logic* (R 478) that he wrote to accompany his Lowell Lectures.

Facts like these demonstrate that Peirce was a key innovator in the development of modern logic. And there is more. As observed, it is the polarity of the outermost ends or portions of ligatures that determines whether the quantification is *existential* (namely that the outermost end or a portion of the ligature rests on a positive area) or *universal* (if it rests on an odd area). Unlike in the Tarski-type semantics, but much in the fashion of what happens in game-theoretical semantics, the preferred rule of interpretation of the graphs is what Peirce termed "endoporeutic": one looks for the outermost portions of ligatures on the sheet of assertions first, assigns semantic values to that part, and then proceeds inwards into the areas enclosed within ovals. (In non-modal contexts, ligatures are not well-formed graphs because they may cross the enclosures.)

The diagrammatic nature of EGs consists in the relationship between forms of relations exhibited in the diagrams and the real relations in the universe of discourse. Peirce was convinced that, since these graphical systems exploit a *diagrammatic syntax*, they—together with extensions and modifications that would cover modalities, non-declarative expressions, speech acts, and so forth—can express any assertion, however intricate. Guided by the precepts laid out by the diagrammatic forms of expression, and together with the simple illative permissions by which deductive inference proceeds, the conclusions from premises can be "read before one's eyes"; these graphs present what Peirce believed is a "moving picture of the action of the mind in thought" (R 298, 1906; LoF 3):

> If upon one lantern-slide there be shown the premisses of a theorem as expressed in these graphs and then upon other slides the successive results of the different transformations of those graphs; and if these slides in their proper order be successively exhibited, we should have in them a veritable moving picture of the mind in reasoning. (R 905, 1907; LoF 3)

The theory of EGs that uses only the notation of ovals and the spatial notion of juxtaposition of graphs is termed by Peirce the Alpha part of the EGs, and as noted corresponds to propositional logic. The extension of the Alpha part with ligatures and *spots*[8] gives rise to the Beta part, and it corresponds to fragments of first-order predicate calculus. What Peirce in 1903 termed the *Gamma* part consists of a number of developments, including various modalities such as metaphysical, epistemic and temporal modalities, as well as extensions of modal graphs with ligatures. In Peirce's repositories one can in addition find many proposals developing graphical systems for *second-order logic* and *abstraction* in the logic of *potentials*, logics of *collections*, and meta-logical theories using the language of graphs to talk about notions and properties of the graphs in that language. The latter include encoding of permissive rules of transformation in such languages of "graphs of graphs". He even proposed this idea also to serve as the method of logical analysis of assertions and meta-assertions. In connection to one of his last remarks on EGs in a letter to the chemist, geologist and astronomer Allan Douglas Risteen (1866–1932; R L 376/R 500, December 6–9, 1911) Peirce mentions that one would also need to add a "*Delta* part in order to deal with *Modals*":[9]

> The better exposition of 1903 divided the system into three parts, distinguished as the Alpha, the Beta, and the Gamma, parts; a division I shall here adhere to, although I shall now have to add a *Delta* part in order to deal with modals. A cross division of the description which

---

8 The spots are the graphical counterparts to the predicate terms, similar to simple rhemas that do not contain any logical constants (see Bellucci 2019; Pietarinen 2015c).
9 A. D. Risteen was "assistant to Professor Charles S. Peirce of Stevens Institute of Technology upon pendulum observations summer of 1886; computer with U.S. Coast and Geodetic Survey 1886–87; editor of Power 1887–88; and also an associate editor of the Century Dictionary; assistant to Professor Peirce in U.S. Coast Survey work at Milford, Pa., May-August, 1888", according to the obituary note in *Yale Obituary Record of Graduates, 1932–1933*, New Haven: Bulletin of Yale University, 15 October 1933, p. 191.

here, as in that of 1903, is given precedence over the other is into the *Conventions*, the *Rules*, and the *working* of the System.

While no evidence remains of the details of what the projected Delta could have been, most likely Peirce thought a new compartment was needed to accommodate the ever-expanding amount of graphical systems that had been mushrooming in the Gamma part. Perhaps he planned the Delta part to capture quantificational multi-modal logics in ways similar to those that can be discerned in how he desired his theory of *tinctured graphs* to look like as it was fledgling since 1905 (LoF 3).

As will be observed from Peirce's writings collected in Volume 3 of LoF, his graphical systems of modal logic included suggestions for defining several types of multi-modal logics in terms of tinctures of areas of graphs. Tinctures enable one to assert, among other things, necessities and metaphysical possibilities, and so call for changes in the nature of how the corresponding logics behave, including the identification of individuals in the presence of multiple universes of discourses. Peirce defined epistemic operators in terms of subjective possibilities which, as in contemporary epistemic logic, are epistemic possibilities defined as the duals of knowledge operators.

Peirce analysed the meaning of identities between actual and possible objects in quantified multi-modal logics. As an example, the two graphs given in Figs. 9 and 10 that he presented in a 1906 draft of the "Prolegomena" paper (R 292a, 1906; LoF 3) illustrate the nature of the interplay between epistemic modalities and quantification:

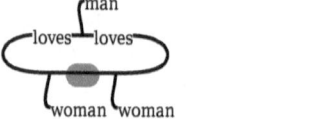

Fig. 9   **Fig. 10**

The graph in Fig. 9 is read "There is a man who is loved by one woman and loves a woman known by the Graphist to be another". The reason is that in the equivalent graph depicted in Fig. 10, the woman who loves is denoted by the name 'A', and the woman who is loved is denoted by the name 'B'.[10] The shaded area is a

---

[10] Fig. 10 is how Peirce presented the graph, apparently forgetting to draw the line of teridentity between the two instances of "loves" and one occurrence of "man", in the same way as in the graph of Fig. 9.

tincture (argent, if given in colours) that refers to the modality of subjective possibility. Thus the graph in Fig. 10 means that it is subjectively impossible, by which Peirce means "is contrary to what is known by the Graphist" (i.e., the modeller of the graph), that A should be B. In other words, the woman who loves and the woman who is loved (whom the graph does not assert to be otherwise known to the Graphist) are known by the Graphist not to be the same person.

Peirce's work on such topics and questions highlights the importance of underlying ideas that were rediscovered significantly later, and often in different guises. In Peirce's largely unpublished works one finds topics that later became known as, for example, multi-modal logics and possible-worlds semantics, quantification into modal contexts, cross-world identities (in R 490 he termed these special relations connecting objects in different possible worlds "references", see Pietarinen 2006b), and what is termed 'Peirce's Puzzle' (Dekker 2001; Hintikka 2011; Pietarinen 2015a), namely the question of the meaning of indefinites in conditional sentences. Peirce himself proposed to analyse the latter in quantified modal extensions of EGs of his own devising.

Far from only anticipating later findings, Peirce's logical innovations have been applied in a number of areas, including philosophical logic, formal semantics and pragmatics, mathematics, mind and language, AI, cognitive and computing sciences, biology, medical diagnosis and prognosis, astrobiology, physics, cosmology and geology, as much as in economics, game and decision theory, history and philosophy of science, archaeology, anthropology, musicology and art studies.[11]

Introduction to Modal Gamma Graphs

This section covers the essentials of Peirce's 1903 theory of modal Gamma graphs that corresponds to propositional modal logic. Peirce introduced it in his lecture notes for the Lowell Lectures. There were many other compartments of logical graphs included in the Gamma chapter that Peirce contemplated during the latter part of 1903, such as second-order logic, logic of potentials, logic of abstraction, logic of multitudes and collections, and even that of logic of continuity. The present introduction is nevertheless confined to describing graphical transforma-

---

[11] For some further work and applications along the lines Peirce had set out to do see, for example, Bellucci & Pietarinen (2020); Bellucci, Pietarinen & Stjernfelt (2014); Brady & Trimble (2000); Lupher & Adajian (2015); Pietarinen (2005b, 2010a,b, 2012a, 2019a,b); Pietarinen, Shafiei & Stjernfelt (2019); Sowa (1984, 2006); Zalamea (2012a,b). For details on Peirce's deductive logic, see the collection of Houser et al. (1997). Hilpinen (2004) is a helpful overview on Peirce's logic.

tion rules of inference that concern the modal logic side of Gamma, without ligatures, and with a focus on Peirce's interpretations for the broken-cut modal operator. The systems here are thus propositional and not those of quantificational modal logic, which Peirce came to propose and study a few years later.

Aside from logical necessity and possibility, Peirce proposed an epistemic interpretation for the broken-cut. Accordingly, he was led to analyse constructions of knowledge in the style of epistemic logic. Peirce also came to propose the normality rule in his gamma system, together with several other noteworthy innovations. It can then be shown how a number of normal modal logics arise from Peirce's graphical logic with the broken-cut notation, and an algebraic semantics defined to establish the completeness of fifteen modal logics of gamma graphs (Ma & Pietarinen 2017b). These are partial fulfilments of Gardner's (1958) prophesies that Peirce's logical graphs are "filled with suggestive hints" expected to be "taken up where he left off and bring his system to perfection".

Gamma Graphs: Inventing Modal Logic

The Gamma part was introduced by Peirce in November 1903 in the pre-lecture drafts of the eight hour-long Lowell Lectures that he delivered in Boston, Massachusetts, in November and December, but which due to the lack of time were introduced to the audience only in passing. Gamma became the third part of his logic of Existential Graphs (EGs), of which the other two were named in those lectures as the Alpha (the propositional logic) part and the Beta (a fragment of first-order logic with identity) part. We may see the germs of modal logic already in Peirce's 1896 writings (such as R 482, R 513; LoF 1). Much later in 1911, Peirce thinks that he would still need to add the fourth, *Delta* part, "in order to deal with modals" (R L 376). Apparently he was left somewhat unsatisfied with his earlier modal approaches and experimentations, though presumably without compelling reasons to really be unsatisfied with what they accomplish.

In the Gamma part Peirce proposes a bouquet of logics beyond the extensional, propositional and first-order systems. Those concern systems of modal logics, second-order (higher-order) logics, abstractions, and logic of multitudes and collections, among others. Peirce erected the third part because of the necessity of investigating "what can logically be asserted of *meanings*" (R 462). Only some of these ideas were taken up and developed further in his later works.

The first innovation in the Gamma graphs was the introduction of a special cut, called the *broken cut*, a dashed oval around graphs: ⊝ . It is used much in the same way as the simple closed continuous curve, termed "the cut" ◯, is used in the Alpha and Beta parts. Its typical reading is a 'weak' negation: ⊝G⊝ means "Possibly, not G". Adding the broken-cut notation to the Alpha system and reformulating the transformation rules to take the broken cut into account extends Alpha graphs into those corresponding to propositional modal logic. Adding it to the Beta graphs would compel one to address important philosophical questions concerning quantification in modal contexts, the topic which Peirce would actively revisit in his later papers on pragmaticism and related issues (LoF 3).

The details of the development of the modal Gamma graphs have remained surprisingly hidden in the historiography of modern logic, despite the fact that in Peirce's Lowell Lectures we have a clear and unambiguous case for the first-ever proposal for systems of modern modal logic. A brief account of Peirce's development of the broken-cut notation for his modal logics is thus in order. The development took place when, beginning in the summer 1903, Peirce began preparing notes for the eight lectures he was assigned to deliver for the Lowell Institute in Boston later in that year, with the title *Some Topics of Logic Bearing on Questions now Vexed*. Lecture IV, which he delivered on December 3, 1903, was entitled "Existential Graphs, Gamma Part" (R 470). Peirce wrote extensive lecture notes of some 50 manuscript pages for it (R 467). Due to strict time constraints in the delivery of the material amassed in his notebooks (each popular lecture was assigned 60 minutes), he was unlikely to have managed in the fourth lecture to communicate much of anything about the broken-cut Gamma system. Certainly at that point Peirce was seriously behind his schedule, as the introduction to the conventions and rules of the propositional Alpha and the first-order Beta parts of his method of EGs during the second and the third lectures took much longer than expected. Lecture five ("The Doctrine of Multitude, Infinity and Continuity") was delivered on December 7, 1903. That lecture did contain something of the proposed Gamma compartment, but only the second-order part of it seemed to have been sketched (R 469–R 471). Most likely nothing was ever delivered on modal logic during the course of eight lectures.

The main goals of the Lowell Lectures were (i) to answer the problem of the soundness of reasoning, (ii) to develop new methods for logical analysis, (iii) to address the question of the nature of mathematical reasoning, and (iv) to present philosophical account of the relation of qualities and laws to forms of thought. In order to reach these goals, from the fifth Lecture onwards Peirce was compelled to move on to another pet topic of his, that of the meta-logical doctrine of the "gamma-possibility" and the allied 'metaphysical' notion of "substantive possibility" (R 464, R 465). Apparently Peirce failed to describe the modal broken-cut notation altogether, among other collateral omissions, as he likewise would fall short of addressing the audience on the logic of abstraction and potentials, too. Luckily, though, fairly extensive lecture notes and supplementary material have been preserved in the archives on what he could have delivered in something like a full semester's course.

Although the modal part of the Gamma graphs was unlikely even to have been presented to a live audience, what about their prospective appearance in some printed form? Just weeks and days before the lectures were to begin, Peirce was busy preparing a handout, *A Syllabus of Certain Topics of Logic*, to complement the lectures. The printed pamphlet of 23 pages distilled from long manuscripts of over 130 autograph pages (located within the Robin folder R 478 of the Harvard Peirce Papers) was distributed to the audience during the fourth and maybe still during the fifth lectures. The handout included a few informal remarks also on the broken-cut representation, interspersed among Peirce's other suggestions on how new systems of intensional and higher-order logic may arise from the Gamma part of EGs. Thus they were likely to have been lost on any of the audience members desperately shifting through the pages of the printed syllabus at the beginning of the fourth lecture.

The broken-cut notation was drafted in a much more detailed manner in alternative and draft versions of the *Syllabus* (R 478, R 478(s)). The shortage of funds did not allow Peirce to include those in the printed version. One of the draft pages presents a list of "special spot-graphs" (R 478, ms p. 147), among which we find graphs for "is necessary", "[is] possible that necessary", and "[is] possible". These three special spot-graphs were omitted from the printed version simply due to the added time and cost constraints resulting from the typographical complications that setting up the types for such special characters would have presented to the printer. The printed *Syllabus* provides only a verbal explanation of the broken cuts in *Convention No. VIII.*: "1. A cut with many little interruptions aggregating about half its length shall cause its enclosure to be a graph, expressing that the entire graph on its area is logically contingent (non-necessary)" (R 478, p. 19; cf. Roberts 1973, p. 82).

A fuller description of the modal system was prepared as a comprehensive lecture note for the planned fourth lecture in one of the numerous thick Harvard Cooperative notebooks (R 467) that Peirce had hoarded during the year. The note appears to be entirely finished and ready for presentation, although it was neither actually delivered nor ever published in Peirce's lifetime. Failures and misfortunes to publicise his logical discoveries persisted, and the Lowell Lectures fared no better than most of his other endeavours to make the writings appear in print. Only some selected and disorganised fragments were included in Volume 4 of *Collected Papers* (CP) in 1933. The prepared fourth lecture in question was partially published in CP 4.510–4.529, where it appears, in a considerably abridged and distorted form, consisting of a number of graphs that were redrawn to be nearly illegible, and with a misleading editorial title "The Gamma Part of Existential Graphs".

Soon after the lectures, Peirce contacts Putnam & Sons (The Knickerbocker Press) to get his Lowell Lectures published. Correspondence with the editors

James McKeen Cattell and George H. Putnam (R L 78) reveals that the publication of the lectures fell through largely for circumstantial and remunerative reasons. The full corpus of his lecture notes consisted of altogether some 1 300 manuscript pages, and despite their enormous complexity, would predictably have made a major contribution to the development of logic of the time—as they without question stand out as a major contribution to logic, especially philosophical logic, putting its historical development into a very different perspective from what the historiographies have hitherto usually revealed.

A close examination of Peirce's original manuscripts evidences that they, together with the details he wrote in the draft versions of the *Syllabus* text and in his related notes and worksheets, indeed mark an inception of modern modal logic. Peirce's incessant drafting of systems and alternative notations and representations in the Gamma part of his graphical method of logic, and only over a few weeks if not days in late 1903, testifies that he was destined to hit upon something of fundamental importance to this new theory of logic and its reformative notation.

Yet it is worth remarking that the creation of the modal part of Gamma graphs was suggested and preceded by what he had accomplished in his previous lectures, namely those in which he had defined the important notions of *alpha-possibility* and *beta-possibility*. He defined these notions in order to gauge the expressive power of these languages and to pinpoint where the limitations of the Alpha and Beta parts lie when having only extensional notions in one's wheelhouse. Among the motivations was thus to provide systematic decision procedures for the logics of the Alpha and Beta parts. Such considerations then led Peirce to invent nothing less than modal logic, together with variations on that theme. His inventions were not limited to the propositional part of modal logic, either, as he in the following years would become increasingly attached to the idea that adding quantifiers to systems of modal logic will yield important insights into the behaviour of those logical signs, and that the application of such extensions would contribute to increasingly better methods of logical analysis of matters of wide philosophical interest. Such ideas soon gave rise to the logically and philosophically significant questions of the interplay of modal operators (the broken cuts) with quantifiers (ligatures), of the meaning of individuals and identity in such modal contexts, as well as the question of the composition of concepts in intensional contexts in which something that is possible is to be composed with something that is actual. It is in such connections some two years later that Peirce is seen to be working hard on the development of (quantified) multi-modal logics, using the approach of the *tinctures* (R 295/292b, Roberts 1973); another and still to date under-explored terrain in modal logic (R 295/292b, R 498–R 499, R 470, R S-36, 1906; LoF 3).

Modal Gamma Graphs: The Broken-Cut Notation

Moving on to technical matters, taking up Peirce's broken cut as the primitive modal operator, one may ask three questions:
(1) How do various modal systems arise from Peirce's assumptions concerning the broken-cut notation?
(2) What are the interesting properties of the resulting systems, including the completeness of their rules?
(3) What did Peirce have to say about the interpretations of this primitive broken cut modality?

To answer such questions, the language of the modal Gamma graphs as produced by the broken cut is described next, comparing it with the language of modern modal logic. Various propositional modal Gamma systems that correspond to different modal logics can be extracted from the material that Peirce left for future generations to develop. Beginning with the modal rules as Peirce had them at his disposal (namely, the "opening" and "closing" of the broken cuts on positive and negative areas, respectively), the resulting system may be compared with standard modal logic. It can then be further shown that Peirce had a *normal* modal logic at his disposal, with the distribution of necessity over conjunction and the distribution of the possibility over disjunction firmly in place. One can then proceed to define a Gamma system that has a new rule (downward monotonicity), and with the aid of that rule go on to build a hierarchy of fifteen modal systems that may be directly erected upon Peirce's basic rules. Defining then an algebraic semantics for modal graph systems, one would then provide the basis for proving the semantic completeness of all these fifteen Gamma logics (on further details, see Ma & Pietarinen 2017a,b).

Peirce's variegated interpretations of modalities arose out of the broken-cut Gamma. They are surveyed in the subsections below, including epistemic, provability and tensed interpretations. One may further argue that Peirce's preferred and most fundamental interpretation of the broken cut was epistemic, and that one important driver for him in developing these systems in the first place was to have a method of logical analysis that is applicable upon various *constructions of knowledge*. It may be concluded that in doing so, Peirce came to propose the first-ever modern type of epistemic logic. But first, let us outline the essentials of modal Gamma graphs.

Modal Gamma graphs arise from Alpha graphs that represent classical propositional logic and correspond algebraically to the two-element Boolean algebra. They can be defined inductively from primitive graphs using the *continuous cut* and, as a new sign, the *broken cut*:

Tab. 1: Two Primitive Cuts

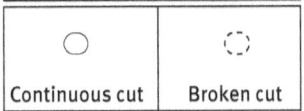

Continuous cut	Broken cut

Recall that the signification of the continuous cut as a Boolean (contradictory) negation is its *derived* meaning: the cut as a negation results from the sign of illation ("the scroll"), by atrophying the inner loop invisibly small (R 455(s); R S-30; Bellucci & Pietarinen 2016, Pietarinen et al. 2020); an argument that Peirce seems to have concocted during the preparation of Lowell Lectures. Since negation is the derived meaning of the cut, its primary service is analogous to the role of parentheses in linear notations, namely denoting the *scope* of the relevant operations, including their mutual logical relationships. Consequently, then, the cut also shows how propositions are to be grouped together, that is, shows where the juxtapositions reside on the sheet of assertion. Furthermore, the cut is also an indicator of the context for subgraphs. Notably, the broken cut serves all these offices (except the first, Boolean negation) just as the continuous cuts do.

In particular, Peirce states that the broken cut expresses that the entire graph that is located on its area is *logically contingent* (that is, non-necessary) (CP 4.410; R 478). Here he considers the enclosures by the broken cut to denote alethic modalities, namely propositions that are of the nature of logical possibilities and logical necessities. Soon, however, he would propose several alternative interpretations of modality, and especially that of an epistemic interpretation, which as will be seen is slated to be the dominant interpretation.

The continuous and broken cuts may both be called *primitive cuts*. Peirce admits that more than two kinds of cuts may be needed in practice, but he also tells in the same breath that he has found real use only for two: the continuous and the broken cut. At first (R S-28, September 1903), he proposes that it is the "mode of dotting the line" that is the relevant notation to identify what the alternative universes are the utterer means when asserting propositions under such modalities (this is his Convention 9 in R S-28). Later, we will observe Peirce rather taking the view that if new and different modes of modalities are needed, then those are better to be represented not by changes in the nature of kind of the line drawn to enclose other graphs (the line really being nothing but the *boundary* between the areas inside and outside of its closure), but by changes in the *quality* of those areas. This approach would then give rise to the proposal of adding tinctures to the graphs (R 295/292b, 1906; LoF 3).

At any event, continuous and broken cuts can be viewed as operations on partial graphs. There are four combinations of continuous and broken cuts. Using them as single compound graph operations, we can give them names as in Table 2.

Tab. 2: Four Compound Cuts

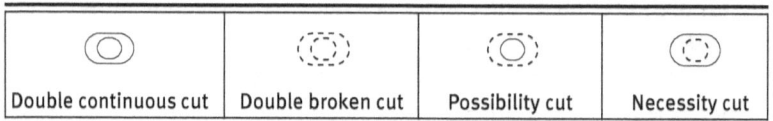

| Double continuous cut | Double broken cut | Possibility cut | Necessity cut |

Compound cuts consist of two cuts, one nested within the other, with nothing but the blank space between them. The two primitive cuts and four compound cuts as stated above may be called *cuts* uniformly. This will be along the lines of Peirce's own proposals. He notes that all Gamma signs "are of those same kinds" as they are in Alpha and Beta parts (R 467). The difference is that in Gamma, "all of the old kinds of signs take new forms" (R 467). Cuts are used as single graph operations that create new graphs from the previously given ones. There are also *primitive graphs*, namely graphs that contain no cuts.

Let us fix a denumerable set of simple propositions Prop the elements of which are primitive graphs. They occur in compound graphs as their basic parts. Following Peirce's account, the sheet of assertion (SA), or the blank graph on which nothing is yet scribed, is also a primitive graph. Henceforth, we may denote the blank in the language of modal Gamma graphs by ⊤ or, when there is no risk of confusion, without any specific notation whatsoever, namely just by the blank of the sheet of paper or of whatever the quality of the medium may be on which the graphs make their appearance. A primitive graph is thus a simple proposition or the blank. Peirce's modal Gamma graphs are defined recursively as follows:

Definition 2.1. The set of all *modal Gamma graphs* $\mathscr{G}_y$ is defined inductively by:

$$\mathscr{G}_y \ni G ::= p \mid \top \mid \textcircled{G} \mid \textcircled{\dashv G \dashv} \mid G_1\, G_2$$

where $p \in$ Prop. The graphs $\textcircled{G}$ and $\textcircled{\dashv G \dashv}$ are read as "the continuous cut of G" and "the broken cut of G", respectively.

Henceforth, when referring to graphs, what is meant are modal Gamma graphs.

Given two graphs G and H, one could define, for reasons of convenience and readability, the simplification of graphs $G \otimes H$, $G \supset H$ and $G \equiv H$ as follows:

$G \oslash H := \;\overline{(\overline{G}\;\overline{H})}\; ; \; G \supset H := \;\overline{(G\,\overline{H})}\; ; \; G \equiv H := \;\overline{(G\,\overline{H})}\;\overline{(H\,\overline{G})}\;.$

To maximise the iconic character of graphs, the practice in what follows is to refrain from using these shortcut notations, however. Peirce would occasionally resort to useful simplifications of the notation in order to "avoid the bewildering number of ovals or other signs of negation" (R 530; LoF 1). Those could well include, when needed, abbreviations for the broken-cut ovals and for the combinations of continuous and broken-cut ovals.

There is a straightforward translation of modal Gamma graphs into sentences of a modern language of modal logic. The modal language $\mathscr{L}_M$ consists of a denumerable set of propositional variables Prop, connectives $\neg, \wedge$, and the modality $\triangleleft$.

Definition 2.2. The set of all modal formulas $\mathscr{L}_M$ is defined inductively by the following rule:

$$\mathscr{L}_M \ni \varphi ::= p \mid \top \mid \neg \varphi \mid (\varphi \wedge \varphi) \mid \triangleleft \varphi,$$

where $p \in \text{Prop}$. Define $\bot := \neg \top$, $\varphi \vee \psi = \neg(\neg\varphi \wedge \neg\psi)$, $\varphi \to \psi := \neg\varphi \vee \psi$ and $\varphi \leftrightarrow \psi := (\varphi \to \psi) \wedge (\psi \to \varphi)$. The dual operator of $\triangleleft$ is defined as $\triangleright\varphi := \neg\triangleleft\neg\varphi$.

The formula $\triangleleft\varphi$ means that φ *is possibly not true*. This is the same meaning with $\overset{\cdot\cdot\cdot}{\varphi}$, the broken cut of φ. Hence $\triangleright\varphi$ means that φ is necessarily not true. The standard modalities of possibility and necessity can be defined in $\mathscr{L}_M$ by $\Box\varphi := \triangleright\neg\varphi$ and $\Diamond\varphi := \triangleleft\neg\varphi$.

The neutral reading of the formula $\Box\phi$ is that it is *necessary that* ϕ is true, and $\Diamond\phi$ that it is *possible that* ϕ is true. The standard modal language takes $\Box$ or $\Diamond$ as the primitive modal operator. Taking $\triangleleft$ as the primitive, however, the translation from modal Gamma graphs to modal formulas is straightforwardly the following:

Definition 2.3. The translation $\pi : \mathscr{G}_\gamma \to \mathscr{L}_M$ is defined inductively by

$\pi(p) = p \qquad\qquad \pi(\top) = \top \qquad\qquad \pi(\,\overline{G}\,) = \neg\pi(G)$

$\pi(\overset{\cdot\cdot\cdot}{G}) = \triangleleft\pi(G) \qquad \pi(G_1\,G_2) = \pi(G_1) \wedge \pi(G_2)$

By the translation π, the following are the translations of compound cuts:

$\pi(\,\overline{\overline{G}}\,) = \neg\neg\pi(G) \qquad\qquad \pi(\overset{\cdot\cdot\cdot}{\overset{\cdot\cdot\cdot}{G}}) = \triangleleft\triangleleft\pi(G)$

$\pi(\overset{\cdot\cdot\cdot}{\overline{G}}) = \Diamond\pi(G) \qquad\qquad \pi(\overline{\overset{\cdot\cdot\cdot}{G}}) = \Box\pi(G)$

Remark 2.1. Scribing a broken cut around an assertion, say "it rains", does not effect a denial of that assertion. For according to Peirce, the graph $\overset{\cdot\cdot\cdot}{\text{it rains}}$ does not assert that it does not rain: "it only asserts that the alpha and beta rules do not compel me to admit that it rains" (R 467). This appears to be an interpretation from ignorance, and it is what Peirce seems to have had in mind as this passage from the third (undelivered) lecture reveals: "[A] person altogether ignorant, except that he was well versed in logic so far as it [is] embodied in the alpha and beta parts of existential graphs, would not know that it rained" (R 467). The interpretation of the broken cut in his example suggests that Peirce's preferred interpretation of primitive modalities was thus epistemic rather than alethic (see below).

Peirce also mentioned the concepts of a partial and entire graph. An *entire graph* is everything that is scribed on the sheet of assertion, while a *partial graph* is "any part of the entire graph which is itself a graph" (R 478). Peirce's definition of partial graphs was handled in terms of the "nests of graphs": "A *nest* is any series of cuts each enclosing the next one" (R 693a, 1904; LoF 1).[12] Peirce's definition of nests is an *explicit* one: "Two nests of cuts may have cuts in common; and one nest of cuts may be within another so as to constitute with it another nest. But of every pair of cuts of the same nest one is immediately or mediately within the other. One cut is said to be *immediately within* another if it is within that other but is not within any third cut that is within that other" (R S-26, 1904, LoF 1; cf. R 650, 1910; LoF 1). This definition can be made precise by defining the construction of the parsing tree of a modal Gamma graph, in the following fashion.

Definition 2.4. For any graph G, the *parsing tree* of G, denoted by $T(G)$, is defined inductively as follows:
(1) $T(p)$ is a single root node p.
(2) $T(\top)$ is a single root node $\top$.
(3) $T(G_1\ G_2)$ is a root node $G_1\ G_2$ with children nodes $T(G_1)$ and $T(G_2)$.
(4) $T(\overline{G})$ is a root node $\overline{G}$ with one child node $T(G)$.
(5) $T(\overleftrightarrow{G})$ is a root node $\overleftrightarrow{G}$ with one child node $T(G)$.
A *partial graph* of a graph G is a node in $T(G)$.

Definition 2.5. For any graph G, the *history* of a node J in $T(G)$, denoted by $h(J)$, is the unique path from the root to J. The position of the root is always on the sheet of assertion.

We say that J is a positive (negative) node of $T(G)$ if there is an even (odd) number of cuts in $h(J)$.

---

[12] The term "nest" was first suggested in July 10, 1903, in his *Logic Notebook* (R 339, LoF 1), so its was already part of the nomenclature by the time of the Lowell Lectures.

This accords with Peirce's rule of interpretation of the diagrammatic syntax of graphs, which is "endoporeutic", that is, proceeds from outside-in (R 650, R 669, LoF 1; R 295/292b, R 293, R 300; LoF 3).

A *position* is a point on the area of a graph (but not on the cut line). Given any graph G, a position in G is *positive* (*negative*) if it is enclosed by an even (odd) number of cuts. Zero (0) is taken to be a positive number. A graph can be scribed at any position.

A *graph context* is a graph $G[\ ]$ with a single slot $[\ ]$, the empty context, which can be filled in by other graphs. The notation $G[H]$ stands for the graph obtained from the graph context $G[\ ]$ by filling the slot by H. An occurrence of a graph J in a graph G is called *positive* (*negative*), notation $G^+[J]$ ($G^-[J]$), if it is a positive (negative) node in $T(G)$.

The *modal depth* of a partial graph H in a graph G is defined as the number of all broken cuts traversed in the history $h(H)$. The *modal degree* of a graph G, notation $md(G)$, is defined as the number of all broken cuts occurred in the longest branch in the parsing tree $T(G)$. A *maximal* (terminal) history ends with a primitive graph or its primitive cut. There is a straightforward correspondence between Peirce's definition of the nesting of the areas of graphs and the histories of the parsing tree, as well as between Peirce's maximal nests (R 650, LoF 1) and terminal histories.

Peirce's Transformation Rules for Modal Gamma Graphs

In this section, Peirce's Gamma rules for modal logics are explored. Peirce stated the rules of transformation for the broken-cut operator in the *Syllabus* manuscript (R 478) and in the lecture notes for his fourth Lowell Lecture (R 467).

First, it does not make any difference as to the polarity of the positions whether the enclosures are given by continuous or by broken cuts. Also, the Alpha rules of *deletion* and *insertion* are allowed with respect to the broken cuts, as these two irreversible rules take the polarity of the area of the graph into account.

Peirce is not fully consistent as to this aspect of the system, however. What he recorded in R 467 was: "Rules of the Broken Cut: *Rule I*. In a broken cut already scribed on the sheet of assertion any graph may be inserted". In the drafts of the *Syllabus* (R 478) he states that the rule of erasure and insertion "applies to the broken cut", which is correct. In what is preserved as the final draft of the *Syllabus* text he states that "The Rule of Erasure and Insertion applies to the broken cut in this form: Evenly enclosed, a full cut can be transformed into a broken cut; while oddly enclosed a broken cut can be transformed into a full one. It makes no difference whether the enclosure here spoken of is by a full or a broken cut. In regard to Graphs the Rule of Erasure and Insertion applies to enclosures by broken cuts precisely as to those by full cuts". This is also correct.

However, there are some marked differences to the Alpha behaviour that are inevitable in the modal case. Peirce proceeds in the next paragraph of R 467 to state that the reversible "Rule of Iteration and Deiteration does not apply to the broken cut", and furthermore that "The Rule of Immaterials [the double-cut rule] and the Pseudograph [contradiction] practically does not apply to broken cuts". This is also correct, supposing here that what Peirce meant was that iteration into the context of a broken cut is not generally permissible and that deiteration from the context of a broken cut likewise is not generally permissible. Having a precise interpretation of such slightly imprecise statements is nevertheless important. What did Peirce think that "does not apply" exactly means? As he provides no further explanation, what he left us with are two different meanings: the phrase could mean that no graph is permitted to cross broken cuts, while it could also mean that no graph containing broken cuts, that is, *no modal assertion* is permitted to be iterated/deiterated across *cuts*, or to be iterated/deiterated across *broken cuts*.

The matter is not rendered much clearer by Peirce's second rule, namely that of the rule of double cuts and the rule of the "pseudograph" (namely, that broken cuts would denote contradiction). As Peirce stated them, the two cases of the second rule "practically" do not apply to broken cuts. One should nevertheless be led to believe that what Peirce meant by this is that no graph (that is, no modal or non-modal graph alike) may be iterated inside the areas governed by broken cuts, and conversely, that no graph may be deiterated from the area governed by broken cuts. Take into account also that, as will be shown below, an empty broken cut is virtually identical to an empty continuous cut (by "empty" meaning an area that is entirely blank). So it is here, in the impermissibility of the rule of iteration and deiteration to be applied on the area surrounded by the broken cut, that the modal Gamma rules of transformation take their departure from those of the proof rules of the Alpha and Beta parts.

After these considerations, Peirce states the following illative rules that he proposed will positively capture the permissible transformations for the language containing modal broken cuts (R 467, R 478):

(Ta) An evenly enclosed standard cut may be transformed (by being half erased) into a broken cut;

(Tb) An oddly enclosed broken cut may be transformed (by being filled up) into a standard cut.

We may call the rule (Ta) the *Rule of Opening a Continuous Cut* and the rule (Tb) the *Rule of Closing a Broken Cut* or, in brief, the Rules of *Opening* and *Closing*. These rules are irreversible: Opening is a permissible operation exactly on positive areas, while closing is permissible exactly on negative areas.

The two rules of opening and closing are the basic rules for the modal Gamma which Peirce chose to advance in his fourth Lowell lecture. Interestingly, he argues that these two rules, (Ta) and (Tb), are gotten from the behaviour of the two fundamental and irreversible operations of logic, namely *erasures* from areas under natural conditions and *insertions* to areas under equally natural conditions, as these two fundamental operations also apply to the cut notation in the modal setting: they just also take into account the way the cut works: one half of the boundary of the full cut, when positioned on a positive area, may be erased and hence turned from a continuous into broken cut, while one half of the broken cut, when positioned on a negative area, may be recovered and thus re-inserted, turning the broken boundary into a continuous one (R 478). There is thus an important notational undercurrent to the reasons why Peirce chose to use the duality between broken and non-broken (continuous) cuts (or smooth vs. non-smooth boundaries) as the best representative of the inferential behaviour the two key modal operators.

We thus have the following inferences:

$$(t)\ \overline{(\dot{g})} \Rightarrow \overline{(g)} \quad (t_1)\ \overline{(\dot{g})} \Rightarrow \overline{(\dot{\overline{g}})} \quad (t_2)\ \overline{(g)} \Rightarrow \overline{(\dot{g})}.$$

The inference (t) is an instance of an application of the rule (Tb), because the inner broken cut is oddly enclosed and can hence by closing be transformed into a continuous cut. The inference (t_1) is an instance of applying (Ta), because now the outer continuous cut is evenly enclosed and can by opening be transformed into a broken cut, resulting in a double broken cut. The inference (t_2) is likewise an instance of the application of the rule (Ta).

Assuming a translation of the broken cut notation into the language of **T**, the inferences given above hold in the standard modal logic **T**. Using a standard double negation equivalence $\phi \leftrightarrow \neg\neg\phi$ and the duality principle $\Box\phi \leftrightarrow \neg\Diamond\neg\phi$, the above three inferences can be represented in the standard modal language as follows:

$$(t)\ \Box g \Rightarrow g \quad (t_1)\ \Box g \Rightarrow \Diamond\Box g \quad (t_2)\ g \Rightarrow \Diamond g.$$

That is, the necessity implies truth, necessity implies the possibility of it, and the truth implies the possibility of it.

Peirce repeated the transformation rules (Ta) and (Tb) in his unpublished notebook sheets R S-1 written while preparing the corresponding lectures (see Section 42, "Fragments"; LoF 2/2). These supplementary (S) sheets and pages cut from the notebooks were rediscovered in 1969 (listed in Richard Robin's supplementary catalogue of Peirce Papers; Robin 1971), but those particular sheets and sketches were never studied before, not even in Zeman (1964), which otherwise is still to date the most extensive and nearly the only study on Peirce's modal Gamma graphs. The following diagrams are found scribed on some of them, among the numerous loose sheets of R S-1 (≺ is, as usual, Peirce's original notation for the logical consequence relation):

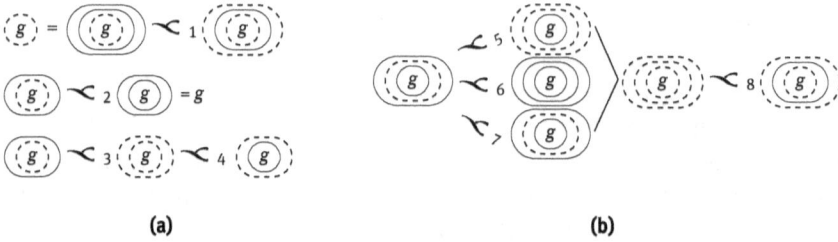

(a)　　　　　　　　　　　　(b)

Figure 1: Peirce's Consequence Relations in the Modal Gamma Graphs (R S-1)

Subindices are added to ≺ in order to provide a further explanation of these implicational relationships. All inferences in these two figures are valid. They are obtained by applying Peirce's modal rules (Ta) and (Tb). The logical consequence relation represented by ≺$_1$ is an application of (Ta), the relation by ≺$_2$ is that of (*t*), the relation by ≺$_3$ is that of (t_1), and so on. Standard modal logic **T**, in which ◁ is the primitive of the language, and using ⇒ instead of ≺ , shows them to correspond to the following valid inferences:

◁g ⇒$_1$ ◇◁g　　□g ⇒$_2$ g　　□g ⇒$_3$ ◇□g　　◇□g ⇒$_4$ ◇g
▷g ⇒$_5$ ◇▷g　　▷g ⇒$_6$ ¬g　　▷g ⇒$_7$ ▷g　　◇□◁g ⇒$_8$ ◇◁g.

Figure 1(b) contains two further lines that Peirce left without comment or explanation. But we can find two more valid inferences: ◇▷g ⇒ ◇□◁g for the top line (from northwest to southeast direction), and ▷g ⇒ ◇□◁g for the bottom line (from southwest to northeast direction). The opposite directions indeed are not valid.[13]

---

[13] In the original diagram depicting these consequences in R S-1, one might suspect that there is also a short line in the middle, suggesting that the thrice continuously-cut g and the thrice brokenly-cut g would be connected with implication both ways, which would represent invalid inference. A close inspection of the sheet reveals that the alleged line—much shorter than the other two diagonal lines are—is accidental, perhaps just an unfinished line as there was nothing to be finished logically.

Peirce then proceeded to write down two cubes, which are shown in Figure 2. These summarise the valid inferences that he had found for the broken cuts.

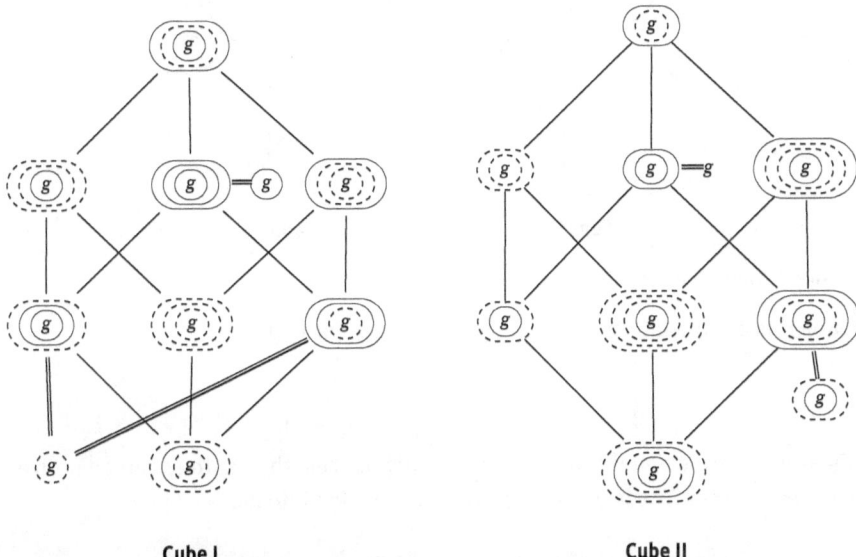

Figure 2: Peirce's Cubes (R S-1)

It is easy to see that Cube I can be obtained from Cube II by replacing g by ⓖ. The direction of inference in both cubes is from top down. All inferences from an upper node to a lower node, linked by a line, are valid. The double line is the sign of equivalence: both graphs can be inferred from each other. These inferences can be translated into valid inferences in modal logic **T**, shown in the corresponding cubes in Figure 3.

Peirce then wrote down some significant equalities for the broken cuts. The following equalities, which we find him having inscribed in the leaves of R S-1, hold in modal logic **K**:

(k)   ⟨ab⟩ = ⟨a⟩ ⟨b⟩
(k_1) ⟨ab⟩ = (⟨a⟩ ⟨b⟩)
(k_2) ⟨(a b)⟩ = ⟨a b⟩ = (⟨a⟩ ⟨b⟩)

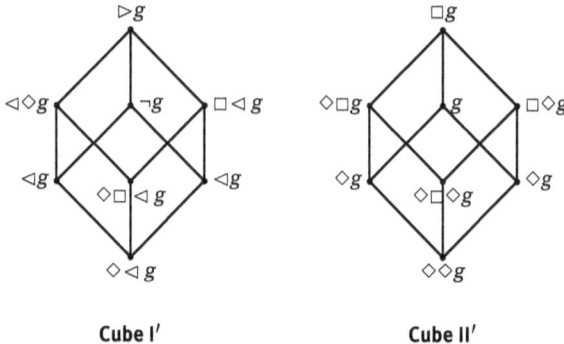

Figure 3: Translation of Peirce's Cubes

Cube I' is obtained from Cube II' by replacing g with $\neg g$.

Clearly the three equalities are logical equivalences, that is, they can be derived from each other. These equalities can be translated into modal logic:

(k) $\Box(a \wedge b) = \Box a \wedge \Box b$
(k_1) $\Diamond(\neg a \vee \neg b) = \Diamond \neg a \vee \Diamond \neg b$
(k_2) $\Diamond(a \vee b) = \Diamond a \vee \Diamond b$.

Keeping (k) as a primitive equality, the remaining equalities are derived. The equality (k) obviously holds. It shows the marrying/divorcing juxtapositions in the universe of modal discourse on necessities. The proposition $a\,b$ is necessarily true if and only if a is necessarily true and b is necessarily true. Thus necessity operator distributes over conjunctions. Likewise, disjunctions are married and divorced in the universes of possibilities. That is, the possibility operator distributes over disjunctions.

Peirce's significant finding, which he also inscribed in the leaves of R S-1, is thus that he figured out this marrying/divorcing behaviour of the broken cut operator in the fashion of these three equalities. He presented them on the same draft sheet as Figures 1 and 2; sheet that was obviously written together with the preparation of his lectures on modal logic as found in the notebook of R 467.

In adjacent leaves of R S-1, Peirce also presented the following two simple graphs:

$$\overline{(\overline{a})} = \Sigma_i \overline{a}_i \qquad \Sigma_i(ab) = \overline{()}$$

The term $\Sigma_i \bar{a}_i$ means that there is a state of things such that a is false. This is the semantic interpretation of the broken cut, or the possibility operator. Modal propositions, as represented in Gamma graphs, are in general descriptions or representations of "certain recognized states of things" (R 339, 1898), including states of things "known to be non-actual" (R 295/292b). Moreover, they are maximally "analytical" such representations, which Peirce notices much later in a letter to Frederick Adams Woods (November 6, 1913, R L 477; LoF 3). The second equality is more meaningful but Peirce did not give any explanation for it. Now the blank inside a broken cut can be translated into the standard modal formula $\diamond \bot$, which is equal to $\bot$. Hence Peirce virtually achieved the equality:

$$\boxed{T} = \{\overline{\overline{T}}\}$$

It suffices to give the interpretation of the term $\Sigma_i(ab)$. When $b = \bar{a}$, we have $\Sigma_i(a\bar{a})$ which is equivalent to the continuous cut of the blank, that is, to the pseudograph or $\bot$, meaning absurdity. Thus the equality $\diamond 0 = 0$ is achieved, which is equal to the rule of necessitation in modal logic (Nec). Namely, if $a = 1$, we have that $\Box a = 1$. The syntactical interpretation of this is that if φ is provable, then $\Box \varphi$ is provable.

A recent paper on Gamma graphs proposes that "some of Peirce's philosophical principles prevented him from formulating an analogue to the basic rule (K) of modal logic" (Ramharter & Gottschall 2011, p. 166). What was shown above was that not only nothing prevented Peirce from formulating the basic rule, but also that he did formulate it, and specifically did so in the context of his original, 1903 presentation of some systems of modal logic. Later he would even go on to remark on what the interpretation of that basic rule ought to be, namely something that should accord to the following principle: "Two graphs in the same *Province*, i.e. on the same continuously tinctured surface will be asserted, not merely as True, but as True *together*" (R 295/292b, LoF 3). The province is the area of the graph enclosed by the cut operators. Therefore, it is only to be expected that we can turn this observation into the general rule which states that any two juxtaposed graphs that are in the same province, and are located in the same universe, can be merged into one province, and that two juxtaposed graphs in the same province may be split, in the same universe, into two graphs. (Notice that in tinctured graphs, there may be differently tinctured provinces in the same graph, giving rise to multi-modal logics, but this does not change the interpretation of the normality rule (K) in any way.)

Gamma Systems for Normal Modal Logics

In this section, several Gamma systems for normal modal logics are formulated upon Peirce's thoughts and definitions on what the modal rules are and what the calculus of the Alpha part is that he already has at his disposal. A Gamma system for the normal modal logic **K** comes first, followed by its extensions.

The Gamma System K^γ

Peirce's systems of the logic of graphs are defined by graph rules. A graph rule is of the form
$$\frac{G_1 \ldots G_n}{G_0}$$
where $G_0, \ldots, G_n$ are graphs. The graph $G_1 \ldots G_n$ is called the *premiss*, and G_0 is called the *conclusion*.

The rules of commutativity, associativity and conjunction may be expressed as follows:
$$\frac{G[H_1 H_2]}{G[H_2 H_1]} \text{ (CM)} \quad \frac{G[H_1(H_2 H_3)]}{G[(H_1 H_2)H_3]} \text{ (AS)} \quad \frac{G \quad H}{GH} \text{ (CN)}$$

The double line means that the reasoning goes both ways, from the upper to the lower graph, and vice versa. These rules express the basic properties of the *ambient space* upon which these graphs appear and whose projections are perceived on the sheet of assertion. The commutativity rule (CM) says that the positions of H_1 and H_2 in a partial graph $H_1 H_2$ of G is immaterial. The associativity is concerned with the order of drawing graphs on the sheet of assertion. The parentheses in (AS) indicate the order of forming the graphs. The rule (AS) says that the order of forming the graphs is immaterial. The rule (CN) says that, if G and H are derived, then $G H$ can be derived. When we have G and H on the sheet of assertion, we obtain $G H$.

Remark 2.2. Since Peirce's *diagrammatic syntax* has certain special characteristics—it is two-dimensional, has no parentheses, and its well-formed graphs that are scribed on the sheet are projections in the ambient space which is continuous, compact, open and non-oriented—we can dispense with explicitly stating either of the rules (CM), (AS) and (CN), as their meaning falls automatically from the properties of the space, namely from the nature of the sheet of assertion (SA). We can take Peirce's characterisation of such a syntax as "diagrammatic" (R L 376) to mean language in which we need not (and properly speaking even *cannot*) state (CM), (AS) and (CN) as particular *rules* of the system to obtain on the sheet of assertion.

Having thus simplified the set of rules, we have the following axiom and the rules of transformation:

Definition 2.6. The Gamma system $\mathbf{K}^\gamma$ consists of the following axiom and rules:
(1) *Axiom:* ⊤ (**SA**)
(2) *Alpha rules:*
 – *Deletion rule:*
$$\frac{G^+[H]}{G^+[\top]} \text{(DR)}$$
 Every positive partial graph H in a graph G can be deleted, leaving blank space in its stead.
 – *Insertion rule:*
$$\frac{G^-[H]}{G^-[JH]} \text{(IR)}$$
 Any graph can be inserted into a negative position in a graph G.
 – *Double cut rule:*
$$\frac{G[H]}{G[(\!(H)\!)]} \text{(DC)}$$
 (DC) means that in any partial graph H of a graph G can be replaced by the double cut of H, and any double cut in G can be deleted.
 – *Iteration/deiteration rule:*
$$\frac{K[GH[J]]}{K[GH[GJ]]} \text{(IT)} \qquad \frac{K[GH[GJ]]}{K[GH[J]]} \text{(DeIT)}$$
 where $H[\;]$ is a broken-cut-free graph context, namely, no broken cut occurs in $H[\;]$. The rule (IT) means that, in any graph $K[GH[J]]$, the partial graph G can be iterated at any position in H. The rule (DeIT) is the converse of (IT).
(3) *Gamma rules:*
$$\frac{J[(\!\!\;\overline{GH}\;\!\!)]}{J[(\!\!\;\overline{G}\;\!\!)(\!\!\;\overline{H}\;\!\!)]} \text{(K)} \qquad \frac{G}{(\!\!\;\overline{G}\;\!\!)} \text{(Nec)} \qquad \frac{(\!\overline{G\,H}\!)}{(\!\!\;\overline{H}\;\!\!\;\overline{G}\;\!\!)} \text{(DMN)}$$

The rule (K) is Peirce's merging/splitting rule as discussed above. (Nec) is the rule of necessitation. (DMN) is the rule of *downward monotonicity* (namely, the inference is antitone).
The double line means that the upper graph can derive the lower graph, and vice versa.

Remark 2.3. Since all derivations begin with the sheet of assertion, which is ⊤, there is no need in the presentation of the rule (Nec) to separately state that the graph G which appears in the premisses needs to be a theorem of the system. That restriction would of course have to be enforced in standard modal logics, in order to distinguish between *local* and *global* consequence relations.

Remark 2.4. The rule (DMN) is new and one should not expect or presume Peirce having presented it anywhere in his vast collection of papers. Rule (K) comes from R S-1, however. (Nec) comes from what he stated in the fourth lecture (R 467). The Alpha rules of (DR), (IR), (DC), (IT) and (DeIT) are usual and they come from a series of papers Peirce wrote between 1896 and 1911 (LoF 1), gravitating to their final formulations largely by August 1898 and ultimately in the 1903 Lowell Institute Lectures.

Remark 2.5. The restriction on the context $H[\ ]$ in the rules (IT) and (DeIT) is important, because application of the rule of iteration/de-iteration in modal contexts may lead to invalid inferences. For example, $(p\,(q))\,(p\,(p\,q))$ serves as a counterexample to the validity of iteration (the antecedent can be true while the consequent is false), and likewise, $(p\,(p\,q))\,(p\,(q))$ is a counterexample to the validity of deiteration. (That is, the graphs of these examples are not valid graphs in modal algebras, see Ma & Pietarinen 2017b.)

A *proof* of a graph G in $\mathbf{K}^y$ is a finite sequence of graphs $G_0, \ldots, G_n$ such that $G_n = G$, and each G_i is either an axiom, or derived from previous graphs by a rule. A graph G is *provable* in $\mathbf{K}^y$, notation $\vdash_{\mathbf{K}^y} G$, if it has a derivation in $\mathbf{K}^y$. A graph rule is *provable* in $\mathbf{K}^y$ if the conclusion is provable whenever the premiss is provable in $\mathbf{K}^y$.

The system $\mathbf{K}^y$ is the modal extension of the Alpha system for classical propositional logic. The following rules are useful and indeed they are provable in $\mathbf{K}^y$:

(1) De Morgan rules:

$$\frac{(G\,H)}{(G)\,(H)}\ \text{(DM1)} \qquad \frac{(G)\,(H)}{(G\,H)}\ \text{(DM2)}$$

(2) Contraposition and transitivity rules:

$$\frac{(G\,(H))}{(H\,(G))}\ \text{(CP)} \qquad \frac{(G\,(H))\quad (H\,(J))}{(G\,(J))}\ \text{(TR)}$$

(3) Prefixing and Modus Ponens:

$$\frac{G}{(H\,G)}\ \text{(PF)} \qquad \frac{G\quad (G\,(H))}{H}\ \text{(MP)}$$

(4) Lattice rules:

$$\frac{G_i\,H}{G_1\,G_2\,H}\,(\&L) \qquad \frac{G\,H \quad G\,J}{G\,H\,J}\,(\&R) \qquad \frac{G\,J \quad H\,J}{G\,H\,\;J}\,(\lozenge L)$$

$$\frac{G\,H_i}{G\,H_1\,H_2}\,(\lozenge R) \qquad \frac{G\,H\,J}{H\,G\,J}\,(NL) \qquad \frac{G\,H\,J}{H\,G\,J}\,(NR)$$

(5) Residuation rules (also known as Peirce's Rule, see Ma & Pietarinen 2017a; LoF 1):

$$\frac{G\,H\,J}{G\,H\,J}\,(RG1) \qquad \frac{G\,H\,J}{G\,H\,J}\,(RG2)$$

Proposition 2.1. The following modal graph rules of *upward monotonicity* and *replacement of equivalents* are provable in $\mathbf{K}^y$ as well:

$$\frac{G\,H}{G\,H}\,(UMN) \qquad \frac{G\,H}{G\,H}\,(UMP)$$

$$\frac{G\,H}{G\,H}\,(UMDB) \qquad \frac{G\,H \quad H\,G}{J\,(J[G/H]) \;\; (J[G/H])\,J}\,(RE)$$

Proof. The rule (UMN) is obtained from (DMN) by the Alpha rule of contraposition:

$$\frac{G\,H}{H\,G}\,(CP)$$

Other upward monotonicity rules are shown similarly. The rule (RE) is shown by induction on the construction of J. □

Proposition 2.2. The following graphs are provable in $\mathbf{K}_y$:

(1) $[\,(G\,H)\;(G)\,]\,(H)$

(2) $(G)\,(G\,H)$

(3) $(G\,H)\,(G)$.

Proof. As to the graph (1), by (K) obviously we have

$$(\!(G)\!)\ (\!(G\,H)\!)\ (\!(G\,(\!(G\,H)\!))\!).$$

Then, we have the following proof:

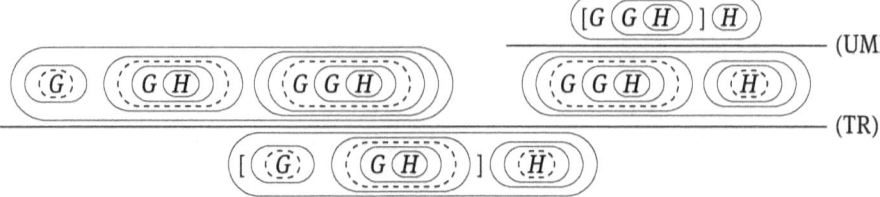

$$\dfrac{[G\,(\!(G\,H)\!)]\,(\!(H)\!)}{}\ (\text{UM})$$

$$\dfrac{(\!(G)\!)\ (\!(G\,H)\!)\ (\!(G\,(\!(G\,H)\!))\!)\qquad (\!(G\,(\!(G\,H)\!))\!)\ (\!(H)\!)}{[(\!(G)\!)\ (\!(G\,H)\!)]\,(\!(H)\!)}\ (\text{TR})$$

The graph (2) is obtained by (IR), and the graphs (3) is obtained by (DR). □

Extensions of K^y

There are extensions of K_y, with additional sequents as their characteristic axioms. The formulation of these characteristic axioms will use the cuts, including the six cuts previously introduced. Following Peirce's standard terminology, let us say that a cut in a graph is *positive* (*negative*) if it is evenly (oddly) enclosed by primitive cuts (either continuous or broken cuts).

A *normal modal Gamma system* is an extension of K^y with a set of graph rules. Given a set of graph rules $\Sigma = \{R_i \mid i \in I\}$, the notation K$\Sigma$ denotes the normal modal system generated by adding the rules in Σ. Let us consider the following rules:

(T) Any positive continuous cut can be transformed into a broken cut. Any negative broken cut can be transformed into a continuous cut.

$$\dfrac{J^+[(G)]}{J^+[(\!(G)\!)]}(T^+)\qquad \dfrac{J^-[(\!(G)\!)]}{J^-[(G)]}(T^-)$$

(D) Any positive necessity cut can be transformed into a possibility cut. Any negative possibility cut can be transformed into a necessity cut.

$$\dfrac{J^+[(\!(G)\!)]}{J^+[(\!(G)\!)]}(D^+)\qquad \dfrac{J^-[(\!(G)\!)]}{J^-[(\!(G)\!)]}(D^-)$$

(4) Any positive necessity cut can be doubled. Any negative possibility cut can be doubled.

$$\dfrac{J^+[(\!(G)\!)]}{J^+[(\!((\!(G)\!))\!)]}(4^+)\qquad \dfrac{J^-[(\!(G)\!)]}{J^-[(\!((\!(G)\!))\!)]}(4^-)$$

(B) Any positive double broken cut can be deleted. Any double broken cut can be inserted into a negative position.

$$\frac{J^+[\,(\!(G)\!)\,]}{J^+[G]}(B^+) \qquad \frac{J^-[G]}{J^-[\,(\!(G)\!)\,]}(B^-)$$

(5) Any positive double broken cut can be transformed into a necessity cut. Any negative necessity cut can be transformed into a double broken cut.

$$\frac{J^+[\,(\!(G)\!)\,]}{J^+[\,(G)\,]}(5^+) \qquad \frac{J^-[\,(G)\,]}{J^-[\,(\!(G)\!)\,]}(5^-)$$

Remark 2.6. The axiom (T) follows from Peirce's presentation of modal logic and its two basic rules in the notes of Lecture IV (R 467). The axiom (D) is gotten from (T) when using both (T^+) and (T^-), and is hence contained in Peirce's own modal systems.

Remark 2.7. One also finds one unique leaf, among the draft pages of the *Syllabus* (R 478(s)), in which he considered the axiom (4), namely the doubling or iteration of the necessity cut (Selection 42, "Fragments"; LoF 2/2). It remains unclear whether in that worksheet leave of R 478(s) Peirce intended to have the sign of consequence ($\prec$) or the sign of equality (=) between $(\!(p)\!)$ and $(\!((\!(p)\!))\!)$, which of course is an important difference. Possibly he first wrote $\prec$ but then crossed it over with =. The latter direction would mean also *density*, that is, a deletion of a doubled necessity around any graph. The latter would produce yet another modal system.

Remark 2.8. As to the axiom (B), Peirce remarked that "there is not much utility in a *double broken cut*. Yet it may be worth [a] notice that $(\!(g)\!)$ and g can neither of them be inferred from the other" (R 467). This is true in general, but a specification is needed to get a new modal system: namely that from top-down the inference in question is permissible when the double broken cut lies on a positive area, while the inverted rule is permissible when g lies on a negative area.

Remark 2.9. A further point of interest concerning the behaviour of the double broken cut is that Peirce took the outer of the broken cuts to be relative not strictly speaking to the state of information "but to a state of reflection", namely to the possibility that the truth of the graph is necessary, and that it is because of the interpretation of the broken cut as *ignorance*, such as that one has "not sufficiently reflected upon the subject" (R 467). Therefore doubt remains whether the truth of the graph obtains or not.[14]

Remark 2.10. Peirce did not have the rules (5^+) or (5^-), and indeed these rules that pertain to the modal system **S5** would have been too strong to argue for a defensible epistemic meaning of the broken cut; indeed Peirce did not take a system with the rule (5) to be a good system for knowledge (R 467; see below).

Definition 2.7. Let $(X) = \{(X)^+, (X)^-\}$ for $X \in \{D, T, 4, B, 5\}$. The following fifteen modal Gamma systems are defined as:

(1) $KD^y = K^y(D)$ (2) $KB^y = K^y(B)$ (3) $K4^y = K^y(4)$
(4) $K5^y = K^y(5)$ (5) $KT^y = K^y(T)$ (6) $KDB^y = KD^y(B)$
(7) $KB4^y = KB^y(4)$ (8) $KD4^y = KD^y(4)$ (9) $KD5^y = KD^y(5)$
(10) $KB5^y = KB^y(5)$ (11) $K45^y = K4^y(5)$ (12) $KTB^y = KT^y(B)$
(13) $S4^y = KT^y(4)$ (14) $S5^y = KT^y(5)$

A modal Gamma system S_1 is a *sublogic* of S_2 if any graph provable in S_1 is also provable in S_2. Then the relationship between above modal Gamma systems can be shown in the following figure where the lower system is a sublogic of the upper system in a branch:

---

[14] An interested reader may compare Peirce's argument to the diversity of similar thoughts that have been presented, ranging from Anselm's ontological proof the status of which has been argued to depend on interpretations of Brouwer's Axiom (Serene 1981), or to the *logic of being informed* (Floridi 2006), or to that of Karl Menger's *logic of doubt* (Menger 1939). Especially the latter portrays itself much in the spirit of Peirce's suggestions: In Menger's logic, being 'doubtful' means not known to be true nor false, that is, it means epistemic contingency. A relevant historical tidbit that sadly tends to be forgotten in mainstream historiographies is that Menger had in 1930 visited Harvard University and met Paul Weiss there, making an early acquaintance of Peirce's works and of the ongoing edition of the *Collected Papers of Charles S. Peirce* that Weiss was editing with Charles Hartshorne. Upon Menger's return to Europe, he would report on American pragmatism, especially as concerns Peirce's works, to the members of the Vienna Circle (Pietarinen 2009a). (The editor's [A.-V. P.'s] autographed copy of Peirce's *Collected Papers* by Karl Menger testifies to this acquaintance, and so do Menger's own memoirs (Menger 1994).) Menger's posthumously published reminiscences include a passage "I thought that Peirce had been professor at Harvard. 'No'', Weiss told me, 'His father and brother were. He himself was on the faculty of Johns Hopkins and only for a short time. People did not like his morals. I thought of the loss that American universities inflicted upon themselves at the turn of the century by rejecting the services of one of the greatest American thinkers" (Menger 1994, p. 162).

Introduction to the Theory of Existential Graphs, Volumes 2/1 and 2/2 — 51

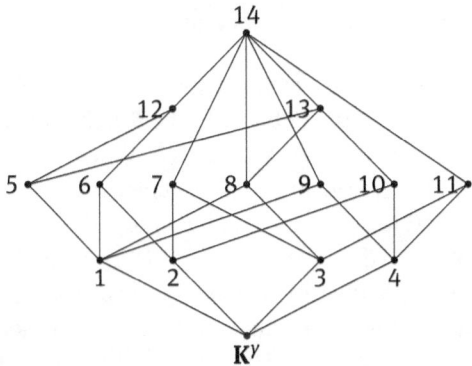

$\mathbf{K}^y$

More precisely, then, Peirce explicitly presented the graph rules for the modal logic $\mathbf{KT}_y$. By the rules (T^+) and (T^-), one can derive in $\mathbf{KT}_y$ the Cube I of Figure 2 and hence the Cube II in Figure 2. The rules (D^+) and (D^-) can be proved in $\mathbf{KT}_y$. The following are the proofs:

$$\frac{J^+[(\!(G)\!)]}{\dfrac{J^+[(\!(G)\!)]}{J^+[(\!(G)\!)]} \; (T^-)} \; (T^+) \qquad \frac{J^-[(\!(G)\!)]}{\dfrac{J^-[(G)]}{J^-[(\!(G)\!)]} \; (T^+)} \; (T^-)$$

Thus the system $\mathbf{KD}^y$ is a sublogic of $\mathbf{KT}^y$. Another example is that (B^+) and (B^-) can be proved in $\mathbf{S5}^y$ as follows:

$$\frac{\dfrac{\dfrac{J^+[(\!(G)\!)]}{J^+[(\!(G)\!)]} \; (5^+)}{\dfrac{J^+[(G)]}{J^+[G]} \; (T^-)}}{J^+[G]} \; (DC) \qquad \frac{\dfrac{\dfrac{J^-[G]}{J^-[(G)]} \; (DC)}{J^-[(\!(G)\!)]} \; (T^+)}{J^-[(\!(G)\!)]} \; (5^-)$$

Thus $\mathbf{KTB}^y$ is a sublogic of $\mathbf{S5}^y$. Other connections between above modal systems can be shown in a similar manner.

One can then proceed presenting the algebraic semantics for modal graph systems (details are found in Ma & Pietarinen 2017b). Since the Alpha system is sound and complete with respect to the class of all Boolean algebra, one may define modal algebras for modal systems and then show that by virtue of the Lindenbaum–Tarski construction that a similar completeness result holds for the Gamma systems:

Theorem 2.1. All fifteen systems in Definition 2.7 are sound and complete with respect to their corresponding modal Gamma algebras.

One may contrast the semantic completeness of graphical modal logic with Peirce's own statements and predictions. In the *Syllabus* he had written (in the non-printed part of the copy-text of the draft R 478) that "for the broken cut, *perfect* rules" may be given. Indeed, at least in so far as the quantifier-free language of the broken-cut modal logic is concerned, its normal systems of rules are completely axiomatizable. And that set of rules arises from what Peirce had originally proposed as the set of basic rules of the modal logic of EGs.

Another of Peirce's terms to describe properties of the system of rules was that its rules comprise "*archegetic* rules of transformation". He explains the meaning of being archegetic as the property of "the rules of any code which is such that none of its rules follows as a consequence from the rest, while all other permissibilities are consequences of its rules" (R 478). This characterises the *independence* of the rules of transformation.

One important feature of these fifteen modal systems is that they are obtained from $\mathbf{K}^y$ by adding pairs of rules. A question that thus arises is whether one rule in a pair is enough for obtaining a complete system. Let S be any one of the fifteen systems. Let S^+ and S^- be the systems obtained from S by dropping the negative rules and positive rules respectively.

Theorem 2.2. For any system S in Definition 2.7, $S^+ - S - S^-$.

Proof. Consider $\mathbf{KT}^+ = \mathbf{K}^y(T^+)$. It suffices to show that (T^-) is provable in $\mathbf{KT}^+$. Assume that $J^-[\langle \widetilde{G} \rangle]$ is provable in $\mathbf{KT}^+$. There are two cases:

Case 1. $J^-[\langle \widetilde{G} \rangle] = J'\ \widetilde{H\ \langle \widetilde{G} \rangle}$. First, it is easy to prove that $(G\ (\langle \widetilde{G} \rangle))$ in $\mathbf{KT}^+$. Then we have the following proof:

Case 2. $J^-[\,G\,] = J'\,(H\,\dot{G})$. We have the following proof:

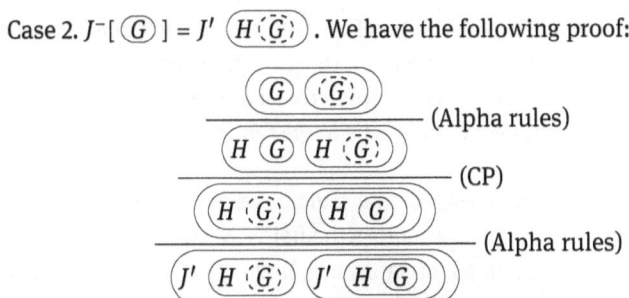

Hence (T^-) is provable in **KT**$^+$. The remaining cases of S are shown similarly. □

In general, algebraic semantics for the Gamma graphs is not intended to capture all aspects of what a comprehensible semantic theory for EGs ought to accomplish; well-known is that Peirce's own interpretation of graphs was set up in the discourse-theoretic framework between the Graphist (the Utterer, the Defender) and the Interpreter (the Hearer, the Antagonist) of the assertion. (For details of such a discourse- or game-theoretic interpretation, see e.g. Pietarinen 2006a, 2013 and the General Introduction to the volumes.) The extension of game-theoretic semantics to modalities is then straightforward, and was noticed to have also been proposed by Peirce in Hilpinen (1995). Yet algebraic semantics is worth developing in its own right. Application of algebra to the theory of graphs is justified from the point of view of Peirce's own logical theory, at least for the following two reasons. First, modal algebraic semantics is a natural continuation of the algebraic tradition of logic that largely originated with Peirce's logical researches. Second, graphical calculi admit of reinterpretations in terms of algebraic rules, thus answering an important remark in Peirce's reply to one of Christine Ladd-Franklin's questions concerning of what bearing he thought logical graphs would have on what the received logic was at that time: "Not much", Peirce answered, "except in one highly important particular, that *they supply an entirely new system of fundamental assumptions to logical algebra*" (R L 237, 1900, latter emphasis added; LoF 3).

Peirce's Interpretations of Modal Gamma Graphs

Modal operators signify intensional notions. For example, the following interpretations have been proposed during the course of the history of modal logic:

(1) If □ is replaced by K_a, the knowledge operator, then $K_a \phi$ means that the agent *a knows* that ϕ is true. The sign of necessity, □, is interpreted as a knowledge operator in *epistemic logic*.

(2) In *provability logic*, the formula **Pr**(ϕ) means that ϕ is *provable* in a system. Here the modality □ is taken to refer to the provability operator.
(3) In linear *temporal logic*, the □ is interpreted as a future necessity **G**. Then **G**ϕ means that ϕ is *always going to be true in the future*.

Variability in interpretations allows modal logic to be applied to philosophical, logical and computational questions across the fields as diverse (but also significantly connected) as epistemology, metaphysics, linguistics, mathematics, cognitive sciences, biology or quantum theory.

By 1903, Peirce had recognised the potential of these interpretations. Aside from alethic modalities, he explored at least three different interpretations of modal logic, and achieved the logic of knowledge, provability and, to a degree, elements of the logic of tensed modalities. He prospected such variations to help analysing the logic of science, the mature doctrine of categories, the nature of mathematical reasoning, and the meaning of intellectual signs, thoughts, concepts and generalities.

Epistemic Interpretation of Gamma Graphs
The interpretation Peirce seems to have been most attracted to is the epistemic reading of the broken-cut modality. This is supported by R S-31, on a page that was cut off from the notebook containing extensive plans of the fourth lecture (R 467):

> ...the general purpose of using different sorts of cuts as practice should prove them to be desirable; but up to this time I have only found occasion for two.
> One of them is the interrupted cut which I draw with little lines about equal to the spaces. Thus, this graph

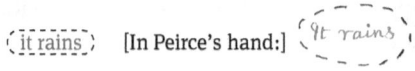

> does not positively deny that it rains, but merely asserts that in some assumed state of information which must be ~~indicated~~ specified by some attachment to a hook of the cut, I do not know that it rains.

What Peirce says may be related to the semantic definition of the broken cut interpreted as an epistemic operator, namely an interpretation which takes modalities to be relative to the states of information. The interpretation of the broken cut thus is, in the first place, an epistemic one: ⦇g⦈ means that an ignorant agent would not know that g. That is, for all that the agent knows, it is so that not g. Modal propositions are about facts that an agent is, as Peirce tells, in "a state of information sufficient to know" (R 467).

Recall that in the standard epistemic logic of knowledge, the formula $K\varphi$ means that the agent knows that φ is true. We can define the dual as $\widehat{K}\varphi := \neg K\neg\varphi$, which means that the agent reckons ϕ possibly true, namely that it does not follow from what the agent knows that $\neg\varphi$ is the case. In other words, φ is the case, for all that the agent knows.

Peirce's broken-cut operator is thus related to the dual version of the knowledge operator as given in Hintikka's *Knowledge and Belief* (Hintikka 1962): an epistemic possibility or not knowing that not g. It is this epistemic possibility, or incompatibility with g, given what the agent knows, that underwrites Peirce's other variations on the interpretation of modalities.

Peirce formalised the following sentences by Gamma graphs (R S-1):
(1) The rules don't know g is true.
(2) They may not know g not true.
(3) They may know g not true.
(4) I may not know that I don't know g true.
(5) I may not know that it is true that I know g.

Peirce's formalization of these five propositions are given in Table 3, where their corresponding formulæ in the standard logic of knowledge are also written down.

Tab. 3: Peirce's Epistemic Reading of the Modal Gamma Graphs

(1)	(2)	(3)
$\neg Kg = \widehat{K}\neg g$	$\neg K\neg g = \widehat{K}g$	$K\neg g = \neg\widehat{K}g$
(4)		(5)
$\neg K\neg Kg = \widehat{K}\widehat{K}g$		$\neg KKg = \widehat{K}\widehat{K}\neg g$

There is yet another novelty that broken cuts have, namely that unlike continuous cuts, they have hooks onto which marks that refer to states of things can be connected. Peirce explains the procedure as follows:

> We should fall into inextricable confusion in dealing with the broken cut if we did not attach to it a sign to distinguish the particular state of information to which it refers. And a similar sign has then to be attached to the simple g, which refers to the state of information at the time of learning that graph to be true. (R 467)

Modalities are thus connected to "states of information" to which they refer.

The passage above is followed by the presentation of the *necessitation rule*, namely that from a graph *g* that has been marked by the attachment to the hook of the broken cut (namely that *one has already learned or proven the graph to be true*), one can infer the necessity of that graph *g*.

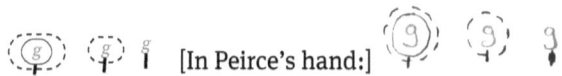   [In Peirce's hand:]

After this, Peirce notices that there are "some peculiar and interesting little rules" (R 467) that he was led to consider from these cases. Among them is the following principle subsequently widely discussed in the literature:

(KK) If I do not know that I know *g* true, then I do not know *g* is true. (R 467)

Using $G \prec H$ to represent that H follows from G, the rule (KK) can be formalised as follows:

$$\boxed{g} \prec \boxed{g} \quad (\neg KKg \rightarrow \neg Kg)$$

Peirce further checked the plausibility of (KK) by reformulating it as "if the rules do not enable me to know that they enable me to know *g*, then they do not enable me to know *g*" (R S-1). This principle is, by contraposition, equivalent to the law of *introspection* in Hintikka's logic of knowledge, namely to the rule that $Kg \rightarrow KKg$ (Hintikka 1962).

One must exercise some caution in the interpretation of such rules, however: knowledge may imply the means of knowing that knowledge, but it by no means follows what knowledge would imply a simple iteration of that very knowledge. According to Peirce:

> There will be some peculiar and interesting little rules, owing to the fact that what one knows one has the means of knowing that one knows,—which is often sometimes incorrectly stated in the form that whatever one knows one knows that one knows, which is manifestly false. For if it were the same to say "A whale is not a fish" and "I know that a whale is not a fish", the precise denials of the two would be the same. Yet one is "A whale is not a fish" and the other is "I do not know that a whale is not a fish". (R 467)

Similar thoughts are found expressed much later as follows:

> It may seem that a mind cannot help being aware of its own states, among which there are the states of knowledge and of belief. At the very least, it seems impossible to doubt that a mind can always become aware of its own states. If I actively believe something, it might be said, surely I must be able to recognize that I do. What could there be preventing me from knowing my own mind? On what authority could anyone say that I do not know what I myself believe? (Hintikka 1962, p. 53)

Peirce is seen to argue, quite rightly, that if a proposition holds in a state of information from which another follows in terms of being related to it (say, in the modern sense of the latter being accessible from the former), then that proposition is necessary in that latter state of information. This is confirmed by what Peirce states in R 467 next, first noted in Zeman (1964) (cf. Pietarinen 2006b):

> The truth is that it is necessary to have a graph to signify that one state of information follows after another. If we scribe

 [P.H.]

> to express that the state of information B follows after the state of information A, we shall have

 [P.H.]

Since Peirce's own rules (Ta) and (Tb) do not give rise to the modal system **S5** and since **S5** is not an adequate logic for the concept of knowledge, the conclusion is that Peirce's preferred interpretation of the broken-cut modality was in terms of knowledge and its veridicality:

> It becomes evident, in this way, that a modal proposition is a simple assertion not about the universe of things but about the universe of facts that one is in a state of information sufficient to know. The graph $(\overline{g})$ without any selective, merely asserts that there is a possible state of information in which the knower is not in a condition to know that the graph g is true, while $(\overline{\overline{g}})$ asserts that there is no such possible state of information. (R 467)

It is worth considering to which extent also *deontic* interpretations—with D but without (5) and possibly without (4)—could have been at the back of Peirce's mind in these days, given that D^+ and D^- are provable in KT_y. Support for deontic interpretations may also be garnered from Peirce's famous conception of logic as a normative science (Pietarinen 2012b).

Provability Interpretation of Gamma Graphs

In addition to the epistemic interpretation, Peirce considered the cases of our knowledge being related to the somewhat more specific and regimented notion of *provability* when using the rules of some systems of logic to perform inferences. Indeed he experimented with what such an interpretation of modal Gamma graphs could look like, and came up with the case of expressing provability by the Beta rules in the modal context. The Beta rules are the rules of transformation for the

Beta part of logic of EGs, which extends the Alpha part with lines of identity, complex lines he termed ligatures, and spots, namely predicate and relation terms. This produces a (fragment of) first-order graphical logic. Peirce's provability reading of modal Gamma graphs is found in R S-1 and it represents the various cases for the rules of the Beta system summarised in Table 4 (see also Selection 42, "Fragments", LoF 2/2).

A natural reading that accords with Peirce's intentions can be supplied to his original proposal. Using the language of provability logic, these four propositions can be formalized as ¬**Pr**(g), ¬**Pr**(¬g), **Pr**(g) and **Pr**(¬g). For example possibility ⬭ corresponds to ¬**Pr**(¬⊤) and necessity ⬭ to **Pr**(⊤).

Two new rules are needed to get the logic of provability going.

- The *distribution* of the provability operator over implication, that is, to permissively infer from ⬭(g g) the graph ⬭(g) ⬭(g), and
- Löb's axiom, namely that of inferring from ⬭(⬭(g) g) the provability of g, namely ⬭(g).

Tab. 4: Peirce's Provability Reading of the Modal Gamma Graphs (R S-1)

	means that beta rules	do not prove that	g is true
	"	"	g is false
	"	prove that	g is true
	"	"	g is false

Whether Löb's axiom is analysable by graph transformations into some more primitive inferential moves remains to be seen. At least the rule (Tb) of closing a broken cut on negative areas does not represent permissible transformations in standard provability logic, as the latter does not instantiate a contradiction (graphically, an empty continuous cut) from a provability of a contradiction. That is, ⬭ does not imply ○, which it would if the closing of the broken cut in the middle of the former graph were to be permitted, followed by an application of an erasure of a double cut.

Semantically, a provability interpretation of the broken-cut modality would mean that there are no infinitely thick 'books of sheets of assertion' that are "tacked together at points", as Peirce depicted them to be in the fourth lecture: "[I]n place of a sheet of assertion, we have a book of separate sheets, tacked together at points, if not otherwise connected" (R 467). This follows from the frame restriction presented by Löb's axiom to those that are *conversely well-founded*, that is, do not form infinitely ascending chains or loops. In the more picturesque, or rather more iconic terms of the Gamma language, the alternative universes of the sheets of assertions that are tacked together (or are accessible through the arrow-relation as shown above), are not open to view without limits: the broken cut only exposes those alternative universes that are bounded—the bottom of the well is to be reachable in a finite number of transitions from one universe to universe.

It is quite possible that Peirce was planning a follow-up to his proposal of those new operations that he presented to his audience at the end of the second lecture (R S-32, R S-34), and perhaps as an opening of the third lecture (R 457, R 462, R 464), which would have showed something of the decidability of formulas as expressed in the language of Gamma graphs. But what could explain Peirce coming close to hitting upon a provability interpretation of the broken-cut notation in the worksheets of R S-1, pages which he wrote contemporaneously with the fourth lecture (R 467)? Right at the end of his second lecture he had explored what the notions of alpha-possibility and beta-possibility, as well as those of the alpha and beta-impossibility amount to, namely a systematic construction of the "state of the universe". Thus the expressivity of the language of the Alpha and Beta graphs was found to be severely limited, motivating Peirce to work out a way to probe the limits of what can be expressed and proven in such systems, from the vantage point of the set of their "perfect" rules.

Broken-Cut Modalities in Graphs of Graphs
Another context in which we find the broken-cut notation being resorted to in novel ways is that Gamma compartment which deals with meta-graphical expressions. Peirce called the result the theory of the *graphs of graphs* (R 467, R S-31), and it seems to have emerged in the wake of the broken-cut's epistemic interpretation. This took place in the course of his planning and writing of the third and the fourth lectures, continuing well into the planning and drafting of his fifth lecture (R 468, R 469, R 470, December 3–7). All of these ideas emerge during his efforts of getting the final version of the *Syllabus* (R 478, R 508) written up and sent to the printer Alfred Mudge & Son of Boston.

The theory of the graphs of graphs concerns the use of graphical expressions and the language of graphs to talk about or represent the properties of that very language and its logic. As such the idea of meta-graphs dates back to some of his earlier writings in 1896, but the novelty of 1903 is to add the modality of the broken cut to the analysis. A particularly significant idea of Peirce's in this regard was thus not only to express the ingredients of Alpha or Beta language and how they are composed using such graphs, but also to express the properties and rules of those systems in the language of graphs. That is, various properties related to the *illative rules of transformation* themselves could then be expressed in the language of modal Gamma graphs. Since representations of illative rules would have to appeal to modalities—after all, illation has the property of being *necessary* inference, and graph transformations concern the issues of what is *permitted* and what is *not permitted* to be scribed on the sheet—the use of the broken-cut modality would strike him as an indispensable asset in graphically modelling the meaning of those permissive transformations.

Let us present three examples out of six such cases that Peirce provided in R S-31, R 468 and R 509 in early December, the detailed explanations of which are given in the survey chapter of the respective selections. These graphs involve special predicates that pertain to the meta-graph compartment of the Gamma graphs, and are denoted by various Greek letters. The main point of interest is the interpretation of the broken cut $(\overline{g})$, which now means that "the rules of logic and graphs do not require g to be true" (R 468). Then the graph in Figure 4a means that "It is always permitted to scribe a line of identity on the sheet of assertion with its extremities attached to blanks" (R 468). The graph in Figure 4b, in turn, means that "If any graph-replica is on the sheet it is not necessary that anything else should be on the sheet" (R S-31). The graph in Figure 4c, indeed much more complicated than the other, means according to Peirce's parlance that "The sheet if is it permitted to carry a graph$_1$ containing a graph$_2$ not a blank and not a cut whose area carries a blank is permitted to carry any graph-replica not differing from that graph-replica$_1$ in any other respect than that it does not carry that graph-replica$_2$" (R 509).[15]

Another and a slightly differently phrased approach is found on the worksheet from February 1909, entitled "The System of Existential Graphs applied to the Examination of Itself" (R S-3, LoF 1). It may be the only place where Peirce actually continued on what he set out to do in his fourth or fifth Lowell Lecture on the theory of the graphs of graphs. A second attempt on this from February 15

---

15 Subscript indices are used here instead of the connecting lines that Peirce had in the original caption of the graph in Figure 4c. Peirce wrote "not quite sure" below this graph.

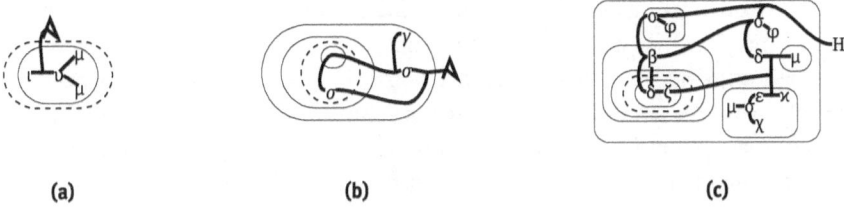

Figure 4: Examples of Peirce's Meta-Graphical Gamma Graphs Concerning Permissions

defines, among others, an interesting precursory gesture at "justification logic", namely that "something justifies something"—perhaps a graph that justifies another graph. In this fragment we also find some Beta-graph-like temporal considerations, such as "a is true at an instant x". The title Peirce gave to the section was "Logic of Time", but it soon breaks off and no continuation of it has been recovered or signalled anywhere else.

The provability interpretation and the meta-logic of the graphs of graphs are connected suggestions, however embryonic, that aimed at giving birth to a meta-logical apparatus that could help analyse the nature of mathematical reasoning better than was possible with the Alpha, Beta or the standard Gamma modalities. Philosophically, graphs of graphs are seen to shift the focus of concern from meanings and significations of the constituents of graphs to the scribing of graph-replicas on the sheet under *material modes of thought*, namely in their mode of being signs. Graphs of graphs are thus not strictly speaking representational at all, or assert anything about graphs as being representations of their objects. Meta-graphs concern purely mathematic definitions of properties of graphs. In Peirce's terms, one has "to be able to speak about every possible graph of a general description", namely to be able to speak under a *suppositio materialis* (see R 2–R 3 and R 511–R 512, both from late 1903, the latter defining some 35 graphs, in natural language, using expressions of the form: "Let it be supposed that...", then using quotation marks to talk about replicas, properties and inferences; LoF 2/2). To do this requires that one has, Peirce states, "learned the language of graphs first", because before one can really conceive graphs in their material modes of thought, one needs to understand what the objects of those graphs are, and those of course are none other than some other graphs and constituents of those graphs.

If one adds to Peirce's statement that in meta-graphs, one has "to be able to speak *uniquely* about every possible graph of a general description", one would make another step towards the idea of Gödel numbering. A full implementation would require prime factorials that were not at Peirce's disposal. The graphs of graphs approach retains its value also as a precursory to later results on hierarchies of truths, inclusions of the truth-predicate within the language, the ensuing hierarchies (such as the Turing ordinal notations), predicativity, and, as noted, the logic of provability. One should notice that in graphs of graphs, one needs to be able to use the notation of graphs to talk about *any* notation of the graphs themselves, and therefore for example the notion of a spot "being attached to" another spot is given in the very language that uses those attachments. This is seen to happen in R 496, for example, in which Peirce inscribed on one of the cut-out sheets the graph A—a—B, meaning by it the graph of "A is attached to B". Here a stands for the two-place relation "is attached to". See the last selection "Fragments" for these details of R 496.

Tense-logical Interpretations

Peirce also wanted to, and to some degree did, develop a logical approach to analyse the concept of time. For example, according to one of the section headings that he gave in 1909 he was planning to embark on a graphical investigation of the "Logic of Time". Be that as it may have been, Peirce famously noticed in the fourth lecture that "Time has usually been considered by logicians to be what is called 'extra-logical' matter. I have never shared this opinion" (R 467; cf. Appendix A of Prior 1964).[16] For example, the very act of asserting graphs is an act of scribing them not only on the surface of the sheet, but also an act of scribing them with respect to the time of that assertion. Surely there is no reason to suppose that propositions that are asserted are eternal, timeless entities.

In order to pursue such ideas somewhat further, Peirce was led in the Gamma compartment to propose some tensed interpretations of modalities. Such interpretations concern not only the broken-cut notation but also some other features of the system. The purported result would be a multi-modal, temporal-epistemic logic:

> But the gravest complications of logic would be involved, in so far as taking account of time to distinguish between what one *knows* and what *one has sufficient reason to be entirely confident of*. The only difference that there seems to be room for between these two is that what one *knows*, one always will have *reason to be confident of* while what one now has ample reason to be entirely confident of one may conceivably in the future, in consequence of a new light, find reason to doubt and ultimately to deny. (R 467)

---

16 On some further and complementary ideas concerning the temporal reading of Peirce's broken-cut Gamma system, as well as Peirce's largely unfulfilled search for the logic of tense, have been put forward in Øhrstrøm (2000) and Zeman (1967).

If one knows *p* now, one will always have a reason to be confident of *p*, so much so that by asserting his knowledge of *p*, one must be prepared to defend *p* in the light of further evidence. Yet if one has a reason to be confident of *p* now, then there may be a point of time in the future in which one begins to doubt *p*, comes to deny *p*, and hence comes to know that not *p*. Pragmatist epistemology indeed takes knowledge to be an *achievement*, which is a result of synchronic, time-dependent processes. What is important is the description of that process, not only its outcome.[17]

The following two examples of tensed conceptions in Peirce's logic of EGs involve the notation from his Beta part, namely ligatures that are attached to predicate terms or spots. First, in the *Logic Notebook* (LN, R 339, January 7, 1909; LoF 1), Peirce proposes a tensed modality attached to truth-values. He presents some Beta graphs such as

 p is true sometimes and *q* true sometimes.

 p and *q* are sometimes true.

 p is true under some circumstances and *q* under others.

Here quantification takes place over moments of time. In Beta graphs these lines denote both quantification, existence and identity. Under tensed conceptions, it is not clear that all the lines could preserve their signification of being those of identity, as well. Indeed the development of quantificational logic over the tensed universe of discourse was left very incomplete, however. The title of his follow-up draft, never fully written either, was "Studies of Modal, Temporal, and Other Logical Forms which relate to Special Universes" (LN [341r], February 16, 1909). In the drafts from these days one finds Peirce's promissory notes on triadic logic, geometrical and topological logic of parts, as well as a few occurrences of graphs with tinctures (LN [342v, 342r, 344r]).

Importantly, in this second part of his three-page study on collections (*Family Record*, R 1601, c.1909; LoF 1) Peirce talks semantics, and proposes 'truth-conditions' for the shaded (tinctured) graphs: "A can be true or sometimes is so"; "Under the presumed conditions A cannot be true"; "B may be true, while A is false"; and so on. Such conditions extend ordinary logic with truth-values of true and false. Moreover, this piece is in fact closely related to his preceding notes found in the *Logic Notebook* and written on January 7, 1909 [340r] (LoF 1), in which Peirce is using the syntax of Beta graphs instead of the Alpha one, but

---

[17] On such pragmatistic interpretations of knowledge and knowability, see Hilpinen (2016), Pietarinen & Chiffi (2020).

the truth-values are similarly phrased, such as "p is true under some/all circumstances"; "p is true some times", and so on. It is quite suggestive that Peirce is using references to "circumstances" and their quantification: indeed objects of the domain may be constituted by circumstances, situations, temporal instances or intervals, for example.

There is one more protrusion of tensed conceptions into logical theories, found in R 496 (Selection 42, "Fragments"; LoF 2/2), a study on loose leaves of undelivered sketches and draft notes for the Lowell Lectures, presumably lectures two and three. Among the leaves one finds tense being introduced into the description of the process of scribing the graphs on the sheet of assertion. To do this, Peirce is seen to develop the following new notation:

This graph means that "A can be scribed at time B on C". Further, the predicate ◇ means that "◇ is a sheet of assertion". Then the graph

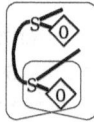

means that "Whatever could be scribed on the sheet at any time when this or that is scribed can be scribed (whatever is or is not scribed) at all times" (R 496).

This notation does not involve the broken-cut modality. With is, Peirce instead proposes to incorporate the denotation of the time of the scribing of assertions into a special three-place spot. In a deleted passage on the verso of a notebook leaf of R 458, initially part of the first draft of his third Lowell Lecture intended to be on the topic of multitudes, a similar spot appears in a graph which was intended "to assert that the graph A is permissibly scribable on [the sheet] within m cuts at the time B, within m cuts being either any whole number including 0 [sic.] There one rule will be and within any n other cuts [end]". This is all very sketchy, but the passage proposes to add an argument 'm cuts' to the spot S, besides the time of scribing and (though omitted in the figure in question) the place of scribing, turning S into a four-place relation.[18]

---

[18] A notable similar 'polarity counter' of cuts, expressed in the very language of graphs, appears in Peirce's February 1909 study entitled "The System of Existential Graphs applied to the Examination of Itself" (R S-3, LoF 1).

In the context of this draft note, Peirce wishes to describe and analyse the process of scribing the graphs, motivated by his attempt to provide a purely mathematical definition of everything that the theory of graphs involves. Such definitions were needed in order to analyse the conceptions of modern mathematics by such novel methods fledging in his multiple notes on the matter. Since "the simplest kind of mathematics would be the mathematics of existential graphs", as he asserts in the opening of that lecture, he would wish to "look at this subject mathematically". Indeed one of the goals of the entire Lowell Lecture series overall was to achieve a strictly mathematical definition of existential graphs, independently of their signification. As the graphs-of-graphs idea may be applied to the description of the process of the very scribing of those graphs, it is only to be expected that some temporal notions would have to be evoked for one to be fully equipped with precisely defined methods to perform that analysis.[19]

Gamma Graphs and Peirce's "Logic of the Future"

Peirce's graphical systems and interpretations of modal logic attest the fecundity and analyticity of the approach catered by the diagrammatic syntax: that non-linear form of language offers new methods and models to think and reason about modalities and their applications. His rules for the broken-cut Gamma graphs form a natural basis from which a hierarchy of modal systems arises. He also presented the rules that correspond to the normality axiom. An algebraic approach to the semantics for Gamma graphs can then provide the completeness of all fifteen normal systems that are defined by the basic rules of transformation for the broken-cut operator that are obtained directly from Peirce's own rules for the broken-cut operator. Furthermore, interpretations of that operator may be endlessly varied; Peirce's preferred interpretation was epistemic and it concerned the universe of subjective possibilities, while he also proposed several others interpretations for difference purposes of analysis by the graphical modal logic.

Since broken cuts are not only signs of modality but also of scope and combination, small variations in the diagrammatic syntax of the language modal Gamma graphs and its rules of inference produce a variety of different modal logics. Given this prolificacy and uberty of the graphical approach, a question that is worth pondering about is why Peirce did not continue working on these broken-

---

[19] On this topic, Peirce's prose forks into at least four very different attempts to look mathematically at the subject of existential graphs and their scribing on the sheet of assertion, only one of which evokes the graphs of graphs approach and the temporal notions. This certainly adds to the difficulty in tracing Peirce's trains of thought in how to best achieve that analysis.

cut modal logics after his 1903 Lowell Lectures? For we find virtually nothing of the broken cuts in his post-1903 writings, although we do find him exploring and using his alternative graphical notations for the analysis of modalities.[20] It can only be part of the answer that his disappointment following the circumstances beyond his powers to have the Lowell Lectures appear in print would have made him give up and forget the significance of modal Gamma graphs altogether, or that his failure to find time to present them during this course of lectures would have meant jettisoning them without further interest in their development, presentation or even mention. In the forthcoming years, he would not give up developing modal-logical instruments of analysis for central philosophical notions; on the contrary, Peirce is soon seen to be to be busy again working on the quantificational part of modal logic as well as on the consequences of the idea of adding tinctures to the graphs to produce something like multi-modal logics (R 292, R 295, R 490, 1906). He would increasingly link modalities with philosophical questions on the nature of meaning, identity and intentions. He saw the need for new methods and tools provided by the diagrammatic syntax to bring his architectonics into completion, namely to show what the philosophical and logical method of analysis and its expression in the form of the maxim of pragmaticism (and its purported proof) ultimately would consist of (Pietarinen 2006a, 2011c). Yet one cannot deny how salient the absence of the broken-cut notation is in anything that Peirce produced after 1903. Even when his writings would address modalities, the nature of real possibilities, continuity, or any of the philosophical, linguistic and epistemological questions analysed by his logic, those studies do not revisit his original broken-cut notation of modal Gamma graphs. Whatever the reasons for its absence, the fact remains that the graphical modal calculi that we see him labouring over in his Lowell Lecture notes never made a comeback.

Soon after 1903, Peirce would have his mind occupied with other developments of the graphical method, especially those increasingly more applicable to profoundly philosophical issues, including the question of how to extend the graphical treatment of modalities to graphs containing ligatures. Any completion of the work that he had set out to do in the Lowell Lectures concerning modal Gamma graphs was expressly remitted to his bequest, as it in any case would be

---

[20] The few instances of the 'broken-cut' emanating from Peirce's hand after 1903 have a different meaning and are merely typographical aids to distinguish between continuous cuts that are oddly enclosed and those that are evenly enclosed; these he used in the period of 1905–1906. His last and possibly the favourite means to illustrate the difference in polarity was in terms of shading the areas that are negative, which he predominantly resorted to in his last writings and sketches of graphs in 1910–1913.

"a labor for generations of analysts, not for one" to achieve the perfection of the "Gamma part of the system of Graphs" (R 478).

Nearly equally salient, however, has been the shortage of the secondary literature on the topic of the modal Gamma during the century that followed. The papers by Caterina & Gangle (2010), Ma & Pietarinen (2017b), Ramharter & Gottschall (2011), Roberts (1973) and Zeman (1964) are among the few exceptions, among which Zeman's dissertation stands out as the first yet the most extensive treatise of modal Gamma graphs to date. The silence is not the mark of there being anything wrong in the very conceptualisation of the idea, however, quite the contrary. Peirce did not give and he did not have any compelling reason to discard the broken-cut notation from the toolkit of the diagrammatic syntax of modal logic, or to replace that notation with something else that could have served his purposes better. The broken-cut notation is not only the basis for a comprehensive hierarchy of graphical modal logics. It also is, in its close resemblance of the notation of the continuous cut one interpretation of which is that of a negation, an analytically superior way to graphically denote modal operators. It fulfills Peirce's goal that whatever the systems of logic in the form of EGs are, they ought to be such that they will exhibit "but one mode of combination of ideas" (R 490, 1906; LoF 3), and that "the relation of *other than* or *not* is here a relation between an existent and a possibility" (R 490). Two years later (LN [322r], September 8, 1908; LoF 1) he summarises the crucial idea by stating that "Negation consists in Necessitation, not Necessitation in Negation" (capitalisation in the original). Negation, as represented by the enclosure, is at bottom a modal notion, and that modality springs out from the opening of the cut into the broken cut, representing a weakening from something 'being other than' to 'possibly, being other than'. Ever since the invention of the mature version of the graphical method in 1896 (LoF 1), Peirce was convinced of its superiority over algebraic languages of logic. In the context of modal Gamma graphs, one can conclude that because less room is afforded in such non-linear, graphical modal logics than in their linear alternatives (that were yet to be properly invented) for different ways of representing the same fact, these more diagrammatic logics were adopted as the preferred instrument for logical analysis.

Ahti-Veikko Pietarinen
Introduction to Volume 2/1: *The Logical Tracts*

In the next two volumes of the *Logic of the Future*, the development of EGs continues along two trajectories. Volume 2 comprises the bulk of Peirce's 1903 Lowell Institute Lectures and is arranged in two stand-alone books, Volumes 2/1 (*The Logical Tracts*) and 2/2 (*The 1903 Lowell Lectures*). Together they tell the story of how Peirce wanted the world to receive that theory, and what his sustained efforts were to communicate the fullest possible account of it to his peers, colleagues and public audience.

In Volume 3, *Pragmaticism and Correspondence*, we see Peirce applying EGs to his ultimate philosophical thoughts, and how he took graphs to deliver the proof of his philosophical theory of meaning, among other late innovations buried in the piles of letters, largely unsent, to his friends, colleagues, collaborators and editors.

The second volume has its textual material organised in fourteen selections, arranged in two parts across two books: three selections belong to *The Logical Tracts* (Part IV) and eleven in *The 1903 Lowell Lectures* (Part V). An account of Part IV, its theoretical background and a description of the texts selected in its individual chapters is provided next.

Part IV: *The Logical Tracts* of 1903

This section contains two subsections. First is an introduction to the topic of the fourth part, *The Logical Tracts*, a large compendium on existential graphs which Peirce prepared in 1903 to aid and accompany his drafting of the Lowell Lectures. Second is a survey of the three main parts that constitute its surviving texts.

Introduction to Part IV: Preparing the Lowell Lectures

From August 1898, Peirce's writings on EGs undergo a nearly five-year intermission until the massive *Logical Tracts* rebounds sometime in summer-fall 1903. His renewed efforts are explained by the upcoming Lowell Lectures later in the fall and winter, which Peirce in early 1903 would learn having been secured for him by his friends and colleagues. Those five years are not entirely vacant from his thinking of the graphs, but they were filled with numerous writing projects largely unrelated to logic. Outputs directly involving EGs are limited to R 493 (LoF 1), *Dictionary of Philosophy and Psychology* articles composed mostly in late 1900 and over 1901 (R 1147, LoF 3); a series of papers on logical notation from late 1901 (R 515, R 516, R 530; LoF 1); a section involving EGs drafted in early 1902 for the *Minute Logic* (R 430, LoF 1), and a few letters in his correspondence with Christine Ladd-Franklin in 1900 (LoF 3). Despite much having been lost from the archives, only a handful of writings and notes on logic and its notation that date from the years 1899–1902 can be documented to have involved sustained thoughts on EGs.

What contributed to the apparent disruption of the development of the theory of EGs and its applications? In the introduction to Volume 1 it was observed that his "The Peripatetic Talks" (R 502–506, LoF 1) and adjacent writings on EGs came to a sudden halt in August 1898, soon after the Peirces had moved permanently back to Milford: Charles in May and Juliette following him in July 1898. In September, he would suffer a typhoid-induced brain fever, from which he is making a slow recovery towards the next spring.[1] Many other writing projects, including numerous translation assignments for the Smithsonian Institution, many book reviews for *The Nation*, and the important but uncompleted History of Science book project for Putnam & Sons arranged by his former Johns Hopkins student James McKeen Cattell, were all necessary to make a living in Milford, and surely took the majority of Peirce's time. Peirce continued to correspond with Paul Carus and the Open Court press in 1898–1900 in his repeated but frustrated attempts to get Carus to publish several of his writings, which Carus refused "from a business standpoint", although "from a scientific standpoint" he held Peirce's contributions very valuable (PC to CSP, October 13, 1898). By the turn of the century, Peirce would suffer many failed attempts to find paid jobs, and the mounting destitution felt after the couple's relocation from New York City to the desolate Arisbe added to the losses. The final blow was the infamous rejection of his massive application "Memoirs on Minute Logic" (R L 75; partly published in NEM IV, pp. 13–73) to the Carnegie Institution to complete and publish the Minute Logic, a nightmare that becomes reality in early spring 1903. His 2500 manuscript and typescript pages on logic and philosophy would now have to be set aside.

With the upcoming Harvard and Lowell Lectures casting some long-awaited light on Peirce's penury, a resurgence is in the air. The year 1903 is destined to become the most productive phase of his life, beginning with the 1903 Harvard

---

[1] A comprehensive medical record of Charles Peirce is now available, compiled by David Pfeifer based on the notes of Max H. Fisch (Pfeifer 2014).

lectures on pragmatism ("Pragmatism as a Principle and Method of Right Thinking") in spring and culminating in the outburst of the long text of *The Logical Tracts*, the full *Syllabus* copy-text and its supplementary material, and the eight Lowell Lectures and their multiple pre-drafts later during the last months of the year, all exceedingly voluminous textual, scientific and educational triumphs.

The exact dating and the time span of Peirce getting the full *Logical Tracts* in shape is unclear, but the project is closely tied in with the preparation of his first planned lectures on graphs.[2] Indeed the text of R 492 reads as a nearly perfect compendium to the first couple of lectures on the definitions and technicalities of the graphical method of logic, brimming with examples of graphs. Its writing is probably immediately preceded by Peirce's long essay on telepathy (R 881), which was nearing its completion in late June.[3] On the verso of one of the final manuscript pages of R 881 on telepathy there exists an incomplete manuscript page 4 of "L Tr I" ("Logical Tracts No. I"), which serves as additional evidence that the telepathy ar-

---

[2] A one-page cover page exists among the collection of assorted pages of R 839, and bearing only the title "The Principles of Exact Logic" and an epigraph in Greek, may be an alternative, and possible Peirce's first attempt to begin writing the tracts. Peirce's Greek epigraph is from Plato's *Phaedrus*, 247c, quoting from Burnet's *Platonis Opera*, 1903 ("It is, however, as I shall tell; for I must dare to speak the truth, especially as truth is my theme").

[3] By the suggestions from William James, Peirce intended his "Telepathy" article to appear in *The Popular Science Monthly*, *The Monist*, or *The Nation* (WJ to CSP, July 10, 1903). The first and probably the longest draft of the article was finished by June 1 (CSP to WJ, June 1, 1903), of which running manuscript pages 1–99 have been preserved at R 881, plus many variants and rejects. The draft breaks off abruptly at the end of the 99th sheet, but a ms page 100 is located among the fragments in R 278(d) ("...well as one can see, points decidedly the other way. Which shall one follow, instinct or reason? The rule cannot be absolute; and what is wisest for one man may not be so for another. Speaking generally, instinct is the lens likely to be in error"). This might be the end of the draft which Peirce nevertheless abandons, explaining the reasons for its abandonment to Welby on December 1 having been that the paper had become "too elaborate": "This very summer I rejected over a hundred consecutive pages of my MS., most painfully and slowly made, simply because it was too elaborate. After all we want to get our thought expressed in short meter somehow" (CSP to VW, December 1, 1903). Although Peirce does not identify to Welby the manuscript by its name or content and says "over a hundred consecutive pages", it is unlikely that he would have meant his another 100-odd production of the year, *The Logical Tracts No. 2*, as that draft was unlikely to have reached its full length of 141 consecutive ms pages during the summer, and as unlike the "Telepathy" article was probably not contemplated for imminent publication (and for "maganization", being "very desirous of making the article so popular as to give me an *entree* to the magazines", CSP to WJ, June 1, 1903) at all. The point is not entirely definite, however, as one can for example find the idea of the "endless nest of seps" (Fig. 73) on the manuscript page 118 of R 492 which could have been written in July or August, in conjunction with (or shortly after) the idea and the same unique graph having been inscribed in the *Logic Notebook* on July 10, 1903.

ticle was in its final stages of completion when Peirce had moved on to composing the initial drafts of the next project, *The Logical Tracts*.

The beginnings of the tracts project also appear to be contemporaneous with Peirce's drafting of the very first Lowell Lecture (R 454) that he had begun planning during those early weeks of the summer. This co-dating is supported, among others, by the same script type that Peirce used in the early version of the second tract (R 492, *Logical Tracts No. 2*, Appendix) to connect words of the sentences that represent propositions in some of his examples of graphs (see especially Figs. 1–7, Fig. 14 and Fig. 19–23 in R 492, albeit the method is rather inconsistently applied towards the later examples). We find the same method of scripting in use when Peirce is inscribing examples of graphs in the first draft of the Lowell Lectures, in which it is justified by Principle II spelled out in the draft ("Anything written shall have its meaning independently of anything else that may be written on another part of the board and that is, not joined to it by any line of connection … Our principles must be perfectly strict … For if the words were separate, they would have to be understood independently of one another", R 454). Other than these couple of early examples in these two writings, R 492 and R 454, such concatenated text as the preferred scripture for expressing linguistic material in graphs nevertheless remained as an experiment that was soon dropped. It is not found in the later, main segment of *Logical Tracts No. 2* nor anywhere else in Peirce's œuvre.

Two sets of drafts survive. The first comprises *Logical Tracts No. 1: On Existential Graphs* (R 491), a brief and unfinished account of three basic "principles of representation" upon which the theory of EGs is erected: the principles one needs to follow in order to rightly notate and use the notions of (i) the sheet, (ii) spots, and (iii) enclosures. To investigate the nature of these representations somewhat further than he had done before, Peirce presents two trichotomies of the sign: first, we find the famous division of signs into *icons*, *indices* and *symbols*, followed by the second trichotomy of dividing symbols into *terms*, *propositions* and *arguments*. The sheet is a graph that asserts the universe to be *definite*, *individual* and *real*. The graphical counterparts to predicate terms are called spots and are now divided into *rhemata* and *onomata*, the latter meaning spots that have individuals that are initially indefinite to be attached to them. *Enclosures* and *polarities* are fully at work when Peirce is defining the quantificational part of the logic of EGs. The distinction between generalities of a representamen *materialiter* (in its mode of being, i.e. as the symbol *is* as a matter of fact and not as it represents its object to be) and *formaliter* (as a signification, i.e. as the symbol *represents* the generality of its object, as the meaning of the representamen), is of further importance in the course that is to follow, and the term "replica" is also coined to speak about *single occurrences* of a symbol.

This first paper of *The Logical Tracts*, numbered No. 1 in some planned sequence of related papers, was probably intended to develop into a representation of Peirce's latest account of his theory of speculative grammar, and then to be followed by a second treatise focussing on explaining the theory and the current state of development of his graphical logic. Peirce abandons this first attempt to write up his projected compendium quite abruptly, however, and moves on to begin his second attempt, *Logical Tracts No. 2* (R 492), for which he gave the subtitle "On Existential Graphs, Euler's Diagrams, and Logical Algebra". It is in this second tract that things really get going. Running nearly 400 manuscript pages, warts and all, R 492 portrays a gigantic enterprise to produce a book-length treatise on virtually everything that the theory of EGs would by now encompass. Together the two tracts form a comprehensive manual for all the needed philosophical, semiotic and logical aspects of EGs, which Peirce now considers as to have matured into a definite theory of the graphical method of logic. *The Logical Tracts* is the most extensive exposition of his graphical systems that Peirce ever undertook to write. But even so, it was left seriously incomplete and was to consist of several more chapters and sections to complement the treatise.

A reconstruction of the Table of Contents reveals that the full version of the tracts was conceived to encompass three large parts. Only the first part was on existential graphs, and those 400 manuscript pages comprise the corpus of that first part. As the subtitle also confirms, part two would add chapters on Euler Diagrams, and part three those on logical algebra. Peirce wrote the part on Euler diagrams sometime in 1903, that material is in R 479. What the part on logical algebra would have consisted of is left on surmises of various degrees of doubt: some of the selections that appear in Volume 1 of *Logic of the Future* on logical notations (such as R 515, R 516 and R 530) could be those of his earlier writings that he wished to use or rewrite for the *Tracts*, among other possibilities.

The full text of *The Logical Tracts* project was to include an extensive glossary. One can find 52 technical terms provided in a separate notebook (R 1589), which was written sometime after the main text. The glossary sits quite well at the end of the first part on EGs, however, and so does the material at the end of the same notebook, describing an "outline of the imaginary Graphist's procedure", which is being followed by the second chapter of the first part on the principles of illative transformation, as it is cross-referenced in the outline.

Here is a reconstruction of the projected Table of Contents based on Peirce's own outlines and collateral textual sources:

Logical Tracts. Number 2.
On Existential Graphs, Euler's Diagrams, and Logical Algebra

[Table of Contents]
- **Part I.** *On Existential Graphs*
    - **Chapter I.** *Principles of Interpretation*
        - **Section i.** *Fundamental Conventions*
            - **Subsection 1.** *Of Conventions Nos. 1 and 2*
            - **Subsection 2.** *Of Convention No. 3*
            - **Subsection 3.** *Of Conventions 4 to 9*
        - **Section ii.** *Derived Principles of Interpretation*
            - **Subsection 1.** *Of the Pseudographs and Connected Signs*
            - **Subsection 2.** *Of Selectives and Proper Names*
            - **Subsection 3.** *Of Abstraction and Entia Rationis*
        - **Section iii.** *Recapitulation.* (Redescription of the system in a compact form)
        - **Appendix.** *Nomenclature* (R 1589)
    - **[Chapter I.]** *Outline of the Imaginary Graphist's Procedure* (R 1589)
    - **Chapter II.** *The Principles of Illative Transformation*
        - **Section i.** *Basic Principles*
            - **[Subsection 1.]** *Categorical Basic Rules for the Illative Transformation of Graphs Dinectively Built up from Partial Graphs not separated by seps*
            - **[Subsection 2.]** *Basic Categorical Rules for the Illative Transformation of Graphs Dinectively Built up from Partial Graphs and from Graphs separated by seps*
            - **[Subsection 3.]** *Basic Categorical Rules for the Illative Transformation of All Graphs*
        - **Section ii.** *Derived Rules of Illative Transformation*
        - **Section iii.** *Recapitulation*
    - **[Chapter III.]** *[Logical Analysis]* (Utility of the system for logical analysis) [not written]
- **[Part II.]** *Euler's Diagrams* (R 479)
- **[Part III.]** *Logical Algebra* [not written]

While large portions of *Logical Tracts No. 2* have been published in the *Collected Papers*, with the title that Peirce had given as the subtitle, "On Existential Graphs, Euler's Diagrams, and Logical Algebra", the manuscript pages transcribed in CP hardly comprise half of what Peirce actually wrote for the first part of the second *Tracts*. It is thus important to provide this work to the readers in as complete a form as possible. This has been done in the present edition, with one concession: as the main segment of R 479—most likely the main chapter of Part II on Euler's diagrams—has in its main been published in CP, it is not included in the present selection. The main segment is nonetheless surveyed in the section below that summarises the individual selections.

Instead, then, what is included in Part IV as its third selection are those segments and texts from R 479 which were not included in CP and which have not appeared in print before. The third chapter, including only the previously unpublished material of R 479, should be read together with the main sequence (manuscript pages 1–66; the original partial publication of it is in CP 4.350–4.371). It is this main sequence that is examined in the survey below.

Peirce's own title, together with the synopsis he provides at the beginning of R 492 on the basis of which the table of contents is reconstructed, tell that Parts II and III would deal with Peirce's improvements on Euler's diagrams and his own general logical algebra, respectively. Notably, these topics are not taken up in the Lowell Lectures or their notes, which suggests that Peirce wanted the lectures to be a progression from what Part I of the *Tracts* jointly covers on EGs with the first four lectures, to the topics of chance, probability and abduction, along the trajectory of the theory of the logic of science rather than along a different trajectory of the theory of logic that the full *Tracts* would have necessitated. Parts II and III were probably seen as somewhat excesses as far as the lectures were concerned. Peirce may never have given much further thought on what ought to be included in the planned last part of the *Tracts* on logical algebra, at least not during the turmoils of the year in progress.

A clear resemblance in content obtains between the *Tracts* and *A Syllabus of Certain Topics of Logic*, another book-length text that Peirce composed in late 1903 to accompany the Lowell Lectures preserved in R 478. There is not that much of exact textual overlap, but both the *Tracts* and the draft *Syllabus* aim at providing a systematic treatise of the fundamentals of the theory of EGs. The second tracts introduces the "Principles of Interpretation", with a detailed exposition of twelve fundamental conventions of the system of graphs (Chapter I). These principles of interpretation are then followed by the "Principles of Illative Transformation" (Chapter II). The promised Chapter III to show "how the system may be made useful" for "logical analysis", and as noted was apparently never written as such. A comparison of the conventions given in the *Tracts*, with those that he articulated in the Lowell Lectures and in the *Syllabus*, indicate that *Logical Tracts No. 2* was written soon after Peirce had finished the first, early draft of the first Lowell Lecture in summer 1903, but certainly well before he had completed the copy-text version of the *Syllabus*. The evidence is that there are twelve conventions in *Tracts No. 2*, while in the lecture drafts he reaches fourteen slightly more elaborate conventions. Some of the additional basic rules (namely those for proper names, selectives and rhemata of second intention), and the derived rules of illative transformation, are missing in the *Tracts* while they do appear in the *Syllabus*. There are also some important terminological changes that take place between *The Logical Tracts* and the *Syllabus* (such as "categorical" set of rules instead of "archegetic" as occurs in the *Syllabus*), but the two also significantly overlap—at places both use nearly identical formulations and definitions. The most salient additions to the *Syllabus* that we do not find in the *Tracts* are the sections dealing with systems of Gamma graphs, especially the modal rules for those systems, plus the logic of potentials which Peirce desperately needed in order to explain the central mathematical and set-theoretical concepts in his fifth Lowell lecture, and in order to analyse the nature of mathematical reasoning. The aim of doing so is clearly stated in the *Tracts*, but it is not until the time to prepare the final lecture drafts approached in the last quarter of the year, and the strict deadline to get the accompanying *Syllabus* text completed and sent to the printer, that we find Peirce inventing the necessary instruments to attempt that analysis.

One can conclude that the writing of the long text of *Logical Tracts No. 2* spanned several months and continued to be written after September 1. Certainly it was completed (or rather, put on hold) well before the Lowell Lectures began on November 23. Most of the material must also have been written and completed before Peirce wrote Section IV of the *Syllabus* on EGs, "Conventions and Rules of Existential Graphs". The entire *Syllabus* text was completed and sent to the Lowell Institute for printing in late October, to its curator William Thompson Sedgwick (1855–1921),[4] who acknowledges its reception on October 30. Probably Peirce was busy at work with the second tract (the first tract could have been written in a

---

[4] Sedgwick was Peirce's junior colleague at Johns Hopkins University in the early 1880s, who presented three papers in the Metaphysical Club in 1880–1883 that Peirce chaired at Johns Hopkins University (Pietarinen & Chevalier 2015). An obituary on Sedgwick mentions an anecdote that "as curator of the Lowell Institute since 1897 he became perhaps more widely known to the citizens of Boston than in any other capacity. He did not confine himself to the abstract task of securing for Boston contracts with the most brilliant teachers of American and European thought; he was almost nightly on hand to act as a personal host and to give the problems of heating and lighting and ventilation an individual attention which made Huntington Hall famous throughout the country" (Winslow 1921, p. 259).

matter of days) through September and possibly still in early October, before his full efforts had to turn to the completion of the *Syllabus* and the final lecture preparations.

Further evidence that Peirce had already started writing the second tract in early to mid-summer 1903 comes from his proposal that "A graph with an endless nest of seps is essentially of doubtful meaning, except in special cases". This is as much as the running figure numbered 73 in the *Tracts*, of which find a copy and the same point (which is a novel one) first being made in the *Logic Notebook* on July 10 (LoF 1): "The graph asserts nothing since $\bar{x} \prec x$ so that it must be true while a must be absurd" (x is the entire graph with endless nests of cuts, and a is a graph scribed in all the areas of that infinitely deep graph). In addition, the notion of "onoma", Peirce's term of art exclusively confined to the corpus of these two *Tracts*, is premiered in the *Logic Notebook* on June 11. This is also the date of revival of his note-taking in the *Logic Notebook* ever since they ceased August 1898. The origins of the early versions of *The Logical Tracts* may thus be traced in the immediate vicinity of Peirce's conversations with William James in early June that were about Peirce's recent and future lessons of the year. The first tract, and perhaps the early version of the second, would thus get to be composed that month, and the latter was soon followed by the writing of the main mature segment of R 492, perhaps as soon as the telepathy article was ready by July 1. Peirce seems to have had a little less than four months to spare in order to amass those nearly half a thousand pages of studies preparatory to his upcoming lectures.

The unfolding complexity of the material might have signalled Peirce that it should not be tried for publication. However, *The Logical Tracts* project should not be seen merely an unfinished collection of preliminary studies that Peirce would just wish to keep to himself or to circulate among a small number of students and colleagues. What one finds instead is a substantial and surprisingly polished-up presentation, approaching the standards of a fair copy-text, that may have been prepared with a potential publication in mind. There is no direct evidence that Peirce offered or even thought to offer the *Tracts* or any part of it to any publisher. What he wanted to get printed was the text of the *Syllabus*. The printer's copy of the full text of the *Syllabus* appears to be the set of leaves in R 478 that are paginated up to 168 manuscript pages, with a gap at pages 106–136 which can be roughly fitted by the pages from R 539. But could *The Logical Tracts*, written on the same paper type as the *Syllabus* (Crane's 1900 Japanese Linen), together with the material that we find in the printed *Syllabus*, be what Sedgwick called Peirce's *magnum opus*, having received that first? What was the body of the work that was sitting at Sedgwick's desk when he was handling the printing of the syllabus for the lectures, when he wrote Peirce that the set of papers that he had just received was no ordinary syllabus?

> I confess that I am somewhat appalled at the large amount of material which you sent and I am wondering if the word 'syllabus' will accurately describe it. At the same time I shall take steps immediately to put it in the hands of an inexpensive printer in order to make the printing go as far as our fifty dollars will allow. I am glad that you will make your own diagrams, this procedure being almost always the most satisfactory for lecturers. (WTS to CSP, October 30, 1903, R L 257)
>
> I find, after consulting three separate printers, that fifty dollars will print about the first hundred pages of your syllabus, which by the way, strikes me as a *magnum opus* rather than a syllabus! This sum will give you one hundred copies on decent paper and another hundred will be only four or five dollars more. I should think that one or two hundred would be sufficient. ... Your syllabus looks most interesting and valuable and is really, it seems to me, a valuable book. (WTS to CSP, November 3, 1903, R L 257)

It could not have been the *Tracts* that Peirce sent to Sedgwick; Peirce would have realised the insurmountable complications and costs that would ensue from getting hundreds of its graphs in their proper shape to be printed. Sedgwick had written Peirce already on October 9 that he can "get many of your diagrams—if not too complex—made for $35.00 and $15.00 ought to print your syllabus unless it is very long" (WTS to CSP, R L 257). Price tags like this would make Peirce quickly realise how remote were the possibilities of getting the material published in the form of the texts he had been preparing until now. From this point on, and as the lectures were approaching in the next month, Peirce was likely to have set the *Tracts* project aside, and after having received Sedgwick's October 9 letter, he would need his full energies to rewrite, in a few short weeks, the projected compendium to fit the idea of a course syllabus.

There is certainly more to the *Tracts* than being just a collection of results, definitions and conventions about EGs known to Peirce by late 1903. For one thing, counting in all the alternative versions as well, the *Tracts* harbours over 150 examples of graphs and explanations of their meanings, many of which are found nowhere else (especially Figs. 5, 15, 50–58, 73, 96, Figs. 6, 8, 9, 33–36 in variants and Figs. 12–17 which occur twice in the appendix to *Logical Tracts No. 2*). The surviving versions of the *Syllabus* (both its copy-text and the printed pamphlet), in contrast, included only two simple examples of Beta graphs (captioned as Figs. 10 and 11, as they were supposed to follow the Figures 1–9 of R 539, "Nomenclature and Divisions of Dyadic Relations"). The *Tracts* tome would certainly fulfill its role as a comprehensive reference text or a handbook written with both the students and the instructor preparing for the actual lectures in mind, but it was unprintable. Indeed one undated early draft (R 450) of the planned second lecture, held on November 27 to introduce the basics of EGs, makes a direct reference to the pagination of the conventions as they were listed in the *Tracts* manuscript.

There is another related detail worth pointing out. In the *Syllabus* manuscript sheet that has been preserved (R 478, ms p. 145) Peirce cut out the two original figures (Figs. 10 and 11) of two Beta graphs and replaced them with rectangular cuts and lines, all with right angles. This was to facilitate easier, faster and cheaper printing, which at the time made no easy allowance for complex images, such as ruling out curved lines and circles, for example.[5] He may have desired to have a few more complex diagrams to be printed, however, which shows in his preparation at the end of the *Syllabus* draft (R 478, ms p. 162, ms alt. p. 162) of some complex second-order diagrams, which represent graphically the relation of inclusion of correlates and which are similar to those that appear towards the end of the pre-draft lecture four (R 467, ms p. 82; R S 31, ms p. 82), in the *Syllabus* having such fully rectangular shapes. In a crossed-out marginal note to R 467 (ms p. 82, actually referring to the diagram on the cut-out page in between, and now located in R S-31, ms p. 82), Peirce lamented, however, that "This diagram [of R S-31, ms p. 82] would be less confusing is the angles were'nt so sharp and the lines so straight and parallel and right angled". The next attempt in re-writing the page (R 467, ms p. 82) sees the cuts taking more ovate shape and the lines of identity increasingly to curve. In the still slightly later pre-drafts and drafts of lecture five, all efforts at such rectangularisations disappear altogether (R 459, R 459(s)). No inscription of the graphs in the *Tracts* project, either, had made any concessions towards printer-friendly rectangular shapes and types. After having received Sedgwick's October 9 letter, Peirce had to begin rewriting at once a much more condensed presentation of the graphs; one that would be altogether stripped of those dozens of complex examples of the sort found in his *Tracts* manuscript. Given Sedgwick's estimated breakdown of the costs in October 9 to be $35.00 for the diagrams and $15.00 for the printing of the syllabus ("unless it be very long"), one may entertain Peirce having switched the strategy of composing the *Tracts* manuscript to another one that he could keep rather long as long as it would be devoid of graphs.[6]

---

5 The same rectangular form is seen to occur in the graphs of the copy-texts used for the printing of the graphs in Peirce's entry "Symbolic Logic, or algebra of logic" in DPP.
6 In his October 9 letter, Sedgwick said to only have guessed the costs, and asked Peirce to send him "some idea of the syllabus and a few specimen drawings or sketches such as you wish turned into roughly-drawn charts" (with "some idea of" and "specimen" as interline additions), so that the Institute could enquire further. Peirce's initial submission of R 478 should then be treated as a body of the work that would cater Sedgwick with an *idea* of Peirce's syllabus, not the final syllabus itself, which he intended to provide later, by means of supplementary material and instructions for selections and revisions. The survey section below includes an account of the compositional history of the *Syllabus* text.

As far as the preparations for the early part of the Lowell Lectures were concerned, *The Logical Tracts* carries out largely the same role as the later *Syllabus* does. Although *The Logical Tracts* is nowhere directly mentioned in the context of the course, the piece is at its best when read together with the lectures; only then will the full panorama of conventions, their elaboration and philosophical background be exposed to view.

The Logical Tracts also communicates well the essentials of how to reason in the language of EGs without translating it into any other language; how in Peirce's terms one is to "learn to think *in* it *about* facts". A couple of pages later, he proceeds to prove the soundness of the "basic categorical rules", remarking further that the "rules for dinected graphs is complete". The set of rules is indeed semantically complete, although Peirce is content with laconically remarking on his notion of completeness that, "This is susceptible of proof, but the proof belongs in the next section of this chapter, where I perhaps insert it. It is not interesting". That next section ("Section II. Derived Rules of Illative Transformation") is preserved only as a one-paragraph draft sheet. The fact that the system with fundamental and derived rules is indeed complete is emphasised in the draft table of contents for the *Syllabus*, which has the section title "IV. Existential Graphs: the Conventions of the System and its Fundamental Rules; with a few deduced rules" and which lists, under the heading "Rules of Transformation Demonstrable from the Archegetic Rules", sixteen further rules. There is no attempt in the surviving pages at proving the completeness of these archegetic (categorical) rules, either.

Peirce's quip on such meta-logical properties, and the overall semantic approach to reasoning that the *Tracts* is seen to promote, are powerful reminders of what he then would set out to do in his opening lecture of the Lowell series, entitled "What Makes a Reasoning Sound?", a lecture delivered in the evening of November 23. Indeed the *Tracts* resemble the very first pre-draft of that first lecture (R 454), which proceeded to develop a meta-logical perspective by which to answer precisely that question. Probably at this point, in early June, Peirce was already progressing well with his plans both for the *Tracts* and for his first lecture pre-draft, since on June 9, 1903, he had added a note on his *Logic Notebook* [119v], in reference to his Theorem XXVI from June 18, 1898, a nearly identical statement of Rule XIV of his sixteen *Syllabus* "rules of transformation demonstrable from the Archegetic Rules" (R 478).

Survey of Part IV: Selections 29–31

This section contains extended headnotes of the items included in Part IV of Volume 2/1. About 500 manuscript and notebook pages comprise the copy-texts and fair copies that appear here in three selections, "Logical Tracts No. 1", "Logical Tracts No. 2" and "Euler Diagrams". Indisputably the whole set, termed here *The Logical Tracts*, is the most extensive exposition of graphical systems of logic that Peirce ever undertook to write. Even so, it was left somewhat incomplete and was planned to include several additional chapters and sections.

Selection 29: The Logical Tracts No. 1. On Existential Graphs

R 491, c. June 1903. *Logical Tracts No. 1: On Existential Graphs* is a brief and unfinished account on three basic "principles of representation" upon which the theory of EGs is erected: (i) the sheet, (ii) the spots, and (iii) the enclosures. In order to investigate the nature of these representations somewhat further than he had done before. First, Peirce presents two trichotomies of the sign: the famous division of *icons*, *indices* and *symbols* is followed by the second trichotomy of dividing symbols into *terms*, *propositions* and *arguments*.

Then, the sheet is a graph that asserts the universe to be *definite*, *individual* and *real*. The graphical counterparts to predicate terms are called spots and are in the text divided into *rhemata* and *onomata*. The latter mean spots that are attached by individuals that are initially indefinite. *Enclosures* and *polarities* are fully at work when Peirce is defining the quantificational part of the logic of EGs. Moreover, Peirce is now consistently defining the enclosures by the *scrolls* and not by the ovals, concluding from this that a single enclosure has the effect of denying the whole graph which it contains.

Third, Peirce introduces the distinction between generalities of a representamen *materialiter* (in its mode of being, i.e. as the symbol *is* as a matter of fact and not as it represents its object to be) and *formaliter* (as a signification, i.e. as the symbol *represents* the generality of its object, as the meaning of the representamen). The term "replica" is then coined to speak about *single occurrences* of a symbol.

Peirce abandons this first attempt to set the basic terminology of logic and graphs in this version of *The Logical Tracts* quite abruptly, however, and moves on to draft the second, *Logical Tracts No. 2* (R 492), which bears the subtitle "On Existential Graphs, Euler's Diagrams, and Logical Algebra". Running nearly 400 manuscript pages, including all its numerous spawning variants, the second tract is an attempt at a book-length treatise on virtually everything that the theory of EGs is now capable of encompassing, rather than just a set of study notes for the upcoming lectures. For example, it contains a "Note A. Recapitulation of Some Points Treated in Tract No. 1", which even though seemingly a summary of his earlier, first tract reads much more like a fresh attempt to revise the material of the first tract pertaining to his fledgling doctrine of the speculative grammar and to embed that within the context of the second. Together, these two tracts certainly form a comprehensive manual on virtually every philosophical, semiotic and logical aspect of the theory of EGs that Peirce is now able to muster, the theory which he now considers to have matured into the definite and the most detailed formulation of that graphical method of logic he set out to have in late 1896 (LoF 1).

Selection 30: The Logical Tracts No. 2. On Existential Graphs, Euler's Diagrams, and Logical Algebra

R 492, June–September 1903. Some time well in advance of the beginning of the Lowell Lectures on November 23, Peirce abandoned the completion of the second of the prospected compendium for the upcoming Lowell Lectures. The contents of *The Logical Tracts No. 2* is far too vast and sublime to admit of any easy synopsis, as Peirce is seen to attempt in it nothing short of a complete description of his theory of EGs, together with an elaborate set of new conventions, definitions, hundreds of examples, planned appendices, and an inordinate amount of technical nomenclature.

In his own summary of the contents of the second *Tracts*, Peirce refers to an appendix that he would attach to the first chapter, which is to provide a "complete discussion" of the reasons that his elaborate set of conventions is intended to meet. The drafts of the Lowell Lectures will soon present some such reasons; however, no appendix survives that Peirce would have written out for *The Logical Tracts* in particular. A small notebook exists in folder R 1589, however, which possesses 52 definitions of technical terms on EGs. As it is proximal to the text of *The Logical Tracts*, albeit probably composed slightly later, those definitions are interpolated into the present selection at a section beginning with an "outline of the imaginary Graphist's procedure", which in turn naturally leads to the second chapter of the *Tracts*. While most of the terms Peirce defines in R 1589 are his standard vocabulary, one also finds examples of some hapax legomena, such as *colors, graven, nomen, seligible, original/actual sheet, original/actual area, natural/artifact graph, solute/alligate graph*. R 1589 may represent some of Peirce's afterthoughts in the wake of the abandonment of the *Tracts*, and thus play the role of an incomplete attempt to patch some of the earlier omissions of the long text. For example, R 1589 consistently resorts to the term "graph-instance" instead of the "graph-replica" familiar from the Lowell Lecture drafts, thus agreeing with the marginal comment on one of the copies of the printed *Syllabus* (R 1600, Box 4) that Peirce had first received on December 3, which stated, "I abandon this inappropriate term *replica*, Mr. Kempe having already (*Math. Form* § 170) given it another meaning. I now call this an *instance*". The term "graph-instance" is appearing in the remarks on graphs preserved from late 1904, such as R 280, "The Basis of Pragmaticism". Thus the glossary of terms (R 1589), although internally suggesting its partial fit with the structure of *Logical Tracts No. 2*, was likely to have been composed slightly later, perhaps around mid-1904, as an attempt at redeeming the promise of the glossary from the *Tracts* text but at the same time introducing certain novelties that did not yet quite exist in 1903.

Given the extraordinary role of his preparatory texts of 1903, including the fact that the *Tract No. 2* was an emerging approximation to how Peirce originally planned his latest theory of semeiotic and EGs to appear in print, there is no other choice than to honor those wishes and publish the relevant writings in their entirety. This means that Part IV is made as complete as possible, including all the variant and alternative versions that can be collated from the surviving papers. Those alternatives are provided in the present selection either as footnotes or in the appendix.

As can be observed from the material collated in the appendix, those versions by no means consist of superseded or redundant texts. What Peirce explores in alternative versions and earlier drafts, especially in the subsection "Note A. Recapitulation of Some Points Treated in Tract No. 1" and its alternatives, is a fresh attempt, including new terminology, to rewrite the second trichotomy of signs by "sisign", "bisign" and "tersign". This supports the hypothesis that at this time Peirce had already planned to carry out an overhaul of his theory of speculative grammar.

Peirce's confessions both in the synopsis of the second tract and in his comments elsewhere reveal an unfulfilled desire to write much more on "How these systems may be made useful" (R 492). The place for this was to be the planned final chapter of the first part on "Logical Analysis". That it is precisely the success of logical analysis that is the ultimate litmus test for the usefulness of Peirce's logical systems is confirmed by an alternative synopsis of the planned third chapter on one of the draft sheets, which reveals that the chapter "will give examples of the utility of the system for logical analysis". Following the chapters on "Principles of Interpretation", which is a detailed exposition of twelve fundamental conventions of the system of graphs, and the "Principles of Illative Transformation", which sets out the basic and derived rules of proofs of the system, the promised third chapter, which was precisely intended to show the system's usefulness for logical analysis, was apparently never written, however.

There are at least two other occurrences of Peirce specifically referring to the usefulness of EGs: One comes from his *Reason's Conscience* ("Logic, Conceived as Semeiotic"), in which he writes that "When you come to find how useful the system is, and what valuable ideas are embodied in the technical terms, you will begin to forgive the trouble they put you to at first" (R 693, LoF 1). Secondly, in one of the planned drafts of "The Basis of Pragmaticism" for his third *Monist* series (R 283, LoF 3), Peirce lists a number of "Useful Systems of Logical Representation", among them mentioning both Entitative and Existential Graphs.

In so far as the representation of logical relations is concerned, Beta graphs are seen as an unparalleled instrument in analysing what is going on in representations of complex relations. Peirce appears to have spotted the special importance of Beta graphs somewhat later than 1903, perhaps by January 1905 (see e.g. *Logic Notebook*, December 15, 1905), which prompted him to supersede the material of R 283 with what would rapidly evolve into the "Prolegomena to an Apology for Pragmaticism", completed by March 1906 and appeared in the October issue of *The Monist*. In that paper and in his coeval drafts and the presentation at the National Academy of Sciences meeting in April (R 490, LoF 3), it is precisely the implications of the meanings of graphs that permit quantification into modal contexts and into the contexts of the conditionals that now give enough confidence to Peirce to state how immensely useful the resulting system would be in performing logical analysis of intellectual concepts and thoughts. So the means, methods and implications of actually being able to carry out the completion of the first part of *The Logical Tracts* were bound to require some years still to be ripened.

Part II of the *Tract No. 2* was planned to be on Euler's diagrams. What looks like near-copy-texts are taken from the manuscript sheets located at R 479. They will make up the topic of the next selection. That selection is limited to those segments and pages from R 479 that were not included in the publication of the main segment from it in the *Collected Papers*. The content of Part III, which was projected to be on logical algebra, was apparently not written at all.

Selection 31: The Logical Tracts No. 2. Part II. On Logical Graphs [Euler's Diagrams]

R 479, Summer–Autumn 1903. Copy-texts of this selection are not what is found as the main segment in the Houghton folder of R 479 (manuscript pages 1–64), as that segment was in its main published in CP 4.350–4.371. Rather, the material for the present selection comes from previously unpublished and discrete variants of that long paper. The main segment presents Peirce's most thorough study of Euler's diagrams and their extensions. The additional pages from the same folder that are collated and transcribed in the present selection are quite different from the main paper, however, and are seen to contain some entirely new developments and ideas concerning Euler's diagrams. Those proposals are found neither in the main segment nor anywhere else in Peirce's *œuvre*.

To put those proposals in the context of the present topic of Euler diagrams, the main innovations of that primary paper need to surveyed first. But even before doing that, a word of warning is in order for those who are to consult the *Collected Papers* for the transcription of that main text. The publication of the long segment on Euler diagrams in CP resulted in several distortions that make the published text far from satisfactory. It has omitted several important paragraphs from the transcription, and two large figures (detailed below) were omitted. The CP edition also results in an imprecise and misleading reproduction of many of the figures that the text does contain. Typographical inaccuracies include using the letter x for the cross × and the number 0 for circles ○, as well as using capital letters as labels that are placed outside the circles.

As to the last point, inspection of the manuscripts shows that Peirce wrote, quite untypically but consistently, the capital letters *on* the line of the circle, not inside or outside. He might have adopted such convention from Johann Christian Lange's 1712 *Nucleus Logicae Weisianae*, the work which Peirce, echoing John Venn, thought "anybody familiar with such literature the title proclaims it to be a work by [Christian] Weise probably with a running commentary or copious notes by Lange" (R 479, ms p. 16). Weise's *Nucleus Logicae* was indeed originally published, as Peirce remarks, in 1691 as a small booklet and it was edited and expanded into an edition consisting of the 834-page *Nucleus Logicae* plus other treatises such as *Conspectus Partium Nuclei Logici Weisiani*[7] adding further 300 pages to the 1712 tome published by Weise's student Johann Christian Lange. Maybe Peirce's labelling practice of placing letters that denote classes on the circle to mean division, namely that a curve standing for the *differentiæ* disposes individuals, depending on their predication, on both sides of the circle, thus forming complementary classes. Hence, the curve both (i) acts as a separation line and (ii) is the object of the label attached to it. The location of the positive and negative terms, standing for the presence and absence of the predicate, is then determined by the shape of the curve and not by its label, a convention that Peirce had adopted already in R 481 (Moktefi & Pietarinen 2016; LoF 1).

The main sequence contains Peirce's criticism of Euler diagrams, listing four of their main shortcomings. (i) The inadequacy of Euler diagrams in dealing with every syllogistic form; (ii) the impossibility of that system to affirm the existence of any description of objects, (iii) the failure of Euler diagrams to represent disjunctions in the general case, and (iv) the drawback that it "affords no means of expressing any other than dichotomous" information. From the last follows the incapability of Euler diagrams to represent relations and thus quantification beyond

---

[7] The earlier booklet is only about 70 pages in length and is devoid of diagrams. In the *Conspectus* part of the edition appears the book *Inventum Novuum Quadratilogic Universalis*, which among others contain plenty of logic diagrams. See Lemanski (2017) for a study of them.

the monadic case. In conclusion, Peirce takes Euler diagrams to be unsuitable as an instrument of logical analysis due to their lack of expressive power. That is, the system "has no vital power of growth beyond the point to which it has been here carried" (CP 4.370; R 491; R 479).

In the main sequence, Peirce explores some ways to overcome these defects and proceeds to improve on the notation and the expressivity of Euler diagrams. But because such diagrams fail to capture the logic and reasoning about relative terms, Peirce's overall interest in them was rather limited and not characterised by mathematical application, problem-solving capacities or fit for logical analysis. Rather, Peirce developed them because of their particular aptness in showing what the basic elements of syllogistic reasoning consist of.

R 479 proposes several improvements over traditional Euler–Venn diagrams. Among them is the suggestion to represent the negation of the copula of inclusion, where the copula of inclusion is a spatial relation of "enclosing only what is enclosed by" ("All Ss are Ms"). Peirce does this by introducing a heavy *dot* • (or alternatively a *cross* ×) to "represent some existing individual" (CP 4.349).[8] Further, if the dot or a cross rests on a closed curve that isolates a boundary of the zone (compartment) of an Euler diagram, Peirce took it to mean that "it is doubtful on which side it belongs" (*ibid.*). A mark on the boundary thus represents logical disjunction. If two or more marks lie on the boundary of the same compartment then there is, Peirce notes, "nothing that prevents their being identical" (*ibid.*). The same holds for marks within the same zone. Thus placing more than one mark inside the same zone does not mean that more than one individual exists.

Figures 1–19 below from R 479 show the basics of Euler diagrams and their modification by Venn.

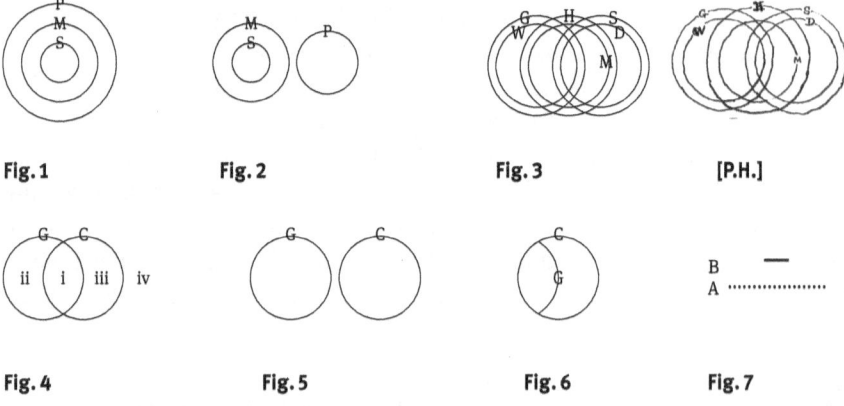

Fig. 1   Fig. 2   Fig. 3   [P.H.]

Fig. 4   Fig. 5   Fig. 6   Fig. 7

---

8 [Dots and crosses are inscribed in red ink in the original.]

Introduction to Volume 2/1: *The Logical Tracts* — **87**

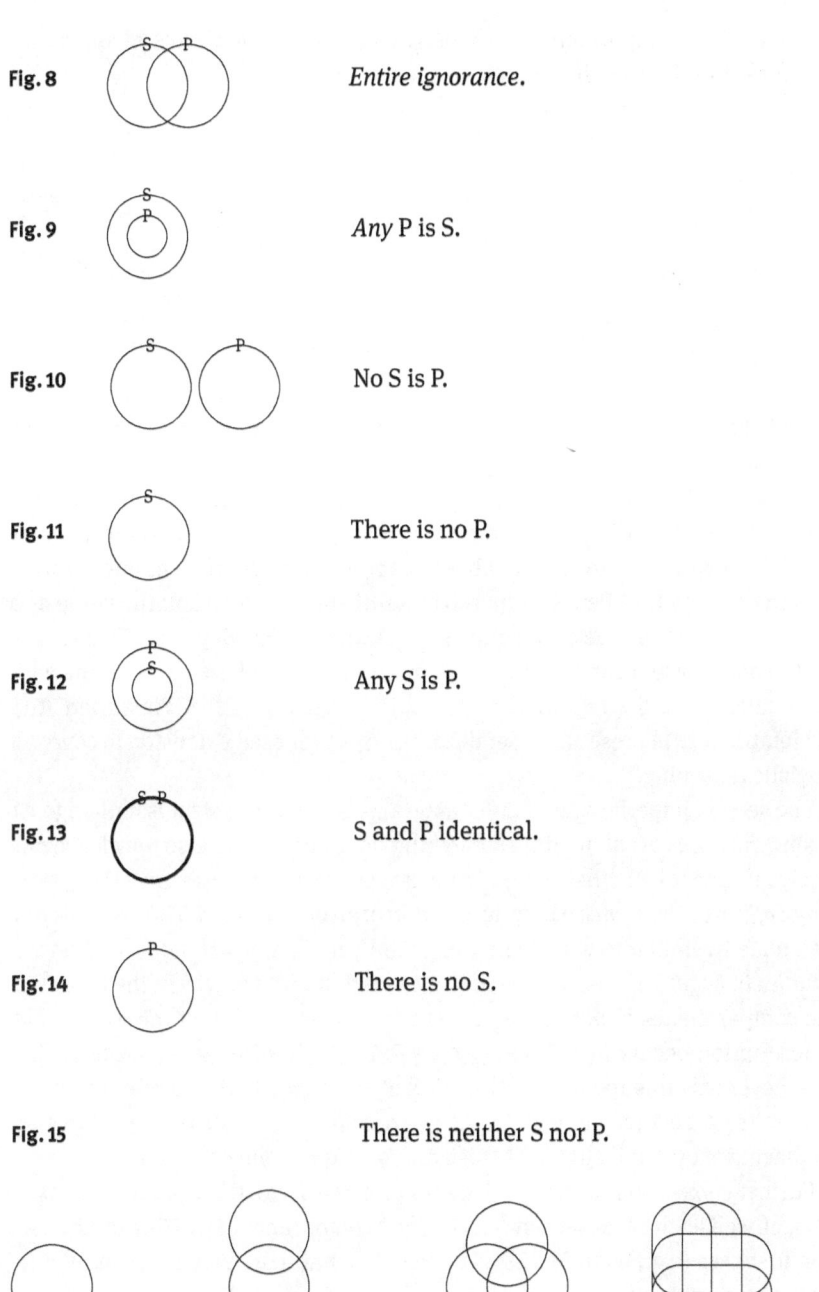

Fig. 8   *Entire ignorance.*

Fig. 9   *Any P is S.*

Fig. 10   *No S is P.*

Fig. 11   *There is no P.*

Fig. 12   *Any S is P.*

Fig. 13   *S and P identical.*

Fig. 14   *There is no S.*

Fig. 15   *There is neither S nor P.*

Fig. 16   Fig. 17   Fig. 18   Fig. 19

Figures 21–23 illustrate Peirce's proposed modification of Venn's modification, which adds the circles to the compartments:[9]

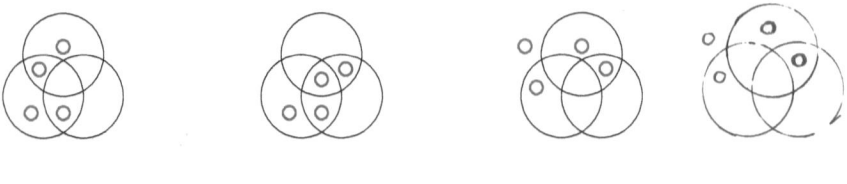

Fig. 21 Fig. 22 Fig. 23 [P.H.]

The first shortcoming, the inadequacy of Euler diagrams to represent every syllogistic form, is addressed in Peirce's R 481 (LoF 1) and in the drafts of his DPP article (LoF 3). In R 479 he just notices the inadequacy and then presents four syllogisms that Euler diagrams, their extension by Venn, and Peirce's own extension of Venn with the circles, are able to capture. A more efficient and a rather ingenious remedy that Peirce proposes in R 481 is to add an infolding curve as a dual to the circular shape of the curves of standard Euler diagrams. This results in 'star' shapes which can show concave interiors of boundaries contrasting with convex interiors of the boundaries of simple circles (Moktefi & Pietarinen 2016 and Pietarinen 2016 present the details of Peirce's proposed extension to cover all syllogistic reasoning.)

The second imperfection of Euler diagrams is that the system is limited to expressing only the case that either something does not exist or else they leave one entirely ignorant of whether something exists or not. In Peirce's terms, the system "*cannot affirm the existence* of any description of an object" (CP 4.356). Now his proposed remedy, similar to what Venn incidentally had proposed in his 1883 review of *Studies in Logic* (SiL), is to draw the cross mark ×, in red, within the Euler diagram compartments, which is then to signify that "something of the corresponding description occurs in the universe" (CP 4.359). (R 855, LoF 1, suggests that Peirce never saw this review; cf. Moktefi & Pietarinen 2015.) The relevant examples are the propositions in Figs. 25–27. The denial of such existence is expressed by replacing × by small circles, ○, also drawn in red in the originals.

Further conventions are needed to interpret cases with three or more compartments, as well as the cases when × lies in one compartment and ○ in another. As to the first case (e.g., as in Fig. 28), Peirce notes that there may be an ambiguity between stating the existence of "Some S that is M but not P", and the existence

---

[9] A marginal note, not in Peirce's hand, states here that "Peirce wrote no 20 for his Figures".

of "Some S that is neither M nor P". He suggests that the disconnected signs in different compartments are to be read conjunctively, and that the connected signs in different compartments are to be read disjunctively. The denial of existence is thus not only a substitution of O for × : one also needs to correctly reverse the connections and disconnections between the crosses.

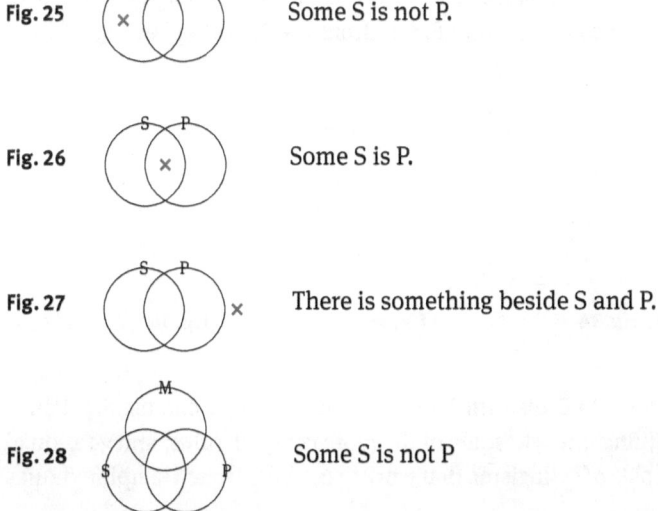

Fig. 25   Some S is not P.

Fig. 26   Some S is P.

Fig. 27   There is something beside S and P.

Fig. 28   Some S is not P

Then, two opposite signs that rest on the same compartment mean that the proposition is absurd (Fig. 29)—unless they coincide, in which case these signs would annul each other (Fig. 30).

Peirce also takes the crosses that rest on the boundary of compartments to be equivalent to the cases in which they occur on both sides of that circumference. Thus *logical disjunctions* can be diagrammatically depicted. A similar method, using connected lines between the dots, was subsequently and independently reinvented in the form of *spider diagrams* (Howse, Stapleton & Taylor 2005). Spider diagrams have become widespread in computational diagrammatic representations and disjunctive Euler–Venn diagrams, among others.

Peirce then presents the rule ("Rule 2. Any sign of assertion can receive any accretion", CP 4.362) by which the assertion in Fig. 31 ("All X are Y and some X are Y") can be transformed into the assertion in Fig. 32 ("All X are Y or some non-X are Y, and some X are Y or all non-X are Y").

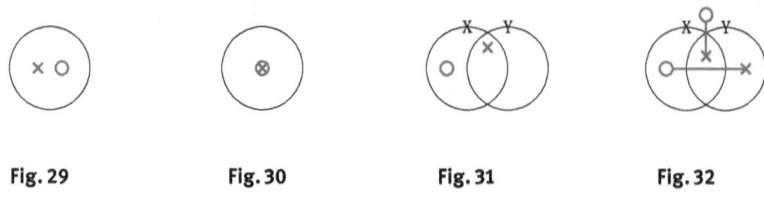

Fig. 29   Fig. 30   Fig. 31   Fig. 32

Moreover, Peirce's fourth rule, which concerns the attachment and detachment of crosses and zeros, entitles one to infer Fig. 34 from Fig. 33, as well as Fig. 36 from Fig. 35:

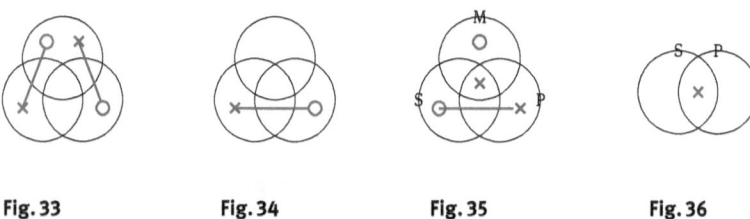

Fig. 33   Fig. 34   Fig. 35   Fig. 36

Six in total, these rules to transform Euler diagrams grow in complexity. Peirce proposes some simplifications to some of the more complex rules, and goes on to present a few examples of syllogisms that work according to such simplified rules (Figs. 39–56 in R 479).[10]

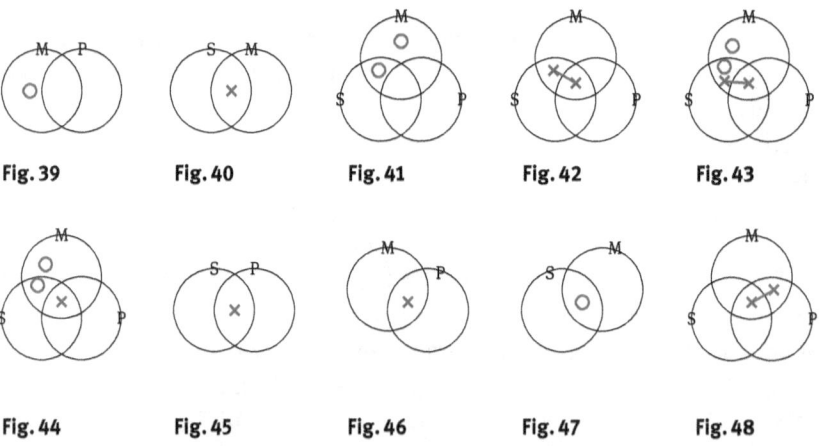

Fig. 39   Fig. 40   Fig. 41   Fig. 42   Fig. 43

Fig. 44   Fig. 45   Fig. 46   Fig. 47   Fig. 48

---

[10] Figs. 37 and 38 were cut out from the manuscript sheet without providing any substitute figures, with an annotation in the place of the cut by the CP editors: "cuts being made".

Introduction to Volume 2/1: *The Logical Tracts* — 91

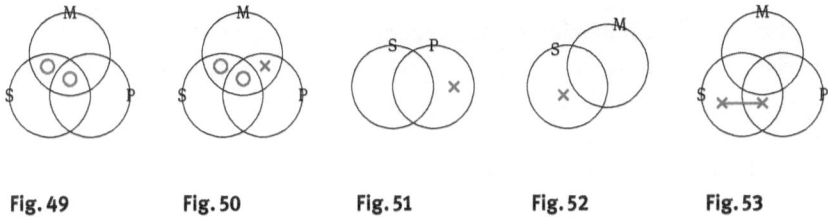

Fig. 49   Fig. 50   Fig. 51   Fig. 52   Fig. 53

The typography of these diagrams must be gotten exactly right. Fig. 56, for instance, was sloppily reproduced in CP 4.363 (therein Fig. 54), and may leave the false impression that the two tokens of × in the intersection are connected. They are not, as may be seen from the original diagrams of Figs. 54–56:

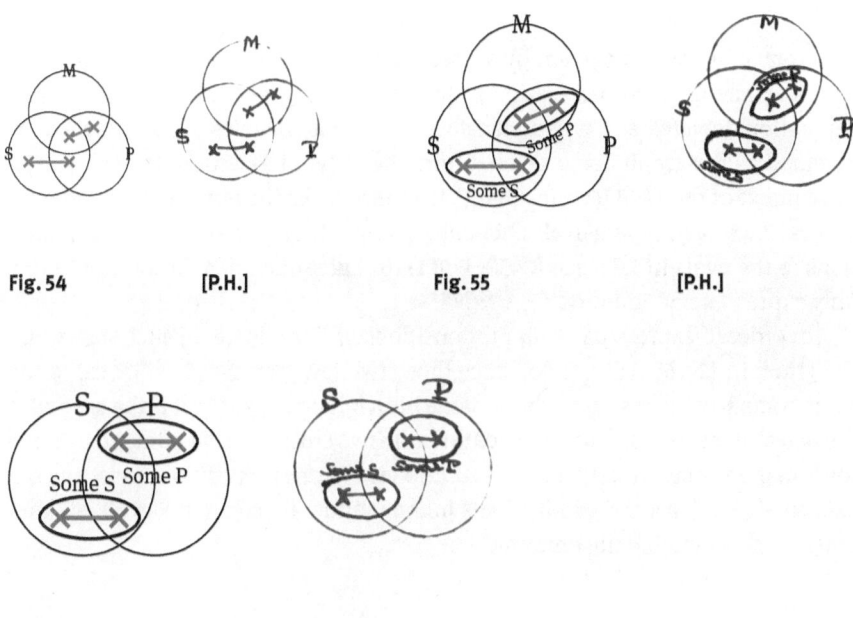

Fig. 54   [P.H.]   Fig. 55   [P.H.]

Fig. 56   [P.H.]

Next, Peirce discusses how one is to express *spurious propositions*, such as that in Fig. 56 which states that "Some S is not some P". Instead of connected crosses he suggests placing × on the boundaries. Thus the graphs in Figs. 57 and 58 express the same proposition. Here an important discovery is seen to emerge. In Fig. 58 the horizontal line in the intersection of S and P tells us that the two tokens of the cross × must not become connected, that is, they must not co-occur within the same region. That line segment, which is what remains from the lower boundary of the circle M in Fig. 57 inside the intersection of S and P, serves the role analogous to the *sign of negation* (or the cut in EGs) that denotes non-equality: it means that the two tokens of × separated by it are not identical. The proposition in Fig. 58 thus expresses the fact that there are at least two individuals that are non-identical, that is, at least two individuals exist:

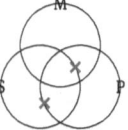

Fig. 57

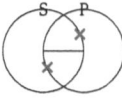

Fig. 58

This way of denoting negation by a linear separation device is notably similar to what became the sign of negation in the early versions of EGs (LoF 1): a linear separation depicted as a one-dimensional oval that encircles a graph, hence understood as the graph being severed from the sheet of assertion. Indeed, it is in the context of the 1903 lectures that Peirce introduces the term "the cut" to refer to these non-overlapping ovals encircling graphs. There are also further significations to the ovals in EGs (see R 430, LoF 1). In Euler diagrams, however, the line only expresses non-identity.

In order to express particular propositions of third degree, Peirce states that the graph in Fig. 59 will not do, since those two lower crosses × adjacent to the same compartment may refer to the same individual. Unlike what is the case with the two topmost crosses, no line separates the two crosses × that border that same lower-region compartment. Peirce's solution is to draw propositions asserting the existence of at least three individuals in the manner depicted in Fig. 60, with no cross-mark remaining unconnected.

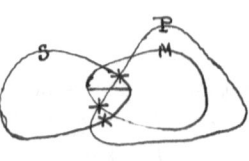

Fig. 59 [P.H.]

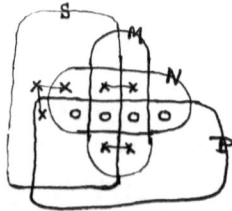

Fig. 60 [P.H.]

The question that naturally arises is whether a systematic method can be found that generalises Euler diagrams to n-degree propositions. In countable universes, numerical statements can be represented by increasing the number of disjuncts. Peirce addresses this question in connection to what he takes to be the third imperfection of the system of Euler circles: its inadequacy to deal with disjunctions in the general case. For example, when it comes to the assertions of disjunctions of conjunctions (disjunctive normal forms), diagrams would soon become disturbingly cluttered. An example is the graph in Fig. 61, which expresses that "Either some A is B and everything is either A or B, or else all A is B and some B is not A".

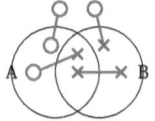

Fig. 61

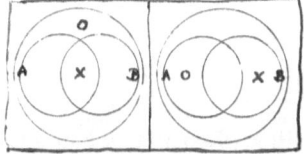

Fig. 62 [P.H.]

Peirce's suggested simplification is to encircle every diagram within yet another circle, and then, for perspicuity, to compartmentalise those 'mother circles' inside rectangles (Fig. 62). The mother circles represent what the *universes of discourse* is commonly taken to be (in Peirce's own terms, it is here the "Universe of Hypothesis"). Hence one can dispense with drawing complex connecting lines as in Fig. 61: now every compartment in Fig. 62 represents *a possible case of the diagram being true*.

Continuing in this manner, an Euler diagram expressing a complex proposition becomes a *sequence* of Euler diagrams, each rectangle or a *frame* depicting one of the disjuncts of that proposition. For instance, the diagram contained within the frame on the left of Fig. 62 expresses that "Some A is B and that there is nothing else in the universe of discourse in that occasion that is either A or B', while the diagrams that is included within the frame on the right expresses, in turn, that "Every A is B and that there are Bs that are not As", just as in Fig. 61.

The box notation became the standard usage by which the universe of discourse is denoted in theories of Euler and Venn diagrams. In speaking of different universes Peirce manages to add a distinctive modal flavour to it—which should not come as a surprise as it is during these very same weeks and months of autumn 1903 that he developed modal logic in the Gamma part of EGs.

A consequence of this remedy to simplify logical disjunctions is that, as in Fig. 63, diagrams encircled by a boundary that denotes the universe of discourse (here with the label A) can now be used to express propositions of the fourth degree ("There are at least four individuals that are As"). And thus its dual, the denial of the proposition that there are at least four individuals that are As, may be expressed as in Fig. 64 ("There are not as many as four As").

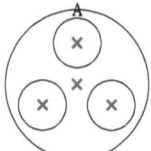

Fig. 63

Fig. 64

It is this method of encircling entire Euler diagrams that Peirce observes to give rise to a generalisation that allows one to express *arbitrary numerical propositions*. He did not develop these possibilities any further, however. Nor did he proceed to study the sequences of frames of Euler diagrams. We may surmise that these ideas are connected to, or are an anticipation of, the "moving pictures of thought" idea that characterise the behaviour or EGs, especially in terms of the application of rules of transformation and the kind of animation of deductive inferences that arises from it (Pietarinen 2006a; Champagne & Pietarinen 2019).

Finally, Peirce introduces a *heavy dot* •; a notation that serves as a 'wild card': it denotes either of the two marks so that any of its tokens means "either a cross or a circle". Thus the inference from Fig. 65 to Fig. 66 is not an inference rule but a *generalised inference schema*:

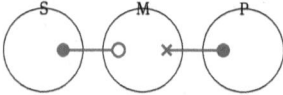

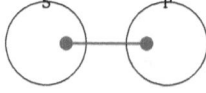

Fig. 65

Fig. 66

An instance of that schema is for instance the valid syllogism of Barbara.

Peirce ends the main sequence of R 479 with a note on the fifth, "fatal defect" of the system of Euler diagram, namely that "it has no vital power of growth beyond the point to which it has been here carried" (CP 4.370). The cap is set by the planar geometry that limits expressive power to first-order logic with monadic predicates. In order to extend the system into an analysis of relative propositions, multitudes or abstractions, that is, to perform reasoning along the lines of general algebra of logic or that of EGs, seemed to be beyond possibility. *Constraint diagrams* (Stapleton, Howse & Taylor 2005) are an example of a modest increase that can be accrued in expressivity up to dyadic relations.

Variant 1. Euler Diagrams with Six Conventions
An alternative, unpublished sequence of R 479 produced within the present selection gives another extension of Euler diagrams with six conventions. The sequence begins with the convention that describes the *universe of discourse*, according to which and much like in EGs the universe is taken to be the subject mutually well-understood between the "drawer" and the "interpreter" of the diagrams. The sheet on which these diagrams are drawn consists, again much like in EGs, of "different possible points" of a "certain individual subject". An important terminological parallel also occurs in this use of the terms "drawer" and the "interpreter", and the "graph-drawer" and "graph-interpreter" in (and only in) one of the rejected early variants of the preceding text of *Logical Tracts, No. 2* (R 492), adding further evidence to our assumption that Peirce's present work on Euler Diagrams and their modifications was largely contemporaneous to his overall *Tracts* project.

Second, ovals drawn on the sheet are connected with an assertion about that universe of discourse, and are denoted by capital letters. Any point outside the oval represents a *possible state of things* in which the assertion would be true of that universe. Any point inside the oval represents a possible state of things in which the corresponding assertion would be false. This suggests that Peirce was contemplating something like a semantic interpretation of modal features as exhibited in Euler diagrams.

Third, these compartments may be *shaded*, and every point on a shaded area means *non-existent individual*. Fourth, any point coloured in *red ink* means that the corresponding *state of things* is "realized at some time or in some reference". Fifth, a *point coloured red and lying on the boundary* of an oval means that "it is not determinate" whether the realised state of things is represented by a point inside of the boundary or outside of that boundary. That is, we can represent logical disjunctions similarly as Peirce did with his other extensions of Euler diagrams. The twist is that Peirce is now giving a model-theoretic gloss on these notions: there are "realised" and "unrealised" "states of things". Sixth, a *box*, which Peirce instructs to be drawn in green ink, marks the *limits of the sheet*. Such boundaries are spurious in EGs as the sheet is assumed to be indefinitely extendible.

Peirce's sole examples found in these draft pages are four (Figs. 1–4). In Fig. 1 the universe of discourse of the diagram is the state of weather in Tompkins Island. The proposition on the left is "It is the dry season" and the proposition on the right is "It is raining". The diagram thus asserts that "It is always either the dry season or is raining on Tompkins Island (or both)". Fig. 2 means that every man is either honest or fool. Fig. 3 means that on Tompkins Island it sometimes does not rain though it is not in the dry season. Fig. 4 means that some man is neither a fool nor honest.

Variant 2. Euler Diagrams on a Sphere

There is another, likewise previously unpublished variant of R 479 in which Peirce presents a rather surprising generalisation: Euler diagrams drawn on a *sphere*. He motivates this by remarking that "there is no particular appropriateness in drawing the diagrams on a plane surface rather than on a sphere", since "the collection of all beings is as a definite a whole as the collection of all mortal beings; and thus the sphere is rather the more appropriate". On the universe living on a sphere, the difference between a dot inside or outside of the oval vanishes. What is the inside (call it, as Peirce proposes, the positive area or an area marked by +) and what is the outside (the negative area, marked by –) of the ovals has therefore to be fixed at the outset. Instead of the two possible positions for the ovals (one inside of the other or else being disjoint), there are now three possible relative positions for two non-intersecting ovals: one in which the uncovered surface of the sphere lies in the middle of the two ovals, one in which the surface lies outside of an outer oval, and one in which two parts of the surface lie outside of the two ovals each.

As an example of these cases, Peirce presents three diagrams, in which the inside/outside of a circle on a sphere is denoted by +/–, meaning "There are no saints that are perfect", "There are no saints that are not perfect" "There is nothing that is neither saint nor perfect", that is, "Everything is either saint or perfect (or both)", respectively.

Peirce prefigures, albeit in a somewhat different sense, the later works e.g. by Edwards (2004; see p. 15 a remark on H. C. Smith) that also extended Venn-like diagrams on spheres. Another recent extension studies Venn–Euler diagrams as three-dimensional objects drawn on closed surfaces or solids (Rodgers, Flower & Stapleton 2012). These two are of course far from equivalent approaches, since the Peirce-Edwards proposal was to draw diagrams on a sphere: $n-1$-spheres and n-balls are different manifolds with different topological properties.

In this second variant, too, Peirce mentions the other defect of Euler diagrams, namely that the ordinary system only represents propositions that express the non-existence of individuals. Euler diagrams can express universal propositions only via expressing non-existence of exceptions. For example "All saints are perfect" means that "There are no saints that are not perfect". But Euler circles do not capture propositions expressing "There is a saint that is not perfect". Peirce's alternative sequence does not proceed to explore remedies to this second defect any further, however.

The second variant of R 479 ends with Peirce recapitulating the history of the invention of Euler diagrams, including Lambert's linear diagrams (see, e.g. Bellucci, Moktefi & Pietarinen 2013). He notes that "no real improvement upon the system was made until Mr. Venn, in 1880, removed the first of the above mentioned defects by simply shading those compartments of the figure that correspond to combinations to be represented as nonexistent". Venn also suggested, Peirce continues to note, to draw ellipses instead of circles, as well as to draw them in fours, in threes, and in pairs. For the number of terms exceeding four, Peirce then proposes the figure in which the diagram for fours is iterated within one big diagram of fours, amounting to a Venn diagram for eight terms drawn on a two-dimensional surface. This method dispenses with introducing additional dimensions that have been proposed to deal with terms beyond four (R 479, p. 13, alt. variant; see Moktefi & Pietarinen 2016).[11]

Summary and Conclusions of R 479
The avenues that Peirce explored in the unpublished parts of the manuscript R 479 are five. (i) Shading or darkening the compartment of ovals, with different shades (we can find up to four different shadings proposed). (ii) Coloring in red any point in the diagram to signify that "the corresponding state of things is realized at some time or in some reference". (iii) Introducing representation of disjunctive statements as colored points on the line of the oval, thus signifying that the realisation of whether the state of things meant is either inside or outside of the oval is "indeterminate", as it is doubtful on which side it belongs. Even more notably, (iv) Peirce is seen to have experimented with the possibility of representing extended Euler diagrams on a sphere rather than on an Euclidean sheet—presumably the first to have not only proposed such an idea but also drawing some observations from having spherical surfaces for Euler diagrams. Last, as is found in the first variant proposing such extensions of Euler diagrams, Peirce (v) enlists six conventions to be used to set up the system. This is vaguely reminiscent of, although less numerous than, the set of conventions of EGs that Peirce had worked out in *The Logical Tracts* around the same time.

---

[11] Gil et al. (2000) on projections of Euler diagrams is a similar and independently discovered idea to this example of Peirce's to have recursive Euler diagrams.

Equipped with these developments and with an improved conceptual clarity and understanding of the system, Peirce is attempting to massage Euler diagrams into something that would possess more of the character of a logical *language* than a *diagram* or a *picture*. This transmogrification would make them better-suited to represent existential statements. The compartments of Euler diagrams may be shaded, and every point on a shaded area would mean a non-existent individual. (This common convention was suggested by John Venn in 1880 and it was reintroduced, in a somewhat different sense, e.g. in Couturat 1914 to strike out all constituents of a certain region and not to demolish a particular individual.) Any point colored in red ink means that the corresponding state of things is "realized at some time or in some reference". Existence can thus refer to objects such as time and other indexicals. A point colored red and resting on the boundary of an oval means that it is not determinate whether the state of things realised is represented by a point inside of the boundary or outside of that boundary. That is, by such borderline cases one can, as noted above, represent disjunctions. The twist is Peirce's semantic prose on "realised" and "unrealised states of things". A rectangular box, which Peirce suggests to be drawn in green ink, is a proposed notation to mark the limits of the sheet on which these diagrams are drawn.

Many of such suggestions have anticipated later and even some quite recent lines of research, such as designing Venn diagrams for more than four terms. Peirce's last example found in the variant pages of R 479 shows his proposal for a diagram of eight terms, in which diagrams for four terms are iterated within the one big diagram of fours. In this way one can draw Venn diagrams for eight terms on a two-dimensional affine plane without introducing further dimensions or other gimmicks. This large iterated Euler diagram was not reproduced in CP. Another is one in which Peirce applies iteration to a logic example taken from Christine Ladd-Franklin's thesis (SiL, pp. 58–61). Peirce explains: "In order to illustrate the method I will apply it (without any preconsideration at all) to the following problem by Mrs. Franklin" (R 479, ms p. 59). A three-page explanation of this example then follows a large diagram on the manuscript page 60, which in its abundant small details and a combination of dozens of marks in both black, red and brown ink unfortunately cannot be conveniently reproduced on a page of the present book.

A number of ideas could be exploited in trying to overcome the defects that haunt ordinary Euler diagrams. Peirce concluded that "the chief interest of non-relative deductive logic is not of the mathematical kind. That is to say, it does not lie in deducing necessary conclusions from assuming hypotheses nor in discovering methods for making such deductions" (R 479, ms p. 58, alt. variant). His desire to overcome the defects might have given some additional reason for him to pursue entirely new kinds of graphical methods that can express relative assertions and quantification free from the standard geometrical restrictions of Euler circles. The relationship between the two, Euler diagrams and relative logic, was to him as wide as that of between the "dichotomic mathematics of non-relative logic" (which is "one dull chapter" and "the very most rudimentary that mathematics can be"—that is, a Boolean algebra) and the "mathematics of plane geometry" (which is "an inexhaustible Proteus"). His quaint analogue in one of the variant draft pages of R 479 is that of "the works of Mother Goose" in comparison to "Voltaire" (R 479, ms p. 55, alt. variant).

Peirce appears to have written all these accounts with a view of having them incorporated into the second part of *Logical Tracts No. 2*. That second part was, at least according to the given subtitle, exclusively to deal with the topic of the theory of Euler's diagrams, with the limitations, extensions and relations it has to the theory of EGs and to the general algebra of logic. Indeed that can be observed in the drafts that survive in R 479. The topic of the general algebra of logic, on the other hand, which was supposed to constitute the third part of the *Tracts*, was apparently never written. Maybe at this point, when Peirce was nearing the completion of the text in the second part of *Logical Tracts No. 2*, the Lowell Lectures—which were not planned to deal with the topic of the algebra of logic at all—were closing in and Peirce had to abandon his plan to bring *The Logical Tracts* into completion.

Conclusions

The year 1903 was the indisputable *annus mirabilis* of Peirce's professional life. That year—even when taking only its second half into account—saw the discovery of modal logics, a decision method for logic (Alpha and Beta-reduct graphs), the theory of meta-graphs, second-order logic of potentials, logic of abstraction, reformation of speculative grammar, and an application of these concepts and tools to the foundations of mathematics, theory of science, epistemology and constructions of knowledge structures, metaphysical and ontological nature of relatives, philosophy of mind and cognition, as well as to the emerging ideas of computation, automated reasoning and logical and intelligent machines.

During the year, Peirce also achieved the perennial classification of the sciences (Kent 1987; Pietarinen 2006c), the formulation of the ethics of notation and terminology, and presented some of the best-known characterisations of abductive reasoning linked to his philosophy of pragmatism. All this happened while having produced a number of paper and lecture drafts, paid book reviews, reports and notices that appeared nearly fortnightly throughout the year (25 such items appeared in *The Nation* that year alone). Obituaries and translation works appeared, while the preserved manuscript papers witness Peirce having recorded a wealth of computations, commentaries, recreational studies and inventions of scientific, mathematical and practical throughout the year. Extensive correspondence was maintained with colleagues, friends and relatives, including the beginnings of an intensive exchange with Victoria Welby (SS).

The Logical Tracts has thus to be set within the context of a textual avalanche that occurred throughout the year. Despite unfinished, it stands out as the most detailed single treatise of the logic of EGs that Peirce ever attempted. Yet its status has remained singularly unacknowledged as such, and its partial publication in the *Collected Papers* in the 1930s does not bespeak the gargantuan and monographic nature of that work.

A lot was at stake for Peirce throughout the year. With his upcoming Lowell Institute Lectures in November and December, Peirce might have hoped to finally have been put in a position from which to make a permanent difference to the way philosophy is being observed and practiced, if not immediately then reassuringly in the long run, by improving on the exact methodology of logic while deepening its relevance to the matters of scientific and intellectual conduct. The second book of Volume 2 of the *Logic of the Future* will attend to what those last months of 1903 had yet to unveil.

References

Only those of Peirce's manuscript writings are included in the reference list below which do not appear in the *Logic of the Future* editions. Titles are those given in the Robin Catalogue, unless otherwise indicated by brackets. The textual sources of Volume 2 are listed in the separate "Catalogue of Peirce's Manuscripts". Peirce's own references are included in the backmatter, listed as "Bibliography of Peirce's References".

Bellucci, Francesco 2017. *Peirce's Speculative Grammar: Logic as Semiotics*. New York: Routledge.
Bellucci, Francesco 2019. Analysis and Decomposition in Peirce. *Synthese*. In press.
Bellucci, Francesco, Moktefi, Amirouche and Pietarinen, Ahti-Veikko 2013. Continuity, Connectivity and Regularity in Spatial Diagrams for N Terms. In Burton, Jim and Choudhury, Lopamudra (eds.), *Diagrams, Logic and Cognition: Proceedings of the First International Workshop on Diagrams, Logic and Cognition*. CEUR Workshop Proceedings 1132, pp. 23–30.
Bellucci, Francesco, Pietarinen, Ahti-Veikko and Stjernfelt, Frederik (eds.) 2014. *Peirce: 5 Questions*. Copenhagen: VIP/Automatic Press.
Bellucci, Francesco and Pietarinen, Ahti-Veikko 2015. Charles Sanders Peirce: Logic. *The Internet Encyclopedia of Philosophy*. http://www.iep.utm.edu/
Bellucci, Francesco and Pietarinen, Ahti-Veikko 2016. Existential Graphs as an Instrument for Logical Analysis. Part 1: Alpha. *The Review of Symbolic Logic* 9(2), pp. 209–237.
Bellucci, Francesco, Chiffi, Daniele and Pietarinen, Ahti-Veikko 2017. Assertive Graphs. *Journal of Applied Non-Classical Logics* 28(1), pp. 72–91.
Bellucci, Francesco, Moktefi, Amirouche and Pietarinen, Ahti-Veikko 2017. *Simplex sigillum veri*: Peano, Frege, and Peirce on the Primitives of Logic. *History and Philosophy of Logic* 39(1), pp. 80–95.
Bellucci, Francesco and Pietarinen, Ahti-Veikko 2017a. Two Dogmas of Diagrammatic Reasoning: A View from Existential Graphs. In K. Hull & R. K. Atkins (eds.). *Peirce on Perception and Reasoning: From Icons to Logic*. New York: Routledge, pp. 174–195.
Bellucci, Francesco and Pietarinen, Ahti-Veikko 2017b. From Mitchell to Carus: 14 Years of Logical Graphs in the Making. *Transactions of the Charles S. Peirce Society* 52(4), pp. 539–575.
Bellucci, Francesco and Pietarinen, Ahti-Veikko 2017c. Assertion and Denial: A Contribution from Logical Notation. *Journal of Applied Logics* 24, pp. 1–22.

Bellucci, Francesco and Pietarinen, Ahti-Veikko 2019. Icons, Interrogations, and Graphs: On Peirce's Integrated Notion of Abduction. *Transactions of the Charles S. Peirce Society* 56(1), pp. 43–62.

Bellucci, Francesco and Pietarinen, Ahti-Veikko 2020. Methodeutic of Abduction. In Shook, John and Paavola, Sami (eds.), *Abduction in Cognition and Action*. Springer. In press.

Bellucci, Francesco and Pietarinen, Ahti-Veikko 2020. Notational Differences. *Acta Analytica* 35, 289–314.

Bellucci, Francesco, Liu, Xinwen and Pietarinen, Ahti-Veikko 2020. On Linear Existential Graphs. *Logique & Analyse* 251, pp. 261–296.

Brady, Geraldine and Trimble, Todd H. 2000. A Categorical Interpretation of C. S. Peirce's Propositional Logic Alpha. *Journal of Pure and Applied Algebra* 149, pp. 213–239.

Brent, Joe 1993. *Charles Sanders Peirce: A Life*. Bloomington: Indiana University Press.

Brünnler, Kai 2003. *Deep Inference and Symmetry in Classical Proof*. PhD thesis. Technische Universität Dresden.

Carroll, Lewis 1895. What the Tortoise said to Achilles. *Mind* 4, pp. 278–280.

Carus, Paul 1910. Non-Aristotelian Logic. *The Monist* 20(1), pp. 158–159.

Caterina, Gianluca and Gangle, Rocco 2016. *Iconicity and Abduction*. Dordrecht: Springer.

Champagne, Marc and Pietarinen, Ahti-Veikko 2019. Why Images Cannot be Arguments, But Moving Ones Might. *Argumentation* 34, pp. 207–236.

Chiffi, Daniele and Pietarinen, Ahti-Veikko 2017. Fundamental Uncertainty and Values. *Philosophia* 45, pp. 1027–1037.

Chiffi, Daniele and Pietarinen, Ahti-Veikko 2018a. Abductive Inference within a Pragmatic Framework. *Synthese* 197, pp. 2507–2523.

Chiffi, Daniele and Pietarinen, Ahti-Veikko 2018b. Assertive and Existential Graphs: A Comparison. In: Chapman P., Stapleton G., Moktefi A., Perez-Kriz S., Bellucci F. (eds.). *Diagrammatic Representation and Inference. Diagrams 2018. Lecture Notes in Computer Science* 10871. Springer, pp. 565–581.

Chiffi, Daniele and Pietarinen, Ahti-Veikko 2019a. On the Logical Philosophy of Assertive Graphs. *Journal of Logic, Language and Information*. 29, pp. 375–397.

Chiffi, Daniele and Pietarinen, Ahti-Veikko 2019b. Risk and Values in Science: A Peircean View. *Axiomathes* 29(4), pp. 329–346.

Chiffi, Daniele, Pietarinen, Ahti-Veikko, Proover, Marika 2020. Anticipation, Abduction and the Economy of Research: A Normative Stance. *Futures: The Journal of Policy, Planning and Futures Studies* 115, 102471.

Chiffi, Daniele, Carrara, Massimiliano, De Florio, C. and Pietarinen, Ahti-Veikko 2019. We Don't Know We Don't Know: Asserting Ignorance. *Synthese*. In press.

Clark, Glenn 1997. New Light on Peirce's Iconic Notation for the Sixteen Binary Connectives. In Houser, N., Roberts, D., Van Evra, J. (eds.). *Studies in the Logic of Charles S. Peirce*. Bloomington and Indianapolis, IN: Indiana University Press, pp. 304–333.

Couturat, Louis 1914. *The Algebra of Logic*. Chicago: Open Court.

Cristalli, Claudia and Pietarinen, Ahti-Veikko 2020. Abstraction and generalization in the logic of science: Cases from the 19th-century scientific practice *HOPOS: The Journal of the International Society for the History of Philosophy of Science*. In press.

Dekker, Paul 2001. Dynamics and Pragmatics of 'Peirce's Puzzle'. *Journal of Semantics* 18, pp. 211–241.

Dipert, Randall 1995. Peirce's Underestimated Place in the History of Logic: A Response to Quine. In Ketner, K. L. (ed.), *Peirce and Contemporary Thought*. New York: Fordham University Press, pp. 32–58.

Dipert, Randall 2006. Peirce's Deductive Logic: Its Development, Influence, and Philosophical Significance. In Misak, C. (ed.). *The Cambridge Companion to Peirce*. Cambridge, Mass.: Cambridge University Press, pp. 257–286.

Edwards, A. W. F. 2004. *Cogwheels of the Mind: The Story of Venn Diagrams*. Baltimore: John Hopkins University Press.

Eisele, Carolyn 1979. *Studies in the Scientific and Mathematical Philosophy of Charles S. Peirce*. The Hague: Mouton Publishers.

Fenster, Della D. 2003. Funds for mathematics: Carnegie Institution of Washington support for mathematics from 1902 to 1921. *Historia Mathematica* 30, pp. 195–216.

Fisch, Max H. 1982. Peirce's Place in American Life. *Historica Mathematica* 9, pp. 265–287.

Fisch, Max H. 1986. *Peirce, Semeiotic, and Pragmatism: Essays by Max H. Fisch*. K. L. Ketner and C. J. W. Kloesel (eds.). Bloomington and Indianapolis, IN: Indiana University Press.

Fisch, Max H. and Turquette, Atwell 1966. Peirce's Triadic Logic. *Transactions of the Charles S. Peirce Society* 2(2), pp. 71–85. Reprinted in Fisch, M., *Peirce, Semeiotic, and Pragmatism: Essays by Max H. Fisch*. K. L. Ketner and C. J. W. Kloesel (eds.). Bloomington and Indianapolis, IN: Indiana University Press, pp. 171–183.

Floridi, Luciano 2006. The Logic of Being Informed. *Logique & Analyse* 196, pp. 1–28.

Frege, Gottlob 1879. *Begriffsschrift: eine der arithmetischen nachgebildete Formelsprache des reinen Denkens*. Halle: Louis Nebert.

Gardner, Martin 1958. *Logic Machines and Diagrams*. New York: McGraw-Hill.

Gentzen, Gerhard Karl Erich 1934. Untersuchungen über das logische Schließen. I. *Mathematische Zeitschrift* 39(2), pp. 76–210.

Gil J., Howse J., Kent S. and Taylor J. 2000. Projections in Venn-Euler Diagrams. *IEEE Symposium on Visual Languages*, pp. 119–126.

Grattan-Guinness, Ivor 2002. Re-Interpreting 'Λ': Kempe on Multisets and Peirce on Graphs, 1886–1905. *Transactions of the Charles S. Peirce Society* 38(3), pp. 327–350.

Grattan-Guinness, Ivor 2007. From A. B. Kempe to Josiah Royce via C. S. Peirce: Addenda to a recent paper by Pratt. *History and Philosophy of Logic* 28(3), pp. 265–266.

Hilpinen, Risto 1982. On C. S. Peirce's Theory of the Proposition: Peirce as a Precursor of Game-Theoretical Semantics. *The Monist* 65(2), pp. 182–188.

Hilpinen, Risto 1995. Peirce on Language and Reference. In Kenneth Laine Ketner (ed.) *Peirce and Contemporary Thought: Philosophical Inquiries*. New York: Fordham University Press. pp. 272–303.

Hilpinen, Risto 2004. Peirce's Logic. In Gabbay, Dov M. and John Woods (eds.). *Handbook of the History of Logic. Vol. 3: The Rise of Modern Logic From Leibniz to Frege*. Amsterdam: Elsevier, pp. 611–658.

Hilpinen, Risto 2016. Peirce, Perfect Knowledge, and the Gettier Problem. *Cognitio* 17(2), pp. 303–312.

Hintikka, Jaakko 1962. *Knowledge and Belief. An Introduction to the Logic of the Two Notions*. Ithaca: Cornell University Press.

Hintikka, Jaakko 1996. The Place of C. S. Peirce in the History of Logical Theory. In Brunning, J. and Forster, P. (eds.). *The Rule of Reason: The Philosophy of Charles Sanders Peirce*. Toronto: University of Toronto Press, pp. 13–33.

Hintikka, Jaakko 2011. What the Bald Man Can Tell Us. In Biletzky, A. (ed.). *Hues of Philosophy: Essays in Memory of Ruth Manor*. London: College Publications.

Holm, Jacob and Rotenberg, Eva 2019. Fully-dynamic Planarity Testing in Polylogarithmic Time. arXiv:1911.03449v2 cs.DS.

Hookway, Christopher 2012. *The Pragmatic Maxim: Essays on Peirce and Pragmatism*. Oxford: Oxford University Press.

Houser, Nathan 1985. *Peirce's Algebra of Logic and the Law of Distribution*. Dissertation. University of Waterloo, Ontario.

Houser, Nathan 1991. Peirce and the Law of Distribution. In: Drucker, T. (ed.). *Perspectives on the History of Mathematical Logic*. Boston: Birkhäuser, pp. 10–32.

Houser, Nathan, Roberts, Don D., Van Evra, J. (eds.) 1997. *Studies in the Logic of Charles S. Peirce*. Bloomington and Indianapolis, IN: Indiana University Press.

Huntington, Edward V. 1904. Sets of Independent Postulates for the Algebra of Logic. *Transactions of the American Mathematical Society* 5, pp. 288–309.

James, William 1988. *Manuscript Lectures*. Cambridge, Mass.: Harvard University Press.

James, William 1907. *Pragmatism, A New Name for Some Old Ways of Thinking*. Popular Lectures on Philosophy. New York: Longmans, Green, and Co.

James, William 2002. *The Correspondence of William James*. Vol. 10: 1902–March 1905. Edited by Ignas K. Skrupskelis, Elizabeth M. Berkeley and John J. McDermott. Charlottesville: University Press of Virginia.

James, William 2003. *The Correspondence of William James*. Vol. 11: April 1905–March 1908. Edited by Ignas K. Skrupskelis, Elizabeth M. Berkeley and John J. McDermott. Charlottesville: University Press of Virginia.

Kempe, Alfred Bray 1886. A Memoir on the Theory of Mathematical Form. *Philosophical Transactions of the Royal Society of London* 177, pp. 1–70.

Kent, Beverley 1987. *Charles S. Peirce: Logic and the Classification of the Sciences*. Kingston and Montreal: McGill-Queen's University Press.

Ketner, Kenneth 1987. Identifying Peirce's "Most Lucid and Interesting Paper". *Transactions of the Charles S. Peirce Society* 23(4), pp. 539–555.

Lemanski, Jens 2017. Logic Diagrams in the Weigel and Weise Circles. *History and Philosophy of Logic* 39(1), pp. 3–28.

Liu, Xinwen 2005. An Axiomatic System for Peirce's Alpha Graphs. In F. Dau, M.-L. Mugnier, & G. Stumme (eds.). *Common Semantics for Sharing Knowledge: Contributions to ICCS 2005*, Kassel: Kassel University Press, pp. 122–131.

Lupher, Tracy and Adajian, Thomas (eds.) 2015. *Philosophy of Logic: 5 Questions*. Copenhagen: VIP/Automatic Press.

Ma, Minghui 2018. Peirce's Logical Graphs for Boolean Algebras and Distributive Lattices. *Transactions of the Charles S. Peirce Society* 54(3), pp. 320–340.

Ma, Minghui and Pietarinen, Ahti-Veikko 2016. Proof Analysis of Peirce's Alpha System of Graphs. *Studia Logica* 105(3), pp. 625–647.

Ma, Minghui and Pietarinen, Ahti-Veikko 2017a. Graphical Sequent Calculi for Modal Logics. *Electronic Proceedings in Theoretical Computer Science* 243, pp. 91–103.

Ma, Minghui and Pietarinen, Ahti-Veikko 2017b. Gamma Graph Calculi for Modal Logics. *Synthese* 195(8), pp. 3621–3650.

Ma, Minghui and Pietarinen, Ahti-Veikko 2017c. Peirce's Sequent Proofs of Distributivity. *Logic and Its Applications: 7th Indian Conference, Lecture Notes in Computer Science* 10119, Springer, pp. 168–182.

Ma, Minghui and Pietarinen, Ahti-Veikko 2018a. Peirce's Calculi for Classical Propositional Logic. *Review of Symbolic Logic* 13(3), pp. 509–540.

Ma, Minghui and Pietarinen, Ahti-Veikko 2018b. A Graphical Deep Inference System for Intuitionistic Logic. *Logique & Analyse* 245, pp. 73–114.

Ma, Minghui and Pietarinen, Ahti-Veikko 2018c. A Weakening of Alpha Graphs: Quasi-Boolean Algebras. In Chapman P., Stapleton G., Moktefi A., Perez-Kriz S., Bellucci, F. (eds.). *Diagrammatic Representation and Inference. Diagrams 2018. Lecture Notes in Computer Science* 10871. Springer, Cham, pp. 549–564.

Ma, Minghui and Pietarinen, Ahti-Veikko 2018d. Let Us Investigate! Dynamic Conjecture-Making as the Formal Logic of Abduction. *Journal of Philosophical Logic* 47, pp. 913–945.

Ma, Minghui and Pietarinen, Ahti-Veikko 2019. Peirce's Logic of Dragon Head (R 501). Preprint.

Majer, Ondrej, Pietarinen, Ahti-Veikko and Tulenheimo, Tero 2009. Introduction to Logic and Games. In O. Majer, A.-V. Pietarinen and T. Tulenheimo (eds.). *Games: Unifying Logic, Language, and Philosophy*. Dordrecht: Springer, pp. ix–xxiii.

Menger, Karl 1939. On the Logic of the Doubtful: On Optative and Imperative Logic. *Reports of a Mathematical Colloquium Notre Dame* 2(1), pp. 53–64.

Menger, Karl 1994. *Reminiscences of the Vienna Circle and the Mathematical Colloquium*. Edited by Louise Golland, Brian McGuinness and Abe Sklar. Dordrecht: Kluwer Academic.

Mitchell, Oscar Howard 1883. On a New Algebra of Logic. In: C. S. Peirce (ed.). *Studies in Logic, by Members of the Johns Hopkins University*. Boston: Little, Brown & Company, pp. 72–106.

Moktefi, Amirouche and Pietarinen, Ahti-Veikko 2015. On the Diagrammatic Representation of Existential Statements with Venn Diagrams. *Journal of Logic, Language, and Information* 24(4), pp. 361–374.

Moktefi, Amirouche and Pietarinen, Ahti-Veikko 2016. Negative Terms in Euler Diagrams: Peirce's Solution. In Jamnik, M. et al. (eds.), *Lecture Notes in Artificial Intelligence* 9781, pp. 286–288.

Moore, Matthew (ed.), 2010. *New Essays on Peirce's Mathematical Philosophy*. Chicago: Open Court.

Newcomb, Simon 1904. The Carnegie Institution. *The North American Review* 178, pp. 172–185.

Øhrstrøm, Peter 2000. Graphs for Time and Modality. In Øhrstrøm, P. & Hasle, R. (eds.) *Temporal Logic: From Ancient Ideas to Artificial Intelligence*, pp. 320–343. Dordrecht: Kluwer Academics.

Pape, Helmut (ed.) 1983. *Charles S. Peirce: Phänomen und Logik der Zeichen*. Frankfurt am Main: Suhrkamp.

Peirce, Charles S. 1867a. On an Improvement in Boole's Calculus of Logic. *Proceedings of the American Academy of Arts and Sciences* 7, pp. 250–261. (Presented March 12, 1867. Reprinted in W2, pp. 12–23; CP 3.1–19.)

Peirce, Charles S. 1867b. On the Natural Classification of Arguments. *Proceedings of the American Academy of Arts and Science* 7, pp. 261–287. (Presented April 9, 1867. Reprinted in W2, pp. 23–49; CP 2.461–516.)

Peirce, Charles S. 1867c. Upon the Logic of Mathematics. *Proceedings of the American Academy of Arts and Science* 7, pp. 402–412. (Presented September 10, 1867. Reprinted in W2, pp. 59–69; CP 3.20–44.)

Peirce, Charles S. 1868. On a New List of Categories. *Proceedings of the American Academy of Arts and Sciences* 7, Boston, pp. 287–298. (Reprinted in W2, pp. 49–59; CP 1.545–559; EP1, pp. 1–10.) [Lowell Lecture's reading list, Lecture III.]

Peirce, Charles S. 1870/1873. Description of a Notation for the Logic of Relatives, Resulting from an Amplification of the Conceptions of Boole's Calculus of Logic. *Memoirs of the American Academy of Arts and Sciences* 9, pp. 317–378. (Communicated on January 26, 1870; a separate publication by Welch, Bigelow, and Company for Harvard University, 1870. Reprinted in W2, pp. 359–429; CP 3.45–149.)

Peirce, Charles S. 1878. *Photometric Researches*. Leibzig: Wilhelm Engelmann.

Peirce, Charles S. 1880. On the Algebra of Logic. *American Journal of Mathematics* 3(1), pp. 15–57. (Reprinted in W4, pp. 163–209; CP 3.154–251.)

Peirce, Charles S. 1881. On the Logic of Number. *American Journal of Mathematics* 4, pp. 85–95. (Reprinted in W4, pp. 299–309.)

Peirce, Charles S. c.1882. [Fragments on Logic] (R 747). Houghton Library.

Peirce, Charles S. 1882. Letter (draft) to Oscar Howard Mitchell, December 21, 1882 (R L 294). Houghton Library.

Peirce, Charles S. 1883a. A Communication from Mr. Peirce (P 245). *Johns Hopkins University Circulars* 2(22) (April 1883), pp. 86–88. (Reprinted in W4, p. 470.)

Peirce, Charles S. 1883b. Note B: The Logic of Relatives. In Peirce, C. S. (ed.). *Studies in Logic*, pp. 187–203. (Reprinted in W4, pp. 453–466; CP 3.328–358.)

Peirce, Charles S. (ed.) 1883c. *Studies in Logic by Members of the Johns Hopkins University*. Boston: Little, Brown, and Company. (SiL) [Lowell Lecture's reading list, Lecture III.]

Peirce, Charles S. 1883d. A Theory of Probable Inference. In Peirce, C. S. (ed.). *Studies in Logic*, pp. 126–181. (Reprinted in W4, pp. 408–450; CP 2.694–754.) [Lowell Lecture's reading list, Lecture VI.]

Peirce, Charles S. 1885. On the Algebra of Logic: A Contribution to the Philosophy of Notation. *American Journal of Mathematics* 7(2), pp. 180–196. (Reprinted in W5, pp. 162–190; CP 3.359–403.)

Peirce, Charles S. c.1886. Qualitative Logic (R 736). Houghton Library.
Peirce, Charles S. 1889a. Notes on Kempe's Paper on Mathematical Forms (R 714). Houghton Library.
Peirce, Charles S. 1889b. Kempe Translated into English (R 715). Houghton Library.
Peirce, Charles S. 1891a. Algebra of the Copula [Version 1]. In *Writings of Charles S. Peirce* Vol. 8 (1890–1892), pp. 210–211. Bloomington and Indianapolis, IN: Indiana University Press, 2010.
Peirce, Charles S. 1891b. Algebra of the Copula [Version 2]. In *Writings of Charles S. Peirce* Vol. 8 (1890–1892), pp. 212–216. Bloomington and Indianapolis, IN: Indiana University Press, 2010.
Peirce, Charles S. 1893a. *How to Reason: A Critick of Arguments*. Division I. Stecheology. Part I. Non Relative. Chapter VIII. The Algebra of the Copula. (R 411). Houghton Library.
Peirce, Charles S. 1893b. *How to Reason: A Critick of Arguments*. Chapter XI. The Boolian Calculus. (R 417). Houghton Library.
Peirce, Charles S. 1893c. *How to Reason: A Critick of Arguments*. Book II. Division I. Part 2. Logic of Relatives. Chapter XII. The Algebra of Relatives. (R 418). Houghton Library.
Peirce, Charles S. c.1894a. [On the Algebra of Relatives] (R 553). Houghton Library.
Peirce, Charles S. c.1894b. [The Three Categories and the Reduction of Fourthness] (R 915). Houghton Library.
Peirce, Charles S. c.1894c. [Logic: Fragments] (R S-64). Houghton Library.
Peirce, Charles S. 1894. Letter to Francis C. Russell, September 6, 1894 (R L 387). Houghton Library.
Peirce, Charles S. 1896. The Regenerated Logic. *The Monist* 7(1) (October), pp. 19–40. (Reprinted in CP 3.425–455; LoI, pp. 170–185.)
Peirce, Charles S. c.1897. Memoir § 4. Algebra of Copula (R 737). Houghton Library.
Peirce, Charles S. 1897. The Logic of Relatives. *The Monist* 7(2) (January), pp. 161–217. (Reprinted in CP 3.456–552; LoI, pp. 186–229.) [Lowell Lecture's reading list, Lecture V.]
Peirce, Charles S. 1898. Reply to Mr. Kempe (K) (R 708). Houghton Library.
Peirce, Charles S. 1901a. New Elements (Kaina stoicheia) (R 517). Houghton Library. (Reprinted in NEM IV, pp. 235–263; EP 2, pp. 300–324.)
Peirce, Charles S. 1901b. [The Logic of Dragon Head] (R 501, R 9, R 11). Houghton Library. (Ma & Pietarinen 2019).
Peirce, Charles S. 1901c. Pearson's Grammar of Science. Annotations on the first three chapters. *Popular Science Monthly* 58, pp. 296–306. [Lowell Lecture's reading list, Lecture VI.]

Peirce, Charles S. and Ladd-Franklin, Christine. 1902. Symbolic Logic, or algebra of logic. In James Mark Baldwin (ed.), *Dictionary of Philosophy and Psychology*. Volume 2, pp. 640–651. [Lowell Lecture's reading list, Lecture III.]

Peirce, Charles S. c.1902. A Treatise on the Calculus of Differences (R 91). Houghton Library.

Peirce, Charles S. 1902. Logic, Regarded As Semeiotic (The Carnegie Application of 1902), Version 1: An Integrated Reconstruction. Joseph Ransdell (ed.), *Arisbe*, preprint. (R L 75), Houghton Library.

Peirce, Charles S. 1903a. *A Syllabus of Certain Topics of Logic*. Boston: Alfred Mudge & Son. (Copies annotated by Peirce located in R 478; R 1600, Box 4; plus two bound in *[Philosophy and minor writings pamphlet]* Phil 2225.5.05*; all at Houghton Library.)

Peirce, Charles S. 1903b. *The Nomenclature and Division of Dyadic Relations*, privately printed (Alfred Mudge & Son). (R 539; R 1600, Boxes 3 and 13).

Peirce, Charles S. 1905a. What Pragmatism Is. *The Monist* 15(2) (April), pp. 161–181. (Reprinted in CP 5.411–437; LoI, pp. 230–244.)

Peirce, Charles S. 1905b. Issues of Pragmaticism. *The Monist* 15(4) (October), pp. 481–499. (Reprinted CP 5.438–463; LoI, pp. 245–258.)

Peirce, Charles S. 1905c. Rough Sketch of Suggested Prolegomena to your [James Mills Peirce's] First Course in Quaternions (R 87). Houghton Library.

Peirce, Charles S. 1906. Prolegomena to an Apology for Pragmaticism. *The Monist* 16(4) (October), pp. 492–546. Errata: *The Monist* 17(1) (January), 1907, p. 160. (Reprinted in CP 4.530–572; LoI, pp. 307–342.)

Peirce, Charles S. 1907. Second Talk to the Philosophical Club and Second Talk. On Deduction. April 12, 1907 (R 754). Houghton Library.

Peirce, Charles S. 1908a. Some Amazing Mazes. *The Monist* 28(2), pp. 227–241. (Reprinted in CP 4.585–593; LoI, pp. 394–403.)

Peirce, Charles S. 1908b. Some Amazing Mazes (Conclusion). Explanation of Curiosity the First. *The Monist* 28(3), pp. 416–464. (Reprinted in CP 4.594–642; LoI, pp. 404–445.)

Peirce, Charles S. 1908c. A Neglected Argument for the Reality of God. *Hibbert Journal* 7, pp. 90–112. (Reprinted in CP 6.452–485; EP 2, pp. 434–450.)

Peirce, Charles S. 1909a. Some Amazing Mazes, A Second Curiosity. *The Monist* 29(1), pp. 36–45. (Reprinted CP 4.643–646; LoI, pp. 446–451.)

Peirce, Charles S. 1909b. Studies in Meaning. March 25–28, 1909 (R 619). Houghton Library.

Peirce, Charles S. 1911a. A Letter (draft) to James Howard Kehler, June 22, 1911 (R L 231, R 514, R 515). Houghton Library.

Peirce, Charles S. 1911b. A Letter (draft) to Allan Douglas Risteen, December 6–9, 1911. (R L 376, marked "moved to R L 376" from R 500, though located at

R 500 in the Harvard's Houghton Peirce Papers at least until 2012). Houghton Library.

Peirce, Charles S. n.d.,a. Note on Kempe's Paper in Vol. XXI of the *Proceedings of the London Mathematical Society* (R 709); Notes on Kempe's Paper (R 710); Notes on Kempe's Paper (R 711); (Kempe) (R 712); (Kempe (R 713). Houghton Library.

Peirce, Charles S. n.d.,b. *[Philosophy and minor writings pamphlet]* Phil 2225.5.05*. Houghton Library.

Peirce, Charles S. n.d.,c. *[Peirce's Reprints and Books from his Library; Editor's Materials and Preliminary Catalogues of the Collection]*. (R 1600), 14 Boxes. Houghton Library.

Pfeifer, David 2014. Peirce Medical History Excerpts. Complied from the Max H. Fisch Records. Mimeograph. Institute for American Thought, IUPUI, Indianapolis.

Pietarinen, Ahti-Veikko 2001. Most Even Budged Yet: Some Cases for Game-Theoretic Semantics in Natural Language. *Theoretical Linguistics* 27(1), 20–54.

Pietarinen, Ahti-Veikko 2003a. Peirce's Game-Theoretic Ideas in Logic. *Semiotica* 144(14), pp. 33–47.

Pietarinen, Ahti-Veikko 2003b. Games as Formal Tools versus Games as Explanations in Logic and Science. *Foundations of Science* 8(1), pp. 317–364.

Pietarinen, Ahti-Veikko 2004. Peirce's Diagrammatic Logic in IF Perspective. *Lecture Notes in Artificial Intelligence* 2980, Berlin: Springer-Verlag, pp. 97–111.

Pietarinen, Ahti-Veikko 2005a. Compositionality, Relevance and Peirce's Logic of Existential Graphs. *Axiomathes* 15(1), pp. 513–540.

Pietarinen, Ahti-Veikko 2005b. Cultivating Habits of Reason: Peirce and the *Logica Utens* versus *Logica Docens* Distinction. *History of Philosophy Quarterly* 22, pp. 357–372.

Pietarinen, Ahti-Veikko 2006a. *Signs of Logic: Peircean Themes on the Philosophy of Language, Games, and Communication* (Synthese Library 329). Dordrecht: Springer.

Pietarinen, Ahti-Veikko 2006b. Peirce's Contributions to Possible-Worlds Semantics. *Studia Logica* 82(3), pp. 345–369.

Pietarinen, Ahti-Veikko 2006c. Interdisciplinarity and Peirce's Classification of the Sciences: A Centennial Reassessment. *Perspectives on Science* 14(2), pp. 127–152.

Pietarinen, Ahti-Veikko 2007. *Game Theory and Linguistic Meaning*. (Current Research in the Semantics/Pragmatics Interface 18). Oxford: Elsevier Science.

Pietarinen, Ahti-Veikko 2008. Diagrammatic Logic of Existential Graphs: A Case Study of Commands. In G. Stapleton, J. Howse, & J. Lee (eds.). *Diagrammatic*

Representation and Inference, Lecture Notes in Computer Science 5223, Heidelberg: Springer, pp. 404–407.
Pietarinen, Ahti-Veikko 2009a. Significs and the Origins of Analytic Philosophy. *Journal of the History of Ideas* 70(3), pp. 467–490.
Pietarinen, Ahti-Veikko 2009b. Pragmaticism as an Anti-Foundationalist Philosophy of Mathematics. In B. Van Kerkhove, R. Desmet & J. P. Van Bendegem (eds.). *Philosophical Perspectives on Mathematical Practices*. London: College Publications, pp. 305–333.
Pietarinen, Ahti-Veikko 2010a. Is Non-Visual Diagrammatic Logic Possible? In A. Gerner (ed.). *Diagrammatology and Diagram Praxis*. London: College Publications, pp. 73–85.
Pietarinen, Ahti-Veikko 2010b. Peirce's Pragmatic Theory of Proper Names. *Transactions of the Charles S. Peirce Society* 46(3), pp. 341–363.
Pietarinen, Ahti-Veikko 2010c. Which Philosophy of Mathematics is Pragmaticism? In M. Moore (ed.). *New Essays on Peirce's Mathematical Philosophy*. Chicago, IL: Open Court, pp. 59–79.
Pietarinen, Ahti-Veikko 2011a. Existential Graphs: What the Diagrammatic Logic of Cognition Might Look Like. *History and Philosophy of Logic* 32(3), pp. 265–281.
Pietarinen, Ahti-Veikko 2011b. Remarks on the Peirce–Schiller Correspondence. In E. H. Oleksy & W. Oleksy (eds.), *Transatlantic Encounters: Philosophy, Media, Politics*. Frankfurt am Main: Peter Lang, pp. 61–70.
Pietarinen, Ahti-Veikko 2011c. Moving Pictures of Thought II: Graphs, Games, and Pragmaticism's Proof. *Semiotica* 186, pp. 315–331. (Translated in Portuguese as 2013, "Grafos, Jogos e a Prova do Pragmaticismo", in Lafayette de Moraes and João Queiroz, *A lógica de Diagramas de Charles Sanders Peirce: Implicacões en Ciêcia Cognitiva, Lógica e Semiótica*. Editora UFJF, pp. 83–104.
Pietarinen, Ahti-Veikko 2012a. Peirce and the Logic of Image. *Semiotica* 2012(192), pp. 251–261.
Pietarinen, Ahti-Veikko 2012b. Why is the Normativity of Logic Based on Rules? In Cornelis De Waal and Kristof P. Skowronski (eds.), *The Normative Thought of Charles S. Peirce*, Fordham: Fordham University Press, pp. 172–184.
Pietarinen, Ahti-Veikko 2013. Logical and Linguistic Games from Peirce to Grice to Hintikka. *Teorema* 33(2), pp. 121–136.
Pietarinen, Ahti-Veikko 2014a. The Science to Save Us from Philosophy of Science. *Axiomathes* 25, pp. 149–166.
Pietarinen, Ahti-Veikko 2014b. A Scholastic-Realist Modal-Structuralism. *Philosophia Scientiae* 18(3), pp. 127–138.
Pietarinen, Ahti-Veikko 2015a. Two Papers on Existential Graphs by Charles S. Peirce: 1. Recent Developments of Existential Graphs and their Conse-

quences for Logic (R 498, R 499, R 490, S-36; 1906), 2. Assurance through Reasoning (R 669, R 670; 1911). *Synthese* 192, pp. 881–922.

Pietarinen, Ahti-Veikko 2015b. Exploring the Beta Quadrant. *Synthese* 192, pp. 941–970.

Pietarinen, Ahti-Veikko 2015c. Signs Systematically Studied: Invitation to Peirce's Theory. *Sign Systems Studies* 43(4), pp. 372–398; Recent Studies on Signs: Commentary and Perspectives, pp. 616–650; [Division of Signs, by Charles Peirce], pp. 651–662.

Pietarinen, Ahti-Veikko 2016. Four Papers Extensions of Euler Diagrams in Peirce's Four Manuscripts on Logical Graphs. In Jamnik, M. et al. (eds.), *Lecture Notes in Artificial Intelligence* 9781, pp. 139–154.

Pietarinen, Ahti-Veikko 2018. To Peirce Hintikka's Thoughts. *Logica Universalis* 13(2), pp. 241–262.

Pietarinen, Ahti-Veikko 2019a. Abduction and Diagrams. *Logic Journal of the IGPL*. In press.

Pietarinen, Ahti-Veikko 2019b. Semeiotic Completeness in the Theory of Signs. *Semiotica: Journal of the International Association for Semiotic Studies / Revue de l'Association Internationale de Sḿiotique* 228, pp. 237–257.

Pietarinen, Ahti-Veikko 2020. How to Justify Deductive Reasoning: Peirce's Solution. *British Journal for the History of Philosophy*. In press.

Pietarinen, Ahti-Veikko and Snellman, Lauri 2005. On Peirce's Late Proof of Pragmaticism. In T. Aho and A.-V. Pietarinen (eds.). *Acta Philosophica Fennica* 79. Helsinki: Societas Philosophica Fennica, pp. 275–288.

Pietarinen, Ahti-Veikko and Bellucci, Francesco 2014. New Light on Peirce's Conceptions of Retroduction, Deduction and Scientific Reasoning. *International Studies in the Philosophy of Science* 28(4), pp. 353–373.

Pietarinen, Ahti-Veikko and Chevalier, Jean-Marie 2015. The Second Metaphysical Club and Its Impact to the Development of the Sciences in the US. *Commens Working Papers no. 2*. Commens: Digital Companion to C. S. Peirce.

Pietarinen, Ahti-Veikko, Shafiei, Mohammad and Stjernfelt, Frederik 2019. Mutual Insights on Peirce and Husserl. In Pietarinen, A.-V. and M. Shafiei (eds.). *Peirce and Husserl: Mutual Insights on Logic, Mathematics and Cognition.* Dordrecht: Springer, pp. 3–15.

Pietarinen, Ahti-Veikko and Chiffi, Daniel 2020. From Knowability to Conjecturability. *Contemporary Pragmatism* 17(2-3), pp. 205–227.

Pietarinen, Ahti-Veikko; Bellucci, Francesco; Bobrova, Angelina; Hayden, Nathan and Shafiei, Mohammad 2020. The Blot. In Pietarinen, A.-V. et al. (eds.), *Diagrammatic Representation and Inference—11th International Conference, Diagrams 2020, Tallinn, Estonia, August 24–28, 2020, Proceedings.* Lecture Notes in Computer Science 12169, Springer.

Putnam, Hilary 1982. Peirce the Logician. *Historia Mathematica* 9, pp. 290–301.
Putnam, Hilary 2011. The Story of Pragmatism. *Comprende* 13(1), pp. 37–48.
Prior, Arthur N. 1964. The Algebra of the Copula. In Moore, E. and Robin, R. (eds.), *Studies in the Philosophy of Charles Sanders Peirce*. Amherst: The University of Massachusetts Press, pp. 79–94.
Ramharter, E. and Gottschall, C. 2011. Peirce's Search for a Graphical Modal Logic (Propositional Part). *History and Philosophy of Logic* 32, pp. 153–176.
Robin, Richard 1971. The Peirce Papers: A Supplementary Catalogue. *Transactions of the Charles S. Peirce Society* 7, 1971, pp. 37–57.
Roberts, Don D. 1973. *The Existential Graphs of Charles S. Peirce*. The Hague: Mouton.
Roberts, Don D. 1997. A Decision Method for Existential Graphs. In Houser, Nathan et al. (eds.). *Studies in the Logic of Charles S. Peirce*. Bloomington and Indianapolis, IN: Indiana University Press, pp. 387–401.
Rodgers, Peter, Flower, Jean and Stapleton, Gem 2012. Introducing 3D Venn and Euler Diagrams. In Chapman, Peter and Micallef, Luana (eds.), *Proceedings of the 3rd International Workshop on Euler Diagrams*. CEUR-WS 854, pp. 92–106.
Royce, Josiah with W. Fergus Kernan 1916. Charles Sanders Peirce. *Journal of Philosophy, Psychology, and Scientific Methods* 13, pp. 701–709.
Russell, Bertrand 1901. Sur la logique des relations avec des applications á la théorie des séries. *Revue de mathématiques/Rivista di Matematiche* 7, pp. 115–148.
Russell, Francis C. 1908. Hints for the Elucidation of Mr. Peirce's Logical Work. *The Monist* 28(3) (July 1908), pp. 406–415.
Serene, E. F. 1981. Anselm's Modal Conceptions. In Knuuttila, S. (ed.), *Reinforcing the Great Chain of Being: Studies of the History of Modal Theories*, pp. 117–163. Dordrecht: Springer.
Schiller, Ferdinand Canning Scott 1903. *Humanism. Philosophical Essays*. London: Macmillan and Co.
Schröder, Ernst 1890. *Vorlesungen über die Algebra der Logik*. Volume 1, Leipzig: Teubner.
Schütte, Kurt 1977. *Proof Theory*. Berlin: Springer-Verlag.
Shields, Paul 1981/2012. *Charles S. Peirce on the Logic of Number*. 2nd ed. Boston: Docent Press.
Shin, Sun-Joo 2002. *The Iconic Logic of Peirce's Graphs*. Cambridge, Mass.: MIT Press.
Sowa, John 1984. *Conceptual Structures: Information Processing in Mind and Machine*. Addison-Wesley.

Sowa, John 2006. Peirce's Contributions to the 21st Century. *Proceedings of the 14th International Conference on Conceptual Structures*. Lecture Notes in Computer Science 4068, pp. 54–69.

Stapleton, Gem, Howse, John and Taylor, John 2005. A Decidable Constraint Diagram Reasoning System. *Journal of Logic and Computation* 15, pp. 975–1008.

Stjernfelt, Frederik 2007. *Diagrammatology: An Investigation on the Borderlines of Phenomenology, Ontology, and Semiotics*. Dordrecht: Springer.

Sylvester, James Joseph 1878. On an Application of the New Atomic Theory to the Graphical Representation of the Invariants and Covariants of Binary Quantics. *American Journal of Mathematics* 1, pp. 64–104.

Venn, John 1883. Review of "Studies in Logic", *Mind* 8, pp. 594–603.

Winslow, C.-E. A. 1921. William Thompson Sedgwick (1855–1921). *Journal of Bacteriology* 6(3), pp. 255–262.

Zalamea, Fernando 2012a. *Synthetic Philosophy of Contemporary Mathematics*. Urbanomic.

Zalamea, Fernando 2012b. *Peirce's Logic of Continuity: A Mathematical and Conceptual Approach*. New York: Docent Press.

Zellweger, Shea 1997. Untapped Potential in Peirce's Iconic Notation for the Sixteen Binary Connectives. In Houser, Nathan et al. (eds.). *Studies in the Logic of Charles S. Peirce*. Bloomington and Indianapolis, IN: Indiana University Press, pp. 334–386.

Zeman, Jay J. 1964. *The Graphical Logic of C. S. Peirce*. Ph.D. dissertation, University of Chicago. Online edition 2002: http://users.clas.ufl.edu/jzeman/graphicallogic/

Zeman, Jay J. 1967. A System of Implicit Quantification. *Journal of Symbolic Logic* 32, pp. 480–504.

Charles S. Peirce's Writings on Existential Graphs

Part IV: **The Logical Tracts (1903)**

29 Logical Tracts. No. 1. On Existential Graphs

[Copy-text is R 491, including draft and variant sequences preserved in the same folder.] "Logical Tracts No. 1" is Peirce's first attempt to produce a compendium for his upcoming Lowell Lectures. In this brief, undated and unfinished piece likely to have been composed in June, Peirce sets out to explain the three basic "principles of representation" of existential graphs: the *sheet*, *spots* and *enclosures*. Despite its abrupt end, Peirce manages to start off the project of writing a book-length treatise of "Logical Tracts", with a fresh investigation into the nature of logical representations. First, the famous division of signs into *icons*, *indices* and *symbols* is here followed by the trichotomy of dividing symbols into *terms*, *propositions* and *arguments*. The *sheet* is then defined to be a graph that asserts that the universe is *definite*, *individual* and *real*. Furthermore, the graphical counterparts to predicate terms, termed the *spots*, are divided into *rhemata* and *onomata*, the latter meaning spots that have initially indefinite individuals attached to them by lines. *Enclosures* and *polarities* are fully at play while Peirce is working out the details of the quantificational part of the logic of EGs. Of note is that enclosures are consistently defined by the *scroll* and not by the ovals, and that the *pseudograph* is introduced as a new constant. Importantly, Peirce concludes that a single enclosure has the *effect* of denying the graph contained within it. The distinction between generalities of a representamen *materialiter* (in its mode of being, i.e. as the symbol *is* as a matter of fact and not as it represents its object to be) and *formaliter* (as a signification, i.e. as the symbol *represents* the generality of its object, as the meaning of the representamen), will be of further importance regarding to what is to follow in the upcoming course, as is the term "replica" which is now coined to speak about single occurrences of a symbol. This text is thus an essential precursor to Peirce's revision of his speculative grammar carried out in October as well as an important initial step towards the desired expansion of the method of EGs that is to happen during the latter half of 1903.

Part I.[1] *Representation* is a relation of one thing,—the *representamen*, or sign—to another,—the *object*,—this relation consisting in the determination of a third,—

---

[1] [Alt.] Logical Tracts. No. 1. On Existential Graphs. Part I. A *pure icon*, or *image*, would be a representamen ([fn:] I call that which represents, a *representamen*. A Representation is that relation of the representamen to its object which consists in it determining a thing (the interpretant representamen) to be in the same relation to that object.) whose special representative character should depend entirely upon qualities or characters which it would possess although its object had no existence. It would therefore represent whatever was like it or analogous to it.

A geometrical figure of a triangle may be taken as an example of an icon. To be sure, no representation can actually take place until there is an object and an interpreter. But still the shape of the figure belongs to it in itself, as much as any character belongs to a thing in itself; [[Alt.]] [...] in itself. The thing so shaped may have existed and been destroyed before anybody ever saw it. A metaphysician may object that the figure's having that shape can only consist in some cognition. But that remark is either quite irrelevant or only confirms the justice of saying that the figure is triangular in itself, apart from any cognition. That metaphysician confounds the character of the cognition in itself, *materialiter*, with the character of what it represents. If to say that the figure has a triangular shape can have no other meaning than that there is a certain

the *interpretant* representamen,—to be in the same mode of relation to the second as the first is to that second.

There are three modes of representation and three corresponding genera of representamens, these being *icons, indices,* and *symbols.* (*Proceedings of the American Academy of Arts and Sciences*, in Boston, for 1867 May 14, Vol. VII, p. 294.)

An *icon, likeness,* or image is a representamen[2] whose representative force depends solely upon characters which it possesses *materialiter*[3] and which it might equally possess though its object had no existence.

For example, a geometrical figure of a triangle is an icon. For though no representation can take place without an object and an interpreter, yet it is the character which the shape has, in the sense in which anything really has characters, which makes it an image of any strict mathematical triangle that there may be.

---

cognition, this completely justifies the acceptance of what that cognition represents and all that is deducible from it. But this will include the judgments that the figure is triangular and the assent to that judgment as true. But a judgment is not true unless it represents matters as they really are, independently of any opinions about them. If, therefore, the metaphysician understands 'The figure is triangular, in itself' in the sense that it is triangular, whatever anybody may think about it, his remark, supposing it to be true, only confirms the truth of this. But if he understands that proposition in any other sense, he is fighting a man of straw.] that is, regardless of anything else, and regardless of how it may be represented. The thing so shaped may have existed and have been destroyed before anybody saw it. A metaphysician may object that a figure's having that shape must consist in some cognition. But this, in an involved way, is substantially like arguing that because that the figure is triangular [it] is a proposition, and thus a representation, therefore it is not triangular independently of being so represented. It simply confuses the character of the proposition as a fact, *materialiter*, with the character of its meaning, *formaliter*.

The *icon* or *image* consists entirely in an appearance. The physical matter of it is not part of the representamen.

An *index* is a sign representamen whose special representative character consists in depends upon its factual connection with its object and is independent of its being interpreted as a sign.

An index may be nearly or quite free from all iconic character; as Bunker Hill Monument, which was intended, as its designer said, merely to say "Here!"

Or it may be predominantly iconic; as a photograph which resembles its object closely by virtue of having been in physical connection with it. The iconic element, as in this case, may be combined with the indexical element in the whole representamen, or these characters may belong to separate parts of the representamen; as when a screw is fastened to the outside of a package of screws in order to show what the screws inside are like. (There is somewhat too much of the symbolic character about this to make it a good example.) one of those hydrometersscopes where a little woman comes out of the house when the air is dry and goes in when it is moist, as a real woman would. This latter kind of index, which conveys definite information is a proposition.

A *symbol* is a representamen whose special representative character depends upon how it will be interpreted. Language is almost wholly symbolic; for most words are no otherwise fitted to be representamens than that they will be so interpreted. All artificial signs are more or less symbolic because some convention is always established concerning [end, fragment abandoned]

It is the appearance that constitutes the image; and any physical existence that may be connected with it is extraneous to it. Considered *strictissime*, it resides in the consciousness of the moment, and usually determines its interpretant by "association by resemblance", calling it up out of the depths of memory. But in practice, it is impossible to keep up to such excessive strictness of language. One sign frequently involves all three modes of representation; and if the iconic element is altogether predominant in sign, it will answer most purposes to call it an icon.

An *index* is a representamen whose representative force depends upon its being factually connected with its object, ~~independently of its functioning as a sign~~ and does not depend upon its being interpreted as a sign.

For example, the symptoms of disease are indices. For though they cannot serve as signs without being interpreted as such, yet that which renders them fit to be the signs they are is their factual connexion with the diseases, which would exist though nobody had remarked it.

An index must essentially be an individual existent fact or thing. *Strictissime*, therefore, it cannot function as an icon too, since an icon is only an appearance in consciousness. But an index must have some appearance connected with it; and according as that does or does not, contribute to its representative force we have an important division of indices into those which give information and those which merely serve to identify individuals. Of identifying indices, the letters which are attached to the singular points of a geometrical diagram are examples. Remembering that an icon—or indeed, any appearance,—has its being only in consciousness, we can readily convince ourselves that any informing index has an icon connected psychologically with it. A symptom calls up in the iatrical mind certain memories of disease. A weather-cock calls up an image of a quarter of the horizon. A toy hydroscope, with its female statuette coming out in fine weather and retiring into the house in foul weather, on the one hand assures us, from its construction, of its dealing with the state of moisture of the air, while on the other hand it recalls the usual conduct of real women. A photograph may be gazed at as a mere appearance, and so considered, is a mere icon. But if we scrutinize a photograph in order to obtain information, we rely on the fact that a physical force makes it accurately represent the object, and it becomes an informant index.

---

2 I call that which represents, a *representamen*. A Representation is that relation of the representamen to its object which consists in it determining a thing (the interpretant representamen) to be in the same relation to that object.

3 That is, as the sign is really, not representatively. *Man materialiter* consists of three letters, but *formaliter* of body and soul.

An informant index is a proposition. For one cannot better define a proposition (as distinguished from the *assertion* whereby one assumes responsibility for its truth) than as a representation of which one part serves, directly or indirectly, as an index of its object, while the other part excites in the mind an image of that same object.

A *symbol*[4] is a representamen whose representative force depends on how it is interpreted.

This sounds like nonsense; for what else is the interpretative force of a representation but its interpretation? But an example will at once show what is meant. The word "man" has the meaning it has simply by virtue of there being a general law, or habit, among English speaking interpreters, to which the interpretations of it will conform. Not only is "man" a "general sign" *formaliter*, or in its signification, but it is also general *materialiter*, in its mode of being as a sign. It is certainly not an existent individual. A book of which millions of copies are in existence contains this word in hundreds of passages, and all these are occurrences of one and the same word "man"; and it is the same word every time it has been pronounced;—not a billion words, but one word. Still less is it an appearance, fitting through the mind, and gone forever. It is evidently of the nature of a habit; not in the physiological sense (if there be any), but in the sense of a *law* to which not merely all interpretations so far (of a given kind) have conformed but to which coming interpretations are really influenced to conform. In short, it is a real general. All modern philosophers teach that generals are "mere" words, or "mere" conceptions, or "mere" symbols of some kind; although they are quite beyond comparison the most important things there are. However this may be, if generals are symbols, no doubt symbols are all generals.

To the single "occurrences" of a symbol,—which are existent individual *indices* exciting in the mind images, which coalesce to form *icons* of the symbol,—I give the name of its *replicas*.

The variety of different kinds of symbols of which logic is, from the nature of things, obliged to take cognizance, is great and bewildering. In addition to that, language, which has grown up under the influence of mens' more or less confused logical notions, and which has furthermore been greatly modified for convenience, presents still other varieties of symbols not strictly necessary for logical purposes but to which it is necessary to pay some attention, on account of the constant use we make of words in reasoning. This superfluity of variety tends to increase the more a language develops. Now the Aryan, or Indo-European, lan-

---

4 Aristotle seems to use σύμβολον quite in this sense. See Waitz, *Organon*, Vol. I, p. 324, on *Perihermeneias*, cap 1, 16a4. There are in all eight passages to be considered.

guages, upon which all our notions of grammar and most of our notions of symbols are founded, are very highly and very peculiarly developed languages. They educate us in conceptions which are very rich in logical power, but are at the same time much more confused than those which a simpler language would produce. Under these circumstances, it will be beyond my power to give a thoroughly satisfactory division of symbols; but I will do my best.[5]

In the first place, every symbol is either a *term*, a *proposition*, or an *argument*.

A *term* (by which I mean something slightly different from what is so called in the books) is any representamen which does not separately indicate its object; as 'kills', 'digs', 'endowed by nature with rich gifts of person and of mind, and a really great poet, but vicious and egoistical'.

A *proposition* is a representamen which separately indicates its object, but does specially show what interpretant it is intended to determine; as 'Brutus killed Caesar', where the pair of men Brutus and Caesar, indicate what object 'killed' is here intended to represent.

An *argument* is a symbol which specially shows what interpretant it is intended to determine; as "Every good catholic certainly adores some woman or other, since there is one woman, Mary, whom they all adore". Here, the substance of the symbol is that Mary is a woman adored by all catholics; but the purpose of recalling this, which the person addressed is supposed to know already, is that [the] person may see that a part of the state of things which this represents is that each catholic adores at least one woman. This last is not asserted by the arguer, if he simply combines himself to arguing. For to assert a proposition is to make oneself responsible for its truth;[6] and the arguer's design is to make the thing so clear to the mind of the person addressed, that he will not ask for any personal guarantee.

The essential difference between term, proposition, and argument, is that they are signs once, twice, and three times over respectively.[7] Thus, the definitions given suggest the question whether or not it is possible for a symbol specially to show its intended interpretant without indicating its object. If we try to produce such a symbol, we shall get something like this: 'If the multitude of atoms is such that any finite whole number being given, a collection of atoms of that number ex-

---

[5] Language is almost wholly symbolic; for most words are no otherwise fitted to be representamens than that they will be so interpreted. All artificial signs are more or less symbolic because some convention is always established concerning [end]

[6] It must be distinctly acknowledged that the logical nature of assertion, enunciation, judgment, assent and so forth, has not yet been definitively nor satisfactorily made clear.

[7] [This antedates Peirce's alternative terminology of sisign, bisign and trisign coined in the early variant of *Logical Tracts No. 2* (R 492, see the next selection under "Recapitulation").]

ists, then the entire collection of atoms is too great for any finite number whatever to count'. But this is evidently nothing but a conditional proposition of which the consequent describes a state of things while the antecedent separately indicates what state of things it is that is so described. Thus, a symbol which separately shows the intended interpretant without separately indicating its object is nothing but a symbol that separately indicates its object without separately showing what interpretant is intended.[8]

Part I. A *Graph* is a diagram consisting of no more than, first, the sheet upon which it is written, secondly, spots (or their equivalents) having various visible qualities (as colors, etc.), third, lines of connection (commonly of only two kinds, those that are drawn and those that are left undrawn), and fourth enclosing ovals.

An *entire graph* is a graph on a sheet otherwise blank. A *partial graph* is a part (possibly the whole) of an entire graph, which part if it were alone upon the sheet would have a meaning as a diagram. A *pseudograph* is a construction out of elements like those of graphs, but which, owing to the way in which these are put together, has no meaning as a diagram of the system to which it belongs.

A *logical graph* is a graph which asserts something, or represents an assertion, concerning a recognized universe, real or ~~imaginary~~ fictive.

An *existential graph* is a logical graph constructed upon a perfectly consistent system of representation such that any unenclosed partial graph shall assert something asserted by the entire graph.

The system of existential graphs herein described, being the only such system heretofore ~~known~~ invented, needs, for the present, no further designation.

Principles of Representation by this System of Existential Graphs

Principle I. *Of the Sheet.* The sheet on which the graphs are written (called the *sheet of assertion*), as well as each portion of it, is a graph asserting that a recognized universe is definite (so that no assertion can be both true and false of it), individual (so that any assertion is either true or false of it), and real (so that what is true and what false of it is independent of any judgment of man or men, unless it be that of the creator of the universe; in case this is fictive); any graph written upon this sheet is thereby asserted of that universe; and any multitude of graphs written disconnectedly upon the sheet are all asserted of the universe.

---

8 [This longest sequence in R 491, of 12 manuscript pages in length plus its variants, ends here. What follows is another and alternative beginning of *Logical Tracts No. 1* of 10 manuscript pages, plus variants.]

Principle II. *Of the Spots.* The spots are of two kinds, *rhemata* and *onomata*, although the former are superfluities of which I make little use. Each onoma is an arbitrary index of an indefinite individual. A connecting line may abut upon it, and this has the effect of attaching the onoma, as a designation, to the individual which that line denotes. I usually write capital letters for onomata. Each rhema is equivalent to a blank form such that if all its blanks are filled with proper names, it becomes a proposition, or symbol capable of assertion. Such a spot has a definite place upon its periphery called a *hook*, corresponding to each blank; and to each hook an extremity of a line of connection may be attached, with the effect of filling the blank with a designation of the individual denoted by the line. When all the hooks have received such attachments, the spots with these attachments becomes a graph signifying a proposition. According as a spot has 0, 1, 2, 3, etc. hooks, it is called a *medad, monad, dyad, triad*, etc. Having more than two, it is a *polyad*. Of these, the medad alone is a graph by itself. I sometimes use ordinary words and phrases for rhemata; and at other times use lower case letters.

Principle III. *Of the Enclosures.*[9] A *scroll* is a line, distinguished from a line of connexion by being drawn lightly or in some other way, which returns into itself after making two complete circuits, once cutting itself. There are thus two parts of the scroll each of which describes a circuit from the node to the node, and is called an *enclosure*. The scroll never cuts a spot nor another scroll, and may, for the present, be considered as ~~dividing~~ separating the entire graph into three partial graphs; one, say a, outside both enclosures; one, say b, inside the outer enclosure but outside the inner one; and one, say c, inside both enclosures. In so far as this separation does not represent the whole effect of the scroll, it will be considered under the head of Principle No. 4.[10]

If no onoma is common to any two of the partial graphs, a, b, c, and if no two are joined by a line of connexion, then the scroll has no effect upon the outermost graph, a, which is independently asserted.[11] But it is to be understood as cutting off its contents from the sheet, the outer enclosure cutting off b absolutely, but

---

9 [Alt.] **Principle III.** *Of the Connections.* Strictly speaking, any two hooks of the same or different spots may be regarded as connected, if not by a heavy line drawn from one to the other, then by the absense of such line. But I call this nex-line restricting the word *connection* to the former mode, unless I speak of an unmarked connection, [end]
10 [Principle 4 does not occur among the preserved pages of *Logical Tracts No. 1*. See *Logical Tracts No. 2*, Convention 3, for a full definition of the enclosures.]
11 [Alt.1] [...] the scroll has no effect upon the outermost graph, a, which is independently asserted. The scroll is to be understood as cutting off its contents assert[ing] that if b is true, c is true, this conditional proposition being understood *de inesse*, that is, in the sense that either b is false or c is true.

the inner enclosure so far restoring c, that it is asserted conditionally upon the truth of b; so that the scroll and its contents may be read 'If b is true, c is true', this conditional proposition being understood *de inesse*, that is, in the sense that either b is false or c is true.

If the inner enclosure of the scroll contains a pseudograph, such as 'The false is true', the scroll and contents means, 'If b is true, the false is true', which reduces b to an absurdity, and thus is equivalent to the denial of b. In that case, by way of simplification, the inner enclosure may be drawn indefinitely small, or may be suppressed. Thus a single enclosure (Fig. 2) has the effect of denying the whole graph which it contains.

(b)

Fig. 2 [end, fragment abandoned]

[Alt.2] [...] the scroll has no effect upon the outermost graph, a, which is independently asserted. The innermost graph, c, is asserted to be true ~~only~~ in case the intermediate one, b, happens to be true; but no assertion is made as to the truth of c in case b happens not to be true, and no affirmation of b is made whether categorical or conditional. Therefore, the scroll with its contents may be said to assert that if b is true then c is true, understanding this conditional proposition *de inesse*, that is, simply in the sense that either b is false or c is true. Or, it might convey the meaning better to say that the assertion of the scroll with its contents is

"If b is true, c is true; but if c is false, b is false";

though this is ~~repetitious~~ tautological. But when the effect of the scroll upon onomata comes to be considered, **[Alts.1,2]** it will be found that a certain distinct precedence must be given to the graph in the outer space; so that, 'If b, then c' is the preferable form of interpretation.

[Alt.1] [...] [it requires] explicit statement. For a puzzle arises from the circumstance that while it is very easy to see that to say that if a person is a mother she is a wife is the same as to say that if a person is a non-wife she is a non-mother, it is sensibly less obvious that to say 'If a person is a mother of anybody she is a wife of somebody' is *not* the same as to say that 'If a person is non-wife to anybody she is non-mother to somebody', but on the contrary is the same as to say 'If a person is non-wife to everybody she is non-mother to everybody'.

[Alt.2] [...] [it requires] explicit statement. An example will best exhibit the complication. Consider this assertion: "There is a woman,—call her arbitrarily, Mary—and if a person,—call him arbitrarily Pedro,—is a catholic, then Pedro adored Mary". That is a very different thing from saying, "If a person,—call him arbitrarily Pat,—is a catholic, then a woman can be found—call her arbitrarily, Bridget,—who is ~~certainly~~ positively a woman, by the way, whether Pat is a catholic or not,—and Pat adores Bridget". An idea of two selections is involved. The woman is to be suitably selected in both cases, while the man is any catholic you like in both cases. But in the one case the woman is selected first, and had to be so selected as to suit any catholic man who might be selected, which in the other case, the catholic man being supposed to be pitched upon, it was only necessary to find a woman who would answer to his individual adorations.

If in place of *c*, a pseudograph be substituted, such as 'What is false is true', the whole may be read: 'If *b* is true the false is true'. This reduces *b* to absurdity, and is equivalent to a denial of *b*. In such case, to simplify the writing, the inner enclosure may be made indefinitely small, or be suppressed; so that Fig. 2 denies *b*; and generally, a single enclosure has the effect of denying the whole graph which it contains. Hence, Fig. 3 asserts that *b* is true and *c* false; while Fig. 4 denies this, that is, asserts that either *b* is false or *c* is true, or, in other words, that if *b* is true, so is *c*.

An onoma, when it is first mentioned, is an indefinite individual. Thus, Fig. 5 may be read, "Something,—call it X,—lives". But if the onoma is denied when first mentioned, this denial is a definite ~~general~~ universal.

Thus, Fig. 6 may be read, "Anything whatever,—say X,—does not live".

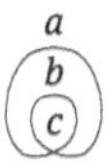

Fig. 1   **Fig. 2**    **Fig. 3** 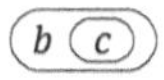   **Fig. 4**   **Fig. 5**   **Fig. 6**

But the universe, which is what is represented by any graph, is both definite and individual. Now a representation must be capable of comparison with the object represented; and therefore in this process the onoma must acquire definiteness and its negative must acquire individuality. In fact, after an onoma has once been named, it becomes definite. For its indefinacy consists in the inapplicability to it of the principle of contradiction. That is, it may be true that *something* lives and *something* does not live. But if we have said "something, call it X, lives", it ceases to be possible that X does not live. So the universality of the denial of the onoma consists in the inapplicability to it of the principle of excluded middle. That is, it may be false at once that "~~Nothing~~ Anything lives" and that "~~Nothing~~ Anything does not live". But, if we have once ~~said~~ denied "Anything whatever,—as X,—lives" we can no longer deny that X does not live. It is convenient to conceive the comparison of an assertion with the real universe to be conducted by a sufficiently informed defender of the assertion and a sufficiently informed opponent of it. The defender chooses the definite individual that is to be represented by an indefinite affirmative onoma,[12] "something"; while the opponent chooses every definite individual which is to be represented by a general denial of an onoma, "anything". Then, it is evident that ~~whoever~~ whichever of the two chooses after the other has

---

[12] [Here Peirce spelled "onoma" as "onomya".]

named his choice has the advantage of being able to adapt his choice to his opponents. Thus, suppose the assertion to be, "Something X loves everything Y". Then the defender first names X and the opponent has only to find something that X does not love. But if the assertion be "Anything, Y, is loved by something, X", the opponent has first to name Y, and the defender has only to find something that loves that Y. It thus appears that there must be a definitely established order of precedence among the first mentions of two onomata of which one first appears "evenly enclosed", that is, encircled by an even number of enclosures (zero being considered an even number), while the other first appears "oddly enclosed", that is, encircled by an odd number of enclosures; and it must be determinate whether the first mention of any onoma is evenly or oddly enclosed. The rule of this system is that what is outside an enclosure is always mentioned before what is inside of it.[13]

---

[13] [The second variant of R 491 is abandoned here. Later in 1906 Peirce coins the term "endoporeutic" to refer to this rule.]

30 Logical Tracts. No. 2. On Existential Graphs, Euler's Diagrams, and Logical Algebra

[Copy-text is R 492, Houghton Library, including most variants and draft versions preserved in the folder.] Sometime around mid-1903, Peirce quite abruptly abandons his first attempt to write up *The Logical Tracts* and moves on to compose another, and much longer version, sequenced as *Logical Tracts No. 2* (R 492), carrying the subtitle "On Existential Graphs, Euler's Diagrams, and Logical Algebra". Nearly 400 manuscript pages in length, this second attempt quickly grew into a book-length treatise on virtually everything that the theory of EGs had encompassed as the year was approaching its final quarter. Together, the two tracts make up a comprehensive manual on the philosophy, semiotics and logic, brought to maturation as a sound and complete graphical method of EGs. Indeed *The Logical Tracts* is the most extensive exposition of logical graphs that Peirce ever undertook to write. Even so, it was left incomplete, and the full treatise was planned to add several more chapters and sections. The ultimate version was projected to consist of as much as three large parts, only the first of them directly concerning EGs as appears in R 492. The second part was to add chapters on Euler Diagrams (see the next selection, R 479), while the third part was reserved for what may have remained as an altogether unwritten treatise on Logical Algebra. The part on Euler–Venn diagrams was separately produced sometime during 1903. As his Lowell Lectures were not meant to address algebra of logic, Peirce seemed to have lost the incentive to actually compose the planned last part. Moreover, an appendix was needed to accompany the first chapter in order to provide a "complete discussion" of the reasons for the introduction of an elaborate set of conventions, the system of norms and definitions upon which Peirce instituted the diagrammatic syntax and semantics of his graphical logic. These conventions are articulated at considerable length in the body of the second tract. His second Lowell Lecture pre-drafts will soon present such reasons as well (see e.g. R 454, R S-31), but no appendix survives among the Peirce Papers that would have been written for the purposes of *The Logical Tracts* in particular. A small notebook exists in folder R 1589, however, which possesses 52 definitions of technical terms on EGs. Proximal to the text of *The Logical Tracts* though probably composed slightly later, those definitions are interpolated into the present selection as the section beginning with an "outline of the imaginary Graphist's procedure", which in turn leads to the second chapter of *The Logical Tracts*. While most of the terms Peirce defines in R 1589 are his standard vocabulary, one also finds examples of some hapax legomena, suggesting that R 1589 may have been Peirce's afterthought in the wake of the abandonment of the *Tracts* project, and preserved as an unfinished but fresh attempt from 1904 to patch some of the earlier omissions of that long text.

The reader will also take particular interest in one of the subsection of the second *Tract*, entitled "Note A. Recapitulation of Some Points Treated in Tract No. 1". Here Peirce makes a fresh attempt to rewrite the second trichotomy of signs in terms of "sisign", "bisign" and "tersign", and communicates his desire to write much more on "How these systems may be made useful", especially in the planned final chapter of the first part that was to be on "Logical Analysis". An alternative synopsis of the planned third chapter, which appears on one of the draft sheets, reveals that such chapter "will give examples of the utility of the system for logical analysis". Following the chapters on "Principles of Interpretation", which is a detailed exposition of the twelve fundamental conventions of the system of graphs, and "Principles of Illative Transformation", which sets out the basic and derived rules of proofs of the system, the promised third chapter that was intended to show the system's usefulness for logical analysis, was apparently never written.

Logical Tracts. No. 2. *On Existential Graphs, Euler's Diagrams, and Logical Algebra*
[Table of Contents][1]
    Part I. *On Existential Graphs*
        Chapter I. *The Principles of Interpretation*
            Section i. *Fundamental Conventions*
                Subsection 1. *Of Conventions $N^{os}.1$ and 2*
                Subsection 2. *Of Convention No. 3*
                Subsection 3. *Of Conventions 4 to 9*
                [Alt.] **Subsection 4.** *Of Convention 10*
            Section ii. *Derived Principles of Interpretation* [Alt.] *Corollaries of Interpretation*
                Subsection 1. *Of the Pseudographs and Connected Signs*
                Subsection 2. *Of Selectives and Proper Names*
                Subsection 3. *Of Abstraction and Entia Rationis*
            Section iii. *Recapitulation.* (Redescription of the system in a compact form)
            [Appendix.] *Nomenclature* (R 1589)
        [Chapter I.] *Outline of the Imaginary Graphist's Procedure* (R 1589)
        Chapter II. *The Principles of Illative Transformation*
            Section i. *Basic Principles*
                [Subsection 1.] *Categorical Basic Rules for the Illative Transformation of Graphs dinectively built up from partial graphs not separated by seps*
                [Subsection 2.] *Basic Categorical Rules for the Illative Transformation of Graphs dinectively built up from partial graphs and from graphs separated by seps*
                [Subsection 3.] *Basic Categorical Rules for the Illative Transformation of All Graphs*
            Section ii. *Derived Rules of Illative Transformation*
            Section iii. *Recapitulation* [not written]
        [Chapter III.] [*Logical Analysis*] (Utility of the system for logical analysis) [not written]
    [Part II.] *Euler's Diagrams* (R 479)
    [Part III.] *Logical Algebra* [not written]

---

1 [The titles and heading numberings are from the main sequence of the text, with emendations indicated by brackets. The Table of Contents itself was not provided by Peirce, and is reconstructed from the synopses he presented of his plans and from the content of the full text of *Logical Tracts No. 2*, as well as from the analysis of the interrelations between versions of the preserved material and collateral sources.]

Part I. On Existential Graphs

A *diagram* is a representamen which is predominantly an icon of relations and is aided to be so by conventions. Indices are also more or less used. It should be carried out upon a perfectly consistent system of representation, founded upon a simple and easily intelligible basic idea.

A *graph* is a superficial diagram composed of the sheet upon which it is written or drawn, of spots or their equivalents, of lines of connection, and (if need be) of enclosures. The type which it is supposed more or less to resemble is the structural formula of the chemist.

A *logical graph* is a graph representing logical relations iconically, so as to be an aid to logical analysis.

An *existential graph* is a logical graph governed by a system of representation founded upon the idea that the sheet upon which it is written, as well as every portion of that sheet, represents one recognized universe, real or fictive, and that every graph drawn on that sheet, and not cut off from the main body of it by an enclosure, represents some fact existing in that universe, and represents it independently of the representation of another such fact by any other graph written upon another part of the sheet, these graphs, however, forming one composite graph.

No other system of existential graphs than that herein set forth having hitherto been proposed, this one will need, for the present, no more distinctive designation. Should such designation hereafter become desirable, I desire that this system should be called the Existential System of 1897, in which year I wrote an account of it and offered it for publication to the Editor of *The Monist*, who declined it on the ground that it might later be improved upon. No changes have been found desirable since that date, although it has been under continual examination; but the exposition has been rendered more formal.

The following exposition of this system will be arranged as follows:

Chapter I will explain the expression of ordinary forms of language in graphs and the interpretation of the latter into the former in three sections, as follows:

Section i will state all the fundamental conventions of the system, separating those which are essentially different, showing the need which each is designed to meet together with the reasons for meeting it by the particular convention chosen, so far as these can be given at this stage of the development. A complete discussion will be given in an Appendix to this Chapter.[2] To aid the understanding of all this, various logical analyses will be interspersed where they become pertinent.

---

[2] [Such an appendix has not been recovered and may not have been provided by Peirce in 1903. In its stead, a glossary from R 1589, written later than the main text and probably in 1904, is interpolated here as the best preserved approximation.]

Section ii will enunciate other rules of interpretation whose validity will be demonstrated from the fundamental conventions as premises. This section will also introduce certain modifications of some of the signs established in Section *i*, the modified signs being convenient, although good reasons forbid their being considered fundamental.

Section iii will redescribe the system in a compact form, which, on account of its uniting into one many rules that had, in the first instance; to be considered separately, is more easily grasped and retained in the mind.

Chapter II will develop formal "rules", or permissions, by which one graph may be transformed into another without danger of passing from truth to falsity and without recurring to any interpretation of the graphs; such transformations being of the nature of immediate inferences. The part will be divided into sections corresponding to those of Chapter I.[3]

Section i will prove the basic rules of transformation directly from the fundamental conventions of the first section of Chapter I.

Section ii will deduce further rules of transformation from those of Section *i*, without further recourse to the principles of transformation.

Section iii will restate the rules in more compact form.

Chapter III will show how the system may be made useful.[4]

CHAPTER I. The Principles of Interpretation

Section i. Fundamental Conventions

Subsection 1. *Of Conventions N°s 1 and 2*

In order to understand why this system of expression has the construction it has, it is indispensable to grasp the precise purpose of it, and not to confuse this with four other purposes, to wit:

First, although the study of it and practice with it will be highly useful in helping to train the mind to accurate thinking, still that consideration has not had any influence in determining the characters of the signs employed; and an expo-

---

3 [Alt.] *Chapter II* will enunciate and prove from the fundamental conventions of the first section of Chapter I the formal "rules", or permissions, allowing the transformation of one graph into another without recurring to interpretation into ordinary language or any other system of expression, and without any danger of passing from truth to falsity; such transformations being of the nature of immediate inferences.

4 [Alt.] *Chapter III* will give examples of the utility of the system for logical analysis.

sition of it, which should have that aim, ought to be based upon psychological researches of which it is impossible here to take account.

Second, this system is not intended to serve as a universal language for mathematicians or other reasoners, like that of Peano.

Third, this system is not intended as a calculus, or apparatus by which conclusions can be reached and problems solved with greater facility than by more familiar systems of expression. Although some writers have studied the logical algebras invented by me with that end apparently in view, in my own opinion their structure, as well as that of the present system, is quite antagonistic to much utility of that sort. The principal desideratum in a calculus is that it should be able to pass with security at one bound over a series of difficult inferential steps. What these abbreviated inferences may best be, will depend upon the special nature of the subject under discussion. But in my algebras and graphs, far from anything of that sort being attempted, the whole effort has been to dissect the operations of inference into as many distinct steps as possible.

Fourth, although there is a certain fascination about these graphs, and the way they work is pretty enough, yet the system is not intended for a plaything, as logical algebra has sometimes been made, but has a very serious purpose which I proceed to explain.

Admirable as the work of research of the special sciences,—physical and psychical,—is, as a whole, the reasoning (employed in them) is of an elementary kind except when it is mathematical, and it is not infrequently loose. The philosophical sciences are greatly inferior to the special sciences in their reasoning. Mathematicians alone reason with great subtlety and great precision. But hitherto nobody has succeeded in giving a thoroughly satisfactory logical analysis of the reasoning of mathematics. That is to say, although every step of the reasoning is evidently such that the collective premisses cannot be true and yet the conclusion false, and although for each such step, A, we are able to draw up a self-evident general rule that from a premiss of such and such a form such and such a form of conclusion will necessarily follow, this rule covering the particular inferential step, A, yet nobody has drawn up a complete list of such rules covering all mathematical inferences. It is true that mathematics has its calculus which solves problems by rules which are fully proved; but, in the first place, for some branches of the calculus those proofs have not been reduced to self-evident rules, and in the second place, it is only routine work which can be done by simply following the rules of the calculus, and every considerable step in mathematics is performed in other ways.

If we consult the ordinary treatises on logic for an account of necessary reasoning, all the help that they afford is the rules of syllogism. They pretend that ordinary syllogism explains the reasoning of mathematics; and books have professed to exhibit considerable parts of the reasoning of the first book of Euclid's *Elements* stated in the form of syllogisms. But if this statement is examined, it will be found that it represents transformations of statements to be made that are not reduced to strict syllogistic form; and on examination it will be found that it is precisely in these transformations that the whole gist of the reasoning lies. The nearest approach to a logical analysis of mathematical reasoning that has ever been made was Schröder's statement, with improvements, in a logical algebra of my invention, of Dedekind's reasoning (itself in a sort of logical form) concerning the foundations of arithmetic. But though this relates only to an exceptionally simple kind of mathematics, my opinion—quite against my natural leanings toward my own creation—is that the soul of the reasoning has even here not been caught in the logical net.

No other book has, during the nineteenth century, been deeply studied by so large a proportion of the strong intellects of the civilized world as Kant's *Critic of the Pure Reason*; and the reason has undoubtedly been that they have all been greatly struck by Kant's logical power. Yet Kant, for all this unquestionable power, had paid so little attention to logic that he makes it manifest that he supposed that ordinary syllogism explains mathematical reasoning, and indeed the simplest mood of syllogism, *Barbara*. Now, at the very utmost, from N propositions only $\frac{1}{4}N^2$ conclusions can be drawn by *Barbara*. In the thirteen books of Euclid's *Elements* there are 14 premisses (5 postulates and 9 axioms) excluding the definitions, which are merely verbal. Therefore, even if these premisses were related to one another in the most favorable way, which is far from being the case, there could only be 49 conclusions from them. But Euclid draws over ten times that number (465 propositions, 27 corollaries, and 17 lemmas) besides which his editors have inserted hundreds of corollaries. There are 48 propositions in the first book. Moreover, in *Barbara* or any sorites, or complexus of such syllogisms, to introduce the same premiss twice is idle. But throughout mathematics the same premisses are used over and over again. Moreover a person of fairly good mind and some logical training will instantly see the syllogistic conclusions from any number of premisses. But this is far from being true of mathematical inferences.

There is reason to believe that a thorough understanding of the nature of mathematical reasoning would lead to great improvements in mathematics. For when a new discovery is made in mathematics, the demonstration first found is almost always replaced later by another much simpler. Now it may be expected that, if the reasoning were thoroughly understood, the unnecessary complications of the first proof would be eliminable at once. Indeed, one might expect that the shortest route would be taken at the outset. Then again, consider the state of topical geometry, or geometrical topics, otherwise called topology. Here is a branch of geometry which not only leaves out of consideration the proportions of the different dimensions of figures and the magnitudes of angles (as does also graphics, or projective geometry—perspective, etc.) but also leaves out of account the straightness or mode of curvature of lines and the flatness or mode of bending of surfaces, and confines itself entirely to the connexions of the parts of figures (distinguishing, for example, a ring from a ball). Ordinary metric geometry equally depends on the connections of parts; but it depends on much besides. It, therefore, is a far more complicated subject, and can hardly fail to be of its own nature much the more difficult. And yet geometrical topics stands idle with problems to all appearance very simple staring it unsolved in the face, merely because mathematicians have not found out how to reason about it. Now a thorough understanding of mathematical reasoning must be a long stride toward enabling us to find a method of reasoning about this subject as well, very likely, as about other subjects that are not even recognized to be mathematical.

This, then, is the purpose for which my logical algebras were designed but which, in my opinion, they do not sufficiently fulfill. The present system of existential graphs is far more perfect in that respect, and has already taught me much about mathematical reasoning. Whether or not it will explain all mathematical inferences is not yet known.

Our purpose, then, is to study the workings of necessary inference. What we want, in order to do this, is a method of representing diagrammatically any possible set of premisses, this diagram to be such that we can observe the transformation of these premisses into the conclusion by a series of steps each of the utmost possible simplicity.

What we have to do, therefore, is to form a perfectly consistent method of expressing any assertion diagrammatically. The diagram must then evidently be something that we can see and contemplate. Now what we see appears spread out as upon a sheet. Consequently our diagram must be drawn upon a sheet. We must appropriate a sheet to the purpose, and the diagram drawn or written on the sheet is to express an assertion. We can, then, approximately call this sheet our *sheet of assertion*. The *entire graph*, or all that is drawn on the sheet, is to express a proposition, which the act of writing is to assert.

But what are our assertions to be about? The answer must be that they are to be about an arbitrarily hypothetical universe, a creation of a mind.[5] For it is

---

5 **[Alt.1]** [...] of some mind. For it is *necessary* reasoning only that we intend to study; and the necessity of such reasoning consists in this, that not only does the conclusion happen to be true in any predesignate universe, but ~~would~~ *will be* true, so long as the premisses are true, howsoever the universe may subsequently turn out to be determined. In order to our fix ideas, we may imagine **[Alt.2]** that there are two persons; on the one hand, a *grapheus*, ~~or graph-drawer,~~ who creates the universe ~~which the graph partially represents, and is at liberty to create it as he likes, and to~~

necessary reasoning alone that we intend to study; and the necessity of such reasoning consists in this, that not only does the conclusion happen to be true of a pre-determinate universe, but *will* be true, so long as the premisses are true, howsoever the universe may subsequently turn out to be determined. Thus, conformity to an *existing*, that is, entirely determinate, universe does not make necessity, which consists in what always *will be*, that is, what is determinately true of a universe not yet entirely determinate. Physical necessity consists in the fact that whatever may happen will conform to a law of nature; and logical necessity, which is what we have here to deal with, consists of something being determinately true of a universe not entirely determinate as to what is true, and thus not *existent*. In order to fix our ideas, we may imagine that there are two persons, one of whom, called the *grapheus*, creates the universe by the continuous development of his idea of it, every interval of time during the process adding some *fact* to the universe, that is, affording justification for some assertion, although, the process being continuous, these facts are not distinct from one another in their mode of being, as the propositions which state some of them are. As fast as this ~~mental~~ process in the mind of the grapheus takes place, that which is thought acquires *being*, that is, *perfect definiteness*, in the sense that the effect of what is thought in any lapse of time, however short, is definitive and irrevocable; but it

---

~~add to it any new characters he likes whenever he chooses to do so. The *interpreter* of the graph, or reasoner, has no such liberty. He must, therefore, be imagined to be another person,~~ and determines its characters as he will; on the other hand a *graphist* who handles the pencil. The *grapheus* communicates to the graphist from time to time his determinations in regard to the character of the universe. Each such communication *authorizes* the graphist to express it. *An authorization once given is irrevocable*: this constitutes the universe to be perfectly *definite*. Should the graphist risk an assertion without authorization, he ~~may receive~~ must hope to receive an authorization later; for *what never will be authorized is forbidden*: this constitutes the universe to be perfectly *determinate*. He is at liberty to transform the graph provided only that ~~the graph is drawn already what is written being true to the creation of the grapheus~~ his transformation shall not be such as to render the graph false to any further determination that the grapheus may thereafter choose to add to the character of his universe.

[Alt.2] [...] that there are two persons, one of whom, called the *grapheus*, creates the universe by declaring from time to time to the other person, the *graphist*, who is meantime modifying the graph (the first writing of it being one of the modifications since the original blank of the sheet is a graph, being *whatever* proposition is then expressed upon the sheet of assertion), what he is authorized to ~~express~~ assert, the grapheus continuing these declarations until the universe is completely described; but not until this process is complete, after which no modification of the graph is possible, does the universe *exist*, since existence consists in entire determinateness of being. Every such ~~authorization~~ declaration is definitive and irrevocable: therein consists the perfect *definiteness*, or *being* of the universe; while its *existence*, or entire determinateness consists in nothing being true of it except what will eventually being [sic.] declared so.

is not until the whole operation of creation is complete that the universe acquires *existence*, that is, *entire determinateness*, in the sense that nothing remains undecided. The other of the two persons concerned, called the *graphist*, is occupied during the process of creation in making *successive* modifications (i.e., not by a continuous process, since each modification, unless it be final, has another that follows *next* after it), of the entire graph. Remembering that the entire graph is *whatever* is, at any time, expressed in this system on the sheet of assertion, we may note that before anything has been drawn on the sheet, the *blank* is, by that definition, a graph. It may be considered as the expression of whatever must be well-understood between the graphist and the interpreter of the graph before the latter can understand what to expect of the graph. There must be an interpreter, since the graph, like every sign founded on convention, only has the sort of being that it has if it is interpreted; for a conventional sign is neither a mass of ink on a piece of paper or any other individual existence, nor is it an image present to consciousness, but is a special habit or rule of interpretation and consists precisely in the fact that certain sorts of ink spots—which I call its *replicas*—will have certain effects on the conduct, mental and bodily, of the interpreter. So, then, the blank of the blank sheet may be considered as expressing that the universe in process of creation by the grapheus is perfectly definite and entirely determinate, etc. Hence, even the first writing of a graph on the sheet is a modification of the graph already written. The business of the graphist is supposed to come to an end before the work of creation is accomplished. He is supposed to be a mind-reader to such an extent that he knows some (perhaps all) the creative work of the grapheus so far as it has gone, but not what is to come. What he intends the graph to express concerns the universe as it will be when it comes to exist. If he risks an assertion for which he has no warrant in what the grapheus has yet thought, it may or may not prove true.

The above considerations constitute a sufficient reason for adopting the following convention, which is hereby adopted:

Convention No. 1. *A certain sheet, called the* SHEET OF ASSERTION, *is appropriated to the drawing upon it of such graphs that whatever may be at any time drawn upon it, called the* ENTIRE GRAPH, *shall be regarded as expressing an assertion by an imaginary person, called the* GRAPHIST, *concerning a universe, perfectly definite and entirely determinate, but the arbitrary creation of an imaginary mind, called the* GRAPHEUS.

The convention which has next to be considered is the most arbitrary of all. It is, nevertheless, founded on two good reasons. A diagram ought to be as iconic as possible; that is, it should represent relations by visible relations analogous to them. Now suppose the graphist finds himself authorized to write each of two entire graphs. Say, for example, that he can draw Fig. 1; and that he is equally authorized to draw Fig. 2.

The pulp of some oranges is red.

Fig. 1

To express oneself naturally is the last perfection of a writer's art.

Fig. 2

Each proposition is true independently of the other, and either may therefore be expressed on the sheet of assertion. If both are written on different parts of the sheet of assertion, the independent presence on the sheet of the two expressions is analogous to the independent truth of the two propositions that they would, when written separately, assert. It would, therefore, be a highly iconic mode of representation to understand Fig. 3, where both are written on different parts of the sheet, as the assertion of both propositions.

The pulp of some oranges is red.
To express oneself naturally is the last perfection of a writer's art.

Fig. 3

It is a subsidiary recommendation of a mode of diagrammatization, but one which ought to be accorded some weight, that it is one that the nature and habits of our minds will cause us at once to understand, without our being put to the trouble of remembering a rule that has no relation to our natural and habitual ways of expression. Certainly, no convention of representation could possess this merit in a higher degree than the plan of writing both of two assertions in order to express the truth of both. It is so very natural, that all who have ever used letters or almost any method of graphic communication have resorted to it. It seems almost unavoidable, although in my first invented system of graphs, which I call *entitative graphs*, propositions written on the sheet together were not understood to be independently asserted but to be *alternatively* asserted, so that Fig. 3 would mean, "Either the pulp of some oranges is red or else to express oneself naturally is the last perfection of a writer's art". The consequence was that a blank sheet instead of expressing only what was taken for granted had to be interpreted as an absurdity.

One system seems to be about as good as the other, except that unnaturalness and aniconicity haunt every part of the system of entitative graphs, which is a curious example of how late a development simplicity is. These two reasons will suffice to make every reader very willing to accede to the following convention, which is hereby adopted.

Convention No. 2. *Graphs on different parts of the sheet, called* PARTIAL GRAPHS, *shall independently assert what they would severally assert, were each the entire graph.*

Subsection 2. *Of Convention No. 3*

If a system of expression is to be adequate to the analysis of all necessary consequences,[6] it is requisite that it should be able to express that an expressed consequent, C, follows necessarily from an expressed antecedent, A. The conventions hitherto adopted do not enable us to express this.[7] In order to form a new and reasonable convention for this purpose we must get a perfectly distinct idea of what it means to say that a consequent follows from an antecedent. It means that

---

[6] In the language of logic 'consequence' does not mean that which follows, which is called the *consequent*, but means the fact that a consequent follows from an antecedent.

[7] **[Alt.1]** […] hitherto adopted do not enable us to express this. We must, therefore, form a new convention for this purpose. In order to effect this, the first thing to be done is to get an exact idea of what it means to say that a consequent, C, follows necessarily from an antecedent, A. It means that in every universe where A is true, C is true also. It makes no difference how it may be in those universes in which A is not true. For we must give to necessary consequence a meaning suitable to the use which the term is to serve. Now the object of distinguishing between what does and what does not follow is to avoid inferences which pass from truth to falsity. If the premiss is false, it makes no difference whether the conclusion is false or not and it would be impossible to find a useful form of inference which should lead from a false premiss to a true conclusion, unless the conclusion [be] necessary, that is, true in all universes whatsoever. [end]

[Alt.2] […] hitherto adopted do not enable us to express this. We must, therefore, form a new convention for this purpose. First of all, let us decide what meaning we shall attach to saying that a conclusion, C, follows necessarily from an antecedent, A. We ought to attach that meaning to it which best adapts the phrase to its purpose, which is to enable us to avoid passing in inference from truth to falsity. Therefore to say that C follows necessarily from A must mean that A's being true C is false is an absurdity not occurring in any *definite* universe. Now A's being true while A is false is an absurdity whenever C's being false is an absurdity. That is to say, from anything absurd everything necessarily follows; and from anything whatever the logically necessary follows. But before we can express that in *every* universe either A is false or C is true, we must find means to express this of a single *determinate* universe. This is the meaning of the form of proposition which logicians call a "conditional proposition *de inesse*". That is to say, it is a conditional proposition which contemplates no general range of possibilities but only a single *determinate* state of things; as when we say "If it is hailing, it is cold"; that is, it either is not hailing or it is cold.

in adding to an assertion of the antecedent an assertion of the consequent we

---

How shall we express a conditional proposition *de inesse*? It might seem that the question launched us upon a sea of possibilities. But the truth is that, disregarding mere external variations in the way of drawing the signs, there is but one way which is thoroughly analytical and which introduces no superfluous sign. In the first place, the conditional *de inesse* is to be *asserted*. It is therefore to be represented by a graph drawn on the field of assertion, in which graph, the antecedent, *a*, and the consequent, *c*, shall be distinctly expressed. But neither *a* nor *c* is asserted in the assertion of the conditional proposition; and therefore neither can be written on the sheet of assertion. The only solution of this puzzle is that an enclosure, meaning an enclosing line, itself drawn on the sheet of assertion, and in a sense with its contents, nevertheless acts to cut off all that is within it from the sheet of assertion; or there may be two enclosures, one for the antecedent and the other for the consequent. In any case the antecedent and consequent must be differently enclosed, since it is one thing to say 'If *a* is true, *c* is true' and another to say 'If *c* is true, *a* is true'. This is strikingly analogous to the geometrical relation of inclusion; so much so that this metaphor is in common use to express the logical relation. It seems to be, on this account, the command of reason that one of the two compartments should be placed within the other. But which is to be the inner one? Shall we express the conditional *de inesse* by Fig. 6 or by Fig. 7?

Fig. 6   **Fig. 7**

I have preferred Fig. 7 because of the greater simplicity of the sign,—only one being necessary instead of two,—and because the transformations are, on the whole, more facile. I shall not argue the question here, however, since the argument must depend upon the developments of other sections and of another chapter; but [Alt.] shall go into the ~~subject~~ question in an appendix. [[Alt.]] [...] must remit the discussion to an appendix to the Part.

As to Fig. 7, the two seps taken together form a curve which I shall call a *scroll*; because it would be inconvenient every time it is to be mentioned to describe it as a bicyclic curve of the sixth class with an inloop. Besides, the node is of no particular significance. It may equally well be drawn as in Fig. 8.

Fig. 8

The only essential feature is that there should be two seps, of which the inner may be called the *inloop*. The node only serves to aid the mind in the interpretation, and will only be used when it will have this effect. The two compartments will be called the *inner*, or *second*, *close* and the

shall be proceeding upon a general principle whose application will never convert a true assertion into a false one. This, of course, means that so it will be in the universe of which alone we are speaking. But when we talk logic—and people occasionally insert logical remarks into ordinary discourse—our universe is that universe which embraces all others, namely THE TRUTH, so that, in such a case, we mean that in no universe whatever will the addition of the assertion of the consequent to the assertion of the antecedent be a conversion of a true proposition into a false one. But before we can express any proposition referring to a general principle, or, as we say, to a "range of possibility", we must first find means to express the simplest kind of conditional proposition the *conditional de inesse*, in which "If A is true, C is true" means only that, principle or no principle, the addition to an assertion of A of an assertion of C will not be a conversion of a true assertion into a false one. That is, it asserts that the graph of Fig. 4, anywhere on the sheet

---

outer close, the latter excluding the former. The outer close together with the loop and its contents will be called [end, sequence abandoned]] In this place, I will develop somewhat the mode of representation which I reject, and which I think everybody will reject, in order that the reader may have the materials for drawing comparisons between the two in the course of what follows.

Whichever method of expressing conditionals be used, it will sometimes be desirable to place in one of the compartments a proposition either absurd or well-understood between the graphist and his interpreter to be false, which may be called an *alogoid* proposition. ([fn:] I prefer this form, because *alogous* might be wanted to mean logically absurd.) If we say that two propositions which will always be true or false together are *equivalent*, then any alogoid proposition is equivalent to 'If anything, then everything'. For logic has no purpose unless some consequence is false; and therefore this must be well-understood between the graphist and his interpreter. In order to express an alogoid proposition, therefore, we need only an expression to which the interpreter shall be free to give any propositional meaning he pleases. Such an expression, introduced into our system of graphs, will not be a graph because it does not represent any possible state of the universe. I shall call it *the pseudograph*; for, however it be written, it remains the same in its equivalence. Since it is the assertion of all propositions, nothing can be added to it; and therefore it may be represented by blackening the whole compartment within which it is placed. Let this convention be adopted. The compartment so blackened may then be made very small or thin. Thus, in the systems of Fig. 6 and Fig. 7 respectively, Fig. 8 and Fig. 9 will express 'If *a* is true, everything is true'; that is, '*a* is not true'.

Fig. 8 **Fig. 9** **Fig. 10** **Fig. 11**

In practice, Fig. 10 would naturally be drawn in place of either Fig. 8 or Fig. 9. Following this practice, Fig. 11 will in either system be another way of writing the pseudograph.

of assertion, might be transformed into the graph of Fig. 5 without passing from truth to falsity.

a

Fig. 4

a c

Fig. 5

This conditional *de inesse* has to be expressed as a graph in such a way as distinctly to express in our system both *a* and *c*, and to exhibit their relation to one another. To assert the graph thus expressing the conditional *de inesse*, it must be drawn upon the sheet of assertion, and in this graph the expressions of *a* and of *c* must appear; and yet neither *a* nor *c* must be drawn upon the sheet of assertion. How is this to be managed? Let us draw a closed line which we may call a sep (*sæpes*, a fence), which shall cut off its contents from the sheet of assertion. Let this sep together with all that is within it, *considered as a whole*, be called an *enclosure*, this close, being written on the sheet of assertion, shall assert the conditional *de inesse*; but that which it encloses, considered separately from the sep, shall not be considered as on the sheet of assertion. Then, obviously, the antecedent and consequent must be in separate compartments of the close. In order to make the representation of the relation between them iconic, we must ask ourselves what spatial relation is analogous to their relation. Now if it be true that "If *a* is true, *b* is true" and "If *b* is true, *c* is true", then it is true that "If *a* is true, *c* is true". This is analogous to the geometrical relation of inclusion. So naturally striking is the analogy as to be (I believe) used in all languages to express the logical relation; and even the modern mind, so dull about metaphors, employs this one frequently. It is reasonable, therefore, that one of the two compartments should be placed within the other. But which shall be made the inner one? Shall we express the conditional *de inesse* by Fig. 6 or by Fig. 7? In order to decide which

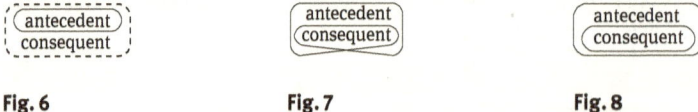

Fig. 6   Fig. 7   Fig. 8

is the more appropriate mode of representation, one should observe that the consequent of a conditional proposition asserts what is true, not throughout the whole universe of possibilities considered, but in a subordinate universe marked off by the antecedent. This is not a fanciful notion, but a truth. Now in Fig. 7, the consequent appears in a special part of the sheet representing the universe, the space between the two lines containing the definition of the sub-universe. There is no such expressiveness in Fig. 6—or, if there be, it is only of a superficial and fanciful sort. Moreover, the necessity of using two kinds of enclosing lines—a necessity which, we shall find, does not exist in Fig. 7—is a defect of Fig. 6; and when we come to consider the question of convenience, the superiority of Fig. 7 will appear still more strongly. This, then, will be the method for us to adopt.

The two seps of Fig. 7, taken together, form a curve which I shall call a *scroll*. The node is of no particular significance. The scroll may equally well be drawn as in Fig. 8. The only essential feature is that there should be two seps, of which the inner, however drawn, may be called the *inloop*. The node merely serves to aid the mind in the interpretation, and will be used only when it can have this effect. The two compartments will be called the *inner*, or *second*, *close*, and the *outer close*, the latter excluding the former. The outer close considered as containing the inloop will be called the *close*.

Convention No. 3. *An* ENCLOSURE *shall be a graph consisting of a* SCROLL *with its contents.*

The SCROLL *shall be a real curve of two closed branches, the one within the other, called seps, and the inner specifically called the* LOOP; *and these branches may or may not be joined at a node.*

The contents of the scroll shall consist of whatever is in the area enclosed by the outer sep, this area being called the close and consisting of the INNER, *or* SECOND, CLOSE, *which is the area enclosed by the loop, and the* OUTER, *or* FIRST CLOSE, *which is the area outside the loop but inside the outer sep.*

When an enclosure is written on the sheet of assertion, although it is asserted as a whole, its contents shall be cut off from the sheet, and shall not be asserted in the assertion of the whole.

But the enclosure shall assert DE INESSE *that if every graph in the outer close be true, then every graph in the inner close is true.*

It would be a grave defect in a system of diagrammatization that its operations should ever be capable of producing a diagram for the interpretation of which no provision has been made. It will be a perfection,—an elegance of reason and a possible utility,—if every visible way of putting together significant elements have a significance[.][8]

---

8 [This segment on Convention No. 3 ends abruptly here.]

Subsection 3. *Of Conventions 4 to 9*

Let a heavy dot or dash be used in place of a noun which has been erased from a proposition. A blank form of proposition produced by such erasures as can be filled, each with a proper name, to make a proposition again, is called a *rhema*, or, relatively to the proposition of which it is conceived to be a part, the *predicate* of that proposition. The following are examples of rhemata:

—is good

every man is the son of—

—loves—

God gives—to—.

Every proposition has one predicate and one only. But what that predicate is considered to be depends upon how we choose to analyze it. Thus, the proposition

God gives some good to every man

may be considered as having for its predicate either of the following rhemata:

—gives—to—

—gives some good to—

—gives—to every man

God gives—to—

God gives some good to—

God gives—to every man

—gives some good to every man

God gives some good to every man.

In the last case the entire proposition is considered as predicate. A rhema which has one blank is called a *monad*; a rhema of two blanks, a *dyad*; a rhema of three blanks, a *triad*; etc. A rhema with no blank is called a *medad*, and is a complete proposition. A rhema of more than two blanks is a *polyad*. A rhema of more than one blank is a *relative*. Every proposition has an *ultimate predicate*, produced by putting a blank in every place where a blank can be placed, without substituting for some word its definition. Were this done we should call it a *different proposition*, as a matter of nomenclature. If on the other hand, we transmute the proposition without making any difference as to what it leaves unanalyzed, we say the *expression* only is different, as, if we say,

Some good is bestowed by God on every man.

Each part of a proposition which might be replaced by a proper name, and still leave the proposition a proposition is a *subject* of the proposition.⁹ It is, however, the rhema which we have just now to attend to. A rhema is, of course, not a propo-

---

9 This, it will be remarked, makes what modern grammars call the direct and indirect objects, as well as much else, to be *subjects*; and some persons will consider this to be a bad abuse of the word *subject*. Come, let us have this out. I grant you that in polite literature usage is, not only almost, but altogether, the *arbitrium et jus et norma loquendi*. And if I am asked *whose* usage, I reply, that of the public whom you are addressing. If, with Vaugelas, you are addressing the court, then the usage of the court. If you are lecturing the riff-raff of a great city, then their usage. If anybody were to dispute this and ask me to prove it, I should reply that whatever ultimate purpose the polite littérateur may have, it is indispensable to that purpose that he should make the reading of what he writes agreeable; and in order that it may be agreeable, it is necessary that it should be easily understood by those who are addressed. But with logical writings it is different. If there be any sciences which can flourish without any words having any exact meanings, logic is not one of them. It cannot pursue its truths without a terminology of which every word shall have a single exact definition. To a great extent it already possesses such a terminology, notwithstanding the frequent abuse of its terms. But where this terminology is unsettled, to follow usage would simply be to prolong the confusion. There are conflicting individual predilections which must be made to give way; and there is only one thing to which they will consent to give way. It is some rational principle; which, stated generally, will recommend itself to all. Where are we to seek such a principle? In experience. He must profit by the experience of those sciences which have had the greatest difficulties with their terminology, and which have successfully surmounted those difficulties. Wherever this has been accomplished, it has been by adopting a rational general principle; and that principle has always been essentially the same. Any taxonomic zoölogist or botanist will tell you what it is. *He who introduces a conception into the science shall have the right and the duty of assigning to it a suitable technical expression; and whoever thereafter uses that expression, technically, in any other sense commits a grave misdemeanor*, since he thereby inflicts an injury upon the science.

Now let us apply this rule to the word 'subject'. This was made a term of logic about A.D. 500 with this definition: "Subjectum est de quo dicitur id quod prædicatur" (*Boethii Opera*, Eds. of 1546 and 1570, p. 823, in *Topica Cic[eronis]*.lib.v.). **[Alt.]** Now unless we were prepared to say that for different languages there are different doctrines of logic (which would be contrary to the essence of logic, as all will admit) we cannot, in this definition, take the preposition *de* in so narrow a sense as to exclude the grammatical accusative, dative, genitive and ablative, of the verb. For dispersed through all the families of speech there are a dozen languages which either habitually or frequently express a proposition completely without putting any noun in the nominative. Among the European languages, Gaelic is an example, in which the principal subject is most commonly put in the genitive. But the logical fact is simply that it frequently makes a difference in the sense of a proposition which of the different nouns naming objects to which the verb refers is considered to be immediately attached to the verb, which to the combination of these two, and so on. Thus, in the sentence, "Some angel gives every man some gift", the verb 'gives' is directly applied to 'some gift', making 'gives-a-gift'; then this action of gift-giving is applied to 'every man'; finally the compound 'gives-gift to every man' is applied to a certain angel; while in the sentence "A certain gift (perhaps, speech) is given to every man by some angel or other" the verb 'is given by' is applied directly to 'some angel', making 'is angel-given to', which is applied to 'every man',

sition. Supposing, however, that it be written on the sheet of assertion, so that we have to adopt a meaning for it as a proposition, what can it most reasonably be taken to mean? Take, for example, Fig. 9.

—is beautiful

—is not beautiful
Everything is true

Fig. 9

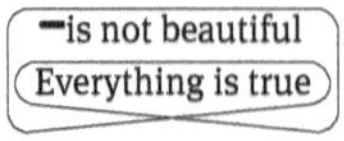

Fig. 10

and then 'is angel-given to every man' is applied to a certain gift. One sentence represents one angel as distributing gifts to all men, the other represents one gift as bestowed by one or another angel on each man. Thus, the subject-nominative is ordinarily of all the subjects the one of which the verb is least directly said. I quite admit that I use the word subject as Boëthius never contemplated its being used; but it would be destructive to science to say that a term must be applied to nothing that its originator did not contemplate its being applied to. It is the definition only that holds.

As a term of grammar, the word *subject* did not come into use until late in the XVIIIth century. It would be somewhat impertinent, therefore, for grammarians to claim that to their usage the millennial usage of those from whom they borrowed the term, must bow. [end]

[Alt.] But that which is, according to him in this passage, predicated is that which I call the *rhema*, and that to which it refers and of which it is spoken (when it is spoken) is, as will be seen, as much any one of several correlates as any other. To restrict it to that which is put in the nominative case would be to leave many propositions in various languages without a subject. For there are languages scattered through all families of speech in which it is common to use a form of sentence which does not raise one of the correlates to that special prominence which the nominative case gives to one of them. One need not go out of modern Europe to find such a language; for in Gaelic it is common to put a subject of a proposition in the genitive without there being any noun in the sentence in the nominative. Now logic remains the same, in whatever language reasoning is conducted. The usage of modern grammarians is of no weight at all in the matter. For they never used the word *subject* until long after the terminology of logic was settled. Neither Priscian nor any predecessor of his used the word; nor had any of them the precise conception now expressed by the phrase "subject nominative". The medieval logic grammarians had the concept; but their word was *suppositum*. The only passage I am able to cite from a medieval grammar in which *subjectum* is used is the following from the *Doctrinale* of Alexander de Villadi (*Noties et Extraits* XXII, 354): "Cum dicitur *[venit]* [Peirce's addition *[venit]* does not appear in the original source of de Villadi (1374) / Thurot (1868) that was in Peirce's possession.] *una sororum*, respectu huius adiectivi *una* consideratur duplex subiectum, scilicet mediatum at immediatum; mediatum voco istud subiectum *sororum*", etc. So here it is a genitive that is subject. The grammatical use is so modern that it does not occur in *The Port Royal Greek Grammar*. Of course, a grammarian of any age might speak of the subject *of a proposition*, that being a term of logic. But the "subject of a verb" is a purely grammatical term and very late.

Shall this, since it represents the universe, be taken to mean that "Something in the universe is beautiful", or that "Anything in the universe is beautiful", or that "The universe, as a whole, is beautiful"? The last interpretation may be rejected at once for the reason that we are generally unable to assert anything of the universe not reducible to one of the other forms except what is well-understood between graphist and interpreter. We have, therefore, to choose between interpreting Fig. 9 to mean "Something is beautiful" and to mean "Anything is beautiful". Each asserts the rhema of an individual; but the former leaves that individual to be designated by the grapheus, while the latter allows the rhema to fill the blank with any proper name he likes. If Fig. 9 be taken to mean "Something is beautiful", then Fig. 10 will mean "Everything is beautiful"; while if Fig. 9 be taken to mean "Everything is beautiful", then Fig. 10 will mean "Something is beautiful". In either case, therefore, both propositions will be expressible, and the main question is, which gives the most appropriate expressions? The question of convenience is subordinate, as a general rule; but in this case the difference is so vast in this respect as to give this consideration more than its usual importance.

In order to decide the question of appropriateness, we must ask which form of proposition, the universal or the particular, "Whatever salamander there may be lives in fire", or "Some existing salamander lives in fire", is more of the nature of a conditional proposition; for plainly, these two propositions differ in form from "Everything is beautiful" and "Something is beautiful" respectively, only in their being limited to a subsidiary universe of salamanders. Now to say "Any salamander lives in fire" is merely to say "If anything, X, is a salamander, X lives in fire". It differs from a conditional, if at all, only in the identification of X which it involves. On the other hand, there is nothing at all conditional in saying "There is a salamander, and it lives in fire".

Thus the interpretation of Fig. 9 to mean "Something is beautiful" is decidedly the more appropriate; and since reasonable arrangements generally prove to be the most convenient in the end, we shall not be surprised when we come to find, as we shall, the same interpretation to be incomparably the superior in that respect also.

Convention No. 4. *In this system, the unanalyzed expression of a rhema shall be called a* SPOT. *A distinct place on its periphery shall be appropriated to each blank, which place shall be called a* HOOK. *A spot with a dot at each hook shall be a graph expressing the proposition which results from filling every blank of the rhema with a separate sign of an indesignate individual existing in the universe and belonging to some determinate category, usually that of "things".*

In many reasonings it becomes necessary to write a copulative proposition in which two members relate to the same individual so as to distinguish these members. Thus we have to write such a proposition as,

A is greater than something that is greater than B,

so as to exhibit the two partial graphs of Fig. 11.

A is greater than—
—is greater than B

Fig. 11

The proposition we wish to express adds to those of Fig. 11 the assertion of the identity of the two "somethings". But this addition cannot be effected as in Fig. 12.

A is greater than—
—is greater than B
—is greater than—

Fig. 12

For the "somethings", being indesignate, cannot be described in general terms. It is necessary that the signs of them should be connected in fact. No way of doing this can be more perfectly iconic than that exemplified in Fig. 13.

A is greater than⏜
⠀⠀⠀⠀⠀⠀⠀⠀⠀is greater than B

Fig. 13

Any sign of such identification of individuals may be called a *connexus*, and the particular sign here used, which we shall do well to adopt, may be called a *line of identity*.

Convention No. 5. *Two coincident points, not more, shall denote the same individual.*

Convention No. 6. *A heavy line, called a* LINE OF IDENTITY, *shall be a graph asserting the numerical identity of the individuals denoted by its two extremities.*

The next convention to be laid down is so perfectly natural that the reader may well have a difficulty in perceiving that a separate convention is required for it. Namely, we may make a line of identity branch to express the identity of three individuals. Thus, Fig. 14 will express that some black bird is thievish. No doubt, it

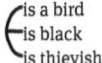

Fig. 14

would have been easy to draw up Convention No. 4 in such a form as to cover this procedure. But it is not our object in this section to find ingenious modes of statement which, being borne in mind, may serve as rules for as many different acts as possible. On the contrary, what we are here concerned to do is to distinguish all proceedings that are essentially different. Now it is plain that no number of mere biterminal bonds, each terminal occupying a spot's hook, can ever assert the identity of three things, although when we once have a three-way branch, any higher number of terminals can be produced from it, as in Fig. 15. We ought to, and must, then, make a distinct convention to cover this procedure, as follows:

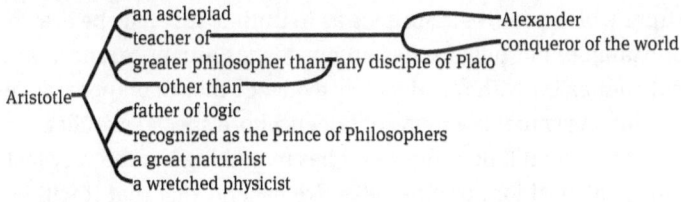

Fig. 15

Convention No. 7. *A branching line of identity shall express a triad rhema signifying the identity of the three individuals, whose designations are represented as filling the blanks of the rhema by coincidence with the three terminals of the line.*[10]

---

10 [Alt.] We now come to the only puzzling feature of this system of diagrammatization. It touches one of the inherent difficulties of logic,—and the only difficulty that logic presents until we climb to its upper atmosphere. This puzzle relates to the combination of the scroll and the connexus in one graph.

Remark how peculiar a sign the line of identity is. A sign, or, to use a more general and more definite term, a *representamen*, is of one or other of three kinds: it is either an *icon*, an *index*, or a *symbol*. An icon is a representamen of what it represents and for the mind that interprets it as such, by virtue of its being an immediate image, that is to say by virtue of characters which belong to it in itself as a sensible object, and which it would possess just the same were there no object in nature that it resembled, and though it never were interpreted as a sign. It is of the nature of an appearance, and as such, strictly speaking, exists only in consciousness, although for convenience in ordinary parlance and when extreme precision is not called for, we extend the term *icon* to the outward objects which excite in consciousness the image itself.

A geometrical diagram is a good example of an icon. A pure icon can convey no positive or factual information; for it affords no assurance that there is any such thing in nature. But it is of the utmost value for enabling its interpreter to study what would be the character of such an object in case any such did exist. Geometry sufficiently illustrates that. Of a completely opposite nature is the kind of representamen termed an *index*. This is a real thing or fact which is a sign of its object by virtue of being connected with it as a matter of fact and by also forcibly intruding upon the mind, quite regardless of its being interpreted as a sign. It may simply serve to identify its object and assure us of its existence and presence. But very often the nature of the factual connexion of the index with its object is such as to excite in consciousness an image of some features of the object, and in that way affords evidence from which positive assurance as to truth of fact may be drawn. A photograph, for example, not only excites an image, has an appearance, but, owing to its optical connexion with the object, is evidence that that appearance corresponds to a reality. A symbol is a representamen whose special significance or fitness to represent just what it does represent lies in nothing but the very fact of there being a habit, disposition, or other effective general rule that it will be so interpreted. Take, for example, the word 'man'. These three letters are not in the least like a man; nor is the sound with which they are associated. Neither is the word existentially connected with any man as an index. It cannot be so, since the word is not an existence at all. The word does not consist of three films of ink. If the word 'man' occurs hundreds of times in a book of which myriads of copies are printed, all those millions of triplets of patches of ink are embodiments of one and the same word. I call each of those embodiments a *replica* of the symbol. This

---

Attention has already been called to [the] fact that a universal categorical proposition understood as not asserting the existence of the subject,—which assertion if made is merely a particular proposition copulated with the universal proposition, "All men are mortal" being equivalent to "If it be true that a man exists, *he* is mortal". [end]

shows that the word is not a thing. What is its nature? It consists in the really working general rule that three such patches seen by a person who knows English will effect his conduct and thoughts according to a rule. Thus the mode of being of the symbol is different from that of the icon and from that of the index. An icon has such being as belongs to past experience. It exists only as an image in the mind. An index has the being of present experience. The being of a symbol consists in the real fact that something surely will be experienced if certain conditions be satisfied. Namely, it will influence the thought and conduct of its interpreter. Every word is a symbol. Every sentence is a symbol. Every book is a symbol. Every representamen depending upon conventions is a symbol. Just as a photograph is an index having an icon incorporated into it, that is, excited in the mind by its force, so a symbol may have an icon or an index incorporated into it, that is, the active law that it is may require its interpretation to involve the calling up of an image, or a composite photograph of many images of past experiences, as ordinary common nouns and verbs do; or it may require its interpretation to refer to the actual surrounding circumstances of the occasion of its embodiment, like such words as *that, this, I, you, which, here, now, yonder*, etc. Or it may be pure symbol, neither *iconic* nor *indicative*, like the words *and, or, of*, etc.

The value of an icon consists in its exhibiting the features of a state of things regarded as if it were purely imaginary. The value of an index is that it assures us of positive fact. The value of a symbol is that it serves to make thought and conduct rational and enables us to predict the future. It is frequently desirable that a representamen should exercise one of those three functions to the exclusion of the other two, or two of them to the exclusion of the third; but the most perfect of signs are those in which the iconic, indicative, and symbolic characters are blended as equally as possible. Of this sort of signs the line of identity is an interesting example. As a conventional sign, it is a symbol; and the symbolic character, when present in a sign, is of its nature predominant over the others. The line of identity is not, however, arbitrarily conventional nor purely conventional. Consider any portion of it taken arbitrarily (with certain possible exceptions shortly to be considered) and it is an ordinary graph for which Fig. 16 might perfectly well be substituted.

—is identical with—

Fig. 16

But when we consider the connection of this portion with a next adjacent portion, although the two together make up the same graph, yet the identification of the something, to which the hook of the one refers, with the something, to which the hook of the other refers, is beyond the power of any graph to effect, since a graph, as a symbol, is of the nature of a *law*, and is therefore general, while here there must be an identification of individuals. This identification is effected not by the pure symbol, but by its *replica* which is a thing. The termination of one portion and the beginning of the next portion denote the same individual by virtue of a factual connexion, and that the closest possible; for both are points, and they are one and the same point. In this respect, therefore, the line of identity is of the nature of an index. To be sure, this does not affect the ordinary parts of a line of identity, but so soon as it is even *conceived* as composed of two portions, and it is only the factual junction of the replicas of these portions that makes them refer to the same individual. The line of identity is, moreover, in the highest degree iconic. For it appears as nothing but a continuum of dots, and the fact of the identity of a thing, seen under two aspects, consists merely in the continuity of being in passing from one apparition to another. Thus uniting, as the line of identity does, the natures of symbol, index, and icon, it is fitted for playing an extraordinary part in this system of representation.

There is no difficulty in interpreting the line of identity until it crosses a sep. To interpret it in that case, two new conventions will be required.

How shall we express the proposition "Every salamander lives in fire", or "If it be true that something is a salamander then it will always be true that *that something* lives in fire"? If we omit the assertion of the identity of the somethings, the expression is obviously given in Fig. 17. To that, we wish to add the expression of individual identity. We ought to use our line of identity for that. Then, we must draw Fig. 18.

Fig. 17   **Fig. 18**

It would be unreasonable, after having adopted the line of identity as our instrument for the expression of individual identity, to hesitate to employ it in this case. Yet to regularize such a mode of expression two new conventions are required. For, in the first place, we have not hitherto had any such sign as a line of identity crossing a sep. This part of the line of identity is not a graph; for a graph must be either outside or inside of each sep. In order, therefore, to legitimate our interpretation of Fig. 18, we must agree that a line of identity crossing a sep simply asserts the identity of the individual denoted by its outer part and the individual denoted by its inner part. But this agreement does not of itself necessitate our interpretation of Fig. 18; since this might be understood to mean, "There is *something* which, if it be a salamander, lives in fire", instead of meaning, "If there be *anything* that is a salamander, it lives in fire". But although the last interpretation but one would involve itself in no positive contradiction, it would annul the convention that a line of identity crossing a sep still asserts the identity of its extremities,—not, indeed, by conflict with that convention, but by rendering it nugatory. What does it mean to assert *de inesse* that there is something, which if it be a salamander, lives in fire? It asserts, no doubt, that there is something. Now suppose that anything lives in fire. Then of that it will be true *de inesse* that if it be a salamander, it lives in fire; so that the proposition will then be true. Suppose that there is anything that is not a salamander. Then, of that it will be true *de inesse* that if it be a salamander, it lives in fire; and again the proposition will be true. It is only false in case whatever there may be is a salamander while nothing lives in fire. Consequently, Fig. 18 would be precisely equivalent to Fig. 19, and there would be no need of any line of identity's crossing a sep. It would then be impossible to express a universal categorical analytically except by resorting to an unanalytic expression of such a proposition or something substantially equivalent to that.[11]

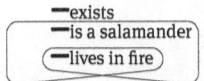

Fig. 19

Two conventions, then, are necessary. In stating them, it will be well to avoid the idea of a graph's being cut through by a sep, and confine ourselves to the effects of joining dots on the sep to dots outside and inside of it.

Convention No. 8. *Points on a sep shall be considered to lie outside the close of the sep so that the junction of such a point with any other point outside the sep by a line of identity shall be interpreted as it would be if the point on the sep were outside and away from the sep.*

Convention No. 9. *The junction by a line of identity of a point on a sep to a point within the close of the sep shall assert of such individual as is denoted by the point on the sep, according to the position of that point by Convention No. 8, a hypothetical*

---

[11] This will be proved in a later note. [Refers to the proof that a point on a sep is outside of the sep.]

conditional identity, according to the conventions applicable to graphs situated as is the portion of that line that is in the close of the sep.

It will be well to illustrate these conventions by some examples. Fig. 20 asserts that if it be true that something is good, then this assertion is false. That is, the assertion is that nothing is good. But in Fig. 21, the terminal of the line of identity on the outer sep asserts that something, X, exists, and it is only of this existing individual, X, that it is asserted that if *that* is good the assertion is false. It therefore means "Somebody is not good".

Fig. 20   **Fig. 21**

On Figs. [23] and [24], the points on the seps are marked with letters, for convenience of reference.[12] Fig. 23 asserts that some~~body~~thing, A, is a woman; and that if there is an individual, X, that is a catholic, and an individual, Y, that is identical with A,

Fig. 23   **Fig. 24**

then X adores Y; that is, Some woman is adored by all catholics, if there are any. Fig. 23 asserts that if there be an individual, X, and if X is a catholic, then X adores somebody that is a woman. That is, Whatever catholic there may be adores some woman or other. This does not positively assert that any woman exists, but only that if there is a catholic, then there is a woman whom he adores.

A triad rhema gives 26 affirmative forms of simple general propositions, as follows:

Fig. 25      Somebody blames somebody to somebody (1)

---

[12] [Figure 22 was not provided; from hereon Peirce probably misnumbered the captions out-of-sequence by one.]

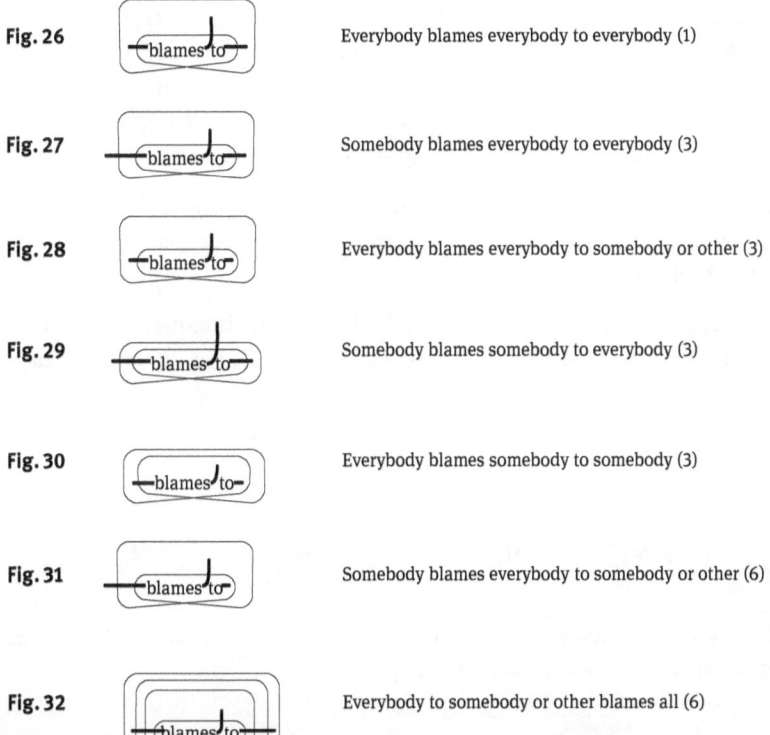

Fig. 26 — Everybody blames everybody to everybody (1)

Fig. 27 — Somebody blames everybody to everybody (3)

Fig. 28 — Everybody blames everybody to somebody or other (3)

Fig. 29 — Somebody blames somebody to everybody (3)

Fig. 30 — Everybody blames somebody to somebody (3)

Fig. 31 — Somebody blames everybody to somebody or other (6)

Fig. 32 — Everybody to somebody or other blames all (6)

Total 26. For a tetrad there are 150 such forms; for a pentad 1082; for a hexad 9366; etc.

Section ii. Derived Principles of Interpretation

Subsection 1. *Of the Pseudographs and Connected Signs*[13]

It is, as will soon appear, sometimes desirable to express a proposition either absurd, contrary to the understanding between the graphist and the interpreter, or at any rate well-known to be false. From any such proposition, as antecedent, any

---

[13] **[Alt.] Subsection 4.** *Of Convention No. 10.* The above shows all the conventions which have hitherto been thoroughly studied. It is certain that something more is needed, but it is uncertain whether it ought to be regarded as an essential part, or indeed, any part at all of this system of representation. I give it the benefit of my doubt, and here insert it.

Suppose we wish to express the algebraic principle that $(x + y) + z = (z + y) + x$. We will

proposition whatever follows as a consequent *de inesse*. Hence, every such proposition may be regarded as implying that everything is true; and consequently all such propositions are equivalent. The expression of such a proposition may very well fill the entire close in which it is, since nothing can be added to what it already implies. Hence we may adopt the following secondary convention.

Convention No. 10. *The* PSEUDOGRAPH, *or expression in this system of a proposition implying that every proposition is true, may be drawn as a black spot entirely filling the close in which it is.*

Since the size of signs has no significance, the blackened close may be drawn invisibly small. Thus Fig. 33 as in Fig. 34, or even as in Fig. 35, Fig. 36, or lastly as in Fig. 37.

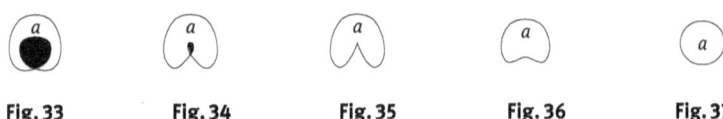

Fig. 33   **Fig. 34**   **Fig. 35**   **Fig. 36**   **Fig. 37**

---

write the letter *s* with three hooks, as in Fig. 33; to express that *w* is equal to a result of adding something equal to *u* to something equal to *v*.

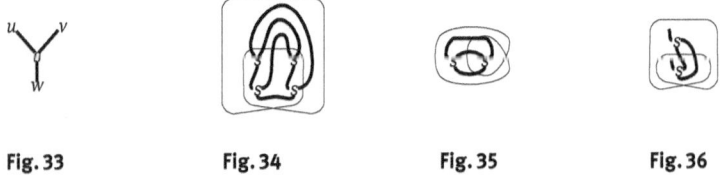

Fig. 33   **Fig. 34**   **Fig. 35**   **Fig. 36**

Then Fig. 34 expresses that, in a universe of values, whatever be the values of *x*, *y*, and *z*, there is a value, *m*, of $x + y$ such that a value, *t*, of $m + z$ is a value of $n + x$ where *n* is a value of $z + y$. Of course, a system of ~~expression~~ representation designed to express all propositions as analytically as possible cannot, from the nature of things, express the mathematical relation with the same elegance as a system designed only to express the special kind of relation in question, and that not analytically, but so as to afford the greatest convenience in transformation. Still, even making proper allowance for that, the graph of Fig. 34 does not express all that it is desirable that it should express. For of the six lines of identity, any three not meeting at one spot might occupy the outer close, the other three being in the middle close, and still the proposition is true, if negative quantities are admitted into the universe. To state this in our notation would require sixteen propositions. They all follow logically, however, from the graph of Fig. 34 by the aid of Figs. 35 and 36, of which the former expresses the commutativeness of addition and the latter the existence of negative quantities. But in order to follow out such a discussion concerning this graph and others, and to prove the results by the use of this very notation, in order to analyze its nature, [end, alternative fragment abandoned]

Interpretational Corollary 1. *A scroll with its contents having the pseudograph in the inner close is equivalent to the precise denial of the contents of the outer close.*

For the assertion, as in Fig. 33, that *de inesse* if *a* is true everything is true, is equivalent to the assertion that *a* is not true, since if the conditional proposition *de inesse* be true *a* cannot be true, and if *a* is not true the conditional proposition *de inesse*, having *a* for its antecedent, is true. Hence the one is always true or false with the other, and they are equivalent.

This corollary affords additional justification for writing Fig. 33 as in Fig. 37, since the effect of the loop enclosing the pseudograph is to make a precise denial of the absurd proposition, and to deny the absurd is equivalent to asserting nothing.

Interpretational Corollary 2. *A disjunctive proposition may be expressed by placing its members in as many inloops of one sep. But this will not exclude the simultaneous truth of several members or of all.*

Thus, Fig. 38 will express that either *a* or *b* or *c* or *d* or *e* is true. For it will deny the simultaneous denial of all.

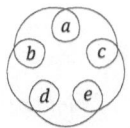

Fig. 38

Interpretational Corollary 3. *A graph may be interpreted by copulations and disjunctions. Namely, if a graph within an odd number of seps be said to be* ODDLY ENCLOSED, *and a graph within no sep or an even number of seps be said to be* EVENLY ENCLOSED, *then spots in the same compartment are copulated when evenly enclosed, and disjunctively combined when oddly enclosed; and any line of identity whose outermost part is evenly enclosed refers to* SOMETHING, *and any one whose outermost part is oddly enclosed refers to* ANYTHING *there may be. And the interpretation must begin outside of all seps and proceed inward. And spots evenly enclosed are to be taken affirmatively; those oddly enclosed negatively.*

For example, Fig. 18 may be read, Anything whatever is either not a salamander or lives in fire. Fig. 23 may be read, Something, A, is a woman, and whatever X may be, either X is not a catholic or X adores A. Fig. 24 may be read, Whatever X may be, either X is not a catholic or there is something Y, such that X adores Y and Y is a woman. Fig. 32 may be read, Whatever A may be, there is something C, such that whatever B may be, A blames B to C. Fig. 39 may be read, Whatever X and Y may be, either X is not a saint or Y is not a saint or X loves Y; that is, Every saint there may be loves every saint. So Fig. 40 may be read, Whatever X and Y may be, either X is not best or Y is not best or X is identical with Y; that is, there are not two bests. Fig. 41 may be read, Whatever X and Y may be, either X does not love Y or Y does not love X; that is, no two love each other. Fig. 42 may be read, Whatever X and Y may be either X does not love Y or there is something L and X is not L but Y loves L; that is, nobody loves anybody who does not love somebody else.

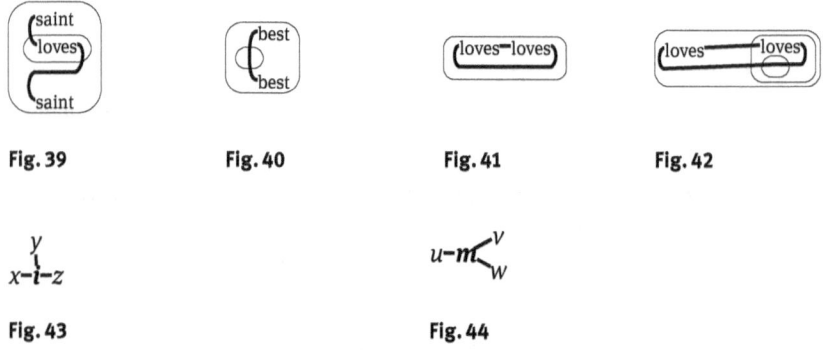

Fig. 39   Fig. 40   Fig. 41   Fig. 42

Fig. 43   Fig. 44

Interpretational Corollary 4. *A sep which is vacant except for a line of identity traversing it expresses with its contents the non-identity of the extremities of that line.*

Subsection 2. *Of Selectives and Proper Names*

It is sometimes impossible upon an ordinary surface to draw a graph so that lines of identity will not cross one another.[14] If, for example, we express that x is a value that can result from raising z to the power whose exponent is y, by means of Fig. 43, and express that u is a value that can result from multiplying w by v, by Fig. 44,

---

14 [Determining the precise cases when this is so has been a difficult problem in graph theory. Known in its puzzle teaser form as "The Three Utilities Problem" since *The Strand Magazine* of 1913, the problem is about how to connect a number of vertices in a mathematical graph without the edges connecting them to cross. Given a graph, is there an effective method to rearrange the lines by insertions and deletions so that there are no intersecting lines (that is, the graph is planar), without having to draw the graph from the beginning? This question was answered only in late 2019 (Holm & Rotenberg 2019). Peirce's graph in Fig. 45 illustrates the unsolvability of the Three Utilities Problem for four vertices (spots).]

then in order to express that whatever values x, y, and z may be, there is a value resulting from raising x to a power whose exponent is a value of the product of z by y which same value is also one of the values resulting from raising to the power z a value resulting from raising x to the power y (this being one of the propositions expressed by the equation $x^{(y^z)} = (x^y)^z$) we may draw Fig. 45; but there is an unavoidable intersection of two lines of identity.

 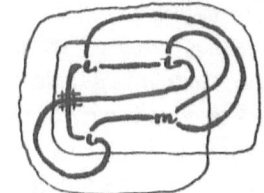

Fig. 45 [P.H. on the right]

In such a case, and indeed, in any case in which the lines of identity become too intricate to be perspicuous, it is advantageous to replace some of them by signs of a sort that in this system are called *selectives*. A selective is very much of the same nature as a proper name; for it denotes an individual and its outermost occurrence denotes a wholly indesignate individual of a certain category (generally a thing) existing in the universe, just as a proper name, on the first occasion of hearing it, conveys no more. But just as on any subsequent hearing of a proper name the hearer identifies it with that individual concerning which he has some information, so all occurrences of the selective other than the outermost must be understood to denote that identical individual. If, however, the outermost occurrence of any given selective is oddly enclosed, then, on that first occurrence the selective will refer to any individual whom the interpreter may choose, and in all other occurrences to the same individual. If there be no one outermost occurrence then any one of those that are outermost may be considered as the outermost. The later capital letters are used for selectives.

For example, Fig. 45 is otherwise expressed in Figs. 46 and 47.

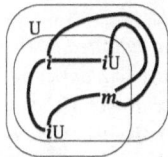 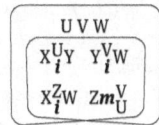

Fig. 46   **Fig. 47**

Fig. 47 may be read, "Either no value is designated as U, or no value is designated as V, or no value is designated as W, or else a value designated as Y results from raising W to the V power, and a value designated as Z results from multiplying U by V, and a value designated as X results from raising Y to the U power, while this same value X results from raising W to the Z power".

Convention No. 11. *The capital letters of the alphabet shall be used to denote single individuals of a well-understood category, the individual existing in the universe, the early letters preferably as proper names of well-known individuals, the later letters, called* SELECTIVES, *each on its first occurrence,*[15] *as the name of an* INDIVIDUAL *(that is, an object existing in the universe in a well-understood category, that is, having such a mode of being as to be determinate in reference to every character as wholly possessing it or else wholly wanting it), but an individual that is* INDESIGNATE *(that is, which the interpreter receives no warrant for identifying); while in every occurrence after the first, it shall denote that same individual.*

Of two occurrences of the same selective, either one may be interpreted as the earlier if and only if enclosed by no sep that does not enclose the other.

A selective at its first occurrence shall be asserted in the mode proper to the compartment in which it occurs.

If it be on that occurrence evenly enclosed, it is only affirmed to exist under the same conditions under which any graph in the same close is asserted; and it is then asserted, under those conditions, to be the subject filling the rhema-blank corresponding to any hook against which it may be placed.

If, however, at its first occurrence, it be oddly enclosed, then, in the disjunctive mode of interpretation, it will be denied, subject to the conditions proper to the close in which it occurs, so that its existence being disjunctively denied, a non-existence will be affirmed, and as a subject, it will be UNIVERSAL *(that is, freed from the condition of wholly possessing or wholly wanting each character) and at the same time*

---

15 [Alt.1] [...] *first occurrence, in case it be evenly enclosed, as the name of a* WHOLLY INDESIGNATE INDIVIDUAL *which it rests with the grapheus to identify (if he has not done so), this individual existing in a well-understood category of the universe* [end]

[Alt.2] [...] *first occurrence, as the name of a* WHOLLY INDESIGNATE INDIVIDUAL *of the well-understood category, existing in the universe (unless it be denied) and of two different occurrences of the same name, that one shall be interpreted as the earlier which is less enclosed. Every occurrence of such a name, when evenly enclosed, shall assert, under the conditions indicated by the enclosing line, that an existing individual is so* DESIGNATED, *and that it fills the rhema-blank corresponding to the hook against which it may be placed; and consequently every occurrence of such a name, when oddly enclosed, shall assert, subject to the conditions of enclosure, either that there is no individual to be so designated or that whatever such there may be does not fill the rhema-blank corresponding to the hook against which it is placed.*

DESIGNATE *(that is, the interpreter will be warranted in identifying it with whatever the context may allow), and it will be (subject to the conditions of the close) disjunctively denied to be the subject filling the rhema-blank of the hook against which it may be placed.*

In all subsequent occurrences it shall denote the individual with which the interpreter may, on its first occurrence, have identified it, and otherwise will be interpreted as on its first occurrence.

Resort must be had to the examples to trace out the sense of this long abstract statement; and the line of identity will aid in explaining the equivalent selectives. Fig. 48 may be read, There exists something that may be called X and it is good. Fig. 49, the precise denial of Fig. 48, may be read "Either there is not anything to be called X or whatever there may be is not good", or "Anything you may choose

X is good   (X is good)

Fig. 48   **Fig. 49**

to call X is not good", or "all things are non-good". "Anything" is not an individual subject, since the two propositions, "Anything is good" and "Anything is bad", do not exhaust the possibilities. Both may be false.

Convention No. 12. *The use of selectives may be avoided, where it is desired to do so, by drawing parallels on both sides of the lines of identity where they appear to cross.*

Thus Fig. 50 asserts that a person whose mother makes a match between two persons to one of whom his father makes a present accuses the other of stealing it.

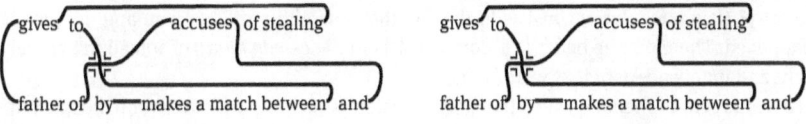

Fig. 50   **Fig. 51**

But Fig. 51 represents the accuser to be himself or herself the spouse of the person accused as well as the person to whom the present was made.

Subsection 3. *Of Abstraction and Entia Rationis*[16]

The term *abstraction* bears two utterly different meanings in philosophy. In one sense it is applied to a psychological act by which, for example, on seeing a theatre, one is led to call up images of other theatres which blend into a sort of composite in which the special features of each are obliterated. Such obliteration is called precissive abstraction. We shall have nothing to do with abstraction in that sense. But when that fabled old doctor, being asked why opium put people to sleep, answered that it was because opium has a dormitive virtue, he performed this act of immediate inference:

> Opium causes people to sleep;
> Hence, Opium possesses a power of causing sleep.

The peculiarity of such inference is that the conclusion relates to something,—in this case, a power—that the premiss says nothing about; and yet the conclusion is necessary. *Abstraction*, in the sense in which it will here be used, is a necessary inference whose conclusion refers to a subject not referred to by the premiss; or

---

16 [Alt.] Subsection 3. *Of Abstraction, Entia Rationis, and allied matters.* [This alternative sequence was to directly follow Convention 12 of the main sequence.] *Abstraction* is a mode of illative transformation of a proposition such that the conclusion has a subject that was not referred to be the premiss, as

> Opium makes whoever takes it sleep;
> Hence, Opium has a dormitive virtue.

A subject which can only be known by abstraction is said to denote an *ens rationis*. Every symbol is an *ens rationis*. On every page of English there are something like a dozen *the*s. All those *the*s are one and the same word. What is that word? What is its mode of being but that of a habit, of a regularity? Now a regularity consists in the fact that something *will* happen, and not merely has happened. Therefore the being of a word consists in the *esse in futuro* of something entirely different and independent of that word.

There are certain rhemata which though predicated of existing individuals and though helping to convey positive information concerning those existents, nevertheless signify what they signify only concerning signs. A striking example is the line of identity which is a dyad rhema without which, or some equivalent for it, it is impossible to convey any information concerning existents. Yet it signifies only identity, which is plainly a relation between two signs of the same thing, not a factual relation between things. These rhemata are called *rhemata of second intention*. They are the special concern of logic. Avicenna, and after him many scholastics, as Raymund Lully, Scotus, Burleigh, and Armandus de Bello Visu, make logic to be the science of second intentions; while Durandus á Sancto Porciano, followed by Gratiadeus Esculanus makes it relate to *entia rationis*. All the rhemata of second intention ought to be provided with special signs in the system.

it may be used to denote the characteristic of such inference. But how can it be that a conclusion should necessarily follow from a premiss which does not assert the existence of that whose existence is affirmed by it, the conclusion itself? The reply must be that the new individual spoken of is an *ens rationis*; that is, its being consists in some other fact. Whether or not an *ens rationis* can *exist* or be *real*, is a question not to be answered until existence and reality have been very distinctly defined. But it may be noticed at once, that to deny every mode of being to anything whose being consists in some other fact would be to deny every mode of being to tables and chairs, since the being of a table depends on the being of the atoms of which it is composed, and not *vice versâ*.

Every symbol is an *ens rationis*, because it consists in a habit, in a regularity; now every regularity consists in the future conditional occurrence of facts not themselves that regularity. Many important truths are expressed by propositions which relate directly to symbols or to ideal objects of symbols, not to realities. If we say that two walls collide, we express a real relation between them, meaning by a

---

The medads of second intention are the proposition which is always true, ~~expressed~~ asserted by every blank space of the sheet of assertion, and the pseudograph which is never true.

The monads of second intention may be written as in Figs. 50 and 51, the former expressing "—is itself", the latter the negative of this. The blank may be considered as equivalent to Fig. 50. So likewise may a dot •.

Of dyadic relations of second intention four are prominent:
- The relation which everything bears to everything else, expressed by Fig. 52 and also by the blank;
- The relation which everything bears to everything else; expressed by Fig. 53;
- The relations which everything bears to itself alone, expressed by the line of identity;
- and the *pseudo-relation* (not properly a relation) which nothing bears to anything, expressed by Fig. 54. An equivalent sign is an empty sep with surrounding blank.

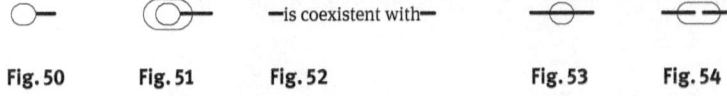

Fig. 50   Fig. 51   Fig. 52   Fig. 53   Fig. 54

A *real relation* such as is expressed by a *spot* (which, by its definition has its hooks *upon its periphery*) implies the existence of its correlates. But a sep with its contents having oddly enclosed hooks does not express a relation between real objects but, on the contrary, says of any possible *assertion* of a relation that it is not true. It thus relates to a symbol, not to an existent.

We can perfectly well talk of a universe of mixed ~~things and words~~ existents and symbols. There is no absolute need of distinguishing between them as individuals, for the reason that what is said of them will sufficiently distinguish between them. For no symbol can be said to be identical with or to be in any real relation with an existent without absurdity. Still, we may as well provide ourselves with means to distinguish the two categories. We may use a dotted boundary round the symbol for this purpose.

real relation one which involves the existence of its correlates. If we say that a ball is red, we express a positive quality of feeling really connected with the ball. But if we say that the ball is not blue, we simply express,—as far as the direct expression goes,—a relation of inapplicability between the predicate blue, and the ball or the sign of it. So it is with every negation. Now it has already been shown that every universal proposition involves a negation, at least, when it is expressed as an existential graph. On the other hand almost every graph expressing a proposition not universal has a line of identity. But identity, though expressed by the line as a dyadic relation, is not a relation between two things, but between two representamens of the same thing.

Every rhema whose blanks may be filled by signs of ordinary individuals, but which signifies only what is true of symbols of those individuals, without any reference to qualities of sense, is termed a *rhema of second intention*.[17] For *second intention* is thought about thought as symbol. Second intentions and certain *entia rationis* demand the special attention of the logician. Avicenna defined logic as the science of second intentions, and was followed in this view by some of the most acute logicians, such as Raymund Lully, Duns Scotus, Walter Burleigh, and Armandus de Bello Visu; while the celebrated Durandus á Sancto Porciano, followed by Gratiadeus Esculanus, made it relate exclusively to *entia rationis*, and quite rightly.

Interpretational Corollary 5. *A blank, considered as a medad, expresses what is well-understood between graphist and interpreter to be true; considered as a monad, it expresses '—exists' or '—is true'; considered as a dyad, it expresses '—coexists with—' or 'and'.*

Interpretational Corollary 6. *An empty sep with its surrounding blank, as in Fig. 52, is the pseudograph. Whether it be taken as medad, monad or dyad, for which purpose it will be written as in Figs. 53, 54, it is the denial of the blank.*

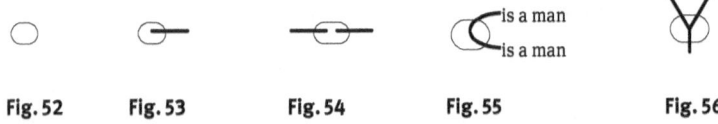

Fig. 52   Fig. 53   Fig. 54   Fig. 55   Fig. 56

---

17 [Alt.] Every combination of parts of a proposition involves a rhema of second intention. If two propositions agree exactly in respect to their rhemata of second intention, differing consequently only in respect to their simple rhemata of first-intention, they are said to have the same *logical form*. If two propositions have precisely corresponding rhemata of second intention, though these are not necessarily the same, they are said to have the same *scheme*.

Interpretational Corollary 7. *A line of identity traversing a sep will signify non-identity. Thus Fig. 55 will express that there are at least two men.*

Interpretational Corollary 8. *A branching point of a line of identity enclosed in a sep, as in Fig. 56 will express that three individuals are not all identical.*

We now come to another kind of graphs which may go under the general head of second-intentional graphs.

Convention No. 13. *The letters $\rho_0, \rho_1, \rho_2, \rho_3$, etc. each with a number of hooks greater by one than the subscript number, may be taken as rhemata signifying that the individuals joined to the hooks, other than the one vertically above the ρ taken in their order clockwise are capable of being asserted of the rhema indicated by the line of identity joined vertically to the ρ.*

Thus, Fig. 57 expresses that there is a relation in which every man stands to some woman to whom no other man stands in the same relation; that is, there is a woman corresponding to every man or, in other words, there are at least as many women as men.[18] The dotted lines between which, in Fig. 57, the line of identity denoting the *ens rationis* is placed, are by no means necessary.

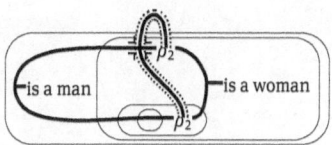

Fig. 57

[P.H.]

Convention No. 14. *The line of identity representing an* ENS RATIONIS *may be placed between two rows of dots, or it may be drawn in ink of another colour, and any graph which is to be spoken of as a thing may be enclosed in a dotted oval with a dotted line attached to it. Other* ENTIA RATIONIS *may be treated in the same way, the patterns of the dotting being varied for those of different category.*

---

18 [The cardinality property of 'at least as many as' indeed is non-elementary, and requires expression in a fragment of second-order logic.]

The graph of Fig. 58 is an example.[19] It may be read, as follows: "Euclid enunciates it as a postulate that if two straight lines are cut by a third straight line so that those angles the two make with the third, these angles lying between the first two lines (τάς ἐτός γονίας) and on the same side of the third, are less than two right angles, then that those two lines shall meet on that same side; and in this enunciation, by a side, μέρη, of the third line must be understood a part of a plane that contains that third line, which part is bounded by that line and by the infinitely distant parts of the plane".

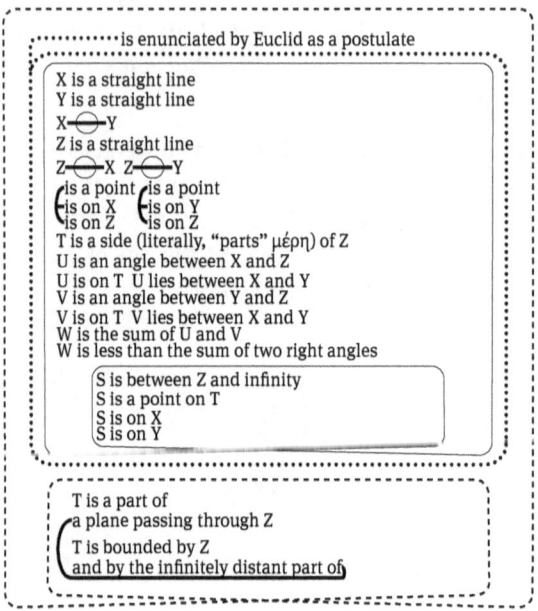

Fig. 58

Euclid's words, literally translated are as follows: [It is postulated] "that if a straight line incident upon two straight lines make the angles that are inside and on the same parts less than two right angles, then those two straight lines being prolonged to infinity shall meet on what parts, the angles were less than two right angles".

---

[19] [The graph of Fig. 58 was erroneously reproduced in the *Collected Papers of Charles S. Peirce* (CP 4.471, Fig. 120). See also a holograph image of the original graph appended to the present selection.]

Section iii

Recapitulation[20]

The principles of interpretation may now be restated more concisely and more comprehensibly. In this *resumé*, it will be assumed that selectives, which should be regarded as a mere abbreviating device, and which constitute a serious exception to the general idea of the system, are not used. A person, learning to use the

---

20 [Alt.1] **Section iii. Recapitulation.** The principles of interpretation of this system of existential graphs may now be restated more concisely and more comprehensively, as follows:
1. The writing of a proposition on the sheet of assertion unenclosed asserts it, independently of anything else.
2. The writing of a name unenclosed ~~asserts~~ affirms the existence of something to which that name applies.
3. A dot or point of a heavy line denotes an existing individual.
4. A dot in the blank of a rhema is the subject filling that blank.
5. An unenclosed sep precisely denies what its entire contents would assert, if written unenclosed.
6. A heavy line asserts the identity of all its points; but no heavy line is to be understood as ~~crossing~~ cutting a sep.
7. The junction of a point within a sep to a point on the sep limits the denial that would be made if the former point were unjoined to the latter so that it only applies to the individual denoted by the latter point.
8. Whatever is enclosed by a dotted line is an *ens rationis*.
9. If a dotted line forms a close, what is in the loop is asserted to be a partial or complete interpretation of what is in the outer close.
10. The sheet of assertion may be conceived to have in[finite extension] [end]

[Alt.2] **Section iii. Recapitulation.** The principles of interpretation may now be restated more concisely and more comprehensively.
1. The writing of a proposition unenclosed on the sheet of assertion is to be understood as asserting it, independently of anything else that may be written. ([fn:] This supposes that selectives, which do not form a regular part of the system, are not used. For a graph containing a selective will not be independent of another partial graph which contains the first introduction of the selective. There is no such dependence when lines of identity are used, because the point of such line on a sep renders the whole enclosure an assertion independent of anything outside of it.)
2. The sheet may be imagined to extend to infinity and whatever we are prepared to assert but have not written may be imagined to be written on very remote parts of the sheet.
3. An unenclosed sep precisely denies what its entire contents would affirm if written unenclosed.
4. Every points of a heavy line denotes an indesignate individual, and drawn unenclosed, affirms the existence of that individual, while the continuity of the line asserts that all its points denote the same individual.
5. The disjunctive denial of the existence of any individual which would be made by the enclosure of a point of a heavy line within a sep will, by the junction of that point by means

system and not yet thoroughly expert in it, might be led to doubt whether every proposition is capable of being expressed without selectives. For a line of identity cannot identify two individuals within enclosures outside of one another without passing out of both enclosures, while a selective is not subject to that restriction. It can be shown, however, that this restriction is of no importance nor even helps to render thought clear.[21] Suppose then that two designations of individuals are to be identified, each being within a separate nest of seps, and the two nests being within a common nest of outer seps. The question is whether this identification can always be properly effected by a line of identity that passes out of the two separate nests of seps, and if desired, still farther out. The answer is plain enough when we consider that, having to say something of individuals some to be named by the grapheus [and] others by the graphist, we can perfectly well postpone what we have to say until all these individuals are indicated, that is to say, the order in which they are to be specified by one and the other party. But if this be done, these individuals will first appear, even if selectives are used, in one nest of seps entirely outside of all the spots; and then these selectives can be replaced by lines of identity.

The respect in which[22] selectives violate the general idea of the system is this; the outermost occurrence of each selective has a different significative force from every other occurrence,—a grave fault, if it be avoidable, in any system of regular

---

of a heavy line to a heavily marked point on the sep, be limited so as only to apply to the individual denoted by the latter point.
6. That which may be enclosed within a dotted line is to be understood as an *ens rationis*.

21 [See R 430, LoF 1; cf. Bellucci, Liu & Pietarinen 2020, on this question of non-planar graphs with lines escaping to third dimension to avoid crossing the cuts.]
22 [Alt.] [...] The respect in which selectives break with the general idea of this system is that in consequence of the outermost occurrence having an altogether different signification from any other occurrence (so that there is an ambiguity in these signs considered in themselves without their relations to one another) assertions on different parts of the sheet of assertion are not always independent of one another. With the lines of identity this fault is avoided by their having at the very sep itself the same signification that they have outside the sep.

Rejecting the selectives, the principles of interpretation can be reduced to half a dozen as follows.
1. The writing of a proposition unenclosed on the sheet of assertion is to be understood as asserting it, independently of anything else that may be written except that any line of identity of one part that is joined to such a line of the other part is [at] the junction asserted to be the same.
2. The writing of a rhema unenclosed asserts it of an indesignate individual for each blank of the rhema.
3. An unenclosed sep precisely denies that which its entire contents would, if unenclosed, affirm.

and exact representation. The consequence is that the meaning of a partial graph containing a selective depends upon whether or not there be another part, which may be written on a remote part of the sheet in which the same selective occurs farther out. But the idea of this system is that assertions written upon different parts of the sheet should be independent of one another, if, and only if, they have no common part. When lines of identity are used to the exclusion of selectives, no such inconvenience can occur, because each line of one partial graph will retain precisely the same significative force, no matter what part outside of it be removed (though if a line be broken, the identity of the individuals denoted by its two parts will no longer be affirmed); and even if everything outside a sep be removed (the sep being unbreakable by any removal of a partial graph, or part which written alone would express a proposition), still there remains a point on the sep which retains the same force as if the line had been broken quite outside and away from the sep.

Rejecting the selectives, then, the principles of interpretation reduce themselves to simple form, as follows:

1. The writing of a proposition on the sheet of assertion unenclosed is to be understood as asserting that proposition; and that, independently of any other proposition on the sheet, except so far as the two may have some part or point in common.
2. A "spot", or unanalyzed expression of a rhema upon this system, has upon its periphery a place called a "hook" appropriated to every blank of the rhema; and whenever it is written a heavily marked point occupies each hook. Now every heavily marked point, whether isolated or forming a part of a heavy line, denotes an indesignate individual, and being unenclosed affirms the existence of some such individual; and if it occupy a hook of a spot it is the corresponding subject of the rhema signified by the spot. A heavy line is to be understood as asserting, when unenclosed, that all its points denote the same individual, so that any portion of it may be regarded as a spot.

---

4. No heavy line crosses a sep; and every point of a heavy line denotes an indesignate individual, and drawn unenclosed, affirms the existence of that individual, while the continuity of the line asserts that all its points denote the same individual.
5. The disjunctive denial of the existence of any individual which would be made by the enclosure of a heavy line within a sep will, by the junction of a point of that line, by means of a heavy line, to a heavily marked point on the sep itself, be so limited as to apply only to the individual denoted by the latter point.
6. That which is enclosed within a heavy line is to be understood as an *ens rationis*.

3. A sep, or lightly drawn oval, when unenclosed, is with its contents (the whole being called an *enclosure*) a graph, entire or partial, which precisely denies the proposition which the entire graph within it would, if unenclosed affirm. Since, therefore, an entire graph, by the above principles, copulatively asserts all the partial graphs of which it is composed and takes every indesignate individual, denoted by a heavily marked point that may be a part of it, in the sense of "something", it follows that an unenclosed enclosure disjunctively denies all the partial graphs which compose the contents of its sep and takes every heavily marked point included therein in the sense of "anything" whatever.

Consequently, if an enclosure is oddly enclosed, its evenly enclosed contents are copulatively affirmed while if it be evenly enclosed, its oddly enclosed contents are disjunctively denied.

4. A heavily marked point upon a sep, or line of enclosure, is to be regarded as no more enclosed than any point just outside of and away from the sep and is to be interpreted accordingly. But the effect of joining a heavily marked point within a sep to such a point upon the sep itself by means of a heavy line is to limit the disjunctive denial of existence, which is the effect of the sep upon the point within it, to the individual denoted by the point upon the sep. No heavy line is to be regarded as cutting a sep; nor can any graph be partly within a sep and partly outside of it; although the entire enclosure (which is not inside the sep) may be part of a graph outside of the sep.

5. A dotted oval is sometimes used to show that that which is within it is to be regarded as an *ens rationis*.

[Appendix.] The Rules of Existential Graphs[23]

Preface. The system of existential graphs is intended to afford a method for the analysis of all necessary reasonings into their ultimate elements. No transformations are permitted except *insertions* and *omissions*, and the result of series of permissible insertions and omissions. The peculiar formal signs are the fewest with which it is possible to represent all the operations of necessary reasonings.

The system was invented in January 1897. *The Monist* refused to publish an account of it.

---

[23] [What Peirce advertises as the "Appendix" is not found in R 492. The following glossary, undated but most likely written later than the main text and perhaps in mid-1904, is taken from R 1589 and is transcribed here in its entirety. The text of R 492 resumes at "Chapter II".]

The Nomenclature. A **graph** is a diagrammatic symbol composed of spots with bonds joining some of them. The spots have usually various qualities called their **colors,** the bonds are sometimes of two or more appearances; but commonly the only distinction is between pairs of spots joined by lines and pairs of spots who[se] relation is expressed by the absence of lines. In this system the character of some of the spots is analyzed, there being other complete graphs within them.

These graphs are called **existential** because the putting upon the sheet of paper or other surface used of a graph signifying a given character means that *something* having that character *exists* in the universe which that sheet or surface represents.

But by a *graph* in this system is meant, a type of a sign which according to the conventions of this system would express a proposition, this type being determinate in all its significant features that are internal, that is regardless of its concomitants, but being indeterminate in all features which are in themselves insignificant. An individual existing embodiment of such a type is called a **graph-instance,** or a[n] **instance** of a graph. I formerly called it a **replica,** forgetting that Mr. Kempe, in his Memoir on Mathematical Forms, § 170, had already preempted this word as a technical term relating to graphs, and that in a highly appropriate sense, while my sense was not at all appropriate. I therefore am glad to abandon this term.[24]

A graph may be said to describe a logically possible state of the universe, though of course it describes it partially in the extreme. If a type of symbol is put together of elements significant in the system, but involves a logical impossibility, say a contradiction, it does not describe a possible state of the universe and I should not say that it expressed a proposition, al[though] I should be peculiar in this terminology. At any rate, it is then no longer, strictly speaking, a *graph*, but may be called **the pseudograph.**

The following examples will illustrate my use of the word graph. A and Ⓐ have the same meaning, or import; for when either is true so is the other, but I do not call them the same graph. Nor are A and AA the same graph. But *a*— and *a*——

---

[24] [Peirce's marginal note on one of his preserved copies of the *Syllabus* (R 1600, No. 1) states that "I abandon this inappropriate term *replica*, Mr. Kempe having already (*Math. Form* § 170) given it another meaning. I now call this an *instance*". This note is repeated, nearly verbatim, on the second preserved offprint of the *Syllabus* from R 1600. Peirce uses the term "graph-replica" consistently throughout the 1903 Lowell Lectures until at least the final drafts of the first lecture composed in the first week of December. The term "graph-instance" appears in the writings preserved from late 1904, such as R 280, "The Basis of Pragmaticism" (LoF 3), as well as in the glossary of terms (R 1589), editorially proposed to be appended to *Logical Tracts No. 2* but likely to have been composed slightly later around mid-1904. The marginal note itself may thus be an insertion from late 1903.]

may be regarded as the same graph since the length of the line is insignificant. On the other hand, since a line is a graph of itself, if we choose to regard a——— as composed of a— and ———, it is from that point of view not the same graph as a—. The graph a is the same graph as the a in ⓐ, although it now means, or may be regarded as meaning, something very different. But external circumstances are not to be considered.

To **scribe** a graph is to embody it in an instance by means of a graphical act.

The **sheet**, or **sheet of assertion**, or **actual sheet**, is that surface upon which any graph that may be scribed will be understood to be thereby asserted of the universe. It is so much of the surface originally appropriated to this purpose as remains unoccupied after part of it has been occupied by instances of scribed graphs. The surface originally so appropriated is called the **original sheet**, as opposed to the *actual sheet*.

When a graph is scribed upon the sheet, although every part of the surface covered by the graph-instance is thereby severed from the sheet, yet the outline of the graph-instance must be conceived to be part of the actual sheet as so cut down, and the whole graph-instance in its entirety is said to lie *on* the actual sheet, as does every part of it which borders upon the actual sheet.

A **cut** is a fine oval line which is not said to be scribed, but **graven**. The whole surface within the oval is called the **original area** of the cut. The surface from which the cut severs its original area is called the **place** of the cut. The cut itself is *on* its place.

Graphs may be scribed on the area of the cut, and the **actual area** of the cut is so much of the original area as remains vacant, including the outlines of whatever graph-instances may be scribed on the area. Although only their outlines are on the actual area, yet each graph-instance which borders upon that area is regarded as lying, in its entirety, on the actual area.

The term **area** is also extended to the actual sheet of assertion.

A cut together with its area and whatever lies upon that area, regarded as a whole is a graph-instance called the **enclosure** of **the cut**.

Any graph-instance which is not entirely composed of two or more graph-instances lying one without the other on the same area is called a **spot**. Thus, an enclosure is a spot. No two spots can overlap each other or have intersecting outlines.

Any vacant part of an area may be regarded as an instance of a graph called **the blank**. But such a graph-instance is not regarded as cutting down the area, as a scribed or graven outline of a graph-instance cuts it down. Evidently no vacant part of an area can be a spot.

The blank is called a **natural graph**, as opposed to an **artifact graph**, which is a graph composed of spots.

The entire contents of an area considered as one graph-instance is called the **entire** graph-instance of the area. Parts of it that are graph-instances are called **partial** graph-instances. The graphs of entire and partial graph-instances are called **entire** and **partial** graphs of the areas. We also speak of entire and partial artifact graphs and graph-instances.

Every graph-instance must lie wholly on a single area.

One cut may be enclosed within another. A graph-instance on the sheet or within an even number of cuts is said to be **evenly enclosed**; but if within an odd number of cuts, it is said to be **oddly enclosed**.

A cut whose entire area is shaded is thereby represented to have all possible graphs scribed upon that area, which is thereby entirely occupied, so that no area remains; and the enclosure of the cut is then said to be **obliterated**.

An **atom** is a graph which has no parts separately significant and united according to the conventions of this system. But most atoms have one or more points upon their outlines where alone their instances may be in significant contact with other graph-instances; and these are called the **valencies** of the graph, and the **hooks** of its instances. The different valencies of a graph have generally different significances.

A peculiar graph in the form of a heavy line is **the line of identity**. It has two valencies, one at either end. Any instance of it is called a **line**, simply. A line may end at the hook of another graph-instance or at an otherwise vacant place, or the line being on the area of a cut may terminate at that cut; in which case, it creates a hook of the enclosure at that point.

Ligature is a name given to a line which is not generally a graph-instance but is a line or collection of lines each in contact with one of the others at an end common to the two on a cut; and the ligature is the whole series of such lines.

The **teridentity** is a graph consisting of the dot in which three lines meet at their ends.[25] Any number, N, of instances of teridentity may sensibly coincide so that $N + 2$ lines will diverge from one point.

An atom with no valency is called a **medad**. An atom with 1, 2, 3, 4, 5, 6, 7, 8, etc. valencies is called (respectively) a *monad, dyad, tetrad, pentad, hexad, heptad, octad*, etc. An atom with more than two valencies is called a **polyad**.

A capital letter used as a monad (best with its valency) beneath is called an **individual** graph. If the letter is one of the early letters of the alphabet, it is usually a **definite individual** graph, or **singular**, or a **nomen**. If it is one of the late letters of the alphabet it is usually an **indefinite individual graph** or **seligible**. In that case,

---

25 [See R 2 (Selection 40) for an equivalent definition of the teridentity as the "dot" at which "three lines meet", namely a "dot of teridentity".]

it cannot occur, at least as for its outermost instance, oddly enclosed. But a middle capital letter of the alphabet [is] an individual graph [and] may occur only oddly enclosed or so enclosed in its outermost instance. But it is only the nomen that properly belongs to the system.[26]

When it is necessary that two lines should cross one another, which seldom happens, they appear thus —⊥⊤— the two small parallels forming what is called a **bridge**.

The **graphist** is the person with whom it lies to make any permissible insertions or omission upon the sheet and the different areas.

The word **may** in the permissions refers to what the graphist is at liberty to do if he likes.

A **scroll** consists of two cuts, one within the other. The outer one is called the **outloop**, the inner the **inloop**. The area of the outloop when there is only the enclosure of the inloop upon it is called the **outer close** of the scroll.

A scroll with nothing on its outer close unless it be lines running from the inloop to the outloop is called a **double-cut**.

A graph not connected with any other by any ligature is called a **solute** graph; if so connected, an **alligate** graph.

CHAPTER I. Outline of the Imaginary Graphist's Procedure

§ 1. A person who desires to put this system to use will usually have to imagine that a Graphist is using it as a calculus, although he himself is presumably using it for the purpose for which it was designed, namely, as an aid in the analysis of reasoning and not at all as a calculus, for which purpose it is not at all adapted.

---

26 [Compare with what Peirce would a little later write as the intended addition to the *Syllabus* text, as its Convention VI (from R 510):]

[i] A selective, or capital letter, is to be substituted for each least enclosed juncture, a juncture not being within a cut unless it is wholly within it, and this is to be repeated until all the junctures are abolished. [ii] Junctures evenly enclosed are to be replaced [by] early letters of the alphabet A to L, [iii] junctures oddly enclosed by late letters Z to M.

The entire graph is to be transcribed, [iv] more enclosed spots being scribed lower down in the same columns and [v] spots enclosed in cuts within the same cut to be in parallel columns, the columns being split by braces.

In place of each evenly enclosed cut is to be placed a single large parenthesis mark to the left and [vii] in place of each oddly enclosed cut is to be placed a single large square bracket to the left. [viii] Oddly enclosed spots are to be put a little further to the right than evenly enclosed spots in the same column.

§ 2. The imaginary Graphist is supposed to receive from time to time special permissions to make then and there special transformations of the entire graph on the sheet.[27] For the present these permissions will be supposed to be ~~given~~ expressed in terms of the system itself. For the translation into these terms of propositions otherwise expressed, see Chap. [I].[28]

§ 3. The Graphist is to be supposed to be always at liberty to leave things as they were.

§ 4. In addition to these special permissions the Graphist is furnished with a Code of Underived General Permissions to make certain described kinds of transformations in certain described kinds of circumstances. See Chap. II.[29]

§ 5. Moreover, the Graphist is supposed to know that there is one transformation which he never will receive permission, whether expressed or implied, to make, provided he has not ~~infringed~~ transgressed the permissions; namely, the permission to obliterate the entire sheet. If, therefore, he finds himself authorized to do this, since the person who is really using the system is able to control the conformity to the general permissions with which he himself is furnished in Chapter II, it follows that the special permissions have been mistaken.

[What Peirce is proposing here is a kind of graph rewriting algorithm, which by following the proposed eight steps would transform existential graphs into a novel, quasi-linear notation. That new linear notation has eliminated junctures from Beta graphs, replacing them with selectives, thus using only notations readily available at the typesetters' facilities, such as line skips, indentations and large multi-line parentheses, brackets and braces. Peirce may have wanted to attempt changing the notation of the graphs for the printed *Syllabus* altogether, in order to be able to have more examples to appear in print. A couple of loose worksheets located in R 278 are also connected to this proposal that was not pursued any further, however (see Bellucci, Liu & Pietarinen 2020 for details).]

27 [R S-36:] The Graphist receives from time to time special external permissions to make specific transformations of the entire graph of the sheet.

He is always at liberty to leave matters as they are.

He independently has certain general permissions under certain kinds of circumstances to make certain kinds of transformations.

He knows that he never will be permitted to obliterate the entire original sheet. Should he find himself in a position in which his general permissions give him the right to do this and no mistake has been made since the start it is a sign that he never would be authorized to scribe what he set out by scribing.

28 [Peirce left the Chapter number blank. It is conjectured to be Chapter I, referring to the first chapter of *Logical Tracts No. 2*.]

29 [Refers to the second chapter of *Logical Tracts No. 2*, provided below.]

CHAPTER II. The Principles of Illative Transformation

Section i. Basic Principles[30]

The first chapter of this tract was a grammar of this language of graphs. But one has not mastered a language as long as one has to think about it in another language. One must learn to think *in* it *about* facts. The present chapter is designed to show how to reason *in* this language without translating it into another, the language of our ordinary thought. This reasoning, however, depends on certain first principles for the justification of which we have to make a last appeal to instinctive thought.

The purpose of reasoning is to proceed from the recognition of the truth we already know to the knowledge of novel truth. This we may do by instinct or by a habit of which we are hardly conscious. But the operation is not worthy to be called reasoning unless it be deliberate, critical, self-controlled. In such genuine reasoning we are always conscious of proceeding according to a general rule which we approve. It may not be precisely formulated but still we do think that all reasoning of that perhaps rather vaguely characterized kind will be safe. This is a doctrine of logic. We never can really reason without entertaining a logical theory. That is called our *logica utens*.

The purpose of logic is attained by any single passage from a premiss to a conclusion as long as it does not at once happen that the premiss is true while the conclusion is false. But reasoning proceeds upon a rule, and an inference is not *necessary*, unless the rule be such that in every case the fact stated in the premiss and the fact stated in the conclusion are so related that either the premiss will be

---

30 **[Alt.] CHAPTER II. The Principles of Illative Transformation. Section i. Basic Principles.** The object of this section is to lay down principles of illative transformation sufficient to justify all such transformations that can be justified. By an illative transformation is meant a transformation permitted by a general rule of permission which will never permit transformation of a true assertion into a false one.

Such transformations will be precisely those which will never assert anything false, assuming that what is already asserted is true. Hence, in deducing the rules, we may assume that all that is asserted is true, and then so frame the rule that **[Alts.1,2]** no assertion of anything false can ever be made under it.

The general principle upon which all the rules will be based (subject to modification when selectives are used) it that, whatever transformation is permissible upon the entire graph is permissible upon every evenly enclosed partial graph while the reverse transformation is permissible upon every oddly enclosed graph. We have to satisfy ourselves, first, that this can never lead to any false rule, and secondly, that it will lead to every true rule.

First, then, suppose that the graph, A, if it were the entire graph, could be illatively transformed into another graph, which we may call B; but suppose that A is, in fact, not the entire

false or the conclusion will be true. (Or *both*, of course. "*Either* A *or* B" does not properly exclude "*both* A and B".) Even then, the reasoning may not be *logical*, because the rule may involve matter of fact so that the reasoner cannot have sufficient ground to be absolutely certain that it will not sometimes fail. The inference

---

graph but is a detached and unenclosed part of the graph, the remainder of which we may represent by R. A and R then are independently asserted [end]

[Alt.1] [...] no assertion of anything false can ever be made under it.

The general principle upon which all the rules will be based (subject to modification when selectives are used) will be that, whatever transformation is permissible upon the entire graph is permissible, upon the same graph when it is an evenly enclosed partial graph, while the reverse transformation is permissible upon every oddly enclosed graph.

We have to make sure, first, that this can never lead to any invalid permission, and secondly, that it will lead to every valid permission.

[Alt.2] [...] no assertion of anything false can ever be made under it.

In this section the aim will be to lay down a series of rules from which the permissibility of every permissible transformation can be deduced without any of these being deducible from the rest. It will further be required that each of the rules of this section shall simply describe the appearance of a class of graphs and categorically assert that any such graph may be transformed in a certain way whose appearance is described, without any reference to the interpretation, and independently of the transformability of any other sort of graph. [The property of independence or admissibility of the rules is what Peirce terms "archegetic rules" in his *Syllabus* draft (R 478).] Finally, the aim will be, while conforming to those conditions to make the rules of this section as few as possible.

Transformations to be taken as basic ought to consist of operations as simple as possible. Since therefore any transformation other than an insertion or an erasure may be conceived to result from an insertion followed by an erasure, operations of these two sorts shall alone be explicitly permitted by rules admitted to this section, and be ranked as basic. This restriction will not prevent the permission of any illative transformation. For if any graph, x, can be illatively transformed into any other, y, it can be transformed into the graph $x y$ which merely asserts the truth of both, and this having been done, it will be permitted to erase the x; so that the transformation into y will be effected in two steps.

All rules of this section will be demonstrated from a single general principle, as follows:

If a graph, A, would be transformable into a graph, B, in case it were the entire graph, standing alone upon the sheet, then, if A is an unenclosed partial graph or is evenly enclosed (whether it be alone in its enclosure or not) it may still be transformed into B, retaining, as far as possible, every connection by a heavy line with the rest of what is written in the same enclosure, but without the addition of any new connections, while B, when oddly enclosed (whether alone in its enclosure or not), may be transformed into A without any new connections with other partial graphs in the same enclosure, but retaining all the connections with those other partial graphs that it had before the transformation, or their equivalents.

This rule has first to be demonstrated; and that having been done, it will still remain to be considered what principle besides this will have to be taken into account in order to furnish us with a complete list of basic rules.

is only logical if the reasoner can be *mathematically certain* of the excellence of his rule of reasoning; and in the case of necessary reasoning he must be mathematically certain that in every state of things whatsoever, whether now or a million years hence, whether here or in the furthest fixed star, such a premiss and such a conclusion will never be, the former true and the latter false. It would be far beyond the scope of this tract to enter upon any thorough discussion of how this can be. Yet there are some questions which concern us here,—as, for example, how far the system of rules of this section is eternal verity and how far it merely characterizes the special language of existential graphs,—and yet trench closely upon the deeper philosophy of logic; so that a few remarks meant to illuminate those pertinent questions and to show how they are connected with the philosophy of logic seem to be quite in order.

Mathematical certainty is not absolute certainty. For the greatest mathematicians sometimes blunder, and therefore it is *possible*,—barely possible,—that all have blundered every time they added two and two. Bearing in mind that fact, and bearing in mind the fact that mathematics deals with imaginary states of things upon which experiments can be enormously multiplied at very small cost, we see that it is not impossible that inductive processes should afford the basis of mathematical certainty; and any mathematician can find much in the history of his own thought, and in the public history of mathematics to show that, as a matter

---

Demonstration of the General Principle. If an unenclosed graph consists of two partial graphs, they must both be unenclosed. For Fig. 59 does not consist of Fig. 60 and Fig. 61.

x ⓨ x y

Fig. 59   **Fig. 60**   **Fig. 61**

Moreover, if the two partial graphs of which an entire graph is composed are connected by heavy lines, these lines (that is, portions of them) belong unenclosed to both the partial graphs, since a graph would cease to be a graph if any unenclosed line of it were entirely removed. For example, a line ending at a sep may be cut off at the sep, but still a heavily marked point will remain on the sep and be unenclosed; and if a line ends at a spot, a heavily marked point must remain on the hook or the graph becomes a mere rhema and not a graph. Further, if the two partial graphs of which an unenclosed graph is composed are connected by heavy lines, the whole asserts no more than the two partial graphs severally assert except the identity of certain indesignate individuals; nor does either partial graph assert anything that the whole does not assert. Let us suppose then that any graph, if it were asserted alone would be illatively transformable into y, that is to say, it is logically impossible that x should be true and y false. Suppose, then, that we have asserted $x\,z$ where x and z may be connected by heavy lines. Then, we must assume that x is true, that z is true, and that certain individuals are identical. Then it must be that y is true and z is true, and if there are any individuals referred to in y that are identifiable with individual [end]

of fact, inductive reasoning is considerably employed in making sure of the first mathematical premisses. Still, a doubt will arise as to whether this is anything more than a psychological need, whether the reasoning really rests upon induction at all. A geometer, for example, may ask himself whether two straight lines can enclose an area of their plane. When this question is first put, it is put in reference to a concrete image of a plane; and at first some experiments will be tried in the imagination. Some minds will be satisfied with that degree of certainty: more critical intellects will not. They will reflect that a closed area is an area shut off from other parts of the plane by a boundary all round it. Such a thinker will no longer think of a closed area by a composite photograph of triangles, quadrilaterals, circles, etc. He will think of a predictive rule,—a thought of what experience one would intend to produce who should intend to establish a closed area.

That step of thought which consists in interpreting an image by a symbol is one of which logic neither need nor can give any account, since it is subconscious, uncontrollable, and not subject to criticism. Whatever account there is to be given of it is the psychologist's affair. But it is evident that the image must be connected in some way with a symbol if any proposition is to be true of it. The very truth of things must be in some measure representative.

If we admit that propositions express the very reality, it is not surprising that the study of the nature of propositions should enable us to pass from the knowledge of one fact to the knowledge of another.[31]

---

[31] Some reader may think that I am expending energy in trying to explain what needs no explanation. He may argue that the mathematician reasons about a diagram in which there appears to be nothing at all corresponding to the structure of the proposition,—no predicate and subjects. Nor does the mathematician's premiss or conclusion at all pretend to represent the diagram in that respect. It may seem to this reader satisfactory to say that the conclusion follows from the premiss, because the premiss is only applicable to states of things to which the conclusion is applicable. If he thinks that satisfactory, the purpose of this tract does not compel me to dispute it. It is only to defend myself against the charge of giving a needless and doubtful explanation that I point out that it is precisely this relation of applicability that requires to be explained. How comes it that the conclusion is applicable whenever the premiss is applicable. I suppose the answer will be that its only meaning is a part of what the premiss means. The "meaning" of a proposition is what it is intended to convey. But when a mathematician lays down the premisses of the Theory of Numbers, it cannot be said that he then intends to convey all the propositions of that theory of which the great majority will occasion him much surprise when he comes to learn them. If to avoid this objection a distinction be drawn between what is explicitly intended and what is implicitly intended, I submit that this manifestly makes a vicious circle; for what can it be *implicitly* to intend anything, except to intend whatever may be a necessary consequence of what it explicitly intended?

We frame a system of expressing propositions,—a written language,—having a syntax to which there are absolutely no exceptions. We then satisfy ourselves that whenever a proposition having a certain syntactical form is true, another proposition definitely related to it,—so that the relation can be defined in terms of the appearance of the two propositions on paper,—will necessarily also be true. We draw up our code of basic rules of such illative transformations, none of these rules being a necessary consequence of others. We then proceed to express in our language the premisses of long and difficult mathematical demonstrations and try whether our rules will bring out their conclusions. If, in any case, not, and yet the demonstration appears sound, we have a lesson in logic to learn. Some basic rule has been omitted, or else our system of expression is insufficient. But after our system and its rules are perfected, we shall find that such analyses of demonstrations teach us much about those reasonings. They will show that certain hypotheses are superfluous, that others have been virtually taken for granted without being expressly laid down; and they will show that special branches of mathematics are characterized by appropriate modes of reasoning, the knowledge of which will be useful in advancing them. We may now lay all that aside, and begin again, constructing an entirely different system of expression, developing it from an entirely different initial idea, and having perfected it, as we perfected the former system, we shall analyze the same mathematical demonstrations. The results of the two methods will agree as to what is and what is not a necessary consequence. But a consequence that either method will represent as an immediate application of a basic rule, and therefore as simple, the other will be pretty sure to analyze into a series of steps. If it be not so, in regard to some inferences the one method will be merely a disguise of the other. To say that one thing is simpler than another is an incomplete proposition, like saying that one ball is to the right of another. It is necessary to specify what point of view is assumed in order to render the sentence true or false.

This remark has its application to the business now in hand which is to translate the effect of each simple illative transformation of an existential graph into the language of ordinary thought and thus show that it represents a necessary consequence. For it will be found that it is not the operations which are simplest in this system that are simplest from the point of view of ordinary thought; so that it will be found that the simplest way to establish by ordinary thought the correctness of our basic rules will be to begin by proving the legitimacy of certain operations that are less simple from the point of view of the existential graphs.

The first proposition for assent to which I shall appeal to ordinary reason is this. When a proposition contains a number of *any*s and *some*s or their equivalents it is a delicate matter to alter the form of statement while preserving the exact meaning. Every *some*, as we have seen, means that, under stated conditions, an individual could be specified of which that which is predicated of the some is true, while every *any* means that what is predicated is true of no matter what individual be specified; and the specifications of individuals must be made in a certain order or the meaning of the proposition will be changed.[32] Consider, for example, the following proposition: "A certain bookseller only quotes a line of poetry in case it was written by some blind authoress, and he either is trying to sell any books she may have written to the person to whom he quotes the line or else intends to reprint some book of hers". Here the existence of a bookseller is categorically affirmed; but the existence of a blind authoress is only affirmed conditionally on that bookseller's quoting a line of poetry. As for any book by her none such is positively said to exist unless the bookseller is not endeavoring to sell all the books there may be by her to the person to whom he quotes the line.

Now the point to which I demand the assent of reason is that all those individuals whose selection is so referred to might be named to begin with, thus: "There is a certain individual, A, and no matter what Z and Y may be, an individual, B, can be found such that whatever, X, may be, there is something C, and A is a book-

---

[32] [Alt.1] [...] the meaning of the proposition will be changed. Consider, for example, the following proposition: "A certain bookseller only quotes a line of poetry in case it was written by some blind authoress all and any of whose books he is desirous of selling to the person to whom he quotes the line". Here the existence of some bookseller is categorically asserted. The existence of a [end, sentence discontinued, followed by the graph below, in **P.H.**, after which the sequence is abandoned:]

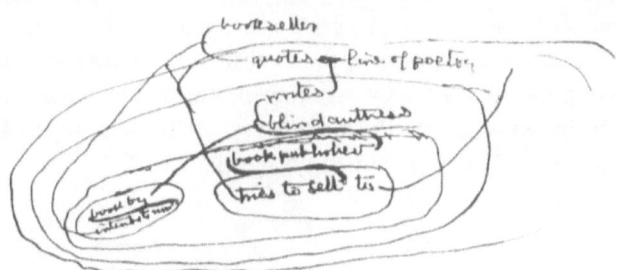

[From top down, the spots in the graph above are: "bookseller", "quotes", "line of poetry", "writes", "blind authors", "book published", "tries to sell to", "book by", "interested in".]

[Alt.2] [...] the meaning of the proposition will be changed. For example, consider the following proposition: "A certain bookseller only quotes a passage in case it is the work of an author all that he desires to sell to the person to whom he quotes it". The existence of a bookseller is here positively asserted. The existence of a book is not asserted that he ever quotes a passage to anybody; but only that if any passage can be found and any person to whom that bookseller quotes that passage, then there is a book [end, fragment abandoned]

seller and if he quotes, Z to Y, and if Z is a line of poetry and Y is a person, then B is a blind poetess who has written Z, and either X is not a book published by B or A tries to sell X to Y or else C is a book published by B and A intends to reprint C". This is the precise equivalent of the original proposition and any proposition involving *somes* and *anys*, or their equivalents, might equally be expressed by first thus defining exactly what these *somes* and *anys* mean and then going on to predicate concerning them whatever is to be predicated. This is so evident that any proof of it would only confuse the mind; and anybody who could follow the proof will easily see how the proof could be constructed. But after the *somes* and *anys* have thus been replaced by letters denoting each one individual, the subsequent statement concerns merely a set of designate individuals.

In order, then, to make evident to ordinary reason what are the simple illative transformations of graphs, I propose to imagine the lines of identity to be all replaced by selectives, whose first occurrences are entirely outside the substance of the graph in a nest of seps where each selective occurs once only and with nothing but existence predicated of it (affirmatively or negatively according as it is evenly or oddly enclosed). I will then show that upon such a graph certain transformations are permissible, and then will suppose the selectives to be replaced by lines of identity again. We shall thus have established the permissibility of certain transformations without the intervention of selectives.

There will therefore be two branches to our inquiry. First, what transformations may be made in the inner part of the graph where all the selectives have proper names, and secondly what transformations may be made in the outer part where each selective occurs but once. It will be found that the second inquiry almost answers itself after the first has been investigated, and further, that the first class of transformations are precisely the same as if all the first occurrences of selectives were erased and the others were regarded as proper names. We therefore begin by inquiring what transformations are permissible in a graph which has no connexuses at all, neither lines of identity nor selectives.[33]

---

[33] **[Alt.]** Here we shall bee much aided by the following principle:

If any graph, x, would if it were written alone upon the sheet of assertion be illatively transformable into another graph, y, then, in any graph without connexuses, where x occurs evenly enclosed it is illatively transformable into y, and where y occurs oddly enclosed it is illatively transformable into x.

For to say that x is illatively transformable into y means simply that, by virtue of its form, it [is] impossible for x to be true while y is false. To say that $a\ x$ is transformable into $a\ y$ is to say that it is, by virtue of its form, impossible for both a and x to be true while either a or y is false. Hence if x is illatively transformable into y, then $a\ x$ is illatively transformable into $a\ y$, whatever graph a may be. That is, if x standing alone on the sheet of assertion would be illatively transformable into y, then x, when it is a detached and unenclosed partial graph, is illatively transformable into y.

But if any graph, u, is illatively transformable into v, then Fig. 59 is illatively transformable into Fig. 60. For to say that this is so is no more than to say that, by virtue of its form, it is impossible for the denial of v to be true and the denial of u to be false, which is the same as to say that, by virtue of its form, it is impossible for v to be false while u is true. But if Fig. 59 is illatively transformable into Fig. 60, then, as we have just seen, Fig. 61 is illatively transformable into Fig. 62. So that if u is illatively transformable into v then Fig. 61 is illatively transformable into Fig. 62. Hence if x is illatively transformable into y, then Fig. 63 is illatively transformable into Fig. 64.

ⓥ	ⓤ	b ⓥ	b ⓤ	b ⓐⓨ	b ⓐⓧ
Fig. 59	Fig. 60	Fig. 61	Fig. 62	Fig. 63	Fig. 64

Hence if a graph would, if written **[Alts.1,2]** alone on the sheet of assertion, be illatively transformable into another it will be so transformable whenever it is an detached partial graph within any even finite number of seps while the reverse transformation will be permissible under any odd number of seps.

Upon any graph standing alone upon the sheet of assertions any one of four illative transformations may be performed that are of such a nature that after any one of them has been performed a reverse illative transformation can undo the effect of it. Namely,

First, the graph may be erased from the sheet while the proposition it expresses be added to the list of those well-understood to be true; and conversely, upon a blank sheet any proposition well-understood to be true may be written in the form of a graph.

[Alt.1] [...] alone on the sheet of assertion, be illatively transformable into another, it will be so transformable whenever it is a dinected partial graph within any even finite number of seps, while the reverse transformation will be permissible under any odd (and therefore finite) number of seps.

What, then, are the illative transformations to which any graph whatever, say that of Fig. 65, may undergo? It can be erased; since there is no falsity in abstaining from any assertion. It can be iterated, as in Fig 66; since this asserts nothing not already asserted. Anything well-understood to be true can be added to it, as in Fig. 67. An *ens rationis* whose being consists, or follows from, the truth of the graph may be asserted to exist in an additional graph; and this may be done in different ways, of which Fig. 68 is an example.

a	a a	a —	a ⟨ a is true ⟩
Fig. 65	Fig. 66	Fig. 67	Fig. 68

[Alt.2] [...] alone on the sheet of assertion, be illatively transformable into another, it will be so transformable whenever it is a dinected partial graph within any even finite number of seps while the reverse transformation will be permissible under any odd (and therefore finite) number of seps.

First of all, let us inquire what are those modes of illative transformation by each of which any graph whatever standing alone on the sheet of assertion may be transformed, and, at the same time, what are those modes of illative transfor-

---

Any graph whatsoever, standing alone upon the sheet of assertion, is susceptible of any one of five illative transformations. Three of these are of such a nature that any graph that could have resulted from either of them would be illatively transformable into the graph from which it could have resulted by such transformation. The remaining two of the five would have been so reciprocally related, were it not that one of the terms of such transformation is not completely expressed as a graph, and is in such a way unexpressed that both operations are performable upon any entire graph whatsoever. If follows, therefore, that the first three ~~operations~~ transformations are ~~performable~~ permissible upon every dinected partial graph, however enclosed, while the fourth and fifth transformations are permissible only upon all evenly enclosed entire or partial graphs while their converse ~~operations~~ transformations are permissible only upon all oddly enclosed entire or partial graphs.

The five universal illative transformations of the entire graph are as follows:

First, the entire graph may be enclosed in two seps; and if the entire graph consists of a sep enclosing nothing but an enclosure, the two outer seps may be removed. **[Alt.3]**

Second, the entire graph may be iterated; and if the entire graph consists of two dinected replicas of the same graph, one of them may be erased.

Third, to the entire graph may be added a graph asserting that there is a true graph that asserts all that the first graph asserted; and if the entire graph asserts that a true graph asserts a proposition, a graph asserting that proposition may be added to it.

Fourth, the entire graph may be erased, when the proposition it asserted will pass into the list of propositions well-understood to be true, but not expressed.

Fifth, to the graph may be added, dinexed and unenclosed, any graph ~~asserting~~ expressing a proposition well-understood to be true, though not ~~yet expressed~~ hitherto asserted.

From these rules follow the following rules of illative transformation of all graphs not involving connexuses:

First, a partial graph expressing a proposition well-understood to be true may be anywhere inserted and anywhere erased.

Second, any evenly-enclosed graph, entire or partial, may be erased; and within any odd number of seps, already drawn, any graph may be inserted.

Third, any partial or entire graph, however enclosed, may be iterated within the same or any additional seps; and if a graph occurs twice within a graph, the inner replica may be erased.

Fourth, two seps of which the one encloses the other and nothing else may be together anywhere drawn or removed.

Fifth, two graphs, one of which simply asserts the other to be true, or merely asserts the existence of a true graph expressing the same proposition that the other asserts may be treated as equivalent, although strictly speaking, they are not so.

These five rules being established, let us return to graphs having lines of identity. Any portion of such a line is a graph, and as such, is necessarily subject to these rules. But it seems not unlikely that it is subject to additional rules, particularly in regard to the junction of two such lines on a sep. It is the second and third rules, in particular, whose sufficiency in such cases seems questionable.

mation from each of which any graph whatever standing alone on the sheet of

By the second rule, Fig. 65 is transformable into Fig. 66.

—(is good)   (—is good)   (—is good)

Fig. 65   **Fig. 66**   **Fig. 67**

It is, therefore, necessary to distinguish sharply between Fig. 66 and Fig. 67; since obviously this might be false though Fig. 65 were true. But this apparent difficulty disappears when we consider that the point on the sep is not enclosed within the sep; so that there would be a difference between Fig. 66 and Fig. 67. Still, Rule 2 would permit the erasure of the point on the sep if it were an ordinary unenclosed point. But it cannot be erased, owing to its effect in limiting the denial of the enclosure. Fig. 67 can be transformed into Fig. 65, as appears from the interpretation. But just so Fig. 68 is illatively transfromable into Fig. 68. This may be explained by saying that Fig. 66 is transformable into Fig. 70 simply because it merely gives a different shape to the external line of identity; and shape is not a significant feature in this system. Then Fig. 70 is converted into Fig. 71 by Rule 2 and Fig 71 into Fig. 69 by Rule 3.

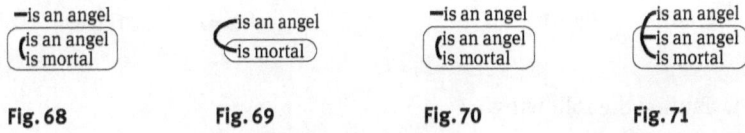

Fig. 68   **Fig. 69**   **Fig. 70**   **Fig. 71**

It is to be noted that a graph cannot be considered as "iterated", unless the two replicas have their corresponding hooks "joined",—that is, either directly connected by lines of identity or indirectly through such lines being joined to the same points on seps. We may say, then, that it is in this same way that Fig. 67 is transformable into Fig. 65, being first transformed, by Rule 1, into Fig. 72.

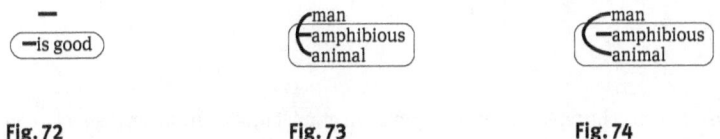

Fig. 72   **Fig. 73**   **Fig. 74**

If it be asked why Fig. 73 is not transformable into Fig. 74 by Rule 3, by deiteration of the graph of identity, the reply is that it is because the line cut out is connected with a line to "is amphibious" to which the line of which it is supposed to be the iteration is not connected.

[Alt.3] Second, the graph may be iterated, that is written a second time on the sheet; and if a graph consists of two dinected occurrences of the same graph either may be erased.

Third, two seps may be drawn round the graph, and if two seps are already drawn with nothing between them, they may be erased.

assertion might result. Let us confine ourselves, in the first instance, to transformations not only involving no connexions, but also involving no *entia rationis* nor seps. Let us suppose a graph, say that of Fig. 59, to be alone upon the sheet of assertion. In what ways can it be illatively transformed without using connexuses nor seps nor other *entia rationis*? In the first place, it may be erased; for the result of erasure, asserting nothing at all, can assert nothing false. In the second place, it can be iterated, as in Fig. 60; for the result of the iteration asserts nothing not asserted already. In the third place, any graph well-understood, before the original graph was drawn, to be true, can be inserted, as in Fig. 61. Evidently, these are the only modes of transformation that conform to the assumed conditions.

Next let us inquire in what manner any graph, say that of Fig. 62, can result. It cannot, unless of a special nature, result from insertion, since the blank is true and the graph may be false; but it can result by any omission, say of *y* from the graph of Fig. 63, whether *y* be true or false, or whatever its relation to *z*, since the result asserts nothing not asserted in the graph from which it results.

a	*a a*	The universe is here *a*	*z*	*y z*
Fig. 59	**Fig. 60**	**Fig. 61**	**Fig. 62**	**Fig. 63**

We may now employ the following:

Conditional Principle No. 1. If any graph, *a*, were it written alone on the sheet of assertion, would be illatively transformable into another graph, *z*, then if the former graph *a*, is a partial graph of an entire graph involving no connexus or sep, and written on the sheet of assertion, *a* may still be illatively transformed in the same way.

Fourth, the graph may be replaced by any equivalent graph introducing an *ens rationis*, and any graph involving an *ens rationis* may be replaced by an equivalent graph.

Finally, the graph may be iterated enclosed in two seps having nothing between them, or be directly so enclosed, as in Fig. 69. It is evident that these are the only elementary transformations which the apparatus of our system will allow us to perform upon every entire graph without exception.

Fig. 69 [end of fragment]

For let *a* be a partial graph of which the other part is *m*, as in Fig. 64.

a m   *z m*

Fig. 64   Fig. 65

Then, both *a* and *m* will be asserted. But since *a* would be illatively transformable into *z* if it were the entire graph, it follows that if *a* is true *z* is true. Hence, the result of the transformation asserts only *m* which is already asserted, and *z* which is true if *a*, which is already asserted, is true.

By means of this principle we can evidently deduce the following:

[Subsection 1.] Categorical Basic Rules for the Illative Transformation of Graphs ~~**without Connexions, Seps, or Entia Rationis**~~ **dinectively built up from partial graphs not separated by seps.**

1. Any partial graph may be erased.
2. Any partial graph may be iterated.
3. Any graph well-understood to be true may be inserted.

It is furthermore clear that no transformation of such graphs is *logical*, that is, results from the mere form of the graph, that is not justified by these rules. For a transformation not justified by these rules must insert something not in the premiss and not well-understood to be true. But under those circumstances, it may be false, as far as appears from the form.

Let us now consider graphs having no connexions or *entia rationis* other than seps. Here we shall have the following

Conditional Principle No. 2. If a graph, *a*, were it written alone on the sheet of assertion would be illatively transformable into a sep containing nothing but *a* graph, *z*, then in case nothing is on the sheet of assertion except this latter graph, *z*, this will be illatively transformable into a sep containing nothing but *a*.

For to say that Fig. 61 is illatively transformable into Fig. 66, is to say that if *a* is true then if *z* were true, anything you like would be true, while to say that Fig. 62 is illatively transformable into Fig. 67 is to say that if *z* is true then if *a* were true, anything you like would be true. But each of these amounts to saying that if *a* and *z* were both true anything you like would be true. Therefore, if either is true so is the other.

Fig. 66 Fig. 67

Conditional Principle No. 3. If a sep containing nothing but a graph, *a*, would, were it written alone on the sheet of assertion, be illatively transformable into a graph, *z*, then if a sep containing nothing but the latter graph, *z*, were written alone on the sheet of assertion, be illatively transformable into the graph, *a*.

For to say that Fig. 67 is illatively transformable into Fig. 62 is to say that by virtue of the forms of *a* and *z*, if *a* is false, *z* is true, or, in other words, by virtue of their forms, either *a* or *z* is true. But this is precisely the meaning of saying that Fig. 66 is illatively transformable into Fig. 61.

By means of these principles we can deduce the following

[Subsection 2.] Basic Categorical Rules for the Illative Transformation of Graphs dinectively built up from Partial Graphs and from Graphs separated by seps.

Rule 1. Within an even finite number (including none) of seps, any graph may be erased, within an odd number any graph may be inserted.

Rule 2. Any graph may be iterated within the same or additional seps, or if iterated a replica may be erased if the erasure leaves another outside the same or additional seps.

Rule 3. Any graph well-understood to be true (and therefore an enclosure having a pseudograph within an odd number of its seps) may be inserted outside all seps.

Rule 4. Two seps, the one enclosing the other but nothing outside that other, can be removed.

These rules have now to be demonstrated.[34] The former set of rules, already demonstrated, apply to every graph on the sheet of assertion composed of

---

34 **[Alt.]** These rules have now to be demonstrated. The former set of rules, already demonstrated, apply to any graph of the sheet of assertions composed of dinected partial graphs not enclosed; for the reasoning by which those rules were demonstrated applies to every such case. Hence, any unenclosed and dinected partial graph may be erased. Now any enclosure, as that of Fig. 68, is transformable into itself, since this in no transformation, and if the enclosure is true, if it is true. Hence, by Conditional Principle No. 2, if the contents of such enclosure be asserted, as in Fig. 62, this is transformable into an enclosure consisting of a sep containing nothing but the former enclosure, as in Fig. 69. Hence, if any graph written on the sheet of assertion, as Fig. 61, is transformable into any graph, as that of Fig. 62, then it is transformable into that same graph enclosed in two seps with nothing between, as in Fig. 69. But by Conditional Principle No. 2, if a

dinected partial graphs not enclosed; for the reasoning of the demonstrations so apply. It is now necessary to demonstrate, from Conditional Principle No. 2, the following *Principle of Contraposition*: If any graph, say that of Fig. 61, is illatively transformable into another graph, say that of Fig. 62, then an enclosure consisting of a sep containing nothing but the latter graph, as in Fig. 68, is illatively transformable into an enclosure consisting of a sep containing nothing but the first graph, as in Fig. 69. In order to prove this principle, we must first prove that any graph on the sheet of assertion is illatively transformable by having two seps drawn round it,[35] the one containing nothing but the other with its contents.

Fig. 68   Fig. 69   Fig. 70   Fig. 71   Fig. 72

For let z be the original graph. Then, it has to be shown that Fig. 62 is transformable into Fig. 70. Now Fig. 68 on the sheet of assertion is illatively transformable into itself, since any graph is illatively transformable into any graph that by virtue of its form cannot be false unless the original graph be false, and Fig. 68 cannot be false unless Fig. 68 is false. But from this it follows, by Conditional Principle No. 2, that Fig. 62 is illatively transformable into Fig. 70; Q.E.D. The principle of contraposition, which can now be proved without further difficulty, is that if any graph, a (Fig. 61) is illatively transformable into any graph, z (Fig. 62) then an enclosure (Fig. 68) consisting of a sep enclosing nothing but the latter graph, z, is transformable into an enclosure (Fig. 69) consisting of a sep

---

graph as that of Fig. 61 is transformable into a graph enclosed in two seps with nothing between, as is Fig. 69, then if the last graph with one sep removed, as in Fig. 68, be on the sheet of assertion, this is transformable into a sep containing only the other as in Fig. 70. Since, therefore, any graph is transformable by erasure when unenclosed, it follows that any graph is transformable by insertion, when it is enclosed in one sep.

35 **[Alt.]** [...] by having two seps drawn round it, the one containing nothing but the other with its contents. That is, any graph, as that of Fig. 62, is transformable into a graph related to it as Fig. 70. For an enclosure consisting of a sep, containing nothing but the graph of Fig. 62, as in Fig. 68, is illatively transformable into itself, since if any graph be true, the same graph is true. Hence, by Conditional Principle No. 2, the graph contained by that sep, as in Fig. 62, is illatively transformable into the graph consisting of a sep containing nothing but the original enclosure, as it Fig. 70. Thus, any graph on the sheet of assertion may have two seps drawn round it with nothing between them. It follows that if any graph, as that of Fig. 61, would, if written unenclosed on the sheet of assertion, be illatively transformable into a second, as that of Fig. 62, it is equally transformable into this latter enclosed in two seps with nothing between them, as in Fig. 70.

containing nothing but the first graph, a. If a is transformable into z, then, by the rule just proved, it is transformable into Fig. 70, consisting of z doubly enclosed with nothing between the seps. But if Fig. 61 is illatively transformable into Fig. 70, then, by Conditional Principle No. 2, Fig. 68 is illatively transformable into Fig. 69. Q.E.D.

Supposing, now, that *Rule* 1 holds good for any insertion or omission within not more than any finite number, N, of seps, it will also hold good for every insertion or omission within not more than $N + 1$ seps. For in any graph on the sheet of insertions of which a partial graph is an enclosure consisting of a sep containing only a graph, z, involving a nest of N seps, let the partial graph outside this enclosure be m, so that Fig. 71 is the entire graph. Then application of the rule within the $N + 1$ seps will transform z into another graph, say a, so that Fig. 72 will be the result. Then a were it written on the sheet of assertion unenclosed and alone would be illatively transformable into z since the rule is supposed to be valid for an insertion or omission within N seps. Hence, by the principle of contraposition Fig. 68 will be transformable into Fig. 69, and by Conditional Principle No. 1, Fig. 71 will be transformable into Fig. 72. It is therefore proved that if Rule 1 is valid within any number of seps up to any finite number it is valid for the next larger whole number of seps. But by Rule 1 of the former set of rules, it is valid for $N = 0$, and hence it follows that it is valid within seps whose number can be reached from 0 by successive additions of unity, that is, for any finite number. Rule 1 is, therefore, valid as stated. It will be remarked that the partial graphs may have any multitude whatsoever; but the seps of a nest are restricted to a finite multitude, so far as this rule is concerned. A graph with an endless nest of seps is essentially of doubtful meaning, except in special cases. Thus Fig. 73, supposed to continue the alternation endlessly evidently merely asserts the truth of a.[36] But if instead of ba, b were everywhere to stand alone, the graph would certainly assert either a or b to

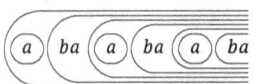
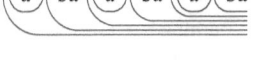

Fig. 73

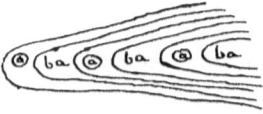

[P.H.]

---

[36] [This proposal of the "endless nest of seps" (Fig. 73) appears on the manuscript page 118 of R 492 and could have been inscribed here sometime in July or August, given that this same unique graph appears in the *Logic Notebook* on July 10, 1903 (see LoF 1).]

be true and would certainly be true if *a* were true, but whether it would be true or false in case *b* were true and not *a* is essentially doubtful.

Rule 2 is so obviously demonstrable in the same way that it will be sufficient to remark that unenclosed iterations of unenclosed graphs are justified by Rule 2 of the former set of rules. Then, since Fig. 74 is illatively transformable into Fig. 75,

a m n   a m a n   a m (a n)

Fig. 74   **Fig. 75**   **Fig. 76**

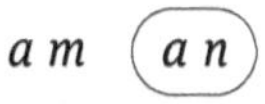

a m (n)   m   m
              (a n a)   (n a)

Fig. 77 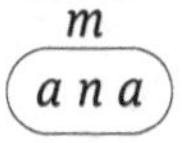   **Fig. 78** 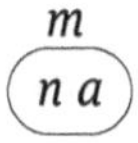   **Fig. 79**

it follows from the principle of contraposition that Fig. 76 is illatively transformable into Fig. 77. Or we may reason that to say that Fig. 75 follows from Fig. 74 is to say that, *a m* being true, *a n* follows from *n*; while to say that Fig. 77 follows from Fig. 76, is to say that, *a m* being true, as before, if from *a n* anything you like follows, then from *n* anything you like follows. In the same way Fig. 78 is transformable into Fig. 79.

The transformations [of] the reverse of these, that is of Fig. 75 into Fig. 74, of Fig. 77 into Fig. 76, and of Fig. 79 into Fig. 78, are permitted by Rule 1. Then by the same Fermatian reasoning by which Rule 1 was demonstrated, we easily show that a graph can anywhere be illatively inserted or omitted, if there is another occurrence of the same graph in the same compartment or farther out by one sep. For if Fig. 76 is transformable into Fig. 77, then by the principle of contraposition, Fig. 80 is transformable into Fig. 81, and by Conditional Principle No. 1, Fig. 82 is transformable in Fig. 83. Having thus proved that iterations and deiterations are always permissible in the same compartment as the leading replica or in a compartment within one additional sep, we have no difficulty in extending this to any finite interval.

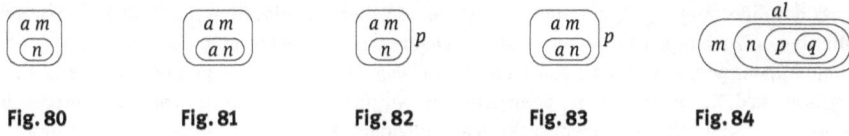

Fig. 80   **Fig. 81**   **Fig. 82**   **Fig. 83**   **Fig. 84**

Thus, Fig. 84 is transformable into Fig. 85, this into Fig. 86, this successively into Figs. 87 to 91. Thus, the second rule is fully demonstrable.

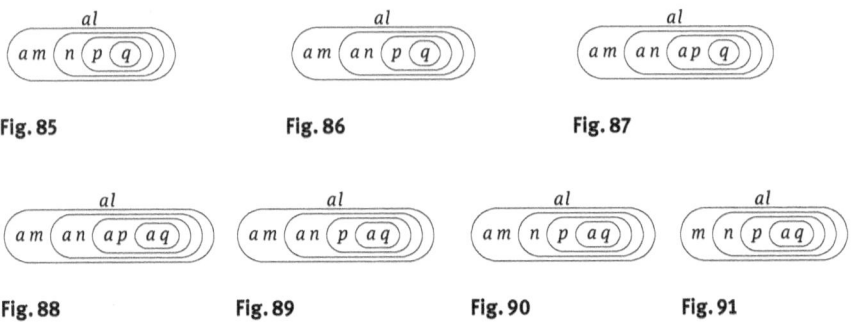

Fig. 85   Fig. 86   Fig. 87

Fig. 88   Fig. 89   Fig. 90   Fig. 91

Rule 3 is self-evident.

We have thus far had no occasion to appeal to Conditional Principle No. 3; but it is indispensable for the proof of *Rule* 4. We have to show that if any graph, which may be denoted by *z*, is surrounded by two seps with nothing between as in Fig. 70, then the two seps may be illatively removed as in Fig. 62. Now if the graph, *z*, occurred within one sep, as in Fig. 69, this, as we have seen, would be transformed into itself. Hence by Conditional Principle No. 3, Fig. 70 can be illatively transformed into Fig. 62. Q.E.D.

The list of rules given for dinected graphs is complete. This is susceptible of proof, but the proof belongs in the next section of this chapter, where I may perhaps insert it. It is not interesting.

We now pass to the consideration of graphs connected by lines of identity.[37] A small addition to our nomenclature is required here. Namely, we have seen

---

37 [Alt.] We now pass to the consideration of graphs connected by lines of identity. Any portion of such a line is a graph, or a rhema (as one chooses to consider it) and as such is necessarily amenable to all the rules given above. But besides its function as a graph, the actual contact of two lines represents indexically what no pure symbol can possibly express,—individual identity. Slight explanations added to the rules suffice to take account of this peculiarity except where the line is joined to a point on a sep. The sep is not inside itself; and therefore a point on a sep does not differ from any other outside point in its general signification. But a line of identity abutting on such a point whether inside or outside the sep, is subject to the conditions of the compartment within which the abuttal occurs. Thus, Fig. 92, where the point of the line on the sep is marked, X, and an arbitrary point of the line within the sep is marked A, may be interpreted as follows: "Some woman is identical with an individual, X, and if any individual, A is identical with X and also with anything ugly, then falsity is truth", or "Some woman is identical with an individual, X, and whatever individual, A, be taken, either A is not identical with X or else A is not ugly". All that is outside the sep may be erased, as in Fig. 93, which will read, "There is an

that a line of identity is a partial graph; and as a graph it cannot cross a sep. Let us, then, call a series of lines of identity abutting upon one another at seps, a *ligature*; and we may extend the meaning of the word so that even a single line of identity shall be called a ligature. A ligature composed of more than one line of identity may be distinguished as a *compound ligature*. A compound ligature is not a graph, because by a graph we mean something which written or drawn alone on the sheet of assertion would, according to this system, assert something. Now a compound ligature could not be written alone on the sheet of assertion, since it is only by means of the intercepting sep, which is no part of it, that it is rendered compound.[38] The different spots, as well as the different hooks, upon which a ligature abuts may be said to be *ligated* by that ligature; and two replicas of the

---

individual, X and whatever individual, A, be taken, this will either not be X or will not be ugly". But the line inside cannot be broken. In Fig. 94, however, the outside line can be prolonged to the sep, because the mere shape and length of a line signifies nothing, and the sep is outside its own ~~enclosure~~ close. We thus get Fig. 95. Then, within the enclosure a line may be inserted joining the point on the line already within the sep, so as to give Fig. 96.

Let us now examine precisely how the four rules are to be understood in the case of graphs connected by lines of identity.

The rule of erasure and insertion is to be understood as allowing the rupture of a line wherever it may be evenly enclosed the junction of any two points oddly enclosed in the same close.

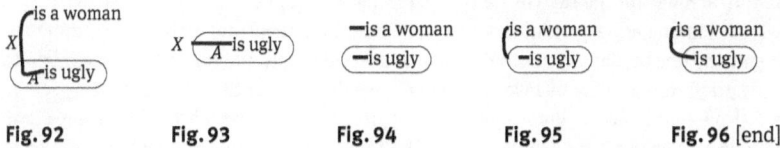

Fig. 92   Fig. 93   Fig. 94   Fig. 95   Fig. 96 [end]

38 [Alt.] [...] part of it, which renders it compound. The hooks or the spots upon which a ligature abuts may be said to be *ligated* by the ligature. When a ligature cuts a sep, the part of it inside the sep may be said to be *joined* to the point on the sep, and through this point to be *transjoined* to the part of the ligature outside. The two parts are *ligated*. The outer part is said to be *extended* to the point on the sep; and it is also *connected* to it. "Ligated" and "connected" are more general expressions than "transjoined" and "extended", being also said of the abuttals of lines and ligatures upon hooks and spots.

Since a line of identity is a graph, all the above rules apply to it, although some of them require to be restated in order to make the mode of their application to lines of identity quite explicit. But besides its function as a ~~symbol~~ graph, — and therefore as a symbol, — a line of identity has a further effect which no pure symbol can have. The truth is that the terms "graph" and "line of identity" are taken in two different accep[ta]tions, just as the word *word* is if we say "One word out of every fifteen to twenty-five in an ordinary English book is the word *the*". Here, when we speak of *the* being everywhere the same 'word', we use the term 'word' in the sense of a symbol, a regularity. But when we refer to the number of other words to each occurrence of *the* as being

same graph are said to have the same *ligations* only when all the corresponding hooks of the two are ligated to one another. When a ligature cuts a sep, the part of

---

from fourteen to twenty-four in number, we use the term 'word' in the sense of the replica of a symbol, which is strictly an index, and not a symbol. I apply these two different acceptations to the terms *graph* and *line of identity*; although ordinarily by a 'graph' I mean the symbol while by a 'line of identity' I mean a replica. But a line of identity, in the sense of a single long strip of ink, is not merely associated with the general conception of identity, so as to be the replica of a symbol, but when it abuts upon a point that denotes an individual, it is forced to refer to the same individual since that point actually becomes a part of the line, and a significant part of it. To denote an individual is beyond the power of a pure symbol, which can *talk of* identifying individuals but cannot *do* it, for the simple reason that the identification is an existential act, which the symbol, as a regularity, is as incompetent to perform as a pure index is to predict what will be. The same thing is true of every replica of a rhema, in so far as it has blanks that can be filled with proper names; and even complete assertions relate to one universe that is here and now; and it is because an assertion is thus an existential act that the assertion of a proposition is different from the proposition itself. Because this is true, every graph-replica resembles a line of identity in that respect; and consequently the rules already laid down are, in ordinary cases, sufficient for graphs containing lines of identity. They only require restatement, so as to render them explicit in regard to the mode of their application to such lines. It is only when the hook upon which the line of identity abuts, instead of being a point upon the periphery of an illaniate spot, is a dot upon a sep and especially when the line is joined to this point on the inside of the sep that a special rule is required. By means of these considerations, we obtain our final list of Basic Rules, as follows:

Basic Categorical Rules for the Illative Transformation of All Graphs.

Rule 1. Within any finite even number of seps (including none) any replica of a graph may be erased and any line of identity may be broken; while within any odd number of seps (already existing) any graph-replica may be inserted and any two lines of identity may be joined.

Rule 2. Any graph may be iterated, the new replica being placed within all the seps that enclose the old replica, and, if desired, within additional seps; but the new replica must have all the ligations of the old replica, and ~~these ligations~~ the requisite ligatures may be scribed by inward extensions of existing ligatures, but must nowhere pass out of any sep that encloses the old replica: and further, any replica of a graph may be erased provided the erasure is a deiteration, that is, leaves a replica of the same graph with the same ligations outside the same or more seps as the erased graph; and along with the graph may be erased its ligatures so far as this can be done by erasures beginning at the erased graph and nowhere proceeding in words, without altering the ligations of unerased graph-replicas in any significant respect.

This rule permits any line of identity to have a branch scribed from any point of it, and permits any free end of a ligature to be prolonged across a sep from the outside to the inside of it.

Rule 3. (Unmodified.) Any graph which expresses a proposition well-understood to be true may be inserted unenclosed.

Rule 4. (Unmodified.) Any *ens rationis* may be created and defined or partially defined by a graph inserted unenclosed; and any proposition whose truth is manifest upon inspection of the graph may be asserted by a graph inserted unenclosed.

Rule 5. Any two seps with nothing between them except a ligature or portion of a ligature may anywhere be removed or inserted.

the ligature outside the sep may be said to be *extended* to the point of intersection on the sep, while the part of the ligature inside may be said to be *joined* to that point.

It has already been pointed out that the mass of ink on the sheet by means of which a graph is said to be "scribed" is not, strictly speaking, a symbol but only a replica of a symbol of the nature of an index. Let it not be forgotten that the significative value of a symbol consists in a regularity of association, so that the identity of the symbol lies in this regularity, while the significative force of an index consists in an existential fact which connects it with its object, so that the identity of the index consists in an existential fact or thing. When symbols, such as words, are used to construct an assertion, this assertion relates to something real. It must not only *profess* to do so, but must really *do* so; otherwise, it could not be true; and still less, false. Let a witness take oath, with every legal formality, that John Doe has committed murder, and still he has made no assertion unless the name John Doe denotes some existing person. But in order that the name should do this, something more than an association of ideas is requisite. For the person is not a conception but an existent thing.

The name, or rather, *occurrences* of the name, must be existentially connected with the existent person. Therefore, no assertion can be constructed out of pure symbols alone. Indeed, the pure symbols are immutable, and it is not them that are joined together by the syntax of the sentence, but occurrences of them,—*replicas* of them. My aim is to use the term 'graph' for a graph-symbol, although I dare say I sometimes lapse into using it for a graph-replica. To say that a graph is scribed is accurate, because 'to scribe' means *to make a graphical replica of*. By 'a line of identity', on the other hand, it is more convenient to mean a replica of the linear graph of identity. For here the indexical character is more positive; and besides, one seldom has occasion to speak of the graph. But the only difference between a line of identity and an ordinary dyadic spot is that the latter has its hooks marked at points that are deemed appropriate without our being under any factual compulsion to mark them at all, while a simple line such

---

Rule 6. A point upon a sep is to be considered, on the one hand, as a hook of the enclosure of the sep considered as a graph, and as such as a portion of a line of identity immediately outside the sep. But on the other hand, any line of identity inside the sep can only be extended to join that point or be disjoined from it according to the rules governing a line so enclosed. That is, if a line inside the sep be evenly enclosed, it may be disjoined from the point on the sep; while if such line be oddly enclosed, it can by the rule of insertion within odd seps be transformed to Fig. 80, and must therefore be interpreted like that "Everything acts on everything"; and not as Fig. 81, "Everything acts on something or other". But if the vacant point on the set could be treated like an ordinary vacant point, Fig. 81 could be illatively transformed into Fig. 79, which the interpretation forbids. [end]

as is naturally employed for a line of identity must, from the nature of things have extremities which are at once parts of it and of whatever it abuts upon. This difference does not prevent the rules of the last list from holding good of such lines. The only occasion for any additional rule is to meet that situation in which no other graph-replica than a line of identity can ever be placed, that of having a hook upon a sep.

As to this, it is to be remarked that an enclosure,—that is, a sep with its contents,—is a graph; and those points on its periphery that are marked by the abuttal upon them of lines of identity are simply the hooks of the graph. But the sep is outside its own close. Therefore an unmarked point upon it is just like any other vacant place outside the sep. But if a line inside the sep is prolonged to the sep, at the instant of arriving at the sep, its extremity suddenly becomes identified,—as a matter of fact, and there as a matter of signification,—with a point outside the sep; and thus the prolongation suddenly assumes an entirely different character from an ordinary, insignificant prolongation. This gives us the following:

Conditional Principle No. 4. Only the connections and continuity of lines of identity are significant, not their shape or size. The connexion or disconnection of a line of identity outside a sep with a marked or an unmarked point on the sep follows the same rules as its connexion or disconnexion with any other marked or unmarked point outside the sep, but the junction or disjunction of a line of identity inside the sep with a point upon the sep always follows the same rules as its connexion or disconnexion with a marked point inside the sep.

In consequence of this principle, although the categorical rules hitherto given remain unchanged in their application to lines of identity, yet they require some modifications in their application to ligatures.

In order to see that the principle is correct, first consider Fig. 73.[39] Now the rule of erasure of an unenclosed graph certainly allows the transformation of this into Fig. 74, which must therefore be interpreted to mean "Something is not ugly", and must not be confounded with Fig. 75, "Nothing is ugly". But Fig. 75 is transformable into Fig. 76: that is, the line of identity with a loose end can be carried to any vacant place within the sep. If therefore Fig. 74 were to be treated as if the end of the line were loose, it could be illatively transformed into Fig. 75. But the line can no more be separated from the point of the sep than it could from any marked

---

[39] [Running numbers of figure captions jump here out of sequence, although the main text appears to comprise one continuous segment. The segment with figure captions continuing with Fig. 92 up to Fig. 96 appears in the alternative variant provided in the note above. In the transcription the original numbering from the manuscript will be preserved throughout.]

point within the sep,—any more, for example, than Fig. 77 "Nothing good is ugly" could be transformed into Fig. 78, "Either nothing is ugly or nothing is good".

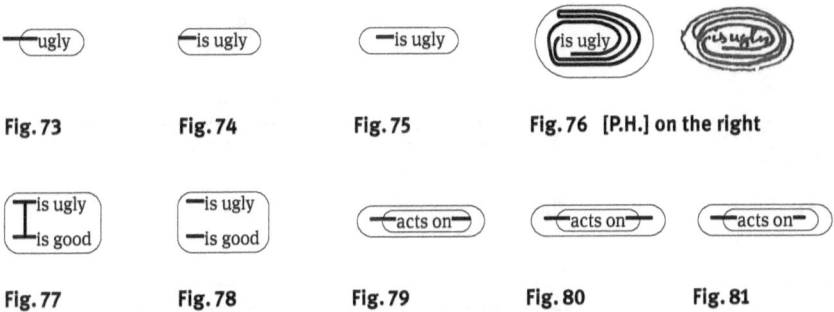

So Fig. 79 can, by the rule of insertion within odd seps be transformed to Fig. 80, and must be interpreted, like that, "Everything acts on everything", and not, as in Fig. 81, "Everything acts on something or other". But if the vacant point on the sep could be treated like an ordinary point, Fig. 81 could be illatively transformed into Fig. 79, which the interpretation forbids. Although in this argument special graphs are used, it is evident that the argument would be just the same whatever others were used, and the proof is just as conclusive as if we had talked of "any graph whatever, x", etc., as well as being clearer. The principle of contraposition renders it evident that the same thing would hold for any finite nest of seps.

On the other hand, it is easy to show that the illative connexion or disconnexion of a line exterior to the sep with a point on the sep follows precisely the same rules as if the point were outside of and away from the sep.

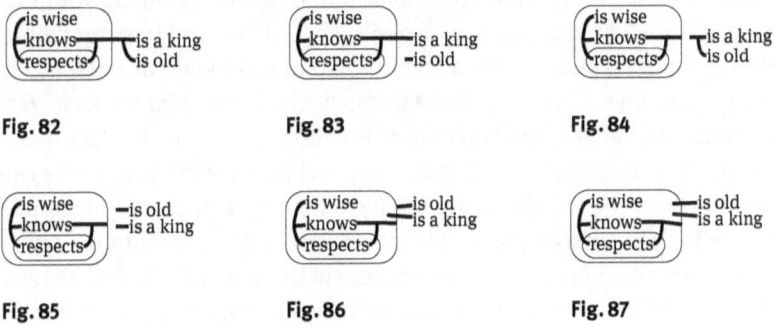

Fig. 88 **Fig. 89** **Fig. 90**

Fig. 91 **Fig. 92** **Fig. 93**

Fig. 94 **Fig. 95** **Fig. 96**

Figs. 82–96 furnish grounds for the demonstration of this. Fig. 82 asserts that there is an old king whom every wise person that knows him respects. The connexion of "is old" with "is king" can be illatively severed by the rule of erasure, as in Fig. 83, so that the old person shall not be asserted to be identical with the king whom all wise people that know him respect; and once severed the connexion cannot be illatively restored. So it is precisely if the line of identity outside the outer sep is cut at the sep, as in Fig. 84, which asserts that somebody is respected by whatever wise person there may be that knows him, and asserts that there is an old king, but fails to assert that the old king is that respected person. Here, as before, the line can be illatively severed but cannot be illatively restored. It is evident that this is not because of the special significance of the "spots" or unanalyzed rhemata, but that it would be the same in all cases in which a line of identity should terminate at a point on a sep where a line inside that sep should also terminate. Fig. 85 shows both lines broken, so that this might equally and for the same reason result from the illative transformation of Fig. 83 or of Fig. 84. The lines being broken as in Fig. 85 can be distorted in any way and their extremities can be carried to any otherwise vacant places outside the outer sep, and afterwards can be brought back to their present places. In this respect, a vacant point on a sep is just like any other vacant point outside the close of the sep. If the line of identity attached to "is old" be carried to the sep, as in Fig. 86, certainly no addition is thereby made to the assertion. Once the ligature is carried as far as the sep the rule of insertion within an odd number of seps permits it to be carried still further, as is done in Fig. 86, with the ligature attached to "is a king". This whole graph may be interpreted "Something is old and something is a king". But this last does not exist unless something is respected by whatever that is wise there may be that knows it. The graph of Fig. 86 can be illatively retransformed into Fig. 85, by first severing the ligature attached to "is a king" outside the sep by the rule of erasure, when the part of the ligature inside may be erased by the rule of deiteration and finally the part outside the close of the sep may be erased by the rule of erasure. On the other hand the ligatures attached in Fig. 86 to "is old" and "is a king" might, after Fig. 86 had been converted in Fig. 87, be illatively joined inside the sep by the rule of insertion, as in Fig. 87, which asserts that there is something old and there is a king; and if there is an old king something is respected by whatever wise thing there may be that knows it. This is not illatively retransformable in Fig. 87. It thus abundantly shows that an unenclosed line can be extended to a point on an unenclosed sep under the same conditions as to any other unenclosed point. For there is evidently nothing peculiar about the characters of being old and of being a king which render them different in this respect from graphs in general. Let us now see how it is in regard to singly enclosed lines in their relations to points on seps in the same close. If in Fig. 82 we sever the ligature denoting the object accusative of "respects", just outside the inner sep, as in Fig. 89, the interpretation becomes, "There is an old king, and whoever that is wise there may be who knows him, respects everybody". This is illatively transformable into Fig. 87 by the rule of insertion under odd enclosures, just as if the marked point on the sep were a hook of any spot. We may, of course, by the rule of erasure within even seps, cut away the ligature from the sep internally, getting Fig. 90, "There is an old king, whom anybody that knows respects somebody or other". The point on the sep being now unmarked, it makes no difference whether the outside ligature is extended to it, as in Fig. 91, or not. It is the same if the ligature denoting the subject nominative of "respects" be broken outside the inner sep, as in Fig. 93. Whether this be done, or whether the line of identity joining "is wise" to "knows" be cut, as in Fig. 92, in either case we get a graph illatively transformable into Fig. 82, but not derivable from Fig. 82 by any illative transformation. If, however, the line of identity within the inner sep be retracted from the sep, as in Figs. 94 and 95, it makes no difference whether the line outside the sep be extended to the unmarked point on the sep or not. One cannot even say that one form of interpretation better fits the one figure and another the other: they are absolutely equivalent. Thus, the unmarked point on the oddly enclosed sep is just like any other unmarked point exterior to the close of the sep as far as its relations with exterior lines of identity are concerned. The principle of contraposition extends this Conditional Principle No. 4 to all seps, within any finite number of seps.

By means of this principle the rules of illative transformation hitherto given will easily be extended so as to apply to graphs with ligatures attached to them, and the one rule which it is necessary to add to the list will also be readily deduced. In the following statement, each rule will first be enunciated in an exact and compendious form and then, if necessary, two remarks will be added, under the headings of "Note A" and "Note B". Note A will state more explicitly how the rule applies to a line of identity; while Note B will call attention to a transformation which might, without particular care, be supposed to be permitted by the rule but which is really not permitted.

[Subsection 3.] Basic Categorical Rules for the Illative Transformation of All Graphs

Rule 1, called **The Rule of Erasure and of Insertion**. In even seps, any graph-replica can be erased; in odd seps any graph-replica can be inserted.

Note A. By even seps is meant any finite even number of seps, including none; by odd seps is meant any odd number of seps.

This rule permits any ligature, where evenly enclosed, to be severed, and any two ligatures, oddly enclosed in the same seps, to be joined. It permits a branch with a loose end to be added to or retracted from any line of identity.

It permits any ligature, where evenly enclosed, to be severed from the inside of the sep immediately enclosing that evenly enclosed portion of it, and to be extended to a vacant point of any sep in the same enclosure. It permits any ligature to be joined to the inside of the sep immediately enclosing that oddly enclosed portion of it, and to be retracted from the outside of any sep in the same enclosure on which the ligature has an extremity.

Note B. In the erasure of a graph by this rule, all its ligatures must be cut. The rule does not permit a sep to be so inserted as to intersect any ligature, nor does it permit any erasure to accompany an insertion.

It does not permit the insertion of a sep within even seps.

Rule 2, called **The Rule of Iteration and Deiteration.** Anywhere within all the seps that enclose a replica of a graph, that graph may be iterated with identical ligations, or being iterated, may be deiterated.

Note A. The operation of iteration consists in the insertion of a new replica of a graph of which there is already a replica, the new replica having each hook ligated to every hook of a graph-replica to which the corresponding hook of the old replica is ligated; and the right to iterate includes the right to draw a new branch to each ligature of the original replica inwards to the new replica. The operation of deiteration consists in erasing a replica which might have illatively resulted from an operation of iteration, and of retracting outwards the ligatures left loose by such erasure until they are within the same seps as the corresponding ligature of the replica of which the erased replica might have been the iteration.

The rule permits any loose end of a ligature to be extended inwards through a sep or seps or to be retracted outwards through a sep or seps. It permits any cyclical part of a ligature to be cut at its innermost part, or a cycle to be formed by joining, by inward extensions, the two loose ends that are the innermost parts of a ligature.

If any hook of the original replica of the iterated graph is ligated to no other hook of any graph-replica, the same should be the case with the new replica.

Note B. This rule does not confer a right to ligate any hook to another nor to deligate any hook from another unless the same hooks, or corresponding hooks of other replicas of the same graphs, these replicas being outside every sep that the hooks ligated or deligated are outside, be ligated otherwise, and outside of every sep that the new ligations or deligations are outside of.

This rule does not confer the right to extend any ligature outwardly from within any sep, nor to retract any ligature inwardly from without any sep.

Rule 3, called **The Rule of Assertion.** Any graph well-understood to be true may be scribed unenclosed.[40]

Note A. This rule is to be understood as permitting the explicit assertion of three classes of propositions; first, those that are involved in the conventions of this system of existential graphs; secondly, any propositions known to be true but which may not have been thought of as pertinent when the graph was first scribed or as pertinent in the way in which it is now seen to be pertinent (that is to say, premisses may be added if they are acknowledged to be true); thirdly, any propositions which the scription of the graph renders true or shows to be true. Thus, having graphically asserted that it snows, we may insert a graph asserting "that it snows is asserted" or "it is possible to assert that it snows without asserting that it is winter".

Rule 4, called **The Rule of Biclosure.** Two seps, one within the other, with nothing between them whose significance is affected by seps, may be withdrawn from about the graph they doubly enclose.

Note A. The significance of a ligature is not affected by a sep except at its outermost part, or if it passes through the close of the sep; and therefore ligatures passing from outside the outer sep to inside the inner one will not prevent the withdrawal of the double sep; and such ligatures will remain unaffected by the withdrawal.

---

40 [In logics that are called *connexive* one makes the assumption that there is at least one true proposition.]

Note B. A ligature passing twice through the outer sep without passing through the inner one, or passing from within the inner one into the intermediate space and stopping there, will be equivalent to a graph and will preclude the withdrawal.

Rule 5, called **The Rule of Deformation.** All parts of the graph may be deformed in any way, the connexions of parts remaining unaltered; and the extension of a line of identity outside a sep to an otherwise vacant point on that sep is not to be considered to be a connexion.[41]

These are all the general basic rules. There are besides special rules for proper names, for selectives, and for rhemata of second intention. It might be supposed that because a line of identity denotes an individual it would require special rules like a proper name or selective. But it will be shown in the next section that no further rules are required for lines of identity than those given.

Section ii. Derived Rules of Illative Transformation

Rule 6. If a line of identity within a sep or nest of seps is connected with no graph without being joined through the seps to the same graph at the same hook, then that line and all its junctions through the seps can be erased.

[Section iii. Recapitulation.]

Appendix [First version]

Logical Tracts. By C. S. Peirce. No. 2. On Existential Graphs, Euler's Diagrams, and Logical Algebra. Part I.

A *diagram* is a representamen which is predominantly an icon of relations and is aided to be so by conventions. Indices are also more or less used. It should be carried out upon a perfectly consistent system of representation, founded upon a simple and easily intelligible basic idea.

A *graph* is a superficial diagram composed of the sheet upon which it is written or drawn, of spots or their equivalents, of lines of connection, and (if need be) of enclosures. The type which it is supposed more or less to resemble is the structural formula of the chemist.

---

41 [The main continuous segment of manuscript pages 1–141 of R 492 ends here. There are no higher page counts than 141 among the preserved drafts and variants of this piece. We do not find, for example, proof or further discussion of Peirce's interesting assertion in the present chapter that "The list of rules given for dinected graphs is complete. This is susceptible of proof, but the proof belongs in the next section of this chapter, where I may perhaps insert it. It is not interesting". What follows as the rest of the main text is found among the assorted pages (ms p. 119, R 492) evidencing that some continuation of the present material might have been written, but no "next section of the present chapter", which according to the reconstruction of the proposed Table of Contents was to be "Section iii, Recapitulation", appears to have been drafted.]

A *logical graph* is a graph representing logical relations iconically, so as to be an aid to logical analysis.

An *existential graph* is a logical graph governed by a system of representation founded upon the idea that the sheet upon which it is written, as well as every portion of that sheet, represents one recognized universe, real or fictive, and that every graph drawn on that sheet, and not cut off from the main body of it by an enclosure, represents some fact existing in that universe, and represents it independently of the representation of another such fact by any other graph written upon another part of the sheet, these graphs, however, forming one composite graph.

No other system of existential graphs than that herein set forth having hitherto been proposed, this one will need, for the present, no more particular designation. The following exposition of the system of Existential Graphs will be arranged as follows:[42]

Chapter I will explain the interpretation of graphs into our usual forms of thinking, and the latter into the former in two sections, of which:

Section i will lay down the fundamental assumptions and will intersperse various logical analyses in the places where they become pertinent; while

Section ii will deduce from these other translations from the one language into the other.

Chapter II will give the principal formal "rules", or permissions, for the transformation of one graph into another without translation into any other system of representation and without danger of passing from truth to falsity. Such transformations are of the nature of immediate necessary inferences. This chapter will consist of two sections related to each as are those of the first chapter; namely:

Section i will prove from the fundamental conventions of Chap. I, Sect. i the basic rules of transformation; while

Section ii will deduce other rules of transformation from those of Section i, without recurring to the principles of Chapter I.

Chapter III will give examples of the utility of the system for logical analysis.

Chapter I. Principles of Interpretation

Section i. Fundamental Conventions

Subsection 1. *Of Convention No. 1*

The purpose of this section is to set forth in a distinct list the fundamental conventions by virtue of which these existential graphs express propositions. These conventions are to be accepted absolutely and not called in question. Still, they are founded in reason; and the design is here to set them forth so that their reasonableness may appear. To do this it will be requisite to call attention to sundry points of logic, some of which may be novelties to the reader and will require some defence. Instead of collecting this matter as an introduction to the explanation of graphs, it will be better to intersperse the logical remarks among those explanations, since the graphs will do much toward making them intelligible and convincing.

This system of graphs is intended to aid the study of necessary ~~reasonings~~ inferences, such as those of mathematics. For this purpose, it must be capable of presenting every such reasoning in a steadily perceptual and controllable form, so that it shall be open to attentive observation and

---

[42] [The first two manuscript pages are missing of this earlier segment of the second *Logical Tracts*, supplied verbatim from the first two pages of the main segment.]

to experimentation. Now, in necessary ~~reasoning~~ inference the fact expressed by the conclusion is involved in the very facts expressed in the premisses. It is therefore requisite that the graphs should be capable of expressing every knowable or supposable state of facts, and that in an analytical manner so far as concerns those connections of its elements upon which any possible inference turns.

What, then, is a *fact*? An entire reality is not a fact. Theodore Roosevelt is not a fact. It is a fact that he exists: it is a fact that he is President, etc. But as for the "entire reality" it could be shown, were it pertinent to do so, that there probably is no such thing. A fact is something separated out from the rest of the real, being so much as is expressible in a proposition. Therefore, the requirement comes to this, that any proposition whatsoever should be translatable into a graph and that in such a manner as to exhibit as distinct any two elements which any given necessary inference may sunder.

So, then, it becomes necessary to inquire into the nature of the Proposition in general. Now every proposition is a partial description of the universe.[43] The logical universe is that object with which the utterer and the interpreter of any proposition must be well-acquainted, and mutually understand each other to be well-acquainted, and must understand that all their discourse refers to it. It is not always the same thing: it may be Shakespeare's world of the Midsummer Night's Dream: it may be a universe created by the utterer for the nonce. But all these universes have their places in one great universe of *The Truth*. At the very outset of forming any intelligible proposition, it is necessary that there should be some sign indicating what universe is meant. In ordinary talk the circumstances in which utterer and interpreter find themselves to be placed form such an index. Before one begins to read a book, one knows from many indications whether it is a work of imagination or with what department of the real world it deals. If we are to write propositions on a sheet, there must be some understanding as to what world they are to deal with. But the moment that this is agreed upon as to a recognizable sheet, that sheet *does* become a sign of that universe. In accordance with that mutual understanding between the writer of the graph—let him be called the *grapheus*,—and the interpreter [of] a proposition written on the sheet, whether in the form of a graph or otherwise,—is *ipso facto* asserted of the universe in question. Before this was written the blank sheet expressed,—that is, caused the interpretation,—that the universe to which it relates had the characters that it was mutually understood to have between grapheus and interpreter. The newly written proposition only makes that representation more determinate.

But innumerable other facts will be true of the universe besides that expressed in the graph that is written, however comprehensive this may be. If, therefore, the system of representation afforded no room to add a further assertion, it would be miserably imperfect; particularly since, in ordinary necessary reasoning, one premiss comes to notice after another. It is, therefore, most desirable that if any proposition, say, 'It snows', is written on the sheet, it should be understood as asserted just as much when another assertion, say, 'It freezes', is written on another part of the sheet, as it would be if no such second assertion were written. Moreover, it is a merit in a diagram to be readily understood; and it will be the more readily understood if its mode of interpretation

---

[43] This luminous idea was obscurely involved in the conception of the logical universe, which was introduced by De Morgan in 1846 (*Cambridge Phil. Trans.* Vol. VIII, p. 380). I do not know where it has been explicitly formulated; but the idea of it is contained in O. H. Mitchell's paper of 1883 (*Studies in Logic by members of the J[ohns] H[opkins] U[niversity]*), one of the greatest contributions that the whole history of logic can show.

is natural. Now certainly it is in the highest degree natural, when two assertions are written on one sheet, to understand that each has the same force as if is stood alone.

But since it has been settled that the sheet, as it was before the first graph was written, should itself be considered as a graph, that is, as the expression of a proposition, namely, that the object it represents, the universe of discourse, has whatever character it has been recognized by grapheus and interpreter to have, which proposition the written graph only serves to amplify by predicating some thing additional of the universe, it follows that if the second graph is to have the same force as if it were written alone, the part of the sheet on which it was written must equally have represented the universe, before this second graph was written on it, just as the whole blank sheet did before anything was written on it.

We are now ready to formulate the first convention of the system, except that two necessary qualifications have to be noticed. We may, and in fact shall, find it necessary in order to express a proposition to refer to another proposition which we do not mean to assert. This latter will have to be written, and therefore must be written on a part of the sheet cut off from the *sheet of assertion*, or sheet upon which any proposition written is asserted. How this is to be effected we need not at this moment consider. In the second place, should two graphs written on the sheet have a common part, they cannot be independent of one another so far as that common part is concerned. With the recognition of those two limitations our first convention will be as follows:

Convention No. 1. *Every portion of the sheet not cut off from the sheet of assertion by an enclosure around it, together with whatever graph or proposition not absurd, may be written upon this unenclosed portion, is to be understood as asserting that whatever it may signify is true of the universe of discourse, this assertion being made independently of the assertion of any other portion of the unenclosed sheet, except so far as this independence is necessarily limited by the two portions having common parts. And every portion of the sheet, not cut by an enclosure, even if this portion is blank, is to be considered as a graph, or proposition, unless what is written be absurd.*

Examples: Fig. 1 asserts that it snows, Fig. 2 that it both snows and freezes:

	It snows	It snows
It snows	It freezes	It does not snow.
Fig. 1	**Fig. 2**	**Fig. 3**

A *graph* represents the universe to be in some conceivable state. Hence, if an absurdity be written, as in Fig. 3, it is not a graph but may be called a *pseudograph*. It would be a violation of Convention No. 1.

Subsection 2. *Of Convention No. 2*

Particular facts, which, if complex, are composed only of simultaneous facts, are not the only facts to be expressed. There are presumably *laws*, as well, that are true of the universe. A law is expressible by a conditional proposition, 'If A, then C'. Such a proposition means that under whatever circumstances A may be true, under these same circumstances C will be true. This refers to a general range of circumstances or of possibilities. In order to construct the system of representation necessary to express such a conditional proposition, it is requisite, in the first place, to supply ourselves with the means of expressing what is called a 'conditional proposition *de inesse*', in which there is no reference to a general range of possibilities, but the only question is, what is true under actually existing circumstances. Understood *de inesse*, 'If A, then C' means merely that if it is a fact that A is true, C is also true; or C is true, unless A is false. Neither A nor C is positively asserted; and therefore neither can be written on the sheet of assertion. They must be cut off from that sheet. Moreover, they must be separated from one another, and in such a manner that they shall not appear as reciprocally related in any one way. They must therefore be in separate enclosures of a different character in one from the other, but connected.

Various different forms of expression present themselves, which would lead to distinct systems of existential graphs, differing materially in their rules. A careful comparison of their respective advantages and disadvantages has led me to prefer to express a conditional proposition *de inesse* by drawing two enclosures, one within the other, and to place the antecedent within one but without the other, while the consequent is placed within both; so that Fig. 4 will mean 'If it is snowing, it is freezing'.

Fig. 4

The word 'enclosure' applies only to the enclosing line. The enclosure with its contents is on the sheet of assertion; but the contents, considered apart from the enclosure is cut off from that sheet. The 'scroll' is composed of two enclosures, one within the other. The node, or point of intersection, has no particular significance. We may regard what is written in the intermediate space between the two enclosures as describing a universe of possibilities subordinate to the main universe of discourse, and what is written within the inner enclosure as a partial description of this universe of possibility. But this is only one of various aspects under which the graph in question may be regarded.

Convention No. 2. *An enclosure written on the sheet of assertion and containing any graph, A, besides an inner enclosure, itself containing any graph or pseudograph, C, shall be understood as asserting that if A is true, then C is true in the acceptation* de inesse *of this conditional proposition.*

Subsection 3. *Of Convention No. 3*

[Alt. A:] Subsection 3. *Of Conventions Nos. 3 and 4*

The apparatus provided by our first two conventions would sufficiently well represent the syllogisms of the ordinary text books; but it is contemptibly inadequate to representing any reasoning less trivial.

It is easily seen that one want there is; and upon examination it turns out to be the principal want. Namely, compare the graph of Fig. 5 with that of Fig. 6.

Something-is-a-bird
Something-is-thievish   Some-bird-is-thievish

Fig. 5   **Fig. 6**

It is desirable,—indeed, quite indispensable for the representation of any reasoning not childish,— that we should be able to express the substance of Fig. 6 in such a manner as to exhibit iconically its relation to Fig. 5. In order to do that, it is only necessary to add to Fig. 5 the assertion that the two "somethings" mentioned are identical. This will be a third assertion; yet it will not do to write it as an independent assertion, as in Fig. 7, since a third something might be mentioned that it was not intended to identify; as in Fig. 8.

~~Something is a bird~~
~~Something is thievish~~
~~The somethings are the same~~

Fig. 7

Something is a bird
Something is a monkey
Something is thievish
Two somethings are identical

Fig. 8

Nor could we describe the somethings meant by their relative situation; for that would be contrary to Convention No. 1, which makes the different graphs independent of one another, and therefore of the *relative* positions. It is evident therefore that we must represent the identity by some sort of visible connection. The sign required must partake of the nature of an *index*, which is a sign which represents its object by virtue of being connected with that object as a matter of fact, like a pointing finger. At the same time, the sign required is not to be *exactly* an index; for it is not to be connected with the things meant but with the representations of those things. Let us call such a sign a *connexus*.

In this system of existential graphs two equivalent forms of connexus will be used. The first form consists of a heavy line joining the signs of the two individuals to be identified. Thus, Fig. 9 would answer the purpose. But there would be no use in writing something twice. We might use Fig. 10. But even this may be simplified by making the line itself to mean that something exists identical with everything represented by a point of the line; and this is the method adopted; so that Fig. 11 will be one of the two ways of expressing analytically that some bird is thievish.

⎛Something is a bird
⎝Something is thievish

Fig. 9

⎧is a bird
Something⎨
⎩is thievish

Fig. 10

⎛is a bird
⎝is thievish

Fig. 11

Such a form of connexus is called a *line of identity*.

The other method of accomplishing the same purpose consists in using different capital letters to denote different indesignate individuals, just as lawyers often do, with one slight but important difference. I find something like the following in a law-book: "A owes B money. But B can find no property of A in A's hands. However, C has in his possession property belonging to A. Then, in the State of Massachusetts, B may sue A on a trustee writ, declaring that C is trustee of A; and if B recovers on this writ, he will have an execution against all A's property in the hands of C". Taking a hint from that use of the capitals, we may write Fig. 12 to assert that something, M is a bird and is thievish. This only differs from the use of A, B, C above in that M denotes *some* individual not specified; while that A, B, C of the legal statement are *any* individuals you please. But lawyers frequently use the letters to mean certain unspecified individuals. Capital letters so used in graphs are called *selectives*. Two selectives of different form, as M and N, may denote different individuals or the same individual; so that Fig. 13 is equivalent to Fig. 5.

M is a bird
M is thievish

Fig. 12

M is a bird
N is thievish

Fig. 13

Of the two forms of connexus, the selective is so inferior to the line of identity that it would deserve no place in this system of graphs were it not that in very complicated graphs it has a simplifying influence for the very reason that it is not so analytical as the line of identity and is therefore less adapted to the purposes of this system.

The selective has the secondary merit of being a remarkably natural sign. Let us compare it with the proper name. The first time we hear a proper name mentioned, say "the Chersonese", we perceive that it denotes an individual; but we get no idea what individual it denotes except from what is said about it: it is a mere something. The next time we hear the name, we identify the something it denotes with the individual we heard mentioned before, and attribute to the present something all that we then learned was true of that individual. Thus, the selective is precisely a proper name; except that every time we pass to a fresh sheet of assertion, it loses its special application and becomes an unknown name for an indesignate individual. The first instance of any selective,—which I call its *first replica*,—denotes an indesignate individual. Every subsequent replica has simply the force of a relative pronoun. This reminds us that in a great many languages of every family of speech,—we may say in all the primitive languages,—a pronoun, relative, demonstrative, or personal, may take the place of the copula "is". Thus, confining ourselves to languages that are not commonly studied in this country, in the old Egyptian ▫𓊃 *pûh*, "it", mostly takes the place of is, in Arabic a personal pronoun, as هُوَ , *hûrva*, "he", is frequent, and so it is in Chaldee, and occasionally in Hebrew. Even in Greek there is a vestige of the use of the article to replace "is", as in ἀχία ἡ κύων τοῦ θρόνου. Even in our own language we can say

and

> Happy the man, and happy he alone,
> He who can call today his own;

and

> Happy the man whose wish and care
> A few paternal acres bound,

> A rosebud set with little willful thorns,
> And sweet as English air could make her, she.

Indeed, we usually find people trying to make themselves understood to foreigners saying, for example, "That man he thief", etc. The explanation of this locution is not primitively or naturally regarded as a name but as involving a verb "is". The stoics regarded the proper noun, ὄνομα, and the common noun, προσηγορία, as different parts of speech. In most languages common nouns, except as parts of verbs, do not exist, or hardly exist. So I find that in analyzing the proposition for the purposes of logic, there is not only nothing to be gained by the separation of "is a man" into verb and common noun, but on the contrary it is better and every way simpler not to do so. Of course, when the *term*, or ultimate logical part of the proposition, is understood as predicative, an identifying pronoun is all that is needed to complete the assertion.

In order to render the interpretation of the line of identity and selective perfectly clear and evidently reasonable in all cases, a good deal of explanation is needed which I shall put into the following two notes, A and B, of which Note A will contain matter abridged from *Tract No. 1*, while Note B will contain logical explanations concerning propositions in general, but not specially relating to graphs.

Note A. Recapitulation of some points treated in Tract No. 1

By the *Phenomenon* is meant whatever is before the mind in any way.

We can distinguish in the phenomenon three kinds of elements which cannot be entirely separated from one another. They are called elements of *Firstness*, elements of *Secondness*, and elements of *Thirdness*.

Of these, the most prominent and easy to make myself understood about, are the elements of Secondness. I will begin with them. A person who is making a muscular effort, say, is pushing against a partly open door, has a double consciousness, a sense of something exerting an effort, and a sense of something resisting that effort. These are not two simultaneous awarenesses, but one and the same. For it would be absurd to talk of having a sense of exertion with no sense of resistance, or of having a sense of a force exerted upon one's self with no sense of counter-exertion. I express this by saying that there is a consciousness of Secondness in such an experience. So if while we are walking on a dark night there is a vivid flash of lightening, self-consciousness is heightened. There is a *shock*, which consists in a double sense of something acting strongly upon us, or disturbing our inertia. Here also is an element of secondness. The idea of reality is the idea that facts are hard and will resist all efforts to annul them. It thus involves a resistance to an imagined effort on our part and to a resistance equal to any exertion that may be put forth.[44] Our ordinary common-sense idea of the impact of bodies is that this impact is a fact,—a real instanta-

---

[44] **[Alt.1]** [...] any exertion that may be put forth. Our ordinary common-sense idea of the impact of bodies, is that it is a real fact that concerns two reacting bodies. What is that instantaneous reaction? We regard it as a real fact in which each of two bodies is as the other compels it to be. There is Secondness again. Thus, by Secondness is meant simply reaction. One reason for calling it Secondness is to mark its relation to Firstness and Thirdness; and another reason is that I desire to indicate that every idea of relationship involves some notion of reaction. Thus, if there are two dots on the paper : , and I think that they each is *not* the other, I do not think of them as actually reacting;—or rather I *do* think of that, but add to that thought, that is is only what their mode of being *fits* them for. If I see a ~~triangle~~ circle and a cross × ○ and think that they are unlike one another, I think of their opposing one another in their ~~influence~~ effects on some third thing, say a[n] image in which the circle and cross each tends to reproduce itself. If I see a pentagon and a heptagon ⬠ , ⭕ , and think of them as being alike polygons in each of which a vertex is opposite to a side, I think of them as acting upon each other, as tending each to be the other, but so that this [end]

[Alt.2] [...] any exertion that may be put forth. Our ordinary common-sense idea of the impact of bodies is that the impact is a fact, a real instantaneous fact, which consists in each of the two bodies being in a state that the other compels. There is Secondness again. All reaction is Secondness. By Secondness I mean a mode of being which consists in something, A, and something, B, being each as it is, A in B's being as it is, and B in A's being as it is, entirely regardless of any third. Genuine secondness requires the two correlates actually to exist and to be individual. There can be no generality in it, since that would involve a third, namely a representation.

Besides elements of secondness, we see in the phenomenon positive qualities, such as *red*, which are such as they severally are in themselves regardless of anything else. For that reason, I call them elements of Firstness. A quality has in itself no identity. So far as it is like another, it *is* that other. They are not in themselves general, since generality refers to representation; but they are perfectly capable of generalization without losing their essential positiveness. Besides, the

neous fact,—which consists in each of the two bodies being in a state that the other compels. Each suddenly resists the other's tendency to continue its state of motion. We do not mean that they *experience* anything; but we do mean that there is something analogous to that. Into the state of being of each there enters an element due to the other. The scientific idea is that all the masses of the physical universe react upon one another in pairs. But we have no need of scientific conceptions. Even to common-sense, it is plain that any two independently existing things are each *other* than the other. Now this mutual otherness is a reaction in so far as the annihilation of either would destroy the otherness to it of the other. To say that a thing *exists* is to say that it reacts with the other things in the universe, being other than every one of them. Hence *existence* is a conception of which Secondness is the principal ingredient. Secondness may be abstractly defined as a mode of being which consists in some thing, A, and something, B, being each as it is, A in B's being as it is, and B in A's being as it is, *entirely regardless of any third*. If every piece of metal in a certain box is being attracted by a certain magnet, then for every piece of metal actually there a fact of Secondness is involved; but that there are no other pieces of metal in the box is not a fact of existence but of non-existence, and as such involves something different from Secondness. Thus, there can be no generality in Secondness. A fact of Secondness must be *hic et nunc*, absolutely determinate in every respect. Otherwise something other than Secondness is involved.

Besides elements of Secondness, we see in the phenomenon positive qualities, such as *red*; and the *positiveness* of them consists in this, that each is as it is, regardless of any comparison or relation whatsoever. This I call *Firstness*. A quality such as red may be called a feeling. That is to say, we can imagine that a being's entire life consisted in one changeless sensation of scarlet or crimson. But every feeling of ours has its degree of *vividness*, which is simply the shock of it and is thus an element of Secondness and no part of the quality itself that constitutes the elements of Firstness. An element of Firstness, in so far as it is such, can have no parts, since parts would be something each not the whole, yet the being of the whole would consist in the being of the parts. The relation of whole to parts is thus a degenerate Secondness. It is quite true that colors, for example, form a system; and that a color, A, may truly be said to consist of a mixture of two colors, B, and C. But not in itself, so far as it is a positive quality; but only in so far as certain comparisons and experiments teach us more than is given in the quality itself. A quality has no identity. For identity is an affair of Secondness, consisting in the applicability of the rule that the object in question either possesses or wants each character. Two qualities, so far as they are alike, are one. A feeling is not in itself general, it is true. That is, is not predicable of many; for that is true only of thoughts, words, or other symbols. But it is capable of generalization without losing all its characteristic positiveness. In that respect, it differs *toto caelo* from an element of Secondness, which loses its essentially individual existence upon the smallest generalization. Besides the qualities of feeling of which we have immediate cognizance, we attribute to things occult qualities upon which their sensible qualities and the applicability to each of this or that law of nature is supposed to depend.

There are in the phenomenon other elements than those of Firstness and Secondness. For example, there is (as I believe, and that makes it phenomenon) no mammal with grass-green hair.

---

qualities of feeling which are immediately known to us, we suppose that things have their occult qualities which are the causes of their sensible ~~experiences~~ appearances and of their behaviour toward one another.

There are in the phenomenon other elements than those of Firstness and of Secondness. [end]

If this is *true*, it represents a *reality*. For to be real is no more than to be as the real object is independently of anybody's opinion or thought *about how it is*. The real object in this case is the earth as it described to be in that negative proposition, or in other words is that negative character in its application to the earth. The assertion involves a prediction in regard to the future; namely, that, hunt the world over as you will, you never will find a grass-green mammal. That, if true, is hard fact. At the same time, this is a fact about words or representations. For it asserts that whatever you may find to which the description "mammal" applies, to that will also apply the description "having hair either white, black, greyish, brown, yellowish, orange or tawny, reddish, purplish, or bluish". Now this assertion would not be falsified by there not being any mammals; so that it cannot be that it concerns any existent things. It may be objected that if it does not concern existing things, it does not concern anything real. But that begs the question. We are supposing the assertion to be *true*; and since it does not assert that there are or that there are not any mammals to be found, it represents a reality which amounts practically to a decree that no green mammals shall be permitted to exist. Such a reality is very well denominated a *law of nature*. It is something real of the nature of a representation; and this I call an element of Thirdness, because a *representamen* (or ~~concrete~~ representing object) may be defined as that whose being consists in its ~~determining~~ having a relation to a second, its *object* represented, such that it determines a third, its *interpretant* representation, to be in this same relation to that [of] second.

Representamens are divisible in two different ways into three classes.[45] In the first way, they are either *Icons*, *Indices*, or *Symbols*.

An *Icon* ~~is a representamen whose special representative force depends upon its qualities as an object a subject of qualities and~~ is independent of the existence of its object. Thus, a geometrical figure of a circle represents a mathematical circle. Strictly speaking, however, it is not the circle on paper, but the image in consciousness, that is the icon. So Fig. 14 is an icon of the identity of the individuals denoted by the selectives A and Z, because it is precisely equivalent to Fig. 15 just as any line is divisible into any desired multitude of partial lines.

A————Z

Fig. 14

A—B B—C C—D...D—J...J—K K—L L—M M—N N—O...O—W...W—X X—Y Y—Z

Fig. 15

Of course, the icon does not function as a representamen unless it is interpreted to be such. But once it is a representamen, it represents whatever its qualities fit it to represent; and these qualities it has even if its object has no existence as in the case of a statue of a centaur.

An index is a representamen of which the special representative force depends upon its being connected in fact with its object represented, independently of whether it is interpreted as a representation or not. In that way, a symptom may be or is to be an index of disease, although it

---

45 [Division of representaments into two tripartite classes instead of three confirms that this part of the text of *The Logical Tracts*, as probably all of it, was written before any drafting of the text of the *Syllabus* (R 478).]

will not actually function as such unless it be interpreted. An index must be an individual existing fact or thing.

A symbol is a representamen whose special representative force depends upon a habit that operates to cause its being interpreted according to that special force. Symbols include language generally and the majority of signs of man's devising together with others that are not of that nature. The symbol itself is of the nature of a habit or general rule. Thus, the word man may occur a hundred times in book of which a myriad copies are printed; but all those million triads of ink spots m a n, will be one and the same word. I call them *replicas* of it. The word itself consists in the habit according to which they will be interpreted in one way.

The other division of representamens is into *sisigns* (*semel signanta*), *bisigns*, and *tersigns*.

- A *sisign* represents its object only once.
- A *bisign* represents its object twice, once more directly, and again as that which is thus represented; or to state it otherwise, it excites an icon and refers to an index of the object of that icon.
- A *tersign* is thrice a representamen; twice in a bisign and then adding an intended interpretant of that bisign.

Sisigns include all icons together with some indices and symbols. Symbols include all tersigns together with some bisigns and signs. There are, besides, bisign indices.

An icon standing alone may be studied in the absence of its object. A sisign index may serve to draw the attention to the object with which it is connected. Thus, the designer of Bunker Hill Monument said that he meant it to say simply, "Here!" Otherwise, sisigns are chiefly useful as parts of bisigns.

Bisigns may convey information. A photograph is a good example of a bisign index. It presents an icon, and at the same time its physical connection with its object seems to afford some guarantee of its fidelity. A bisign symbol is a proposition proper. It has a predicate which excites a sort of composite photograph or generalized image of its object, ~~abstracting~~ emphasizing certain features by abstraction from others; and besides, it has a subject which serves the purpose of an index in identifying its object. But though a proposition certainly has two parts as described, it is more or less arbitrary where the line is to be drawn between them. Thus if the proposition is 'Some bird is thievish', we may regard 'Some bird' as the subject and 'is thievish' as the predicate, or we may regard 'Something' as the subject and 'is at once a bird and thievish' as the predicate, or we may regard 'Something thievish' as the subject and 'is a bird' as the predicate. The distinction between the three concerns methodeutic or rhetoric but not critical logic, which has only to consider the fact represented.

A proposition is usually intended to govern the conduct or reason of the person who is to interpret it. In order that it may do so, some act has to be performed to render it effective. If it is a mental proposition addressed to oneself, an act of the will, called a resolve, may be performed in order to create a disposition to be governed by the proposition. If another person is addressed, a hypnotic "suggestion" may be made by a serious and emphatic manner of enunciation and expression; or a fact may be created which is designed to serve the interpreter as an argument to convince his reason of the truth of the proposition, as when the utterer voluntarily subjects himself to a penalty in case it be not true.

Tersigns are arguments (in the sense of argumentations, not as the word is used above) or inferences. The conclusion is the interpretant sign which is intended to be determined. But this is represented by the *fact* which is itself represented in the premiss. The premiss is usually a copulative proposition. The praemitted fact may be a sign of the conclusion in various ways. [End of Alt.1]

[Alt.2] In a graph, the representation of any rhema which is not represented analytically, but is merely signified as a whole is called a *spot*. A spot occupies a certain area of the surface; and upon the periphery of this spot, there must be a special place appropriated to each blank of the rhema that the spot represents. Each such place on the periphery of a spot may be called a *hook*. The following are examples of the attachments of lines of identity to dyads and polyads.

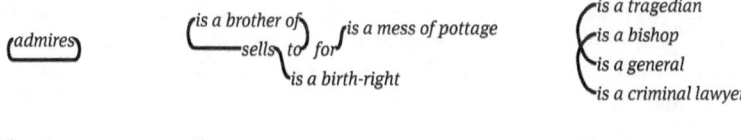

Fig. 10   Fig. 11   Fig. 12

Fig. 10 asserts that something admires itself; Fig. 11, that something sells a birthright to its brother for a mess of pottage; Fig. 12 that somebody is at once a tragedian, a bishop, a general, and a criminal lawyer.

Before a proposition can be of any avail in reasoning it must be put into a form in which it shall show itself to be a whole consisting of partial propositions. Thus, Fig. 11, which might have been written either as in Fig. 13, as in Fig. 14, or as in Fig. 15 is, in Fig. 11 represented as consisting of four propositions, or more.

⌜sells his birth-right for a mess of pottage to a brother of⌝

Fig. 13

—sells̸his̸/birth-right̸for̸a̸mess̸of pottage̸to̸his̸/brother

Fig. 14

This will appear more clearly if we replace the lines of identity of Fig. 11 by selectives, as in Figs. 15, 16, 17.

	M has a brother, N
M has a brother, N	M' sells P to N' in exchange for Q
M sells P to N in exchange for Q	P' is a birthright
P is a birthright	Q' is a mess of pottage
Q is a mess of pottage	M is identical with M'
	N is identical with N'
	P is identical with P'
	Q is identical with Q'

Fig. 15   **Fig. 16**

M has a brother *N*
M" sells *P* to *N"* for *Q*
P" is a birthright
Q" is a mess of pottage
M is identical with *M'*   *M'* is identical with *M"*
N is identical with *N'*   *N'* is identical with *N"*
P is identical with *P'*   *P'* is identical with *P"*
Q is identical with *Q'*   *Q'* is identical with *Q"*

Fig. 17

The peculiarity of a line of identity [is] that it can be regarded as composed of as many propositions as we like is advantageous for the use of graphs, in several ways; but for ordinary purposes, Fig. 15 is better than Fig. 16 or Fig. 17; and for that reason we will not ordinarily regard propositions merely asserting the identity of the individuals denoted by two selectives as parts of the whole proposition.

[Alt.3] It is furthermore usually requisite that there should be enclosures. A graph which is a whole consisting of partial graphs, other than mere lines of identity (which are strictly speaking graphs) may be termed a *syntactic graph*. Two modes of division of the entire class of syntactic graphs are important. On the one hand, a syntactic graph must be of one (and one only) of the following descriptions:

1. It may be *hypothetoid*, that is, composed of medads.
2. It may be *categoroid*, that is, composed of parts of which two at least are monads, but none are dyads or polyads.
3. It may be *grammode*, that is, may have at least one dyad part but no polyad part.
4. It may be *epipolode*, that is, may have one or more polyad parts.

On the other hand, a syntactic graph of any of the above classes, according as it is related to its parts, will either be[46]

1. *Copulationary*, that is, will be true only if each of its parts simply conforms to a certain condition as to truth or falsity and will be false if any part fails to conform to the condition; or
2. *Disjunctionary*, that is, will be false only if each of its parts singly fails to conform to a certain condition as to truth or falsity, but will be true if any part conforms to its condition.

For example, Fig. 16 is copulationary hypotheloid [end] [Fig. 17 is disjunctionary hypetheloid; Fig. 18 is copulationary categoroid; Fig. 19 is disjunctionary categoroid]:

It snows
It blows

(It thunders)
(It lightens)

It freezes
(is indoors
is warm

It freezes
(is warm
is indoors)

Fig. 16   **Fig. 17**   **Fig. 18**   **Fig. 19** [End of Alt.3]

---

46 [Defining these two classes of syntactic expressions are Peirce's attempts at what later were singled out as *conjunctive* and *disjunctive normal forms* of sentential (propositional) logic, respectively.]

[Alt.2, cont.:] There are two ways of combining propositions to which attention must be specially directed. They may be called *direct* combinations, for a reason which will presently appear. They are called *Copulationary* combination and *Disjunctionary* combination.

Copulationary combination, or combination to a *copulate* whole, is such a combination of partial propositions to constitute a whole proposition, that the whole proposition is *true* in case each one of the partial propositions *conforms* to a certain condition as to truth, which condition need not be the same for all the partial propositions; but if a single one of the partial propositions *fails to conform* to the requisite condition the whole is *false*.

Disjunctionary combination, or combination to a *disjunct* whole, is such a combination of partial propositions to constitute a whole proposition, that the whole proposition is *false* in case each one of the partial propositions *fails to conform* to a certain condition as to truth; but if a single one of the partial propositions *conforms* to its condition, the whole is *true*.

For example, the proposition, "It snows and blows but neither freezes nor hails", is a copulate whole, which is true in case the partial propositions that it snows and that it blows are true while the partial propositions that it freezes and that it hails are false. But unless all four conditions are fulfilled the whole is false.

The conditional proposition *de inesse*, considered as a combination of its antecedent and consequent is a disjunct whole. Thus 'If it is hailing, it is cold' is false in case 'it is hailing' fails to be false while 'it is cold' fails to be true; but if either condition is fulfilled, that is, if it is not hailing, or if it is cold, then the conditional proposition *de inesse* asserts nothing false and is therefore true.

Now there is an important principle of logic which is concerned with these two modes of combination. To make it clear, it is necessary to recall (as will be done in the next paragraph) certain points established in *Tract No. 1*.

There are three kinds of representamens, or signs: *icons*, or images; *indices*; and *symbols*, or general signs. An icon is a sign by virtue of resembling its object, which may not even exist; as for example, a statue of a centaur is an image. But strictly speaking, the image is in consciousness. The outward statue is an image only in the sense that it excites an image in consciousness. An index represents its object by virtue of being connected with it in fact, and is necessarily an existing thing or fact. A photograph is an index. For, although it calls up an image, yet it conveys positive information about its object only because we know that physical forces have compelled it to be a faithful likeness. This actual fact ~~gives the photograph~~ imparts to the photograph a representative efficiency, whether the person who looks at it is aware of the fact or not. A *symbol* is a representamen whose representative virtue lies in its being interpreted as having such value. This, for example, is the character of language. Something is whispered in the ear of a king. The result may be that thousands of men lose their lives, that thousands are born who would not otherwise have been born, and that the moral character of a nation is modified. This is not sufficiently accounted for by the fact that the whisper excited an image in the mind of the king, or that the acoustic vibrations were physically connected with any facts; nor even by any force being put upon the king's subjects to do as they did. Unless you hypnotize a man you can hardly put any force upon him of any considerable amount. When we speak of compelling a man to do something, what we mean is that we cause considerations in regard to the future to influence him so as to induce him to act in a given way. The representative force of language and of every other symbol depends upon the symbol's being made such as it is for the sake of the future. This influence of the future is what we call *reason*. It is futile to endeavor to show that it can result in any way from any combination of *imaging* (which is only the vestige of the past) and of *force* (which can only be exerted by what is here and now). The influence of the future must evidently be a third element. It cannot actually be in consciousness, although we can have an indication of it in consciousness as we can on paper. It is strictly a habit governing thought; and as the representative force of the symbol is of this nature, the mode of being of the symbol is of the same nature. Thus, the word 'man' may occur hundreds of times in a book, and of this book there may be myriads of copies. Yet every one of these millions of imprints are one and the same word. The word consists in the habit of thinking about a succession of three characters, m a n, in a certain way. It is the same with any symbol. Each mass of ink spread upon paper in a shape sufficiently like man to be recognized for that, may be called a *replica* of the symbol. All symbols that are created now-a-days,—and I doubt not it was so from the very first,—have forms derived more or less according to general habits and dispositions of symbolizing. But in case the meaning of a symbol is mainly arbitrary the replica in which we first meet with it, which may be called its *introductory* replica for us, will be very indefinite, as above remarked.

All representamens are either *sisigns* (*semel signa*), *bisigns*, or *tersigns*, according as they are once signs, doubly signs, or triply signs. An icon can only be a sisign: a symbol alone can be a tersign. The tersign appeals to the reason of the interpreter to accept it, and does not concern us here. A photograph is an example of a bisign. For on the one hand the manner in which it has been produced necessitate its fidelity to nature, while on the other hand, it presents an image of that nature. It thus affords information; and this is the distinguishing characteristic of the typical bisign. But the symbolic bisign is markedly different from the indexical bisign. The latter represents the state of things at the moment. It is true that the light may be years in coming from the star photographed to the photographic plate; nor is the action on the plate instantaneous. But as to the former objection, it is the incident rays that constitute the object photographed; and as to the latter objection, it misses the point which is that the index represents the facts at the very time when the action takes place, which time no doubt is always a variable of an integral of action. But a symbolic bisign never primarily represents the present time but always future time. It always assumes that the truth, the very truth is destined to be discovered. It does not assert this. Far from that, its utterer probably believes no such thing. But he goes on that supposition in so far as this utterance does; and what he asserts,—subject to that condition,—is that something will be discovered. The proposition represents a fact, which is, as it were, a rag torn out of reality. But the proposition need not be understood as asserting that the reality is a patch-work of facts. But in the process of discovery knowledge comes in bits, and it is such **[Alts. 4, 5]** an item of discovery that the proposition represents. Accordingly, the proposition can only express itself by analysis of the fact; yet it by no means represents that the fact represented is in itself so analyzed.

The following terminology will be used:

Two propositions are said to represent the same *fact* or *truths*, if, and only if, in each supposable state of the universe either both are true or both false. A proposition viewed as identical with every proposition which asserts the same fact may be termed a *nunce* (*nuntius*, message).

Two propositional expressions are said to express the same *proposition*, if, and only if, they not only represent the same fact or truth, but if further in both this same fact is regarded as a combination of the same immediate parts all combined in the same way, and if this is true of all the parts to which the analysis leads.

By different propositional *expressions* are to be understood, not mere *replicas*, but symbols, or general modes, or habits, of representation. One may express a proposition orally, another in English writing, a third algebraically, etc.

If two propositions not only express the same facts but are composed of the same rhemata of first intention, though differently combined, they are said to be *materially equivalent*.

Rhemata of *first intention* are those rhemata which express differences of real fact. Rhemata of *second intention* are those which express differences between symbols. The principal simple rhemata of second intention are as follows:

Medads	What is well-known to be true.
	What is well-known to be false.
	—exists
Monads	—does not exist
	—is identical with—
	—is other than—
Dyads	—is co-existent with—
	—is not co-existent with—
	—is identical with—and with—
	—is other either than—or than—
	—is co-existent with—and with—
Triads	—is incompossible either with—or with—
	—exists and—is identical with—
	Either—does not exist or—is other than—
	etc. etc.

It will be remarked that since we have already seen that to repeat the name of an individual is to introduce the rhema '—is identical with—', it follows that it is impossible to represent that A, B, C are all identical without the triadic rhema '—is identical with—and with—' which is a simple rhema. But the assertion that A, B, C, D are all identical can be made by two triads; and so for greater collections. Similar remarks apply to other triadic rhemata of second intention. [end]

[Alt.4] [...] an item of discovery that the proposition represents. Moreover, the proposition is forced to avail itself of analysis; but it certainly does not represent such analysis as in the fact. Nobody but a metaphysician ever dreams of such an idea. On the contrary we constantly hear two persons uttering propositions very different in form, and yet saying of the others' utterance "that is just what I say". It is difficult, if not impossible, to say just what modification destroys the identity of a proposition, unless we adopt the rule that if of two propositions one might conceivably be false and the other true, they are different propositions, but if not they are the same. At any rate we certainly must distinguish between the proposition and the *mode of expression* of the proposition. [end]

[Alt.5] [...] an item of discovery that the proposition represents. Moreover, the proposition is forced to avail itself of analysis; yet it does not represent such analysis as belonging to the fact represented. For two propositions making very different analyses may be true and false together in all conceivable states of the universe. The following terminology may be used:

Two propositions are said to represent the same *fact* if, and only if, in every conceivable state of the universe they are either both true or both false.

Two propositional expressions are said to express the same *proposition*, if, and only if, representing the same fact, they analyze that fact into the same immediate parts and the same parts of parts to ultimate parts of the same form and meaning.

Two expressions of the same proposition may differ by depending on different conventions or habits of symbolization. Thus, one may be a graph; another may be written in English; another written in Arabic; etc. But if two replicas differ only in respect which are not interpreted as representatively different, as for example, if one is written in English, and the other spoken in the same dialect of English (the two principal dialects of English being the printed and the vernacular, which must use words that are identified but whose principles of interpretation differ considerably), then they are said to be two replicas of the same expression; and there will be no need, in logic, of any general term to express their possible modes of difference.

Triads	—is identical with—and— —is other either than—or than— Some two of—and—and—are identical All three of—and—and—are non-identical —is co-existent with—and— —is incompossible with—or with—

[End of Alt. A.] [The body of the main variant resumes, from **Subsection 3.** *Of Convention No. 3.*] The apparatus provided by the first two conventions would be sufficient to represent the stuff which the ordinary text-books of logic give for syllogistic. It would only be necessary to consider the universe as composed of a single individual. But its insufficiency is manifest. Consider the graph of Fig. 5,

Something—is—a—bird
Something—is—thievish.

Some—bird—is—thievish.

Fig. 5

Fig. 6

and compare it with that of Fig. 6. It is desirable to be able to express the substance of the latter, so as to exhibit iconically its relation to the former. To do that, it is necessary to add to Fig. 5 the assertion that the two somethings mentioned are identical. "Something" denotes an individual; but is indefinite, so that it is not absurd to write Fig. 7, which is, indeed, true of our universe of

Something—is—a—bird
Something—is—not—a—bird.

⟨is a bird
⟨is thievish

Fig. 7

Fig. 8

experience; although it is not true of any definite individual that it is at once a bird and not a bird. There are two obvious ways of adding to Fig. 5 what is requisite to make it equivalent to Fig. 6. Perhaps the more obvious of the two is that shown in Fig. 8, where the heavy line asserts that all the points of it represent identically the same existing individual and that its extremities are to be taken as completing the propositions upon whose predicates they abut; so that Fig. 7 may be read, 'There is something identical with something that is a bird and identical with something that is thievish', that is, 'There is a thievish bird'. The other way, which is occasionally useful, is to use the capital letters as designations each of one individual (the different letters not necessarily denoting different individuals), which is indefinite upon the first use of the letter, but as soon as it has been used, becomes confined to such use as will avoid contradiction.

Thus, Figs. 9 and 10 will have precisely the same meaning, but Fig. 11 will be a pseudograph and not equivalent to Fig. 7.

Something is a bird	M is a bird	M is a bird
		M is not a bird
Fig. 9	**Fig. 10**	**Fig. 11**

A blank form which, when every one of its blanks is filled with a proper name, becomes a proposition, is called a *rhema*. Thus, the following are rhemata

—teaches a boy
A man teaches—
—teaches—.

Rhemata of 0, 1, 2, 3, etc. blanks are called respectively *medads*, *monads*, *dyads*, *triads*, etc.; so that a *medad* is a complete proposition. By a *polyad* is meant a rhema of more than two blanks. In drawing graphs, rhemata may be written out in ordinary language or may be represented by lowercase letter. But in either case a special place called a *hook*, on the periphery of the sign of the rhema, must be recognized as proper to each blank. The expression of the rhema with its hooks is called a *spot*. If the heavy line is employed (called a *line of identity* or a *connexus*), this is to have an extremity abutting upon a hook in order to assert that the rhema is true of [the] individual it denotes. Or the blank may be filled by a capital letter, called an *onoma*, by writing this against the hook. For example, Fig. 12 asserts that somebody is a brother of somebody to whom he sells a birth-right for a mess of pottage; and Fig. 13 asserts that somebody loves himself.

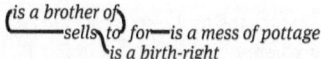

Fig. 12   **Fig. 13**

With this apparatus everything goes smoothly until onomata or lines of connection come to be used along with enclosures, when certain difficulties arise which it will be the province of the next section to explain.

Two things only have to be said here on this subject. First it is a part of our understanding which hardly needs explicit mention that lines of identity do not lose their force in traversing enclosures; nor do onomata cease to perform the function of identification when one is without and one inside an enclosure. Thus Fig. 14 means that there is a certain people which if the Bible is true, is favored of God.

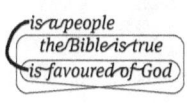

	A is a ray	Q is a plane
	B is a ray	A is in Q
	P is a plane	B is in Q
	A is in P	(P is Q)
	B is in P	
		Y is a point
	X is a point	Y is in A
	X is in A	Y is in B
	X is in B	(Y is X)

Fig. 14   **Fig. 15**

So also Fig. 15 means that if there is a ray, say A, and if there is a ray, say B, and if there is a plane, say P, and if the ray A is in the plane P and the ray B is likewise in the plane P and if furthermore it would follow that if there were any plane, Q, and A were in Q, and B likewise were in Q, then Q must be identical with P, then there is a point X, such that X is in A and X is in B, and if Y is a point such that Y is in A and Y is in B, then Y is identical with X; or in more condensed language, two rays lying in one plane and both in only one plane contain in common one point and only one point. When one sees that so relatively simple a mathematical proposition is really as complicated as this, one judges less severely those who have a difficulty in following the older mathematicians, whose statements are apt to be incomplete and whose reasonings are not always flawless.

Since it is the plan of this tract to place all fundamental logical remarks that need to be made in this section, it will be well to call attention here to two points. In the first place, when an indefinite individual is mentioned in the antecedent of a conditional proposition, the designation ceases to be indefinite and ceases to be individual, becoming a universal designation. Thus in Fig. 16, which may be read, 'if it be true that there is a man who is translated, then God has favorites', we are really speaking of any man whatsoever, and are saying that 'if any man whosoever is translated God has favorites'.

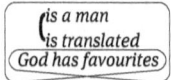

Fig. 16

If we write the antecedent outside the enclosure, as in Fig. 17, it means that *a suitable individual being taken*, it may at once be a man and be translated. But when it is enclosed, as in Fig. 15, it means that *taking any individual object in the universe you please*, if it be a man and be translated, then God has favorites. So the interpretation of Fig. 15 may begin thus: 'Take any objects, A, B, and P, that you please, and if A is a ray and B is a ray and P is a plane, etc.' But it is different with Q and X which are first introduced under two enclosures, for the interpretation will proceed thus: 'and if A and B are in P then, either it is possible to find a plane Q besides P in which both A and B lie or else it is possible to find a point X that lies in both A and B and in that case any object you please if it be a point and lie both in A and in B will be identical with X'. It will be seen that all those onomata which on their first mention occur under an even number of enclosures, or as we may say, are *evenly enclosed*, are indefinite individuals, while those which first occur *oddly enclosed*, that is, within an odd number of enclosures are definite universals. The following definitions will make this clear.

(*is a man*
is translated

Fig. 17

A *subject* of a proposition is any part of it for which a proper name of a known existing individual may be substituted without otherwise modifying the meaning.[47]

---

[47] It will be observed that this makes what modern grammars call the direct and indirect objects to be subjects. The word subject is a term of logic, and the exigencies of logic must determine

A subject is either *general* or *singular*. A *general* is "quod aptum natum est dici de multis"; that is that which of its nature might be applicable to more than one real thing.

A *singular* subject is a subject both *individual* and *definite*.

An *individual* subject is a subject, S, such that, whatever monad rhema P may be, it is either true that S is P or that S is not P. A subject not individual is *universal*. For example, it may be false that *Any man* is rich and yet equally false that *Any man is not rich*.

A *definite* subject is a subject, S, such that whatever monad rhema P may be, it is either false that S is P or else is false that S is not P. A subject not definite is *indefinite*. For example, it may be true at once that *Some man is rich* and also that *Some man is not rich*.

The universe of discourse,—at any rate, the highest universe, to which all propositions alike refer, that of 'the Truth', or the aggregate of all reals,—is singular. If, therefore, a general subject is used, it must be understood that it is capable of replacement by a singular. The proposition may intend to leave the choice of the singular instance to the interpreter, which is the case when the subject is universal; as in 'Any man is a sinner'; or the proposition may intend to reserve the choice of the singular instance for further information to disclose, which is the case when the subject is indefinite; as in 'Some king of Egypt made the Sphinx'. Evidently, the specification of the singular instance cannot be at once reserved and be left to the interpreter, and therefore no subject can be at once universal and indefinite, although it may be neither.

If one subject is universal while another subject of the same proposition is indefinite, the proposition will be equivocal unless it expresses which specification of a singular instance is to be made first. For of two parties, the one having to specify the singular which one subject may be taken to denote, and as utterer of it is desirous of showing that the proposition is true, while the other has to make the specification for the other subject, and as interpreter is properly critical of its truth, that one who makes his choice after the other has announced his will manifestly have the advantage. Understanding, therefore, as in our language we usually do,[48] that the selections are to be made in the order in which the subjects are mentioned, it will assert more to say that

---

the meaning that is to be given to it. It was not used by ancient or medieval grammarians. Even *The Port Royal Greek Grammar* does not contain it. The subject nominative is not the only kind of subject. The word first occurs in Boethius who defines it thus: "Subjectum est id de quo dicitur id quod praedicatur". Now any *rhema* in a proposition may be regarded as its predicate and therefore my definition of subject is correct.

48 Other locutions are in use. The word "given" is used to mean previously chosen. Thus we may say, "Although there is a ~~quantity~~ number closer to the value of π than is any *given* approximation to π, yet there is an approximation to π closer to it than is any *given* number". In a graph, π being a singular quantity will be represented by a capital letter; and the proposition will be represented as follows:

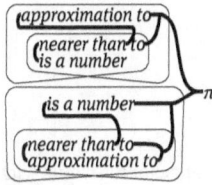

Fig. 18

Somebody is loved by everybody, than to say that Everybody is loved by somebody.

It will, therefore, be necessary that in our system of graphs there should be some rule as to the order in which onomata and lines of identity are to be understood as having to be taken in such specification. But it will be shown in the next section that such a rule is implicitly given in our second convention.

Convention No. 3. *A heavy line (called a line of identity or line of connexion) shall assert the identity of an indefinite individual represented by all its points and makes this individual the subject filling any blank of a rhema upon the corresponding hook of the spot for which rhema this line may abut.*

Any one onoma (usually written as a capital letter) having replicas attached to two or more hooks shall have the same force as a line of identity connecting them.

Section ii. Corollaries of Interpretation

Subsection 1. *Of Interpretational Corollary No. 1*

Since any blank portion of the sheet may be considered as meaning that the universe is singular (as it is mutually understood by grapheus and interpreter to be), it follows that if the space between two enclosures is blank, they have no effect. Thus, Fig. 19 may be read "If the universe is, God is good", which is just the same

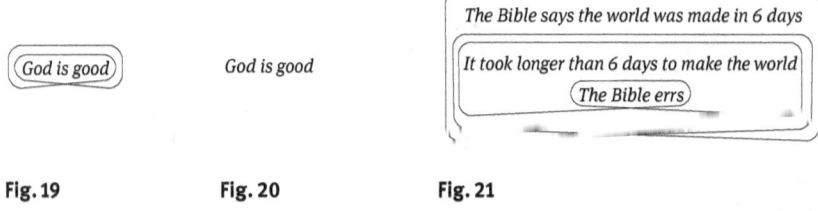

Fig. 19   **Fig. 20**   **Fig. 21**

as Fig. 20. Again, Fig. 21 may be read, "If the Bible says the world was made in six days, then if it took more than six days to make the world, the Bible errs". But the space between the second and third enclosures is blank, and the proposition is evidently equivalent to Fig. 22, "If the Bible says the world was made in six days, while it took more than six days to make the world, then the Bible errs"; so that again two enclosures with nothing between have no effect.

Fig. 22

Corollary 1. *Two enclosures with nothing between them are equivalent to none.*

Subsection 2. *Of Interpretational Corollaries Nos. 2, 3, and 4*

If the inner enclosure of a scroll contains a pseudograph, or absurdity, the effect of the whole will be to deny the truth of the graph in the intermediate space. Thus, Fig. 23 amounts to denying that assassination is right. Conversely, if it be false that the Great Pyramid has fallen down, Fig. 24 is true. For it is an assertion, and an assertion which contains nothing false is true. Now a conditional proposition *de inesse*, relates merely to the truth or falsity of its antecedent and consequent and in case the antecedent is false asserts nothing of the truth of the consequent. Hence if the proposition between the enclosures

Fig. 23 **Fig. 24**

of a scroll is false, the assertion of the scroll with its contents is true; and consequently a pseudograph may then be placed in the inner enclosure. Therefore, a scroll with a pseudograph in the inner enclosure is precisely equivalent to a denial of the graph in the intermediate space.

But a scroll with a pseudograph in the outer enclosure is, taken with its contents, always true, since a conditional proposition with a false antecedent is, as we have just seen, always true. In other words, a pseudograph has the same effect as erasing the first enclosure within which it is written. For a blank is also always true.

Hence, when a pseudograph is written in the inner enclosure of a scroll it is the same as if that inner enclosure were erased. But it is also equivalent to the denial of what else there is in the outer enclosure. Hence, a single enclosure has the effect of denying the entire graph within it.

Corollary 2. *An enclosure has the precise effect of a denial of the entire graph within it.*

It follows that Fig. 25 is a pseudograph; for it denies what is always true.

Then Fig. 4 may be analyzed as follows.

Fig. 25 **Fig. 25** **Fig. 26** **Fig. 27**

Fig. 26 means "It does not freeze". Fig. 27 means, "It snows but does not freeze"; and Fig. 4 precisely denies this, asserting that "It either does not snow or it freezes", or, what is the same thing, "If it snows, it freezes", understood *de inesse*. The node of the scroll is of no consequence, as already remarked. Yet for psychological reasons, it often facilitates interpretation, and should be employed with judgment for that purpose.

According to the traditional, and therefore [the] only correct, terminology of logic, a *hypothetical* proposition is a proposition compounded of propositions not connected by any relative pronoun or any equivalent expression. Hypothetical propositions are either *copulative* or *disjunctive*. A *copulative* proposition is a proposition consisting of members so connected that the copulative proposition is true if all the members are true and is false if any one is false. A *disjunctive* proposition is a proposition consisting of members so connected that the disjunctive proposition is false if all the members are false but is true if any one is true. Consequently the denial of a copulative proposition is a disjunctive proposition and *vice versa*.

An ordinary categorical proposition is a proposition compounded of members of which subjects are identified by a single relative pronoun or its equivalent. If the members are copulatively combined the relative pronoun must be an indefinite individual; for otherwise, the categorical proposition would degenerate to a mere hypothetical one. Thus, "Something which is generous is rich" is a categorical copulative. But "Anything is both generous and rich", is merely a hypothetical copulative, "Anything is generous and anything is rich". Such a categorical copulative proposition asserts existence, and is called a *particular* proposition. So likewise, if the members are disjunctively connected, the relative pronoun must be a definite universal, or the categorical sinks to the condition of a mere hypothetical proposition. Thus, "Anything is either mortal or not a man" is a categorical disjunctive; but "Something is either mortal or is not a man" merely asserts that "Either something is mortal or something is not a man",—unless it be taken as implying more than it expresses *de inesse*. A categorical disjunctive proposition denies the existence of something and is termed a *universal* proposition. In this view of the matter, a conditional proposition is merely a special kind of disjunctive. But it is quite as just, if not more so, to regard the conditional form as primitive.

A relative proposition is a proposition compounded of members whose subjects are identified by more than one relative pronoun or their equivalents. It is subject to somewhat the same conditions but of far greater complexity. We have as the simplest modes of combination,

> Everything is at once a lover and a teacher of something
> Something is at once a lover and teacher of something
> Everything is to everything either lover or teacher
> Something is to everything either lover or teacher.

The propositions, Everything is to something either lover or teacher, and Something is to everything both lover and teacher are mere categoricals; while Something is to something either lover or teacher and Everything is to everything both lover and teacher are mere hypotheticals.

Corollary 3. *Evenly enclosed graphs express existence; oddly enclosed, nonexistence.*

An evenly enclosed onoma or connexus is indefinite; oddly enclosed it is universal. Evenly enclosed elements are combined copulatively; oddly enclosed, disjunctively.

Corollary 4. *An affirmative disjunction is expressed by placing each member of the disjunction in an enclosure and enclosing all these enclosures.*

Thus, it either rains, snows, or sleets is expressed by Fig. 28.

Fig. 28

Subsection 3

The question may properly be asked whether Fig. 29 means that something N is loved by all saints or whether it means that each saint loves something. This question may be resolved with certainty in various ways. One way is to compare two graphs like Figs. 30 and 31. Fig. 30 asserts that it storms and in addition, that it either does not thunder or else it does not fail to lighten.

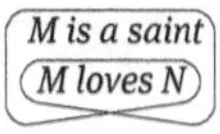

(M is a saint) (M loves N)	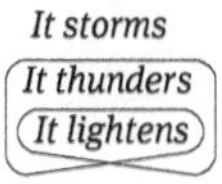 It storms (It thunders It lightens)	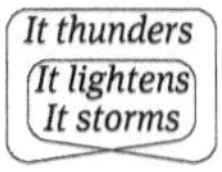 (It thunders) (It lightens It storms)
Fig. 29	**Fig. 30**	**Fig. 31**

That is, it either storms and does not thunder or else it storms and lightens. Fig. 31 means that it either does not thunder or else it both storms and lightens. It is plain that the former asserts all that the latter does and more besides; namely, that if it does not storm and lighten both, it still storms, which Fig. 30 asserts while Fig. 31 does not assert it. Now Figs. 32 [end][49]

---

49 [No continuation of this early variant segment of *Logical Tracts No. 2* has been preserved. The sequence ends abruptly at the end of manuscript page 41, and neither Fig. 32 nor anything to continue the present sequence of Section ii, Subsection 3, beyond page 41 has been identified in R 492 or elsewhere in the Houghton Peirce Papers.]

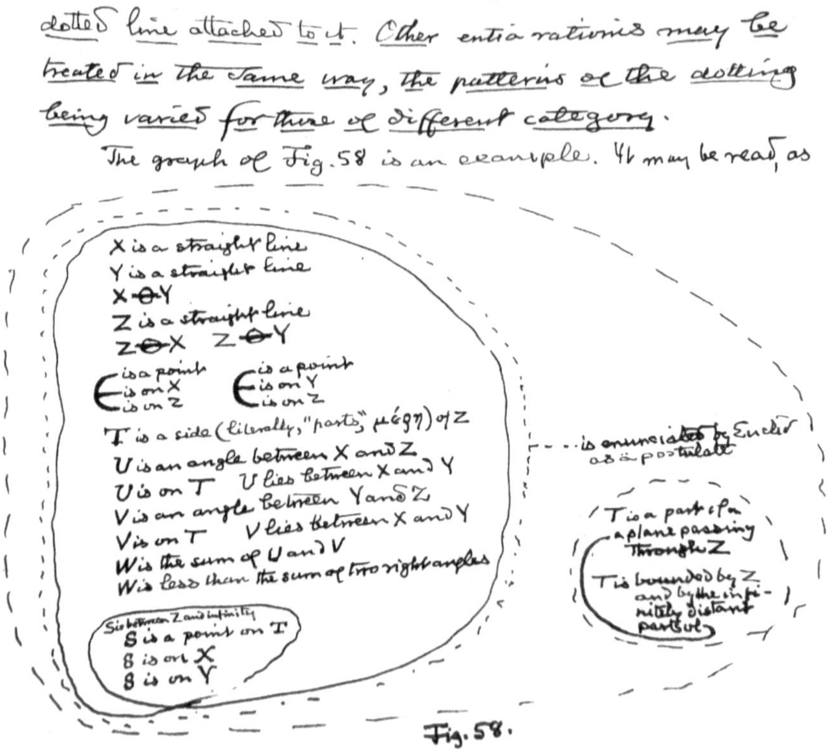

dotted line attached to it. Other entia rationis may be treated in the same way, the patterns of the dotting being varied for those of different category.

The graph of Fig. 58 is an example. It may be read as

X is a straight line
Y is a straight line
$X \ne Y$
Z is a straight line
$Z \ne X \quad Z \ne Y$
E is a point, E is a point
  is on X,   is on Y
  is on Z,   is on Z
T is a side (literally, "parts" μέρη) of Z
U is an angle between X and Z
U is on T — U lies between X and Y
V is an angle between Y and Z
V is on T — V lies between X and Y
W is the sum of U and V
W is less than the sum of two right angles
S is between Z and infinity
S is a point on T
S is on X
S is on Y

...is enunciated by Euclid as a postulate

T is a part of a plane passing through Z
T is bounded by Z and by the infinitely distant parts

Fig. 58.

[A holograph page of R 492, showing Peirce's proposal for depicting abstractions (Harvard Peirce Papers).]

[A mutilated page of R 492, showing abundant editorial marks and cut-and-paste clippings by the editors of the *Collected Papers* (Harvard Peirce Papers).]

31 On Logical Graphs [Euler Diagrams]

[Copy-text is from R 479, variants and draft versions.] Part II of *The Logical Tracts* was planned to be on Euler diagrams. A rich and nearly complete set of texts on Euler diagrams, prepared most likely sometime in 1903, is found in the folder R 479, and it contains a continuous segment of manuscript pages 1–64 (in Peirce's pagination), with a significant number of discrete variants and alternative explorations. Those texts present the most thorough and detailed studies on Euler diagrams and their proposed extensions that has been preserved in the Peirce collection at Harvard's Houghton Library. The main segment of the text, which Peirce designated with a doubly underlined short title ("*Graphs*") in the margins of the sheets, has in most part been published as CP 4.350–4.371. The present selection, in contrast, contains those variants, additional drafts and study notes from R 479 that have not been previously published and do not belong to the main segment. These variants document Peirce's further explorations on Euler diagrams many of which are new, including proposals to erect a theory of (i) Euler diagrams on six modified conventions, (ii) Euler diagrams drawn on a sphere, and (iii) iterated Euler–Venn diagrams to represent more than four terms. Peirce may have experimented on such ideas with a view of having them incorporating into the second part of *The Logical Tracts*, as the goal of the second part was to expose both the limitations of the standard notation of Euler diagram and to present a number of ideas to overcome those limitations. He may also have wanted to contrast Euler's diagrams both to the theory of EGs and to the general algebra of logic, and to do so in more detail and length than he was actually able to do in the present situation at that time. Although the topic of the general algebra of logic was supposed to constitute the third part of the *Tracts*, it apparently was never written as at this point of Peirce nearing the completion of the second part of *Logical Tracts No. 2*, the first term of the course was quickly approaching and he had to move on producing those more pressing lecture drafts and pre-drafts collected in the second part of the present edition.

On Logical Graphs. The word graph was introduced into algebra either by William Kingdon Clifford or by the great Sylvester,—I believe they attribute the invention to each other reciprocally,—to designate a diagram of dots and lines, similar to those by which the chemists represent the constitution of compounds, used as an icon of the relationships involved in invariants. Similar diagrams, though not called graphs, were employed by Kempe in his remarkable memoir on Mathematical Form to represent relationships of all kinds between individuals. I subsequently proposed (*The Monist* Vol. VII, pp. 161–217) a system capable of representing all facts of relation between classes as well as between individuals; but this was no sooner seen by me in type than I perceived that it was one of a pair of twin systems of which the other was to be preferred, and I wrote at once an elaborate paper on the subject, for which I vainly endeavored to find an asylum. At that time, I drew up an elaborate definition of a graph contemplating all sorts of possible generalizations; but I have since bestowed a great deal of study upon the matter both in its details and in its general aspects, and have been led to prefer a very much simpler definition which includes diagrams already in general use among logicians, — being one of the few things which all schools unite in finding valuable, and this catholic confession would seem to be an argument in favor of that intuitional theory of reasoning which was so forcibly defended by Friedrich Albert Lange.

I propose to use the term *logical graphs* to designate any diagram which iconizes logical relations[.]

William Kingdom Clifford introduced the term *graphs* to denote diagrams of spots and lines drawn on a surface to represent singular states of a continuum, such as the invariantive forms of an algebraic expression. The suggestion of such diagrams came from those employed by chemists to represent the constitutions of compounds.

By a logical graph, I mean any superficial geometrical diagram intended to represent logical relations. In this paper I intend to describe three systems of logical graphs and to show that all such systems belong to one or other of two general systems very simply related to each other.

I. Eulerian Diagrams. It is one of the signs that the study of philosophy has not yet attained the scientific stage of development that even to this day any one philosopher deems the lucubrations of any other philosopher to be not worth reading, until once in a while a work appears which, for one reason or another, is generally read. Such was the book of the celebrated mathematician Leonard Euler, and Antiwolfian, entitled *Lettres à une princess d'Allemagne sur quelques suject de physique et de philosophie*, which appeared in two volumes in 1768 and 1772. This book seems to have made logicians generally acquainted with the use of geometrical diagrams in syllogistic. Yet essentially the same method (in a less elegant shape, lengths taking the place of areas) had been employed in one of the most celebrated of works on logic, the *Neues Organon* of the mathematician Lambert published in two volumes in 1764, and precisely Euler's form of the diagrams had been published in the *Nucleus Logical Weisianae* of Johann Christian Lange published in 1712, where the authorship of these diagrams is attributed [to Juan Luis Vives] [end]

On Logical Graphs. I. The so-called diagrams of Euler are well-known. They have been traced back to Laurentius Valla in the fifteenth century, and there is no knowing how much older they may be. It certainly does not seem at all unlikely that Aristotle aided his syllogistic by diagrams; for such a hypothesis would explain a number of his expressions.

Euler's diagrams will here be described in the improved form given to them by Mr. Venn, adding an additional improvement. The system of representation being so modified, the conventions are as follows:

1. The diagram shall be drawn on a sheet, called the *sheet of the diagram*. The different points of this sheet shall represent the different possible states of a certain individual subject, it being well-understood between the drawer and the interpreter of the diagram what this subject is. Let this subject be termed the *Universe of Discourse*.
2. Different ovals may be drawn upon the sheet, and each of these shall be connected with some assertion about the Universe of Discourse, which assertion may be written along the oval line or otherwise indicated; and the connection shall be such that every point of the sheet outside the oval shall represent a possible state of things in which the corresponding assertion would be true of the universe of discourse, while each point inside the oval shall represent a possible state of things in which the corresponding assertion would be false.
3. Areas of the sheet may be shaded or darkened, and every point of a darkened area are to be regarded as non-existent, or excluded from the sheet of the diagram in so far that known facts exclude the state of things which would be represented as possible if the point had existed on the sheet of the diagram.
4. The coloring red of any point of the diagram shall signify that the corresponding state of things is realized at some time or in some reference.
5. If a point colored red lies on an oval line, the signification of this circumstance shall be that whether the realized state of things is such that it is represented by a point inside or outside of the oval is indeterminate.
6. A rectilinear border in green shall mark the limit of the sheet of the diagram.

Illustrations. In Fig. 1, the universe of discourse is the state of the weather in Tompkin's Island.[1] The proposition connected with one oval is "It is the dry season"; that connected with the other oval is "It is raining". The diagram asserts that it is always either the dry season or is raining on Tompkin's Island. It may be both. For

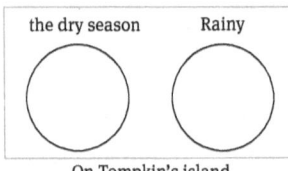

On Tompkin's island

Fig. 1

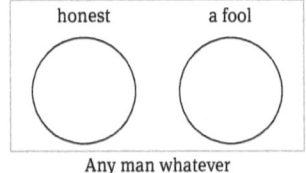

Any man whatever

Fig. 2

---

1 [In Figs. 1–4, the rectilinear borders are drawn in green ink in the original copy-text, and the dots in Figs. 3–4 are drawn in red ink.]

there are no points enclosed by both ovals. So Fig. 2 expresses that every man is either honest or a fool. Fig. 3 expresses that on Tompkin's Island, it sometimes does not rain though it is not in the dry season. Fig. 4 expresses that some man is neither a fool nor honest.

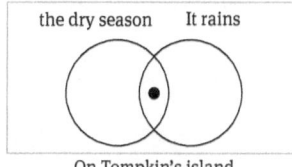

Fig. 3

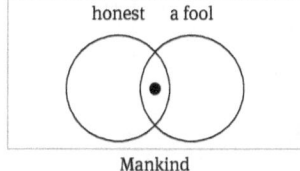

Fig. 4

I. Of Eulerian Diagrams.[2]

The general attention of logicians was called to these diagrams by the description of them in 1772 in the second volume of Leonard Euler's *Lettres à une princesse d'Allemagne sur quelques sujects de physique et de philosophie*. In order to exhibit the nature of the syllogism,—say of this one

> All men are mortal
> All saints are men;
> ∴ All saints are mortal;—

imagine all the saints to be brought together and an imaginary circle, S, to be drawn round them enclosing nothing else. Imagine at the same time all men to

---

2 **[Alt.1] On Eulerian Diagrams.** Let a surface topically [be] like that of a sphere, so that any undetermined line separates it into two parts, represent the whole range of possibility, but not in such a sense that two portions of the surface represent incompossibles.

Let points marked on this surface represent existing individual objects of any kind. It is assumed that there is room on the surface for a collection of distinct points of *any multitude whatsoever*.

Let the two parts into which the surface is divided by a closed line represent [end]

[Alt.2] On Eulerian Diagrams. Let a surface [be] such that any closed line separates it into two parts, represent the whole range of predication.

Let the two parts into which the surface is separated by any closed line represent two mutually contradictory predicates.

Let a point marked on any part [of] the surface represent an existing individual of which the predicate represented by that part is true. It is assumed that there is room on the surface for a collection of points of any multitude whatsoever. If a point is placed on a line, it is doubtful on which side it belongs.

be brought together,—those who are not saints as close as possible to those who are,—and an imaginary circle, M to be drawn round them, enclosing nothing else.

A diagram based on these assumptions is a Eulerian diagram. Such diagrams very clearly illustrate simple syllogisms; but I do not see how they can be further extended, since they afford no means of representing relations or even logical aggregation.

The following diagrams illustrate different forms of syllogism.

No A is not B
No B is C
∴ No A is C

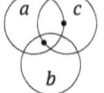

No A is not B
Some C is not B
∴ Some C is not A

Some A is B
Some C is not B
∴ Some A is not some C

Some A is not some B; i.e. Some A is X; some B is not X.
No B is not C
∴ Some C is not some A; i.e. Some C is not X; some A is X.

[P.H.]

Some A is not some B
Some C is not B
∴ Some A is not something that is not some C.

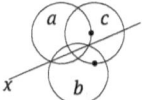

Some A is not some B (1)
Some C is not B (2)
∴ Some C is not something (2) that is not something (1) that is not some A.

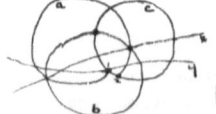

[P.H.]

Some A is B
Some B is C
∴ Some A is coexistent with some C; i.e. There is some A; there is some C.

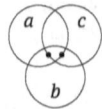

Plainly the circle M must enclose the circle S. Finally, let all mortal beings be brought together, and an imaginary circle, P, to be drawn round them enclosing nothing else.

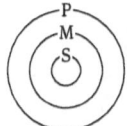

Fig. 1

Then because what is enclosed in something enclosed by anything, P, is itself enclosed in P, it follows that the circle S must be enclosed in the circle P. But all saints are in S and nothing but mortal beings are in P. Hence, all saints must be mortal beings. But the theory is that, instead of reasoning in this way, one simply looks at the diagram and sees that it is so. It is, however, not the question how some or all men *do* perform reasoning, but what is essential to its validity. One sees that a relation exists; but can one see that it *must* be? Still, the analogy between the logical relation and the geometrical relation is unquestionable.

It is evident however that the relation of enclosure can only be the basis of an inference in three cases; namely in that of Fig. 1,

$$\text{S is within M}$$
$$\text{M is within P}$$
$$\therefore \text{S is within P}$$

in the case of Fig. 2,

Some two different A's are B
Some C is not B
∴ Some C is different from ~~either~~ both of two different A's.

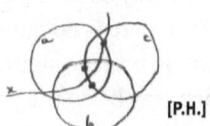

[P.H.]

Although such syllogisms are among the easiest examples in the logic of relatives, it seemed worth while to show how they could be solved by Eulerian diagrams, especially since Lange holds that such diagrams are the foundation of logic. [End of Alt.2]

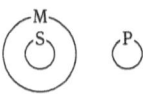

S is within M,
M is entirely outside P;
∴ S is entirely outside P,—

Fig. 2

and in the case of Fig. 3

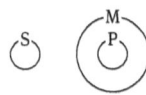

S is entirely outside M
M encloses P
∴ S is entirely outside P.

Fig. 3

The last two cases become the same, as soon as it is recognized that to say that S is entirely outside P is the same as to say that P is entirely outside S.

So little are logicians given to the easy but most serviceable habit of generalizing that there are books of leaders in the science which mention the fact that there are only these two ways in which one circle can entirely separate two circles from one another as an instance of the perfect aptitude of these diagrams to represent the relations of logic. But there is, at any rate, no particular appropriateness in drawing the diagrams on a plane surface rather than on a sphere. The collection of all beings is as definite a whole as the collection of all mortal beings; and thus the sphere is rather the more appropriate. But drawing either diagram on a sphere make the circle P a great circle of that sphere and the difference between Fig. 1 and Fig. 2 becomes infinitely little. Indeed on a sphere there is evidently no essential difference between the *inside* and the *outside* of a circle. It is simply that a circle has two sides either of which may arbitrarily [be] called the positive side, and the other the negative side. There are then *three* possible relative positions of two non-intersecting circles, namely:

First, each may be on the negative side of the other, so that there is no part of the surface at once on the positive side of both.

Second, one may be on the negative side of the other, which is on the positive side of it, so that there is no part of the surface at once on the negative side of the former and on the positive side of the latter.

Third, each may be on the positive side of the other, so that there is no part of the surface on the negative side of both.

There are also these three logical relations. Thus, the classes of *saints* and *perfect* beings may either be related in the first way, so that

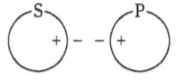 There are no saints that are perfect; or in the second way, so that

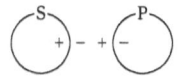 There are no Saints that are not Perfect, or in the third way so that

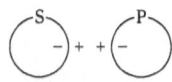 There is nothing that is neither Saint nor Perfect, i.e. Everything is either Saint or Perfect (or both).

Unquestionably two classes may be related in this last way. Every being is either finite or cognoscitive; every whole number above three either differs by one from a multiple of six or is composite. Yet two circles cannot exhibit this relation, if their insides correspond to the positive terms.

Another defect of the system is that it only represents those propositions which declare some description of thing to be *non-existent*. It does not represent the precise denial of such a proposition which declares the same description of thing to be existent. It can express "All saints are perfect", because, or provided, that means "There are no saints that are not perfect". But it has no way of ~~representing~~ expressing "There is a saint that is not Perfect". To be sure, there is a way of remedying this defect; but the way commonly used introduces an inconsistency, so that the clearest-headed logicians do not attempt to use the system in these cases.

It is a singular proof of the unscientific stage of development of logic, that different logicians look so little into one another's books that down to 1834 when Hamilton began his public lectures, Euler was always credited with the authorship of this system; and indeed, it may very well be that he reinvented it for himself. But another mathematician, a German son of a French father, Johann Heinrich Lambert, had given substantially the same system in his *Neues Organon* only a few years previously, in 1764.³ Lambert, instead of areas, used the stretch of horizontal parallels but with a complication hard to comprehend and certainly erroneous. Thus he draws

to signify 'Some A is B'. But 'Some A is B' expresses the same relation as 'Some B is A', which he would represent by

---

3 [These historical notes were expanded in the main segment of the text (R 479 manuscript pages 11–19), published as CP 4.353.]

```
A  ───
B  ·············
```

differently from the very same relation expressed with a very slight grammatical difference.

Hamilton first pointed out, in modern times, the claim made for Christian Weise, who died in 1708,[4] to the merit of inventing the Eulerian circles. Hamilton's expression is "I find it in the *Nucleus Logicæ Weisianæ*, which appeared in 1712"; but Hamilton is so reckless in his statements that this very likely refers to the fact that Johann Heinrich Lambert in his *Architektonik* appears to attribute to Weise the use of circles and squares to represent the relations expressed in propositions. But Lambert's ideas were far from clear in this matter, and since his *Architektonik* appeared in 1771, the year before the publication of the second volume of Euler's *Lettres*, it is very doubtful, and since nobody but Hamilton ~~claims~~ has testified since to having examined the original work explaining Weise's system, it remains very doubtful whether he really did anticipate Euler. Hamilton in the same passage says "Lambert's method… by parallel lines of different length is to be found in the *Logic* of Alstedius, published in 1614"; but Hamilton's own editors flatly contradict this, and Venn (*Symbolic Logic*, 1st Edition, p. 423) copies the passage of Alstedius and shows that Hamilton's assertion is unwarranted. In 1877, however, Friedrich Albert Lange remarked that the celebrated Juan Luis Vives, who died 1540, in his *De Censura Veri* used substantially the Eulerian method, except that in place of circles he uses open triangles. The passage and figure are given by Venn (*loc.cit.*) and fully bear out the assertion of Lange.

No real improvement upon the system was made until Mr. Venn, in 1880, removed the first of the above mentioned defects by simply shading those compartments of the figure that correspond to combinations to be represented as non-existent. At the same time, Mr. Venn suggested ~~making~~ drawing ellipses instead of circles arranging these in fours thus ⊛ or in threes ⚛ or in pairs ◎. The method is not well adapted for cases in which the number of terms exceeds four, although the accompanying figure (where four of the terms are each represented by sixteen ovals) shows how it may be adapted to eight terms.

---

4 [Christian Weise, April 30, 1642–October 21, 1708.]

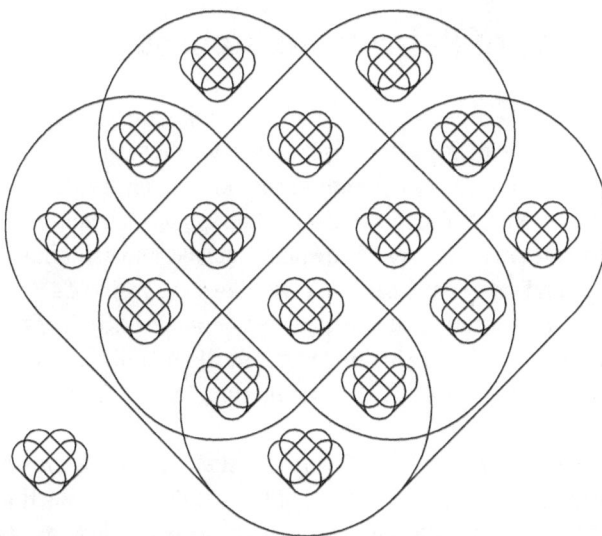

Such a figure is a blank form of which a supply (multiplied by lithography or otherwise) may be kept on hand. A covariant form of oval is that of the curve $x = \sqrt{7 - y^2/9 - y^2}$, or $y = \sqrt{\frac{7-9x^2}{1-x^2}}$, as shown in the figure [end][5]

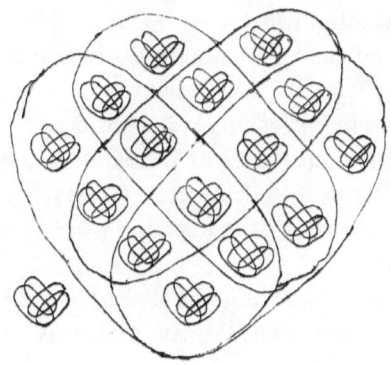

[P.H.]

---

5 [The segment and the sentence ends abruptly in the top part of this last manuscript sheet (ms p. 14). The only preserved additional draft page that has its title in margin singly underlined (ms p. 20) and which does not interpolate well with the material in the main segment with a doubly underlined title (ms pp. 1–64), suggests that this earlier segment, of which manuscript pages 3–14 have been preserved, was at least five manuscript pages longer than what remains in R 479 or in the Harvard Peirce Papers.]

Bibliography of Peirce's References

This bibliography encompasses those books, volumes and editions that Peirce referred or is most likely to have referred to in the relevant parts of the texts included in the volumes of the *Logic of the Future*. His self-references are included in the bibliography at the end of the introductory chapters of each volume.

At various times in his life, Peirce owned extensive and valuable collections of books, journals and reference works that was likely to consist of several thousand items. Details of the editions that Peirce owned or had in his possession when producing the relevant studies are included after the item information, and if known, with their present provenance (JHU = Johns Hopkins University, Special Collections).

The list below comprises approximatively some 1/30 of the books that Peirce might have acquired during his lifetime. Sadly the bulk of his collection, including countless books rife with marginalia, is no longer recoverable as most of the items that once belonged to his library have been lost, damaged, discarded, destroyed, stolen, given away or sold to collectors over the years.

Abelard, Peter (Abelardus Petrus). *Ouvrages Inédits d'Abelard Pour Servir À l'Histoire De La Philosophie Scolastique En France*. Edited by Victor Cousin. Paris: Imprimerie Royale, 1836. (Peirce's Library) [Only mentioned by name, no specific book detailed. This edition was owned by Peirce.]

Agrippa, Cornelius (Heinrich Cornelius Agrippa von Nettesheim). *De incertitudine et vanitate scientiarum et artium*. Parisiis: Apud Ionnem Petrum, 1531.

Alstedius (Alsted), Johann Heinrich. *Sientiarum omnium encyclopaediae*. Lyon: Hvgetan and Ravavd, 1649. (Peirce's Library, two copies of the same item, JHU) [Peirce's reference is to Alstedius's *Logic*, 1614, as referred to by W. R. Hamilton (LoF 2).]

Apuleius, Lucius. *Opuscula quæsunt de philosophia*. Edition A. Goldbacher, 1876.

Aquinas, Thomas. *Summa totius logicae Aristotelis*. Edidit Hieronymus Monopolitanus. 1496. [Of Thomas Aquinas's works, Peirce owned at least three incunabula, with Peirce's marginal notes: *Quaestiones de anima* (Venice: F. Renner, 1472), *Opuscula* (Venice, 1508), and *Quaestiones de quodlibet* (Nüremberg: Johann Sensenschmidt & Andreas Frisner, 1474). *Opuscula* is identified as "From the Library of Ludovico Manini [1726–1802], Doge of Venice". Provenance JHU.]

Aquinas, Thomas. *Opuscula sancti Thome: quibus alias impressis nuper hec addidimus videlicet Summam totius logice. Tractatum celeberrimum De usuris nusquam alias impressum*. Venice: cura & ingenio Giacomo Penzio mandato & expensis Peter Liechtenstein, 1508. (Peirce's Library, JHU) [Peirce's reference is: "Aquinas ... or the writer of the treatise on logic attributed to him" (LoF 3), probably referring to the *Summa logicae*. It is this particular edition that was in Peirce's possession.]

Aristotle. *Aristoteles Graece*. Two volumes. Edited by Theodor Waitz. Leipzig: Georg Reimer, 1831. (Peirce's Library, JHU) [Peirce mentions a few books in Aristotle's œuvre by name: *Metaphysics, Prior Analytics, Posterior Analytics, Perihermeneias* (ed. F. Michelis) and *Sophistical Elenchi*.]

Aristotle. *Aristotelis Organon graece*. Edited by Theodor Waitz. Lipsiae: Sumtibus Hahnil, 1844–1846. (Peirce's Library, JHU)

Arnauld, Antoine & Pierre, Nicole. *The Port Royal logic*. [*l'Art de Penser*] Translated by T. S. Baynes. 5th edition. Edinburgh: James Gordon, 1861. (Peirce's Library) [Lowell Lectures reading list. Peirce refers to the 5th edition of 1861 (R 454; LoF 2). This translation contains Leibniz's *Mediationes de Cognitione, Veritate et Ideis* (1684). Peirce's Library contained the 1851 edition, Edinburgh: Sutherland and Knox.]

Bachmann, Carl Friedrich. *System der Logik: Ein Handbuch zum Selbststudium*. Leipzig: F. U. Brockhaus, 1828. (Peirce's Library, JHU)

Bayes, Thomas. "An essay towards solving a problem in the doctrine of chances". *Philosophical Transactions of the Royal Society* 53(1763): 370–418.

Berkeley, George. *A Treatise Concerning the Principles of Human Knowledge*. Dublin: Jeremy Pepyat, 1710.

Berkeley, George. *The Works of George Berkeley, D.D. Late Bishop of Cloyne in Ireland—To which is added An Account of His Life, and several of his Letters to Thomas Prior, Esq., Dean Gervais, and Mr Pope*. In Two Volumes. Dublin: John Exshaw, 1784. (Peirce's Library, JHU)

Bertrand, Joseph Louis François. *Calcul des probabilités*. Paris: Gauthier-Villars et fils, 1889. [Lowell Lecture's reading list, Lecture VI.]

Boethius. *Anitii Manlii Severini Boethi: opera omnia*. Two Volumes. Basileæ: ex officina Henricpetrina [1570], 1546. (Peirce's Library, JHU. Peirce owned or attempted to acquire also the Migne edition of Boethius's *Opera*.)

Boltzmann, Ludwig. "Über die Grundprincipien und Grundgleiehuugen der Mechanik". In *Clark University 1889–1899: Decennial Celebration*, Edited by W. E. Story et alii, (261–309). Worcester, Mass., 1899.

Bolzano, Bernard. *Wissenschaftslehre: Versuch einer ausführlichen und größtentheils neuen Darstellung der Logik mit steter Rücksicht auf deren bisherige Bearbeiter*. Sultzbach: J. E. v. Seidel, 1837.

Bolzano, Bernard. *Paradoxien des Unendlichen*. Leipzig: C. H. Reclam sen., 1851.

Boole, George. *The Mathematical Analysis of Logic: Being an Essay Towards a Calculus of Deductive Reasoning*. Cambridge: MacMillan, Barclay, and MacMillan, 1847.

Boole, George. *An Investigation of the Laws of Thought, On which are founded the mathematical theories of logic and probabilities*. London: Walton & Maberly, 1854. [Lowell Lecture's reading list, Lecture VI.]

Bosanquet, Bernard. *Knowledge and Reality. A Criticism of F. H. Bradley's "Principles of Logic"*. London: Swan Sonnenschein & Co., 1892. [Lowell Lecture's reading list, Lecture I.]

Bossuet, Jacques-Bénigne. "Logique". Oeuvres inédites de Bossuet, évêque de Meaux dédiées à S. A. R. Monseigneur le Duc de Bordeaux. Paris, 1828.

Boutell, Charles. *The Handbook to English Heraldry*. London: Cassell, Petter, & Galpin, 1867.

Bradley, Francis Herbert. *The Principles of Logic*. London: Kegan Paul, Trench & co., 1883. [Lowell Lecture's reading list, Lecture I.]

Bradley, F. H. *Appearance and Reality: A Metaphysical Essay*. London: Swan Sonnenschein & Co, 1899. (Peirce's Library, Harvard University Robbins Library)

Byrne, James. *General Principles of the Structure of Language*. Two volumes. London: Trübner & Co, 1885.

Cantor, Georg. "Beiträge zur Begründung der transfiniten Mengenlehre". *Mathematische Annalen* 49(1897): 207–246. [Lowell Lecture's reading list, Lecture V.]

Cantor, Georg. *Zur Lehre vom Transfiniten: gesammelte Abhandlungen aus der Zeitschrift für Philosophie und Philosophische Kritik*. Halle: Pfeffer, 1890.

Cantor, Georg. "Une contribution à la théorie des ensembles". *Acta Mathematica* 2(1883): 311–328. [Peirce's reference is: "Acta Mathematica Vol. II, p. 321" (LoF 3).]

Cantor, Georg. "De la puissance des ensembles parfaits de points". *Acta Mathematica* 4(1884): 381–392.

Cantor, Moritz. *Vorlesungen über Geschichte der Mathematik*. Volume 2. Leipzig: B. G. Teubner, 1900.

Carus, Paul. *Ursache, Grund und Zweck: Eine philosophische Untersuchung zur Klärung der Begriffe*. Dresden: R. von Grumbkow, 1883.

Castrén, Matthias. *Grammatik der samojedischen Sprachen*. St. Petersburg: Buchdruckerei der Kaiserlichen Akademie der Wissenschaften, 1854. [Mentioned by name ("…Castrén, a grammarian of those [Samoyeed] languages…", LoF 1).]

Cayley, Arthur. "Fifth Memoir on Quantics". *Philosophical Transactions of the Royal Society of London* 148(1858): 429–460.

Cayley, Arthur. "Metrics". In: Salmon, George. *A Treatise on the Higher Plane Curves: Intended as a Sequel to A treatise on Conic Sections*, (108–128). Dublin: Hodges, Foster & Figgis, 1879.

Clarke, Frank Wigglesworth. *Data of Geochemistry*. Bulletin No: 330. Series E, Chemistry and Physics, 54. Washington: Government Printing Office, 1908.

Clifford, William K. *Lectures and Essays*. London: Macmillan, 1879. (Peirce's Library)

Darwin, Francis, Sir. *The Life and Letters of Charles Darwin: Including an Autobiographical Chapter*. Three volumes. London: John Murray, 1887.

Davidson, Thomas. *Aristotle and Ancient Educational Ideals*. New York: C. Scribner, 1892.

Dedekind, Richard. *Stetigkeit und irrationale Zahlen*. Braunschweig: F. Vieweg und sohn, 1872.

Dedekind, Richard. *Was sind und was sollen die Zahlen?* Braunschweig: Vieweg, 1887.

Dedekind, Richard. *Essays on the Theory of Numbers, 1. Continuity and irrational numbers. 2. The Nature and Meaning of Numbers*. Translated by Wooster Woodruff Beman. Chicago: Open Court, 1901. (Peirce's Library) [A copy of this book was sent to Peirce on July 13, 1903, by Fred. Sigrist, printer and compositor from Open Court who corresponded with Peirce on Carus's alleged plagiarism and misconduct issues in 1903 (FS to CSP, July 13, 1903, R L 77). Its present provenance is unknown. Included in the Lowell Lecture reading list, Lecture V, with reference to "Authorized translation by W. W. Beman. Chicago, 1901".]

De Morgan, Augustus. "On the Structure of the Syllogism". *Transactions of the Cambridge Philosophical Society* 8(1846): 379–408.

De Morgan, Augustus. *Formal Logic, or The Calculus of Inference, Necessary and Probable*. London: Taylor & Walton, 1847. (Peirce's Library) [The book has Peirce's abundant marginalia and its provenance has in the past been at the Harvard University's Library System. The item is no longer to be located in Harvard's collections.]

De Morgan, Augustus. "On the syllogism no: II. On the symbols of logic, the theory of the syllogism, and in particular the copula". *Transactions of the Cambridge Philosophical Society* 9(1850): 79–127.

De Morgan, Augustus. "On the syllogism no: III and on logic in general". *Transactions of the Cambridge Philosophical Society* 10(1858): 173–230.

De Morgan, Augustus. "On the syllogism no: III and on the logic of relations". *Transactions of the Cambridge Philosophical Society* 10(1860): 331–358.

De Morgan, Augustus. *A Syllabus of a Proposed System of Logic*. London: Walton & Maberly, 1860.

Descartes, René. *Geometria*. Second Edition. Amstelædami: apud Ludovicum & Danielem Elzevirios, 1659. (Peirce's Library, Harvard Robbins Library)

Diogenes Laertius. *Diogenis Laertii de vitis, dogmatibus et apophthegmatibus clarorum philosophorum libri X, Graece et Latine*. Volumes 1 and 2. Amstelædami: Apud Henricum Wetstenium, 1692. (Peirce's Library, JHU)

Drummond, William. *Academical Questions*. London: W. Bulmer and Co., 1805. [Peirce refers to Diodorus Cronus, "as related by Cicero toward the end of the Lucullus' book of his Academical Questions" (LoF 3).]

Erdmann, Benno. *Logik. I. Band: Logische Elementarlehre. Zweite, völlig umgearbeitete Auglage*. Halle a. S.: Max Niemeyer, 1907.

Erdmann, Johann Eduard. *Outlines of Logic and Metaphysics*. Translated by B. C. Burt. London: Sonnenschein, 1896. [Lowell Lecture's reading list, Lecture I.]

Euclid. *Euclidis Opera Omnia*. Edited by J. L. Heiberg & H. Menge. 8 Volumes. Lipsiae: B. G. Teubneri, 1883–1916. [Peirce's reference is: "Heiberg admits 27 corollaries as genuine in the Elements" (LoF 1).]

Euler, Leonhard. *Lettres à une princesse d'Allemagne sur divers sujets de physique & de philosophie*. Saint-Pétersbourg: Imprimerie de l'Académie Impériale des Sciences, 1768–1772.

Flint, Robert. *Philosophy as Scientia Scientiarum and A History of Classifications of the Sciences*. New York: Charles Scribner's Sons, 1904. [Peirce's Library]

Girard, Albert. *Invention nouvelle en l'algèbre*. Amsterdam: W. J. Blaeuw, 1629.

Glanvill, Joseph. *Saducismus triumphatus. or, Full and plain evidence concerning witches and apparitions. In two parts. The first treating of their possibility. The second of their real existence*. London: Printed for J. Collins & S. Lownds, 1681.

Goethe, Johann Wolfgang von. "Den Originalen", 1812. In *Berliner Ausgabe. Poetische Werke (Band 1–16)*. Band 1, Berlin, 1960.

Grassmann, Robert. *Der Formenlehre oder Mathematik*. Five Volumes. Volume three, *Die Bindelehre oder Combinationslehre*. Stettin, 1872. (Peirce's Library, JHU)

Hamilton, William Rowan. "Recent Publications on Logical Science". *Edinburgh Review* 58(1833): 194–238.

Hamilton, William Rowan. *Lectures on Metaphysics and Logic. Volumes III and IV. Logic I and II*. London: William Blackwood, 1860.

Helmholtz, Hermann von. "On the Conservation of Forces". *Popular Lectures on Scientific Subjects*, (317–362). Translated by Edmund Atkinson. New York: D. Appleton & Co., 1885.

Hibben, John Grier. *Hegel's Logic. An Essay in Interpretation*. New York: Charles Scribner's Sons, 1902. (Peirce's Library) [Lowell Lecture's reading list, Lecture III.]

Hume, David. *A Treatise of Humane Nature*. London: Printed for John Noon, 1738.
Hume, David. *An Enquiry Concerning Human Understanding*. In Volume 2 of *Essays and Treatises on several Subjects*. London: Printed for T. Cadell, 1788.
Isidorus Hispalensis (Isidorus of Sevilla). *Isidori Hispalensis episcopi Etymologiarum sive Originum*. In J.-P. Migne, *Sancti Isidori Hispalensis Episcopi: Opera Omnia*. Paris, 1830. [No information on the year or publisher of the edition that Peirce would have consulted in found in his text. References are to "Isodorus Hispalensis about A.D. 600 refers to [obelus] as an old sign" (LoF 1), "A.D. 600 by Isidorus Hispalensis (*Etymologiarum* lib.I.cap.xxi.3) as [obelus] being an old sign" (LoF 1) and to "his great work usually called his *Origines* (lib.XIII, cap.xi.tertus 2)" (LoF 1).]
James, Henry. *Substance and Shadow. On Morality and Religion in their Relation to Life: An Essay upon the Physics of Creation*. Boston: Ticknor and Fields, 1863. (Peirce's Library)
James, William. *Pragmatism, A New Name for Some Old Ways of Thinking*. Popular Lectures on Philosophy. New York: Longmans, Green, and Co, 1907. (Peirce's Library) [Peirce received a copy of this book from James on June 13, 1907.]
James, William. "Experience of Activity". In: *Essays in Radical Empiricism*. Edited by Ralph Barton Perry, (155–190). New York: Longman Green & Co, 1912. [Mentioned in a letter to Josiah Royce in June 30, 1913, but may refer to an earlier edition from 1909 (LoF 3).]
Jevons, William Stanley. *Pure Logic or the Logic of Quality apart from Quantity: with Remarks on Boole's System and on the Relation of Logic and Mathematics*. London: Edward Stanford, 1864. (Peirce's Library, JHU)
Jevons, William Stanley. *The Principles of Science: a Treatise on Logic and Scientific Method*. London: Macmillan & Co., 1877. [Peirce makes multiple references e.g. to Jevon's •|•, but no specific book or source is mentioned (LoF 1). The Lowell Lecture's reading list, Lecture VIII, has a reference to "2d edition. London, 1877". Peirce owned also Jevons's *Studies in Deductive Logic*, London, 1880, and *Substitution of Similars*, London, 1889; the provenance of all four volumes is JHU.]
Jordan, Camille. *Traité des substitutions et des équations algébriques*. Paris: Gauthier-Villars, 1870.
Kant, Immanuel. *Kritik der reinen Vernunft*. Part 2 of *Sämmtliche Werke*. Edited by K. Rosenkranz & F. W. Schubert. Leipzig: L. Voss, 1838. (Peirce's Library, JHU)
Kant, Immanuel. *Disputatio de mundi sensibilis atque intelligibilis forma et principiis*. Part 1 of *Sämmtliche Werke*. Edited by K. Rosenkranz & F. W. Schubert. Leipzig: L. Voss, 1838. (Peirce's Library, JHU)

Kant, Immanuel. *Critique of Pure Reason*. Translated from the German of Immanuel Kant by J. M. D. Meiklejohn. London, Henry G. Bohn, 1855. (Peirce's Library, Houghton) [Heavily annotated, virtually every page up to p. 160, including extensive corrections which bear mostly on the terminology of the translation, together with extensive marginal notes on the content. A separate leaf on Bacon is glued on p. 278. Very few annotations from the beginning the second division and virtually no annotations from p. 365 onwards (Div. II, Chap. III, Sect. IV).]

Kempe, Alfred Bray. "A Memoir on the Theory of Mathematical Form". *Philosophical Transactions of the Royal Society* 177(1887): 1–70. [Lowell Lecture's reading list, Lecture II. Peirce's abundant marginalia appears on nearly every of the first 40 pages of his offprint of Kempe's article located in R 1599.]

Kepler, Johannes. *Astronomia Nova* αιτιολογητος *seu physica coelestis, tradita commentariis de motibus stellae Martis ex observationibus G. V. Tychonis Brahe*. Heidelberg: Vogelin, 1609. [Peirce refers to this as "De Motu stellas Marties", not *Astronomia Nova*, but this is the most likely source, as it contains *De Motibus Stellae Martis* (LoF 3).]

Ladd-Franklin, Christine. "On the Algebra of Logic". In: Charles S. Peirce (ed.), *Studies in Logic, by Members of the Johns Hopkins University*. Boston: Little, Brown & Company, 17–71, 1883.

Lambert, Johann Heinrich. *Anlage zur Architektonik, oder Theorie des Einfachen und Ersten in der philosophischen und mathematischen Erkenntnis*. Riga: Hartknoch, 1771.

Lambert, Johann Heinrich. *Neues Organon oder Gedanken über die Erforschung und Bezeichnung des Wahren und dessen Unterscheidung vom Irrthum und Schein*. Two Volumes. Leipzig: Johann Wendler, 1764. (Peirce's Library, JHU) [No marginalia or annotations by Peirce.]

Lange, Friedrich Albert. *Logische Studien: Ein Beitrag zur Neubegründung der formalen Logik und der Erkenntnistheorie*. Iserlohn: J. Baedeker, 1877.

Lange, Johann Christian (Langii, Iohannis Christiani). *Nucleus Logicae Weisianae*. Auctore Christiano Weisio (Weise, Christian). Gissae-Hassorum: Henningi Mülleri, 1712. [The Heidelberg Edition, Universitätsbibliotek Heidelberg.]

Laplace, Pierre-Simon. *Théorie analytique des probabilités*. Paris: Ve. Courcier, 1812.

Laurent, Hermann. *Traité du calcul des probabilités*. Paris: Gauthier-Villars, 1873. [Lowell Lecture's reading list, Lecture VI.]

Legendre, Adrien-Marie. *Éléments de géométrie*. Paris: F. Didot, 1794.

Leibniz, Gottfried (Godefridus Guilielmus Leibnitius). *Meditationes de Cognitione, Veritate et Ideis*. Acta Eruditorum Lipsiensum, 1684. [Peirce's own copy at Houghton Library is Leibniz's *The Monadology and Other Philosophical Writ-*

ings, translated with introduction and notes by Robert Latta, London: Oxford at the Clarendon Press, 1898, with Peirce's marginalia. His Arnault & Nicole 1861 includes translation of the *Meditationes*.]

Leibniz, Gottfried. *Nouveaux Essais sur l'entendement humain* (New Essays on Human Understanding). In *Oeuvres philosophiques latines & francoises de feu*, Amsterdam et Leipzig: Chez Jean Schreuder, 1765.

Le Jeune Dirichlet, Gustav. "Beweis des Satzes, dass jede unbegrenzte arithmetische Progression, deren erstes Glied und Differenz ganze Zahlen ohne gemeinschaftlichen Factor sind, unendlich viele Primzahlen enthält". *Abhandlungen der Königlichen Preußischen Akademie der Wissenschaften zu Berlin*, 48(1837): 45–71.

Listing, Johann Benedict. "Vorstudien zur Topologie". *Göttingen Studien* 2(1847): 811–875.

Listing, Johann Benedict. *Vorstudien zur Topologie*. Göttingen: Vandenhoeck und Ruprecht, 1848. [Peirce's reference is: "J. B. Listing, who was a colleague of Gauss in Göttingen. He published two papers on *Topologische Studien*. One of these in an octavo publication called as well as I remember *Göttingen Studien*, or something like that, the other later on in the quarto Vandenhoeck und Ruprecht" (LoF 1).]

Listing, Johann Benedict. "der Census räumlicher Complexe, oder Verallgemeinerung des Euler'schen Satzes von den Polyädern". *Abhandlungen der Königlichen Gesellschaft der Wissenschaften zu Göttingen* 10(1862): 97–182.

Locke, John. *An Essay concerning Humane Understanding*. London: Awnsham and John Churchill, 1694. (Peirce's Library, JHU) [Second edition.]

Lutosławski, Wincenty. *The Origin and Growth of Plato's Logic; with an account of Plato's style and of the chronology of his writings*. London, New York and Bombay: Longmans, Green, and Co., 1897. (Peirce's Library, Houghton).

Mach, Ernst. *Popular Scientific Lectures*. Translated by T. J. McCormack. Second edition. Chicago, 1897. [Lowell Lecture's reading list, Lecture VIII.]

MacColl, Hugh. "The calculus of equivalent statements". *Proceedings of the London Mathematical Society*, 9(1877): 9–22. [Peirce's citation is "McColl, (1877)" (LoF 1). Three out of the series of eight papers were published in 1877.]

Mansell, Henry Longueville. *Prolegomena Logica: an Inquiry into the Psychological Character of Logical Processes*. London: Whittaker and Co., 1851.

Maxwell, James Clerk. *A Treatise on Electricity and Magnetism*. Two Volumes. Oxford: Clarendon Press, 1873.

Mill, John Stuart. *A System of Logic, Ratiocinative and Inductive*. New York, 1846. [Peirce mentions "the first edition of his *System of Logic, Ratiocinative and Inductive*, published in March, 1843" (LoF 3), and that "Mill's went through 9 editions (though with the advantage of containing no special novelty)"

(LoF 3). Peirce's copy at Houghton is a heavily annotated *A System of Logic, Ratiocinative and Inductive: being a connected view of the principles of evidence and the methods of scientific investigation*. Longmans, Green, and co., 1886 edition (London), "People's edition". [Lowell Lecture's reading list, Lecture VI, with reference to "New York, 1846" edition.]

Mitchell, Oscar Howard. "On a New Algebra of Logic". In *Studies in Logic by Members of the Johns Hopkins University*. Charles S. Peirce, editor. Boston: Little Brown & Company, 1883, 72–106. (Peirce's Library, Houghton)

Müller, Max. *Three Introductory Lectures on the Science of Thought*. Chicago: Open Court, 1887. [Peirce's reference is "two little books by Max Müller published by the Open Court Co. at a quarter each" (LoF 1).]

Müller, Max. *Three Lectures on the Science of Language*. Chicago: Open Court, 1889. [Peirce's reference is "two little books by Max Müller published by the Open Court Co. at a quarter each" (LoF 1).]

Murphy, Joseph John. *Habit and Intelligence Vol. II*. London: Macmillan & Co., 1869. (Peirce's Library)

Newton, Isaac. *Philosophiæ naturalis principia mathematica*. London: Jussu Societatis Regiae ac typis Josephi Streater, 1687. Glasgow: G. Brookman; London: T. T. and J. Tegg, 1833.

Ockham, William. *Tractatus Logicae*. Paris: Johann Higman, 1488. [Peirce borrowed this incunabulum of his, now at JHU, to a Harvard graduate student, with a contract; the item's provenance is now at Houghton Library. He refers to it as "The distinction [between *objectively general* and *subjectively general*], so far as I know, was first drawn, though not very accurately, by William Ockham, as is stated in his book variously called *Summa logices*, *Tractatus logicae* and *Logica aurea*, Pars 1ma, cap. xiiii, and in the two following chapters is made the basis of his variety of nominalism, which denies the reality of subjective generality" ("The First Part of an Apology for Pragmaticism", R 296; LoF 3). Peirce owned three other works of Ockham from the late 15th century.]

Pearson, Karl. *The Grammar of Science*. 2nd edition. London: Adam & Charles Black, 1900. (Peirce's Library) [Lowell Lecture's reading list, Lecture VI.]

Peirce, Benjamin. *An Elementary Treatise on Plane and Solid Geometry*. Boston: James Munroe, 1837. [Charles Peirce refers from memory to his father's "textbook of Elementary Geometry, 1832" (LoF 3).]

Peirce, Benjamin. *A System of Analytic Mechanics*. Boston: Little, Brown & Company, 1855. (Peirce's Library) [Peirce probably refers to this item from memory as "1852" (LoF 3).]

Peirce, Benjamin. *Linear Associative Algebra*. A Memoir read before the National Academy of Sciences in Washington, 1870. By Benjamin Peirce. With Notes

and Addenda, by C. S. Peirce, Son of the Author. New York: Van Nostrand, 1882. (Peirce's Library)
Petrus Hispanus (Hispani, Petri/John XXI). *Summulae logicales (ff. 1 r. -84 v.) followed by a Propositio exponibilis (in a different hand) elucidating obscure points in the foregoing treatise.* de Ricci, Census, 753, no. 1. 15th Century. (Peirce's Library, JHU)
Petrus Hispanus (Hispani, Petri/John XXI). *Compendiarius parvuorum logicalium.* Vienna: Vietor, 1512. (Peirce's Library, JHU)
Philodemus. *On Signs and Semiotic Inferences* (Περὶ Σημείων καὶ Σημειώσεων/ Περὶ Φαινομένων καὶ Σημειώσεων). T. Gomperz. *Herkulanische Studien, i Philodem über Induktionslüsse.* Leipzig: Teubner, 1865. (Peirce's Library)
Plato. *Platonis Opera.* Edited by John Burnet. Oxford Classical Texts, Oxford University Press, 1903. (Peirce's Library)
Prantl, Karl von. *Geschichte der Logik im Abendlande.* Three volumes. Leipzig: S. Hirzel, 1855.
Priscianus Caesariensis. *Priscianus Caesariensis Grammatici Opera, ad vetustissimorum codicum, nunc primum collatorum, fidem recensuit, emaculavit, lectionum varietatem notavit et indices locupletissimos adiecit Augustus Krehl.* Two volumes. Edited by Krehl, August Ludwig Gottlieb. Lipsiae: Weidmann, 1819–1820.
Recorde, Robert. *The Whetstone of Witte.* London: Jhon Kyngstone, 1557.
Renouvier, Charles Bernard. *Essais de critique générale.* Four volumes. Paris: Bureau de la Critique Philosophique, 1854–1864. [Peirce's citation is "Essai de philosophie critique" (LoF 3).]
Risteen, Allan Douglas. *Molecules and the Molecular Theory of Matter.* Boston and London: Ginn & Co., 1895. Reprinted 1896.
Royce, Josiah. *The World and the Individual.* New York: Macmillan, 1900.
Russell, Bertrand. *The Principles of Mathematics.* Vol. 1. Cambridge: Cambridge University Press, 1903. (Peirce's Library, Houghton) [Peirce's copy is lightly annotated, and includes two EGs in the margin (p. 18): "Carroll is not right. $\overline{q\;\overline{r}}$ $\overline{p\,q\,r}$ for if q is absurd $q \prec r$ and $q \prec \bar{r}$ may both be true". Lowell Lecture's reading list, Lecture V, with reference to "London, 1903" edition.]
Salmon, George. *A Treatise on the Higher Plane Curves.* Dublin: Hodges, Foster & Figgis, 1879.
Sayce, Archibald Henry. "Grammar". *Encyclopaedia Britannica.* 11th edition, 1911.
Schaff, Philip. *History of the Christian Church.* Translated by Edward D. Yeomans. New York: Scribner, Armstrong & Co., 1874. ["Now no single creed of christendom,—as I can say by a painstaking study of Dr. Schaff's three volumes,—was ever put forward of which the principal purpose was not to

proclaim somebody to be damned" (LoF 2). Schaff published eight volumes under the same title in 1858–1890.]

Schönflies, Arthur. "Die Entwickelung der Lehre von den Punktmannigfaltigkeiten". *Jahresbericht der deutschen Mathematiker-Vereinigung* 8, part 2(1900): 1–250.

Schröder, Ernst. *Der Operationskreis des Logikkalküls*. Leipzig: B. G. Teubner, 1877.

Schröder, Ernst. *Vorlesungen über die Algebra der Logik*. Three volumes. Leipzig: B. G. Teubner, 1890–1895. [Lowell Lecture's reading list, Lecture II.]

Schubert, Hermann. *Kalkül der abzählenden Geometrie*. Leipzig: B. G. Teubner, 1879.

Sigwart, Cristoph von. *Logic*. Second edition, enlarged and revised. Translated by Helen Dendy. London: Swan Sonnenschein & Co., 1895. [Lowell Lecture's reading list, Lecture I.]

Smith, James & Smith, Horace. *Rejected Addresses: or, The new theatrum poetarum*. London: John Murray, 1879.

Southey, Robert. *The Doctor*. New York: Harper & Brothers, 1836.

Stout, George Frederick. *Analytic Psychology*. London: Swan Sonnenschein & Co., 1896.

Trendelenburg, Friedrich Adolph. *Elementa Logices Aristotelicae*. Berolini, 1836. [Lowell Lecture's reading list. Peirce owned its 1862 edition, Berlin: Gustavi Bethae, JHU.]

Trendelenburg, Friedrich Adolph. *Logische Untersuchungen*. Berlin: S. Hirzel, 1840. [Lowell Lecture's reading list, Lecture I.]

Tucker, Abraham. *The Light of Nature Pursued*. (Together with some account of the life of the author by John Mildmay). Cambridge: Hilliard and Brown, 1831.

Überweg, Friedrich. *System der Logik und Geschichte der logischen Lehren*. Bonn: Bei Adolph Marcus, 1865. (Peirce's Library, JHU)

Ueberweg, Friedrich. *System of Logic, and History of Logical Doctrines*. Translated by T. M. Lindsay. London: Longmans, Green, & Co., 1871. [Lowell Lectures reading list, Lecture I.]

Überweg, Friedrich *Grundriss der Geschichte der Philosophie*. 9te Auflage. Herausgere M. Heinze. Four volumes.

Valla, Laurentius (Valla, Lorenzo; Laurentius, Vallensis). *Dialecticae Disputationes contra Aristotelicos*. Venice, 1499. Original publication c.1439. Printed in the *Laurentii Vallae Opera*, Basel, 1540, reprinted with a second volume, Turin: Bottega d'Erasmo, 1962, and as *Dialectical Disputations*. Latin text and English translation the *Repastinatio* by B. P. Copenhaver and L. Nauta. The I Tatti Renaissance Library, Cambridge: Harvard University Press, 2012. [Peirce's reference occurs in his library book list of R 1574: "Laurentius Valla, Dialecticae Disp (1499) or Opera *containing this*". The list contains several items that Peirce was canvassing from libraries in Boston or in Cambridge, Mass., in 1903.]

Vaugelas, Claude Favre de. *Remarques sur la langue française*, Paris: Vve J. Camusat et P. Le Petit, 1647. (Peirce's Library)

Venn, John. *The Logic of Chance. An Essay on the Foundations and Province of the Theory of Probability, with Especial Reference to Its Application to Moral and Social Science*. London: Macmillan & Co., 1876. (Peirce's Library) [Lowell Lecture's reading list, Lecture VI, with reference to "3d edition. London, 1888".]

Venn, John. *Symbolic Logic*. First edition. London: Macmillan & Co., 1881.

Venn, John. *The Principles of Empirical or Inductive Logic*. London and New York: Macmillan & Co., 1889. [Lowell Lecture's reading list, Lecture VIII.]

de Villadi, Alexander (Alexander of Villedieu). *Doctrinale puerorum* XXII, 1374. [Peirce's reference is to p. 354 of his copy of Thurot, Charles. *Notices et extraits de divers manuscrits latins pour servir á l'histoire des doctrines grammaticales au moyen age*. Notices et extraits des manuscrits de la Bibliothéque nationale 22.2, Paris: Imprimerie Impériale, 1868.] (Peirce's Library, JHU)

Vives, Juan Luis. "De Censura Veri et falsi". In: *De disciplinis Libri XX*. Antwerp: Michael Hillenius Hoochstratanus, 1531. (Peirce's Library)

Wadding, Luke (ed.). *Scotus, Duns. Ioannis Duns Scoti Opera Omnia*. Twelve Volumes. London: Laurent Durand, 1639. (Peirce's Library, JHU) [Peirce owned Volumes 1–4 of Duns Scotus's *Opera Omnia*, together with at least thirteen other 15th, 16th and early 17th century works by Scotus (JHU). Thomas of Erfurt's *Tractatus de modis significandi sive Grammatica Speculativa* is included in Volume 1 of the Wadding edition.]

Watts, Isaac. *Logick, Or, the Right Use of Reason in the Inquiry After Truth. With a variety of rules to guard against error, in the affairs of religion and human life, as well as in the sciences*. London: Printed for J. Buckland, T. Caslon etc., 1772. (Peirce's Library, JHU)

Welby, Victoria. *What is Meaning? Studies in the Development of Significance*. London: Macmillan and Co., 1903. (Peirce's Library)

Whately, Richard. *Elements of Logic*. 4th edition. London: B. Fellowes, 1831. (Peirce's Library) [Lowell Lecture's reading list (New York, 1875).]

Whewell, William. *History of Scientific Ideas. Being the first part of the Philosophy of inductive sciences*. London, 1858. [Lowell Lecture's reading list, Lecture VIII.]

Whewell, William. *History of Scientific Ideas. Being the second part of the Philosophy of inductive sciences*. London, 1858. [Lowell Lecture's reading list, Lecture VIII.]

Whitehead, Alfred North. "The logic of relations, logical substitution groups, and cardinal numbers". *American Journal of Mathematics* 25(1903): 157–178. [Lowell Lecture's reading list, Lecture II.]

Wilkins, John. *An Essay towards a Real Character, And a Philosophical Language.* London: Printed for Sa. Gellibrand, and for John Martin Printer to the Royal Society, 1668. (Peirce's Library, JHU) [Inscribed, on the frontleaf (not in Peirce's hand): "This design was pursued with great application, but has failed in the success, it was expected, would attend it. Nevertheless, the Book us very valuable, as containing a general reduction of things to their proper heads, and exhibiting at once an entire analytical system of the Universe. Some divisions perhaps are not exactly agreeable to the Philosophy now in vogue, or that which will come after, But. Who expects a perfect work to see, Expect what never was, not is, nor e'er will by, [undersigned] $\mathcal{M}$."]

Wilson, John Cook. *On the Traversing of Geometrical Figures.* Oxford: Clarendon Press, 1905. (Peirce's Library)

Wolff, Christian. *Vernünfftige Gedancken Von den Kräfften des menschlichen Verstandes Und ihrem Richtigen Gebrauche In Erkäntnißder Wahrheit.* Halle im Magdeburgischen Renger Halle, Saale Halle, 1713. [Peirce's citation is "*Vernünftige Gedanken von den Kräften des menschlichen Verstanden*, 1710" (LoF 1). Peirce owned at least thirteen volumes of Wolff's works, provenance JHU.]

Woods, Frederick Adams. *Mental and Moral Heredity in Royalty.* New York: Henry Holt & Co, 1906. (Peirce's Library)

Wundt, Wilhelm Max. *Logik, eine Untersuchung der Prinzipien der Erkenntnis und der Methoden Wissenschaftlicher Forschung.* 2nd edition. Stuttgart: Ferdinand Enke, 1893–1895. [Lowell Lecture's reading list, Lecture I.]

Catalogue of Peirce's Writings

This list references Peirce's writings—manuscripts, letters, papers and pieces—that have been included in Volumes 2/1 (Selections 29–31) and 2/2 (Selections 32–42) of *Logic of the Future*. The writings are in an approximate chronological order. Peirce did not date most of the notebooks and drafts; the third lecture and its drafts are a notable exception and are written during the first part of October. The prefaces of the syllabus manuscript R 478 have a (possibly post-dated) designation of November 1, R 468 has a date of December 4, and R S-28 is dated to the first part of September. All the rest of the material included in the present volume is undated; uncertainties remain as to the exact timing of their composition or relative ordering. It is not known, for example, whether Peirce worked on the lectures in sequence or whether he may have produced some of his pre-lecture drafts in parallel and was led to rearrange and revise them sometime later.

Alternatives, variants and pages from collateral sources are included and are also listed as separate items only if they bear a separate original title, label, designation or indication of their approximate contents and purpose. Label inscriptions appearing on the notebook covers and first pages are included. Some notebooks are without labels and some cover information was added by the editors of the *Collected Papers of Charles S. Peirce*. The details as well as references to sources from the published papers of Charles S. Peirce are included in the introductory essays and surveys of individual selections.

R 454 What Makes a Reasoning Sound?
   Lowell Lecture I [Early Draft]
   – Spring–Summer 1903. *Selection 32.*
   "Lectures on Logic, to be delivered at the Lowell Institute. Winter of 1903–1904"

R 491 *The Logical Tracts No. 1*. On Existential Graphs
   – Early Summer (June) 1903. *Selection 29.*

R 492 *The Logical Tracts No. 2*. On Existential Graphs, Euler's Diagrams, and Logical Algebra
   – Summer–Autumn (July–September) 1903. *Selection 30.*

R 479 *The Logical Tracts No. 2*. Part II. On Logical Graphs [Euler's Diagrams]
   – Summer–Autumn 1903. *Selection 31.*

R S-28 The Conventions.
   Lowell Lecture II(a)
   – September 1–15, 1903. *Selection 33.*

R S-28 [Fragments.]
  – September, 1903.   *Selection 42.*
R S-27 Graphs, Little Account.
  Lowell Lecture II(a)
  – September 1903.   *Selection 33.*
R 450 A System of Diagrams for Studying Logical Relations. Exposition of it begun. (Existential Graphs—Alpha & Beta).
  Lowell Lecture II(a)
  – September 1903.   *Selection 33.*
R S-29 Existential Graphs: The Initial Conventions.
  Lowell Lecture II(b)
  – September 1903.   *Selection 34.*
R 455 A System of Diagrams for Studying Logical Relations. Exposition of it begun. (Existential Graphs—Alpha & Beta).
  Lowell Lecture II(b) (Includes R 455(s), R 456 and pages from R S-29, R S-32, R S-33, R S-34)
  – Late September–early October 1903.   *Selection 34.*
  "Lowell Lectures by C. S. Peirce"
R 1333 [Fragments.]
  – Before October 1903.   *Selection 42.*
R 496 [Fragments.]
  Lowell Lecture V(c).
  – Before October 1903.   *Selection 42.*
R 458, R 458(s) The Doctrine of Multitude, Infinity and Continuity. (Multitude.)
  Lowell Lecture V(c).
  – Before October 1903.   *Selection 38.*
  "May be useful for 3rd or 4th. Lecture 3. First Draught"
R 459 The Doctrine of Multitude, Infinity and Continuity. (Multitude.)
  Lowell Lecture V(a) (Includes pages from R 459(s), R 466)
  – Before October 1903.   *Selection 38.*
  "Lowell Lectures. by C. S. Peirce. 1903. Lecture 3. Won't do"
R 466 The Doctrine of Multitude, Infinity and Continuity. (Multitude.)
  Lowell Lecture V(a)
  – Before October 1903.   *Selection 38.*
  "? Useful for Third or Fourth ?"
R 457 The Three Universal Categories and their Utility. (General Explanations. Phenomenology and Speculative Grammar.)
  Lowell Lecture III(b)
  – October 2, 1903.   *Selection 36.*
  "1st Draught of 3rd Lecture"

R 462 The Three Universal Categories and their Utility. (General Explanations. Phenomenology and Speculative Grammar.)
Lowell Lecture III(a) (Includes pages from R S-31)
– October 5, 1903.   *Selection 35.*
"The Main holt of Lecture 3. C. S. P's Lowell Lectures of 1903. 2nd Draught of 3rd Lecture. Begun 1903 Oct 5, 10:30am"

R 464 The Three Universal Categories and their Utility. (General Explanations. Phenomenology and Speculative Grammar.)
Lowell Lecture III(b) (Includes pages from R 464(s), R 465, R S-34)
– October 8, 1903 (R 464, R 464(s)); October 12 (R 465).   *Selection 36.*
"Lowell Lectures of 1903. Lecture III. Second Draught"

R 464(s) "Part I of the 3rd Draught of the Third Lecture"
Lowell Lecture III(b)
– October 8, 1903.   *Selection 36.*

R 465 "Second Part of the Third Draught of Lecture III"
Lowell Lecture III(b)
– October 12, 1903.   *Selection 36.*
"To be used. Lecture III. Vol. 2. C. S. P's Lowell Lectures of 1903. 2nd Part of 3rd Draught of Lecture III"

R 478 *A Syllabus of certain Topics of Logic.* (Includes pages from R 478(s), R 508, R 509)
– October 1903 (R 478, R 478(s) written before October 30).   *Selection 41.*

R 508 Existential Graphs. Rules of Transformation. Pure Mathematical Definition of Existential Graphs, regardless of their Interpretation (Syllabus B)
– Late October–early November 1903.   *Selection 41.*

R 509 Gamma Graphs.
– Late October–early November 1903.   *Selection 41.*

R 510 [Fragments]
– November 1903 (Includes pages from R 278)   *Selection 42.*

R 2, R 3, R 511, R 512 On the Simplest Branch of Mathematics, Dyadics.
– November 1903.   *Selection 40.*

R S-1 Notes on the Theory of Multitude.
Lowell Lecture IV (Notebook pages 61–85 are on existential graphs)
– From July to early December, 1903.   *Selection 42.*

R 460 Lowell Lecture IV
– November 30–December 3, 1903.   *Selection 37.*
"Lect. III a̶ b d"

R 467 Exposition of the System of Diagrams Completed. (Existential Graphs: Gamma Part.)
Lowell Lecture IV (Includes pages from R 468, R S-31)

– Late November–early December, 1903. *Selection 37.*
"C. S. Peirce's Lowell Lectures 1903. Lecture 4. Vol. 1. Lowell Lectures for 1903"

R 468 Introduction to Lecture V.
Lowell Lecture IV
– December 4, 1903. *Selection 37.*
"C. S. P's Lowell Lectures of 1903. Introduction to Lecture 5. 1903 Dec 4"

R 469 The Doctrine of Multitude, Infinity and Continuity. (Multitude.)
Lowell Lecture V(d) (Including R 470)
– December 3–7, 1903. *Selection 39.*
"1903. Lowell Lectures. Lecture 5. Vol. I"

R 470 The Doctrine of Multitude, Infinity and Continuity. (Multitude.)
Lowell Lecture V(d) (including R 471)
– December 3–7, 1903. *Selection 39.*
"1903. Lowell Lectures. Lecture 5. Vol. 2"

R 1070 [Fragments.]
– post 1903. *Selection 42.*

R S-46 [Fragments.]
– late 1905. *Selection 42.*

Name Index

Anselm 50
Aristotle; On diagrams 229 ; On symbols 122
Armand de Bello Visu 162, 164
Avicenna 162, 164

Baldwin, James Mark 2
Boethius 146; On Subject 221
Boole, George 1
Burleigh, Walter 162, 164

Carroll, Lewis 247
Cattell, James McKeen 16, 31, 70
Cicero 242
Clifford, William Kingdon 228, 229
Couturat, Louis 98

De Morgan, Augustus 1; Universe of discourse 204
Dedekind, Richard 134
Durandus á Sancto Porciano 162, 164

Euclid 134, 166 ; *Elements* 134
Euler, Leonhard 235; *Lettres...* 229, 231, 236

Fermat, Pierre de 191
Fisch, Max H. 70
Franklin, Christine see Ladd-Franklin, Christine
Frege, Gottlob XIII, 2

Gardner, Martin 15, 28
Gratiadeus Esculanus 162, 164

Halley, Edmund XV
Hamilton, William Rowan 235, 236
Hartshorne, Charles 50

James, William VIII, 2, 3, 12, 16, 77

Kant, Immanuel; *Critic* 134 ; On logic 134
Kempe, Alfred Bray 6; *A Memoir on the Theory of Mathematical Form* 171, 228

Ladd-Franklin, Christine 53, 70, 98
Lambert, Johann Heinrich; *Architektonik* 236 ; *Neues Organon* 229, 235
Lange, Friedrich Albert 229, 236
Lange, Johann Christian 229

Menger, Karl 50
Mitchell, Oscar Howard 23, 204

Newton, Isaac XV

Peano, Giuseppe 133
Peirce, Benjamin 50
Peirce, James Mills 50
Peirce, Juliette 15, 70
Putnam, George Haven 31, 70

Raymundus Lullus 162, 164
Risteen, Allan Douglas 25
Robin, Richard S. XV, 22, 39

Schiller, Ferdinand Canning Scott 16, 17
Schröder, Ernst 134
Scotus, Duns 162, 164
Sedgwick, William T. 76–79

Tarski, Alfred 24, 51

Valla, Lorenzo 229
Vaugelas, Claude Favre de 145
Venn, John 97, 98, 229 ; *Symbolic Logic* 236
Vives, Juan Luis 229, 236

Waitz, Theodor 122
Weise, Christian 236
Weiss, Paul 50
Woods, Frederick Adams 43

Keyword Index

Abduction XIII, XVI, 1, 75
Abstraction 25, 27–29, 95, 130, 162, 212, 226 ; two meanings of 162
Aggregation 232
Algebra 216; Algebraic logic 133, 135 ; Algebraic notation 155
Alogoid 141
Argument 72, 81, 119, 123, 212
Argumentation 212
Arithmetic 134
Association 150; and signification 195
Atom 163
Atom (graph) 173
Axiom; Euclid's axioms 134

Blank 172

Chemistry; Chemical graphs 131, 202, 228, 229
Collections 25, 27, 63, 238
Commutativity 156
Conditionals; Methods of expressing 141
Consciousness; and icon 121, 150, 211, 215 ; Dyadic consciousness 209
Continuity XVI, 13, 27, 29, 66, 152, 167, 169, 196, 252
Continuum; line continuum 152
Copula; and pronoun 208 ; hypothetical copulative 224
Critical logic 1, 212
Cut see also Existential Graphs; Actual area 172 ; Enclosure of 172 ; Obliterated 173 ; Place of 172

Decidability 59
Deduction XIII, 1, 13, 23, 24, see also Reasoning, necessary
Diagram 131, 135, 202 ; and Aristotle 229 ; and icon 137 ; and mathematics 179 ; Eulerian 86–99, 229 ; geometrical 121 ; Spider diagrams 89 ; Venn diagrams 86–99
Diagrammatic syntax 10, 20, 24, 37, 44, 65–67, 129

Diagrammatization 138, 143, 149
Dinected graphs 74, 80, 130, 183–185, 187–189, 192, 202
Disposition 150, 212, 216

Endoporeutic principle 24, 37, 128
Ens Rationis; and graphs 167–170, 183, 186, 194
Entitative Graphs 84, 138, 139
Epistemic Logic 26, 28, 32, 53–55
esse in futuro 162
Ethics; and logic 1 ; of terminology 145
Existential Graphs see also Endoporeutic principle, Grapheus, Graphist, Hook, Line of Identity, Nex, Replica, Rhema, Selective, Sheet, Spot; Alpha-possibility 31 ; Beta-possibility 31 ; Cut 172 ; Delta graphs 25, 26, 28 ; Double-cut 174 ; Evenly enclosed 128, 157, 160, 170, 173, 174, 182, 220, 224 ; Gamma-possibility 29 ; Inloop 174 ; Oddly enclosed 128, 159, 160, 163, 170, 173, 174, 182 ; Outer close 174 ; Outloop 174 ; Principles of Representation by the system 124 ; Province 43 ; Pseudograph 38, 124, 127, 141, 155–157, 163, 164, 171, 188, 205, 206, 218, 222, 223 ; Scroll 125, 126, 143, 149, 157, 174, 222, 223 ; Tincture 26, 27, 31, 33, 43, 63, 66 ; Unenclosed 167, 169
Experience 145, 151, 209, 210, 218
Experimentation; and graphs 204 ; and mathematics 178, 179

Feeling; Qualities of feeling 164, 210
Firstness 209, 210

Geometry; Analogy between logical and geometrical relation 233 ; figure 211 ; Metric 135 ; relation of inclusion 140, 142
Graph 171; Alligate 174 ; as a symbol 152 ; Bridge 174 ; Definite individual 173 ; Entire graph 36, 124 ; Existential 171 ; Individual 173 ; Logical graph 124, 229 ; Natural and Artificial 172 ; Scribing 172 ;

Seligible 173 ; Solute 174 ; Valency of 173 ; versus Calculus 133, 174
Graph-instance 19, 20, 22–24, 82, 171–173, see also Replica ; Partial 173
Graph-replica 18, 60, 61, 82, 171, 194, 196, 200, 201
Grapheus 22, 135–137, 147, 160, 168, 204, 205, 222
Graphist 22, 26, 27, 136, 137, 168, 174, 175
Graphist and Interpreter 137, 141, 147, 155, 164
Grave 172
Gödel numbering 61

Habit 137, 150 ; and meaning 122 ; and regularity 162 ; as law 122
Hook 125, 147, 149, 156, 160, 161, 163, 165, 169, 173, 178, 195, 196, 199–201, 213, 219
Hypnotism 212

Icon 120, 212 ; and Diagram 131, 202 ; and geometrical diagrams 150 ; Association by resemblance 121 ; Iconicity of relations in EG 131, 137, 138, 142, 148, 152, 203, 206, 218, 228
Incompossibility 231
Indefinite individual 125, 127, 173, 218, 220, 222, 223
Indesignate individual 147, 148, 159, 160, 169, 170, 178, 207, 208
Indeterminateness 171, 230
Index 121, 122, 150, 151, 195, 211, 212, 215 ; and Line of Identity 152 ; Bisign 212 ; Informant 121, 122 ; Sisign 212
Induction; and mathematics 178
Inference XIII, 17, 28, 39, 133, 135, 139, 162, 163, 176, 180, 203, 204, 212 ; Immediate 132, 162 ; Mathematical 134 ; Necessary 203, 204
Interpretant 120, 121, 123, 211, 212 ; and argument 123
Interpreter 22, 137, see also Graphist and Interpreter ; and drawer 230 ; and icon 120 ; and indesignate individuals 160 ; and index 121, 151 ; and pure icons 150 ; and selectives 159 ; and Universals 221

Languages; and Existential Graphs 176, 178, 180 ; and logic 122, 145 ; and pronoun in place of copula 208 ; Arabic 208 ; Egyptian 208 ; Gaelic 145 ; Greek 208 ; Hebrew 208
Law 205; and graphs 152 ; and habit 122 ; and interpretation 151
Ligature 19, 173, 193, 198, 200 ; Compound 193
Line of Identity 19, 148, 164, 173, 195, 196, 198, 207, 208, 214 ; and connexus 219 ; and graphs 152, 193 ; and individual identity 152 ; and Loose end 201 ; as a sign 150–152, 162 ; Branching 149
Logic; as science of second intentions 162
Logica Utens 176
Logical equivalence 26, 42
Logical Graphs see Entitative Graphs, see Existential Graphs, see Graph
Löb's axiom 58, 59

Mathematics; Logical analysis of mathematical reasoning 134 ; Mathematical certainty 178 ; Reasoning in 133–135
Meaning; of a proposition 179
Methodeutic XVI, 2, 212
Modal Logic 26–29, 31, 32, 35, 41–44, 46, 52, 54, 65–67, 93
Modality XVI; subjective possibility 27
Multi-modal Logics 26, 27, 31, 43, 62, 66
Multitude 28, 95, 124, 190, 231

Necessity; Physical and Logical 136
Nominalism 246

Obelus 243
Onoma 72, 77, 81, 125–127, 208, 219, 220, 222, 224
Origina area 172

Peirce's Puzzle 27
Peirce's Rule 47
Perception; Perceptual form of graphs 203
Phaneron 1
Phenomenology 1
Phenomenon 209; Tripartite division of 209
Photograph; Iconicity and indexicality of 121, 150, 151, 212, 215

Pons asinorum see Euclid
Possibilities 139, 205 ; Range of 141 ; Universe of 142
Potentials 25
Pragmaticism VIII, XIII, XIV, 2, 3, 29, 66, 83, 84, 171, 246
Pragmatism XIII, 16, 17, 50, 71
Predication 231
Prescissive abstraction 162
Principle of contradiction 127
Principle of contraposition 189, 191, 199
Principle of excluded middle 127
Proper names XIII, 145, 158, 159, 182, 208, 219, 220, see also Selective
Proposition; governing the conduct of the interpreter 212
Provability 32, 54, 57–59, 61, 62
Psychology 133; and logic 179

Quantifiers XIII, 2, 31, 52

Reaction; and existence 210
Real; Real general 122 ; Real relation 163, 164 ; Reality and existence 163 ; Reality and fact 204 ; Reality and Secondness 209 ; Reality as independence of beliefs 211 ; Reality of laws 211
Reasoning; as self-controlled thought 176 ; in philosophy and special sciences 133 ; Intuitional theory of 229 ; Necessary 135, 170, 204 ; Syllogistic 134
Replica 122, 137, 150, 152, 171, 195, 212, 216, 217, 222 ; Graph-replica 195
Representamen 72, 81, 119–123, 131, 150, 151, 164, 202, 211, 212, 215, 216
Residuation see Peirce's Rule
Resistance and Effort 209, 210
Resolve 212
Retroduction XVI, 1
Rheme 25, 125, 144, 145, 147, 160–162, 164, 165, 167, 169, 178, 198, 213, 216, 217, 219, 221, 222 ; Triad 149, 154

Science; and logic 235 ; and philosophy 229
Scriptibility 6, 64
Second intention 164; graph 165 ; Medads of 163 ; Monads of 163 ; Rhemata of 162, 164, 202, 217 ; Triadic rhemata of 217

Secondness 209, 210 ; Degenerate 210
Selective 159–161, 202, 208 ; and Existential Graphs 161, 167–169, 177, 182, 207, 208
Sheet 124; Actual and Original 172 ; and universe 131, 203 ; Blank 136–138, 163 ; of assent 18 ; of assertion 18, 124, 135, 137, 172 ; of insertions 190 ; of the diagram 230
Sign; Bisign 83, 212, 216 ; Sisign 83, 212, 216 ; Tersign 83, 212, 216 ; Triadicity of 120, 150, 211, 215
Speculative Grammar 1, 18, 73, 81, 83, 119, 252
Speculative Rhetoric see Methodeutic
Spot 125, 147, 163, 169, 172, 198, 213 ; Color of 171
Stoics; and proper noun 208
Subconscious 179
Syllogism 133, 206, 218 ; and diagrams 229, 232 ; Barbara 134
Symbol 122, 162, 163 ; and *ens rationis* 163 ; and conduct 151 ; and conventions 151 ; Icons of symbol 122 ; Pure 151, 152 ; Term/Proposition/Argument 123

Teridentity 26, 173 ; Graph of 173
Thirdness 209; and law of nature 211
Topology 63, 134, 135
Transformability 6
Transformation rules; Deiteration 200 ; Disjunction 157 ; Erasure 200 ; Insertion 200 ; Iteration 200
Transformations of graphs 177; Archegetic 52 ; Basic Categorical Rules of Illative 200 ; Completeness of Rules 192 ; Derived Illative 202 ; Illative 162, 176, 178, 180, 182, 185–192, 196, 197, 199
Truth 141
Type; and graph 171

Universe 124, 135 ; logical 204 ; of discourse 230 ; of Truth 204
Utterer XIII, 22, 33, 53
Utterer and Interpreter 204

Vexed questions of logic 3

www.ingramcontent.com/pod-product-compliance
Lightning Source LLC
Chambersburg PA
CBHW030104170426
43198CB00009B/491